Circuits of Visibility

CRITICAL CULTURAL COMMUNICATION

General Editors: Sarah Banet-Weiser and Kent A. Ono

Circuits of Visibility

Gender and Transnational Media Cultures

Edited by

Radha Sarma Hegde

NEW YORK UNIVERSITY PRESS

New York and London

NEW YORK UNIVERSITY PRESS
New York and London
www.nyupress.org

References to Internet websites (URLs) were accurate at the time of writing.
Neither the author nor New York University Press is responsible for URLs that
may have expired or changed since the manuscript was prepared.

Library of Congress Cataloging-in-Publication Data
Circuits of visibility : gender and transnational media cultures
edited by Radha S. Hegde.
p. cm. — (Critical cultural communication)
Includes bibliographical references and index.
ISBN 978-0-8147-3730-9 (cl : alk. paper)
ISBN 978-0-8147-3731-6 (pb : alk. paper)
ISBN 978-0-8147-9060-1 (e-book : alk. paper)
1. Sex role in mass media.   2. Sex role and globalization.
3. Women in mass media.   4. Feminism and mass media.
5. Mass media and globalization.   6. Mass media and culture.
I. Hegde, Radha Sarma, 1953–
P96.S5C57   2011
302.23—dc22   2011004010

New York University Press books are printed on acid-free paper, and their binding
materials are chosen for strength and durability. We strive to use environmentally
responsible suppliers and materials to the greatest extent possible in publishing our
books.

Manufactured in the United States of America

c 10 9 8 7 6 5 4 3 2 1
p 10 9 8 7 6 5 4 3 2 1

Contents

Acknowledgments

My inspiration to work on this project came from teaching a graduate seminar, "Gender and Globalization," at New York University. The stimulating discussions with my students about gender and sexuality spanned intertwined contexts of war, migration, neoliberal shifts, labor, technology, and media flows. My undergraduate students in the course "Gender, Sex, and the Global" kept me engaged with news items about the intersections of globalization and gender, whether it was the controversy about the veil, legislating sexuality in various parts of the globe, sex trafficking, or changes in immigration law. The questions from my students have been central to my commitment to understanding globalization from the lived practices of the everyday.

Conversations with Angharad Valdivia, Sujata Moorty, and Radhika Parameswaran about feminist research and globalization at various conferences were significant in the development of this book. Angharad Valdivia's enthusiastic support of this endeavor encouraged me to get moving on this project. Thanks to David Morley for his input and comments on earlier iterations of this project.

I offer my deepest thanks to the contributors who worked with me in record time and persevered with patience through the process. Their scholarship opens up a conversation across multiple locales and themes. Thank you for your involvement and partnership on this project.

I greatly appreciate the collegial environment offered by the Department of Media, Culture, and Communication at New York University. In particular, I wish to express my gratitude to my colleagues Deborah Borisoff, Allen Feldman, JoEllen Fisherkeller, and Arvind Rajagopal for their friendship and intellectual support. To Helen Nissenbaum, my friend and colleague, very special thanks for motivating me to adhere to my writing schedule and deadlines. To Robert Wosnitzer, my thanks for providing me a constant flow of books, articles, images, and ideas. Rajeswari Sunder Rajan has been a source of inspiration, and I extend my thanks for her support and interest in this project.

In Chennai, India, where I spent my sabbatical and did most of the work for this book, I would like to acknowledge the support of my sisters, Sudha Ramesh and Rajini Balachandran. Thanks to my friend Nirmala Lakshman, who readily provided help and logistical assistance during my time in India.

To Nirupama Shree Hegde, for her keen editorial eye and sense of humor, a very special thank you. And Krishna, thanks for everything.

Courtney Wolf was a skillful research assistant and worked with me across time zones. I am very grateful to Amanda Vega, who brought her amazing efficiency and sense of organization to the book on its final path to completion. My thanks to Jaclyn Rohel for her editorial assistance and being ever so generous with her time.

My thanks to Kent Ono and Sarah Banet-Weiser, the series editors, for their invaluable guidance and positive response to the intellectual goals of this project. I thank the reviewers for their sharp and astute comments. To Eric Zinner and Ciara McLaughlin at NYU Press, I extend my thanks and appreciation for their encouragement, advice, and support throughout the process of working on this book.

Introduction
Radha S. Hegde

The past decade has seen an internationalization of cultural studies scholarship and an emerging interest in interdisciplinary approaches to the study of globalization. Recent developments on the world stage, such as the global economic crisis, political violence, urban terror, militarization, and migrant flows, all reveal the complex interplay between economic, cultural, and political processes. Although issues of gender and sexuality are woven into these exigencies, the manner in which they come into public view demands critical attention. *Circuits of Visibility* is an attempt to create an intellectual space in order to engage with the gendered politics of visibility in the context of globalization.

Gendered Subjects and Global Visibility

Visibility, writes Foucault, is a trap. It assures the automatic functioning of power whose force lies "in a certain concerted distribution of bodies, surfaces, lights, gazes; in an arrangement whose internal mechanisms produce the relation in which individuals are caught up."[1] Following that logic, the gendered subject of globalization, far from being self-evident or transparent as often assumed, has to be situated within shifting formations of power. There is scholarly consensus that gendered categories being reproduced under transnational conditions need more nuanced research attention.[2] Global flows of media technologies, migration, and the unfettered mobility of capital rework old logics of domination in new global forms. The subject of sexuality and cultural politics gets caught in the global crossfire, and the issues are no longer contained within national borders and local domains.[3] The uneven formations of global cultures and their implications are a point of political and intellectual concern to scholars and activists alike.[4]

The essays in *Circuits of Visibility* track the ways in which gendered subjects are produced and defined in transnationally networked, media-saturated environments. Driving this production is the flow of capital, with its complex global infrastructure of commodities, resources, and bodies. Media technologies, systems of representation, and information networks constitute the circuitry that transport modalities of power, producing what Grewal and Kaplan term "scattered hegemonies."[5] Hence, transnational media environments serve as a crucial site from which to examine gendered constructions and contradictions that underwrite globalization. Globalization represents a complex disjunctive order that is clearly not captured by the popular rhetoric of easy fusion and smooth cultural transitions; rather, it is marked by jagged contours which can no longer be captured in terms of simple binaries that characterize center-periphery models.[6] Taking this shift as a point of departure, the essays in this collection engage with debates about gender and sexuality as they are reconfigured in various parts of the globe.

The rhetoric of securitization and the neoliberal marketplace are key registers through which gendered subjectivities are currently being defined, disciplined, and deployed across spatial and temporal boundaries. Since sexuality has historically played a central role in the ways in which dominant Western views on cultural differences are coded, sexual politics continues to be highly racialized in globality. In the context of global economic fluctuations and mobility, resorting to simple reductive binaries has become a paradigmatic mode of response to describe difference. These evocations, when layered within other political and economic assemblages and scripts, have material implications. As Joan Scott reminds us, the "ruses of essentialism, in whatever guises they come, ultimately perpetuate inequalities and militate against change."[7]

How does the problematic of gender surface and morph within the space of transnational public cultures? Inderpal Grewal advances a persuasive argument for thinking about "the heterogeneous and multiple transnational connectivities that produced various meanings of the term global."[8] She cautions that a theory of connectivity should be historicized and include incompleteness, exclusions, and unevenness. To produce a gendered understanding of globality is to show how these absences and invisibilities are produced and sustained through mediated reiterations that cross borders and communities. In that spirit, by way of introducing the issues, let me offer a few examples drawn to highlight how particular types of gendered visibility are normalized within the asymmetries of transnational linkages.

The Afghan woman, whose body provided the moral justification for the war on terror, stands out as the most enduring and iconic image of gendered oppression. Her abject body surfaces only to consolidate cultural differences in terms of a civilizational clash and set the stage for pastoral power of Western benevolence. Visually captured and circulated by the media, the gesture of recue and foregrounding of Afghan women as victims reinforces the superiority of the West. By default, the West is seen as the haven of democracy, secularism, and an enlightened citizenry fortified with agency and choice. In Europe, recent political controversies have once again made the Islamic veil signify the split between Western modernity and the Islamic world. The wearing of the Islamic veil, in most of its forms, has been conflated with oppression, patriarchal control, and subordinate status of Muslim women. The subject of gender is predictably drawn into public view and grafted onto other social and political agendas. The rhetoric about veiling today is being recuperated in the context of widespread resistance to Muslim migration. Defending a total ban on the veil, French prime minister Nicolas Sarkozy declared that the veil is an attack on French ideas of how to live together: "Citizenship has to be lived with an uncovered face."[9] A similar statement sparked national debate about the very possibility of a multicultural society in Britain in 2006 when Jack Straw, a British Labor Party politician, stated that the *niqab* was a "visible statement of separation and of difference."[10] The veiled body of the Muslim woman is singled out as the one that refuses integrations with the national community through a sartorial barrier. What stands out in these examples is how questions of modernity and tradition are inserted into public culture and managed in terms of symbolic meaning and material practices.[11] Transnational communities and the presence of deterritorialized cultures unsettle dominant definitions of publics and citizenship. The veil sets the Muslim woman apart as incapable of participating in a communicable modernity, thereby perpetuating the view of the West as the end point—the destination for the rest of the world, which, as Dipesh Chakrabarty notes, is delegated to the waiting rooms of history, lacking contemporaneity with the West.[12]

In the context of American exceptionalism and the war against terror, the regulation of sexualities has lately mobilized an assemblage of discourses once again linking nationalism, heteronormativity, whiteness, and citizenship. The transnational production of sexualized bodies works in concert with power and technology, as seen in the digital circulation of the torture images from Abu Ghraib prison in Iraq. The Abu Ghraib photographs publicizing the inhumane treatment meted out to Iraqi prisoners shocked the world. The image of Private Lynndie England holding a leash attached to the neck of a crawling, naked Iraqi prisoner digitally flashed across the world, evoking outrage about American brutality and arrogance and the dehumanization of Muslim men. The pictures of England and the detainees, according to Allen Feldman, represent a visual circuitry of gender reversal. Iraqi prisoners are emasculated and stripped of their sexual power by the white woman soldier, who in her pose of dominance serves as the emblematic figure of these rites of gender inversion.[13] The Abu Ghraib scandal, with its complex figurations of race, sexuality, and gender, has to be situated against the framework of U.S. nationalism. Here sexuality, as Jasbir Puar writes, is not a situation out of control, but rather "it constitutes a systemic, intrinsic, and pivotal module of power relations."[14]

With the transnational circulation of media images, the hegemony of the West is reproduced in the global imaginary as the site of progressive sexual politics and cosmopolitan modernity. As Inderpal Grewal and Caren Kaplan write, "the United States and Europe are figured as modern and thus as the sites of progressive social movements, while other parts of the world are presumed to be traditional, especially in regard to sexuality."[15] It is this assumption, for example, that drives the problematic immigration tests which measure the assimilability of would-be immigrants by gauging their response to supposedly progressive Dutch values about sexuality.[16] Ironically what signifies a liberal worldview associated with the West is deployed as an instrument of "shock and awe" for potential immigrants. Sexuality, mobility, and scripts of modernity are deeply intertwined in the production of the transnational subject.

Popular discussions, according to Ara Wilson, conflate Western, modern, and globalization as the source of sexual modernity, particularly nonnormative sexuality, reproducing what she calls "a general framework of an import-export calculus."[17] For example, on July 2009, when the New Delhi High Court decriminalized homosexuality in India, many in the media termed the victory "India's Stonewall."[18] The developmental narrative with the West as the site of sexual liberation stays intact in these scripts.[19] The hegemony of the West and its sexual modernity has been an important form of control since the colonial civilizing mission; today, its presence and power is pervasive due to the global media flows.

Sexual cultures of postcolonial societies continue to have a tangled and contested relationship to Western modernity and its public manifestations in the world of consumption. In January 2009, a group of activists in India belonging to a Hindu right-wing organization physically attacked women in a bar in the town of Mangalore, stating that the women were indulging in activities that went against the grain of Indian culture. India's media went full throttle, covering the event with sensational titles such as "Talibanisation of India." The clips of the women being brutally beaten and dragged were replayed over and over again in the media. There was heated debate about the moral policing and "domestic terrorism" that was being directed against women. A very successfully managed campaign lashed back at the conservative Hindu group, rallying support through the Internet.[20] The political organizing and retaliation by urban youth was made possible though social networking technologies. The blogosphere created a vibrant space for a new form of feminist debate using the language and tactics of the marketplace.

The incident forced a repetition of the familiar discourse of protection. The attackers justified their violence as necessary response to restrain women from their anti-Indian activity of being in a bar. The men claimed that they were suspicious of young women who were independent and "Westernized," thereby reviving a civilizational discourse in which *moral* and *local* are conflated and are held in opposition to *degenerate* and *global*. An Indian politician affiliated with the Hindu right-wing party (BJP) commented on the incident and what he perceived as global contamination of Indian values: "India cannot remain India if it becomes America."[21] America, as transnational imaginary, was contaminating authentic expressions of sexuality through a penetration of new consumption practices and desires.[22]

The politics and performance of sexuality, as demonstrated by these various examples, are situated within the complex histories and economies of the local, the structures of global capitalism, and transnational media flows. The move to study globalization through a gendered optics and from different material sites is particularly relevant in the context of conspicuous consumption. Packaging market-driven interests as social values, neoliberalism reshuffles the meaning of public responsibility and citizenship into the language of private choices and entitlements. This neoliberal ethic in its transnational travels is rapidly reshaping social formations and cultural practices, with gendered consequences.[23] However, global consumer culture, in its commodification of difference, actively erases historical memory in the production of newer forms of power. Using textual and ethnographic data from various global sites, the essays in *Circuits of Visibility* discuss how gender and sexuality are constituted, come into public visibility, and in the process get entangled within transnational configurations of power.

The literature on globalization, according to Saskia Sassen, needs to address "gendered instantiations" of the moment in order to render visible what is now evicted from the account.[24] The objective of this collection is to gain a more nuanced understanding and active consideration of global transformations and their impact on gendered subjectivities and sexual politics. Globalization and transnational flows have received extensive academic attention across disciplines. As Jacqui Alexander and Chandra Mohanty write, "There is an ongoing theoretical challenge to uncover the cultural, political, and economic interplay between the very categories of the global and the local."[25] This challenge to decenter categories takes on new dimensions with changes in the global social and political landscape. Scholars have undertaken this critical task by addressing how new modes of power inscribe sexuality and gender within assemblages spanning domains such as nationalism, citizenship, governmentality, public-sphere formations, and flows of labor and capital.[26] Motivated by feminist concerns and postcolonial critique, *Circuits of Visibility* attempts to provide deep and textured contextualization of gender and sexual politics.

Mediated Cultures

In the global context, questions of culture, subjectivity, and everyday life have to be situated against the ubiquitous presence and proliferation of communication technologies and their ability to transcend time and space. Increasingly embedded in the circuits of social life, media forms collide with established cultural practices, forcing reconfigurations of categories such as private/public, tradi-tion/modernity, and global/local. The pervasiveness of these processes and the level of media saturation necessitate a critical defamiliarization of media pres-ence in everyday life and culture. As W. J. T. Mitchell and Mark B. N. Hansen write, media can no longer be dismissed as neutral or transparent, subordinate or merely supplemental to the information they carry. Instead they "broker the giving of space and time within which concrete experience becomes possible."[27] The cultures and practices developed around media forms provide an analytical space from which to examine how the global is performed, reproduced, and con-tested within the material specificities of everyday life. Local moments, as Saskia Sassen argues, are found to be at the center of the global, rather than being the nonglobal.[28] Taking a broad perspective on media and media forms, the essays in *Circuits of Visibility* direct focused attention to the ways in which gender and sex-uality are constituted and regulated via transnational media flows and networks.

The pathways of media that crisscross national boundaries create a virtual sensorium that permeates the local and cultural life of communities. As Brian Larkin argues, the meaning attached to technologies and "the social uses to which they are put are not an inevitable consequence but something worked out over time and in the context of considerable cultural debate."[29] These cultural trans-formations are located within the instabilities of transnational political and eco-nomic linkages. The approach of the essays in this book shares the perspective of media anthropology and interdisciplinary media scholarship, which situate media as social practice.[30] This enables a reading of the constitution of everyday life, the workings of power, and the production of individual and collective iden-tities.

The essays engage with global dynamics of media in order to render visible the selective promotion of gendered identities within new cultural, political, and eco-nomic configurations. According to Arjun Appadurai, because of the multiplicity of forms and the speed in which they move through daily life routines, electronic media provide resources for self-imagining as an everyday project.

> Thus the biographies of ordinary people are constructions (or fabrications) in
> which the imagination plays an important role. Nor is this role a simple matter of
> escape (holding steady the conventions that govern the rest of social life), for in the
> grinding of gears between unfolding lives and their imagined counterparts a variety
> of imagined communities ... is formed, communities that generate new kinds of
> politics, new kinds of collective expression, and new needs for social discipline and
> surveillance on the part of elites.[31]

Further, this work of the imagination, Appadurai argues, cannot be assumed to be wholly emancipatory or entirely disciplined but stands as a space of contestation where individuals work the global into their own practices of the modern.[32] This process is steeped within the historical and political trajectories of the nation and is most visible in the spaces of consumption and popular culture where narratives of desire, gender, and commodity overlap in particular formations.

The circulation of media images and commodities draws the global consumer into the circuits of the global cultural economy and its distinct ideological imprints. Consumers in the Global South flex this commodity space in order to create new responses to the scripts of Western modernity. In Kathmandu, for example, Mark Liechty notes that people use fashion as a means both to identify with other fashionable people locally and to forge imaginative links with the global culture of urban modernity.[33] Here is an illustrative response from one of Liechty's respondents: "According to our religion . . . , it's written that women shouldn't be prostitutes, dancers, and all this. But just for society I have to wear *makeup*, lip stick, eye makeup, fancy clothes, . . . or else they'll say, Eh! What a hillbilly . . . she is !"[34] Fashion stands in as a marker of global cosmopolitanism, although it is perceived as frivolous in the local context. It is interesting that the respondent in Liechty's ethnography supports her claim about cultural authenticity not only by citing the textual authority of religion but also by referring to a rural/urban divide which in turn serves as a proxy for local/cosmopolitan.

Cinema works with the consumer market in mobilizing alternative versions of modernity in various parts of the Global South and among immigrant groups.[35] In India, the Bollywood industry has had a dramatic influence on the fashion industry and in the creation of a new Indo-Western aesthetic in contemporary women's fashions in which Western functionality, or what is locally called "modern," meets ethnic design and traditional norms of feminine decorum and modesty. These mediated pathways of consumer discourse make available alluring global subject positions which are flexed and made pliable enough to accommodate local ideologies of gendered bodily comportment, thereby creating an interactive form of modernity.[36]

These adaptations and overlay are not always so smooth; they are more often the sites of violent contestations, especially when the sexualized body becomes the flash point and the surface on which other anxieties about globalization and modernity are contested. The situation of women working in the export-processing zones of Mexico and China or even the call centers of India are illustrative of how the global labor market reorganizes social worlds, with violent consequences.[37] The manner in which questions of gender and sexuality gain publicity is a commentary on how social worlds are produced and regulated. As Arvind Rajagopal writes, relations between individuals tend to be mediated more and more through markets and media, increasing the distance between individuals even as, in imagination, they grow closer.[38]

The essays in *Circuits of Visibility* engage with media imaginaries and the manner in which they are inserted into the complex scripting and orchestration of gendered meanings and subject positions in globality. The essays in this book all speak to the fact that social relations are constituted in highly mediated environments which are no longer bound within the insularity of nations. The presence of media and technology, in all the various sites examined in *Circuits of Visibility*, enables the exploration of complex transnational circuits that connect capital to the routines of everyday life. The prodigious discourse generated through the labyrinth of communication systems, technologies, and platforms does not necessarily translate into the creation of a democratic transnational public sphere. The media are part of the global machinery that discounts history in its populist emphasis on the present and the future. It is also the presence of media technologies that is assumed to deliver societies into the threshold of a hegemonic Euro-American modernity. At this juncture when technology holds sway, it is important, as David Morley reminds us, "to pay attention to the particularities of the media, without reifying their status and thus isolating them from the dynamics of the economic, social and political contexts in which they operate."[39]

Tracking Transnational Circuits

The essays in *Circuits of Visibility* collectively advance a discussion about sexual politics, mediated environments, and cultures of globality. They do so by mapping how forms of visibility and invisibility, with reference to the gendered body, are produced and sustained across borders, markets, and communities. In addition to a general inattention to issues of gender, accounts of globalization have been critiqued for the assumption that mapping the facticity of economic linkages and population flows is sufficient to account for current cultural forms and subjective interiorities.[40] The study of the mediated and transnational production of gender and sexuality requires deep contextualization. The intellectual challenge is to rethink categories such as nation, tradition, modernity, culture, and gender in mobile and pliable terms rather than as territorial and fixed. To do so, critical practice has to work against familiar models of cultural critique that rest on essentialized dichotomies, universalism, and an unquestioned Eurocentrism. Postcolonial feminist scholars have long argued for the need to highlight the politics of transnational linkages and problematize the lines cutting across center and periphery.[41] The sign of the transnational is used here, in both its descriptive and heuristic sense, to capture the layering of social, political, economic, and mediated processes that exceed conventional boundaries. The transnational provides an analytical framework to open the terrain of media cultures, gender, and everyday life in dynamic interrelationality. The transnational as an optic and approach "creates a space to imagine options for social transformation that are obscured when borders, boundaries and the structures, processes and actors within them are taken as given."[42] The contributions engage with the strategic processes and follow the mediated circuits through which gendered categories travel.

A variety of questions animates the discussion raised in this collection of essays: What forms of publicity do gender politics take in a transnational world? How does the pervasive presence of an ethos of consumerism and the hypermobility of capital flows influence various sites of cultural production? In the wake of neoliberal transformations, what types of hybrid and gendered performances follow or are expected to come into being? How are newer forms of racialized tensions, nativism, and violence worked into global scripts of sexuality? How have debates on the private/public distinctions been mediated and mobilized globally? How has the history and genealogy of knowledge production impacted the framing of these debates? What are the terms of admittance into the transnational public sphere, both in terms of discourse and materiality of experience? How do media forms and technologies reframe, merge, and morph the debates on gender in transnational registers?

The essays in this book engage with these questions and more from multiple global locations and theoretical perspectives. The four-part structure of the book is determined by the central problematics that emerge from the essays around the subjects of visibility, ideology, capital, and technology. The essays track the circulation of bodies, aesthetics, media forms, and technologies across national borders and map the ways in which dominant power structures frame sexual identities and practices.

Part 1, "Configuring Visibilities," presents chapters about the travel of visual practices of modernity, the creation of a neoliberal aesthetic, the transnational hegemony of whiteness, and the mediated circulation and global reproduction of ethnic categories. These essays all deal with the processes and intricate routes through which issues regarding gender come into visibility. Since the global circulation of media and the technologies of social networking have exploded the notion of a singular public, it is far more productive to find ways to engage with the public sphere as a field of discursive connections.[43] Within these multiple ways of imagining social worlds, certain discourses gain public attention with particular ideological inflections, relegating other issues to the largely invisible confines of the private domain. Tracking such configurations poses a methodological challenge and necessitates a multisited approach in order to highlight the interconnections between levels of discourse and the cultural practices of everyday life.

Susan Ossman asks how certain regimes of gendered visibility dictate the publicizing of the nation and its leadership. Through an examination of the visual cultures of royal display in Morocco, Ossman advances a larger argument about the consolidation or reinforcement of gendered forms of power. The introduction of Princess Salma in representations and portraiture of the royal family is interpreted by Ossman as transnational management of a visual grammar of the nation. As sartorial choices stand in as indices of modernity, managing visibility and calibrating appearances assume dynamic transnational dimensions in the Arab world.

Stripping history of controversy is the way of the neoliberal marketplace. It is also the same logic that drives the publicity for a Balkan singer with a complicated affiliation to the violence of her nation's past. Through a close reading of singer Ceca's highly sexualized performance and research with her fans, authors Zala Volčič and Karmen Erjavec show how the Balkan diva leverages her iconic national status in redefining herself as a borderless celebrity. The global media machinery ensures that the malleability of celebrity presence trumps Ceca's nationalist politics.

Angharad Valdivia focuses on how the transnational flow of media reproduces types of racial normativity. An examination of received forms of hybridity enables Valdivia to engage with power structures that define the gendered face of Latinidad, as deployed by popular culture. Revisiting popular sites of mediated cultural production and the global travel of form, artifacts, and actors enables Valdivia to question the limits of cultural categories as revealed through the scalar collision of the national and the transnational.

Radhika Parameswaran provides a critical treatment of whiteness against a transnational web of visual technologies as they permeate the fabric of everyday life in India. Blending textual analysis and ethnography, Parameswaran shows how whiteness, evoked within the national space of India through various media technologies, impacts the performance and lived experience of gender. The politics of the "fluctuating epidermis" is premised on the complex transnational histories of whiteness and colonialism.

Part 2, "Contesting Ideologies," follows with a multisited discussion on gendered regimes of normativity that underlie the production of transnational spaces. In a world connected by media technologies, new lines of power shape social norms, social interactions, and ways of being in the world. Global ideoscapes collide with local cultures and traditions, placing gendered bodies right at the center of the crossfire. Normative scripts of nationalism, intact with exclusionary forms of admittance and regulation of populations, constitute the basis for the policing of gendered bodies. When projected on the transnational screen, the structures of Western modernity and sexual hegemony are inscribed over non-Western bodies, thereby consolidating new forms of domination.

Islam and sexuality have been assigned a visible place in public debate as media spectacles, mainly through the yoking of disparate issues and players. Examining Islamic practices of self-making that are distinct from the Western liberal scripts reveals alternate social imaginaries and the new mediated, public face of Islam. Nabil Echchaibi in his essay captures modes of projecting Islam into public visibility through alternative formulations of mediated masculinity. The transnational circulation and reach of new media technologies enable Muslim televangelists to articulate an Islamic modernity in cosmopolitan terms. Echchaibi engages with how this project of religious revivalism recasts the gendered debate within Islam in a new global paradigm.

Globalization has precipitated the suturing of issues where various forms of disciplinary power coalesce. Nowhere is this better seen than in the immigration system, where surveilling techniques place immigrants within a wide centralized network of power. Felicity Schaeffer-Grabiel discusses global media outreach against sex trafficking. In this context, metaphors of slavery are used to foment gendered panics and then inevitably slide into debates on boundaries and exclusions. Media forms create what Schaeffer-Grabiel calls a "culture of repetition," in which Western nations have to be quarantined from the cross-border contamination of expendable gendered bodies.

Julie Thomas turns our attention to the media space of the Petit Palais museum in Paris and its remaking of immigrant women as producers and consumers of commodified nationalism. Thomas examines the institutional role of the museum in circulating national culture and the penetrative power of its civilizing mission in France. This essay takes us through the Petit Palais to demonstrate that to be modern is to act like the West.[44] Like the garments featured in the exhibition, behavior for immigrant women, writes Thomas, must be "customized" and "reinvented" in order to be deemed assimilable.

Extending the gendered implications of the project of modernity and the narrative of humanitarianism, Spring-Serenity Duvall turns the focus to celebrities and their place in the neoliberal framework and dispensation of care. This essay demonstrates the coming together of the marketplace, media spectaclization of celebrity, and images of motherhood. Angelina Jolie as the postfeminist mouthpiece and savior of the Global South mobilizes a new politics of transnational care that is carefully grounded within the frames of U.S. exceptionalism. The travel of celebrities from the West and their projection of care continue a familiar West-rest/North-South script. These dichotomies are reinforced and replayed by the media in the exotic visual coverage of Jolie in distressed global regions.

Part 3, "Capital Trails," transports the discussion to the ways in which gender and the subject of sexuality are deployed through media technologies in the construction of commodities and labor. Mainstream accounts of globalization, as noted earlier, often proceed on purely economic and gender-neutral terms. By bringing in mediated influences and opening up the space of analysis, the essays in this section situate the meanings of gendered labor against a broad canvas of intersecting forces. Aihwa Ong states that economic rationalities of globalization and the cultural dynamics that shape human and political response have to be brought together in the same analytical frame.[45] Economic lines of power have historically been deeply entrenched within the materialities of race and gender divisions. In globality, the media exacerbate the tensions within these intersections.

Minoo Moallem offers an exploration of the world of connoisseur books and their historical investments in the circulatory value of the Persian carpet. Moallem tracks the transnational connections between the history of commodities, modes of economic exchange, mediated knowledge, and women's labor in carpet production. Distancing the carpet from the gendered and embodied experience surrounding its production, this system of expert knowledge is embedded in a scopic economy that displays total mastery of the Other and the "not-so-civilized" cultures of the East.

The saga of modernity takes aggressive new turns in India with the emergence of economic liberalization and technologized work environments. My chapter examines how the neoliberal economy seeps into everyday practices of local lives, enabled by the support of local infrastructures. The rape of a call-center employee in Bangalore opens up a discussion of the discursive grammars through which the gendered body is made visible in the articulation of global modernities. I engage with the asymmetries that underwrite the creation of a transnationally positioned yet locally bound and malleable labor force.

The subject of mobility is central to the next two essays, which map migration within the pathways of global capital. Through a blending of ethnography and textual readings, Wanning Sun notes that the circuit of transnational capital is inhabited not only by power elites but also by invisible laboring bodies. Here we see the coming together of the dynamics and flexibility of global mobility cast against the limitations of translocal movements. The figure of the Chinese migrant domestic worker serves to frame Sun's argument that class and gender intersect to produce specific conditions of subjection in China's globalized capitalist market.

In globality, both state and corporate actors are vested in the creation of a citizenry oriented to the consumption of global products. Jan Maghinay Padios shows through careful ethnographically informed examination how the overseas Filipino community is transformed into a transnational migrant market. A global media machinery both creates and sustains a transnational imaginary within which the affective structures of immigrant lives are played out. Gendered roles and images of motherhood are leveraged in the neoliberal campaign to rearticulate citizenship in terms of consumption.

Part 4, "Technologies of Control," explores how the intimacies of capitalism, governmentality, and new technologies establish the terms on which sexuality is foregrounded. Through a range of subjects—human rights, queer subjectivities, cultural citizenship, and diasporic politics—the authors follow an assemblage of regulatory practices instituted and transported through mediated channels and mechanisms. The ubiquity of new media technologies and their power to morph between platforms are often equated to their transparency and liberatory potential. Deconstructing these claims through a close reading of the technologized frames that define sociality, these essays probe the lines of power within the economies of visual and digital media.

While new technologies enable the rapid global circulation of information and images of human rights violations, Sujata Moorti shows how visual documentation of civil crises in the Global South reinscribe a digital colonialism. In her analysis of the teachers' strike in Oaxaca and the protests in Myanmar, she argues that the Internet and cell-phone footage from citizens-turned-journalists have transformed the narration of human rights from national and local registers into spectacles for transnational consumption. In the process, paradoxically, the Internet recenters the West and reproduces geopolitical asymmetries of race and gender.

The production of public queer cultures as sites of media consumption is the subject of Audrey Yue's essay. Sexuality is used strategically in Singapore to promote consumption and further the state's image as a global media hub. While homosexuality is illegal and actively policed, it is incorporated into the cultural and mediated life of the city, following the market-driven dictates of the neoliberal economy. Yue examines what consumption practices, especially for lesbians, reveal about claims to citizenship and participation in transnational networks.

Saskia Witteborn's chapter looks at diasporic imaginaries and cultural politics as defined outside the boundaries of nation. The focus of this chapter is on the persona of Rebiya Kadeer, who spearheads a political agenda for the Uyghur diasporic community. Using the tropes of motherhood and nature, Kadeer scripts a global media presence for the cause. A transnational politics of visibility for the Uyghurs is predicated on the deployment of conventional gender scripts which stand in for tradition and history. Communication technologies, in this case, become the site and conduit for reconstruction of lost localities and cultures.

Noor Al-Qasimi turns her focus to the questions of governmentality and the regulation of queer subjectivities in cyberspace. For the "post-oil" generation in the United Arab Emirates, the use of social networking websites has led to the creation of a transnational pan-Gulfian queer imaginary that unsettles notions of sovereignty and territoriality. Cyberspace, argues Al-Qasimi, provides a political space for transgressive expression. However, the question remains to what extent it displaces the governance of gender that is embedded within the framework of the state's preoccupation with its global image and the preservation of an authentic, regional cultural identity.

The essays in their diversity reveal that the politics of sexuality is never a discrete area of practice. Traveling through various global sites, the questions raised address crosscutting issues that exceed conventional boundaries of the nation. The essays resist linear characterizations and attempt the critical work of bringing issues into productive crisis.[46] *Circuits of Visibility* initiates a collective conversation and political critique about the mediated global terrain on which sexuality is defined, performed, regulated, made visible, and experienced.

NOTES

1. Michel Foucault, *Discipline and Punish: The Birth of the Prison*, trans. Alan Sheridan (New York: Vintage Books, 1979), 200, 202.

2. For more on this subject, see Amrita Basu, Inderpal Grewal, and Lisa Malki, eds., "Globalization and Gender," special issue, *Signs* 26, no. 4 (Summer 2001).

3. See Yukiko Hanawa, "Circuits of Desire: Introduction," *Positions* 2, no. 1 (1994): v–xi; Jasbir Puar, "Global Circuits: Transnational Sexualities and Trinidad," *Signs* 26, no. 4 (Summer 2001): 1039–1065; Jigna Desai, "Homo on the Range: Mobile and Global Sexualities," *Social Text* 20, no. 4 (Winter 2002): 65–89; Anjali Arondekar, "Border/Line Sex," *Interventions* 7, no. 2 (2005): 236–250.

4. Many of these ideas were first formulated in Radha S. Hegde, "Transnational Feminist Media Studies," in Wolfgang Donsbach, ed., *International Encyclopedia of Communication* (Malden, MA: Blackwell, 2008), 1794–1799; Radha S. Hegde, "Globalizing Gender Studies in Communication," in Julia Wood and Bonnie Dow eds., *Handbook on Gender Studies in Communication* (Thousand Oaks, CA: Sage, 2006), 433–449.

5. Inderpal Grewal and Caren Kaplan, eds., *Scattered Hegemonies: Postmodernity and Transnational Feminist Practice* (Minneapolis: University of Minnesota Press, 1994).

6. Appadurai argues that globalization constitutes "a complex overlapping, disjunctive order that cannot any longer be understood in terms of existing center-periphery models." See Arjun Appadurai, *Modernity at Large: Cultural Dimensions of Globalization* (Minneapolis: University of Minnesota Press, 1996), 32.

7. Joan Wallach Scott, "Feminist Reverberations," *Differences* 13 (2002): 8.

8. Inderpal Grewal, *Transnational America: Feminisms, Diasporas, Neoliberalisms* (Durham, NC: Duke University Press, 2005), 22–24.

9. Lizzy Davies, "Nicolas Sarkozy's Cabinet Approves Bill to Ban Full Islamic Veil," *Guardian* (May 19, 2010), http://www.guardian.co.uk/world/2010/may/19/nicolas-sarkozy-defends-veil-ban/ (accessed May 17, 2010).

10. Jack Straw, "I Want to Unveil My Views on an Important Issue," *Telegraph* (October 10, 2006), http://www.telegraph.co.uk/news/main.jhtml?xml=/news/2006/10/06/nveils106.xml (accessed August 3, 2007).

11. For more on this subject, see Radha S. Hegde, "Eyeing New Publics: Veiling and the Performance of Civic Visibility," in Daniel C. Brouwer and Robert Asen, eds., *Public Modalities* (Tuscaloosa: University of Alabama Press, 2010), 54–172.

12. Dipesh Chakrabarty, *Provincializing Europe: Postcolonial Thought and Historical Difference* (Princeton, NJ: Princeton University Press, 2000); Joan Wallach Scott, *Politics of the Veil* (Princeton, NJ: Princeton University Press, 2007).

13. Allen Feldman, "On the Actuarial Gaze: From 9/11 to Abu Ghraib," *Cultural Studies* 19, no. 2 (March 2005): 203–226.

14. Jasbir Puar, *Terrorist Assemblages: Homonationalism in Queer Times* (Durham, NC: Duke University Press, 2007), 113.

15. Inderpal Grewal and Caren Kaplan, "Global Identities: Theorizing Transnational Studies of Sexuality," *GLQ: A Journal of Lesbian and Gay Studies* 7, no. 4 (2001): 663–679.

16. Gregory Crouch, "Dutch Immigration Kit Offers a Revealing View," *New York Times* (March 16, 2006), http://www.nytimes.com/2006/03/16/world/europe/16iht-dutch-5852942.html (accessed August 3, 2007).

17. Ara Wilson, "Queering Asia," *Intersections: Gender, History and Culture in the Asian Context* 14 (November 2006), http://intersections.anu.edu.au/issue14/wilson.html (accessed June 18, 2008).

18. Mansi Poddar, "India Decriminalizes Gay Sex," *Huffington Post* (July 2, 2009), http://www.huffingtonpost.com/2009/07/02/india-decriminalizes-gay_n_224656.html (accessed May 19, 2010).

19. For more on this theme, see Martin F. Manalansan, "In the Shadows of Stonewall: Examining Gay Transnational Politics," *GLQ: A Journal of Lesbian and Gay Studies* 2 (1995): 425–438; Gayatri Gopinath, *Impossible Desires: Queer Diasporas and South Asian Public Cultures* (Durham, NC: Duke University Press, 2005); Lisa Rofel, *Desiring China: Experiments in Neoliberalism, Sexuality, and Public Culture* (Durham, NC: Duke University Press, 2007).

20. Nisha Susan, "Why We Said Pants to India's Bigots," *Guardian* (February 15, 2009), http://www.guardian.co.uk/commentisfree/2009/feb/15/india-gender (accessed May 20, 2010).

21. AlJazeeraEnglish, "Indian Extremists Want to Limit Women's Freedom," *YouTube* (February14, 2009), http://www.youtube.com/watch?v=yTNPZGWPqIY&NR=1 (accessed June 17, 2008).

22. Grewal, *Transnational America*.

23. Angela McRobbie, *The Aftermath of Feminism: Gender, Culture and Social Change* (London: Sage, 2009).

24. Saskia Sassen, *Globalization and Its Discontents* (New York: New Press, 1998).

25. M. Jacqui Alexander and Chandra Talpade Mohanty, "Introduction: Genealogies, Legacies, Movements," in M. Jacqui Alexander and Chandra Talpade Mohanty, eds., *Feminist Genealogies, Colonial Legacies, Democratic Futures* (London: Routledge, 1997), xi.

26. It is beyond the scope of this introduction to review the growing body of literature on gender and sexuality and globalization. I draw attention to some select contributions which have been significant in retheorizing gender and sexuality from a transnational framework: Alexander and Mohanty, *Feminist Genealogies, Colonial Legacies, Democratic Futures*; Grewal and Kaplan, *Scattered Hegemonies*; Ella Shohat, ed., *Talking Visions: Multicultural Feminism in a Transnational Age* (Cambridge, MA: MIT Press, 2001); Ella Shohat and Robert Stam, *Multiculturalism, Postcoloniality and Transnational Media* (New Brunswick, NJ: Rutgers University Press, 2003); Anne McClintock, Aamir Mufti, and Ella Shohat, eds., *Dangerous Liaisons: Gender, Nation, and Postcolonial Perspectives* (Minneapolis: University of Minnesota Press, 1997); Caren Kaplan,

Norma Alarcon, and Minoo Moallem, eds., *Between Woman and Nation: Nationalism, Transnational Feminisms, and the State* (Durham, NC: Duke University Press, 1999); Andrew Parker, Mary Russo, Doris Sommer, and Patricia Yaeger, eds., *Nationalism and Sexualities* (New York: London, 1992); Marianne DeKoven, ed., *Feminist Locations: Global and Local, Theory and Practice* (New Brunswick, NJ: Rutgers University Press, 2001); Sara Ahmed, Claudia Castañeda, Anne-Marie Fortier, and Mimi Sheller, eds., *Uprootings/Regroundings: Questions of Home and Migration* (Oxford, UK: Berg, 2003).

27. W. J. T. Mitchell and Mark B. N. Hansen, *Critical Terms for Media Studies* (Chicago: University of Chicago Press, 2010).

28. Saskia Sassen, "Afterword: Knowledge Practices and Subject Making at the Edge," in Melissa Fisher and Greg Downey, eds., *Frontiers of Capital: Ethnographic Reflections on the New Economy* (Durham, NC: Duke University Press, 2006), 307.

29. Brian Larkin, *Signal and Noise: Media, Infrastructure, and Urban Culture in Nigeria* (Durham, NC: Duke University Press, 2008), 3.

30. Faye D. Ginsburg, Lila Abu-Lughod, and Brian Larkin, introduction to Faye D. Ginsburg, Lila Abu-Lughod, and Brian Larkin, eds., *Media Worlds: Anthropology on New Terrain* (Los Angeles: University of California Press, 2002), 1–38; Kelly Askew and Richard R. Wilk, eds., *Anthropology of the Media* (Malden, MA: Blackwell, 2002); Nick Couldry and Anna McCarthy, eds., *MediaSpace: Place, Scale and Culture in Media Age* (London: Routledge, 2004).

31. Appadurai, *Modernity at Large*, 54.

32. Ibid., 4.

33. Mark Liechty, *Suitably Modern: Making Middle-Class Culture in a New Consumer Society* (Princeton, NJ: Princeton University Press, 2003).

34. Ibid., 137.

35. On this point, see the work of Brian Larkin Signal, *Noise: Media, Infrastructure, and Urban Culture in Nigeria* (Durham, NC: Duke University Press, 2008); and Dilip Gaonkar, *Alternative Modernities* (Durham, NC: Duke University Press, 2001).

36. For more on interactive modernity and public culture, see Arjun Appadurai and Carol Breckenridge, introduction to Carol Breckenridge, ed., *Consuming Modernity: Public Culture in Contemporary India* (Delhi: Oxford University Press 1996), 1–20.

37. On this issue, see Melissa Wright, *Disposable Women and Other Myths of Global Capitalism* (New York and London: Routledge, 2006); Melissa Wright, "The Private Parts of Public Value: The Regulation of Women Workers in China's Export-Processing Zones," in Joan W. Scott and Debra Keates, eds., *Going Public: Feminism and the Shifting Private Sphere* (Chicago: University of Illinois Press, 2004), 99–122; Kathleen Staudt, *Violence and Activism at the Border: Gender, Fear, and Everyday Life in Ciudad Juarez* (Austin: University of Texas Press, 2008).

38. Arvind Rajagopal, "Technologies of Perception and the Cultures of Globalization," *Social Text* 68 (Fall 2001): 1–9.

39. David Morley, *Media, Modernity and Technology: The Geography of the New* (London: Routledge, 2007), 1.

40. I draw this idea from Elizabeth A. Povinelli and George Chauncey, "Thinking Sexuality Transnationally," *GLQ: A Journal of Lesbian and Gay Studies* 5, no. 4 (1999): 439–450; Sassen also makes a similar point in *Globalization and Its Discontents*.

41. Grewal and Kaplan, "Global Identities"; Inderpal Grewal and Caren Kaplan, "Introduction: Transnational Feminist Practices and Questions of Postmodernity," in Grewal and Kaplan, *Scattered Hegemonies*, 1–33; Aihwa Ong, *Flexible Citizenship: The Cultural Logics of Transnationality* (Durham, NC: Duke University Press 1999); Chandra Talpade Mohanty, *Feminism across*

Borders: Decolonizing Theory, Practicing Solidarity (Durham, NC: Duke University Press, 2003); Caren Kaplan, "Transporting the Subject: Technologies of Mobility and Location in an Era of Globalization," in Ahmed et al., *Uprootings/Regroundings*, 207–223.

42. Peggy Levitt and Sanjeev Khagram, introduction to Peggy Levitt and Sanjeev Khagram, eds., *The Transnational Studies Reader: Intersections and Innovations* (New York: Routledge, 2007), 9.

43. Craig Calhoun, "Imagining Solidarity: Cosmopolitanism, Constitutional Patriotism, and the Public Sphere," *Public Culture* 14, no. 1 (Winter 2002): 147–171; Craig Calhoun, "Introduction: Habermas and the Public Sphere," in Craig Calhoun, ed., *Habermas and the Public Sphere* (Cambridge, MA: MIT Press, 1992), 1–50.

44. Timothy Mitchell, "The Stage of Modernity," in Timothy Mitchell, ed., *Questions of Modernity* (Minneapolis: University of Minnesota Press, 2000), 1.

45. Ong, *Flexible Citizenship*, 5.

46. According to Gayatri Spivak, to bring something into productive crisis is a necessary part of the maintenance of a practical politics of the open end. See Gayatri Spivak, *Postcolonial Critic: Interviews, Strategies, Dialogues* (New York: Routledge, 1990), 105.

Configuring Visibilities

1 Seeing Princess Salma

Transparency and Transnational Intimacies

Susan Ossman

In raising questions of how spaces of global media shape feminine visibility we find ourselves entangled in discussions about modernity and transparency that have remained lively for several decades. Women's exposure to the eyes of particular men, or of random publics, and concerns about what their clothing covers or what it reveals have often been used to demonstrate the position of entire societies or classes or families with respect to ideals of equality and liberation. Yet at the same time as women alter their skirts in sync with international fashion, their sartorial choices are also asked to stand for national or ethnic or religious identities; pictured in *burqas* or ball gowns, they become tiles in the mosaic of world cultures. An image of a world of flows or the idea of a kind of liquid society may be enticing and, indeed, may even correspond to the sensations engendered by the speed with which we can connect to people in faraway places via Internet or travel.[1] But such impressions of flowing and floating are often produced through the speeding up, multiplication, and blurring of fixed images. With respect to women, a scale of liberation that weighs them is calibrated first to weigh their clothing, then to examine what body parts are covered. The types of dress are inventoried, as are the kinds of occasions at which they are to be worn. A complex collection of scenes and types informs our interpretation of where an individual or group of women is located on the path of progress, indicating that more than attention to transparency or concealment is at work in shaping the politics of feminine visibility. Although much attention has been paid to the role of the veil, the *hijab*, when this "protection" appears as a piece of clothing that can be modeled, photographed, and worn, it is merely another picture in this evolving typology. It may act as an index of backwardness and a symbol of self-empowerment for others, but even the fully covered body can operate as a meaningful image in this system. What is difficult to tolerate is the absence of depiction. When meaning arises through the interplay of images that portray social positions and personal opinions, to refuse to present oneself or another in images becomes a problem.

In this chapter, I focus on one such conspicuous absence by following the media journey of Salma Bennani, who became the first publicly recognized wife to a Moroccan king in 2002. Princess Salma's appearance in royal family photos on the event of her marriage to the young king Mohammed VI pointed to the absence of the figure of the king's wife during the reigns of previous Moroccan kings. It also drew attention to the continuing refusal of other leaders elsewhere in the Arab world to admit their wives, following what have become international expectations regarding the composition and representation of first families. Without globally circulating norms for the composition of the family, tales of tumultuous affairs among international royalty would seldom be so eagerly reported in the popular press. The image of the first family in Morocco has progressively come to be based on the marriage of "one man and one woman," as the current rhetoric of conservative America would have it. Of course, in the United States, the issue of polygamy has been extremely peripheral to this debate, which has focused on gay marriage.[2] One might interpret King Mohammed VI's introduction of the first royal wife to the national and international arena as indicating his willingness to become more like other world leaders, whose wives act as both accessories and spokeswomen for their husbands.[3] But it would be wise not to forget that by publicizing himself as part of a couple, Mohammed VI did more than implicate himself and his princess into a new position with respect to global first couples. He also played on the limits of the Arab world and monarchy itself by coming out as a married man. Not only did his wife's picture now appear beside well-known female representatives of visible Arab wives such as the Jordanian queens, but it was also projected against the background of the invisible wives of other Arab leaders. Monarchs such as Abdullah of Jordan and Mohammed VI of Morocco publicize their monogamy in nations where polygamy is legal, and they display their wives as indicative of their modernity and the degree of liberation of women in their nations. In so doing they play not only on increasingly global norms of the family but also with the very ways in which tropes of progress and modernity have been associated with the increased transparency and visibility of women's bodies.

While I followed pictures as they moved to shape the nation and reinstate borders in Morocco under King Hassan II, I found that it was not sufficient to notice how the king's portraits showed him first in military uniform and then as a playboy, in religious garb, or in a cowboy hat.[4] The political import of these images was to be found not only in how they fixed certain notions of the monarch following globally circulating notions of various kinds of masculinity but also in what they excluded, what we forgot in viewing them. As pictures of the king moved across national borders into European magazines, Algerian newspapers, or American televisions, one could easily imagine that the sometimes scantily clad and always stylish princesses beside their father reflected the pro-Western alliances of the kingdom. Moroccans did often remark the absence of the children's mother in family portraits, and they were thrilled when the national television offered a furtive glance of her at the wedding party of one of her daughters.

The woman whom Hassan II referred to only as "the mother of my children" never appeared in family portraits. Meanwhile a tidal wave of pictures of the king and other members of his family circulated around the world. One might interpret this flow of pictures of his daughters and sons and grandchildren as a tactic to obscure the disparity between King Hassan's family photos and those of other nation's leaders, who appeared with their spouses.

By responding to this perceived absence of a wife, King Mohammed VI was generally seen as making a political statement on women's equality and drawing Morocco ever closer to the West.[5] He shifted his own position by this visible adherence to dominant international norms of what makes up a family. While Salma's presence at the king's side filled a striking gendered absence, it also revealed a logic of publicity that claims transparency while being at odds with the basic tenets of equal access and open communication. Discourses of human rights, democratic governance, and the ideal Habermasian public sphere are typically conceived as unimpeded spaces of dialogue among equals. But this attention to the free flow of ideas does not allow us to engage with some very important truths about political communication that are clearly evident in Princess Salma's coming out. In what follows, I thus part company with those writers who take the side of "free communication" and measure the progress of a nation according to narratives of progressive enlightenment. There is more behind what meets the eye in the introduction of the royal couple as a figure on the international political scene.[6]

While media reports in Morocco and internationally have tended to focus on the introduction of Mohammed VI's wife as a part of the royal family as indicative of the present king's modernity and progressiveness, I argue that Salma's appearance is more about the transnational management of the king's image. I draw on an analytic model of "three worlds" that I first developed through ethnographic research on social interactions, meaning, and judgment among women in the beauty salons of Casablanca, Paris, and Cairo.[7] This model of "three worlds" links day-to-day social interactions to distinct ways of making sense of things, being with others, and making judgments. In a series of studies, I have worked through the way access to particular kinds of social spaces teaches people to think and take action according to "worlds" that I label as proximate, rational, and celebrated. Here I cannot provide details to the entire chain of connection that tie together social spaces to these different ways of configuring truth. What I will do is to draw on the model to disentangle the multiple ways that the appearance of Salma repositions the king firmly within the heterosexual contract of marriage, allowing the Moroccan royal family the possibility of repositioning itself on the stage of regional and world politics. By following the interplay of several coexisting ways of making sense of Salma's image, we realize that what is really at stake in such representations is the figure of the king himself. The introduction of his wife to the world must be interpreted as a way of extending his own political reach and roles. This is possible not simply because of how the people of Morocco weave proximate, rational, and celebrity worlds into their lives but also because these social and cognitive worlds are no longer contained within national boundaries.

Selecting Salma

Salma Bennani was a young student when her sister introduced her to her fiancé, the soon-to-be King Mohammed VI. In the weeks leading up to her wedding, the Moroccan press made sure that everyone in the kingdom knew that she had lost her mother as a child, had lived in an ordinary family environment, and had excelled in math and science. She was indeed ranked first in her class at engineering school and gave up a scholarship to go to Canada to pursue her studies when she agreed to marry the king. In addition to her academic credentials, she appears to have been a model daughter. The highly complimentary coverage of the life of the soon-to-be princess emphasized her beauty, good upbringing, and morality. Some more religiously conservative people criticized her for shamelessly revealing her beautiful, long, red hair in the many photographs that accompanied the news of the upcoming marriage; for others, these pictures indicated the possibility that the king might champion the demands of liberal groups for women's rights. In online chat rooms and international discussions about the princess, her red hair and freckled pallor were sometimes taken as a sign of her foreign heritage, but among Moroccans, these traits represented her Fasi heritage and were discussed in terms of the king's close connection with Fez, a city known for its cultural prestige and wealthy, intellectually prominent families.[8]

While some religiously inspired critics referred to the princess as "the actress," implying that she displays herself in ways that connote sexual impropriety, others critiqued the rags-to-riches story of a poor orphan turned princess, a story disseminated by the national and European media. For all the accounts of how the king was smitten by the beauty and intelligence of his soon-to-be bride, all the people I interviewed in Morocco shortly after the wedding insisted that a royal wedding could not be so "spontaneous," arguing that potential spouses would have been carefully examined. When the bride-to-be is the very first wife of a nation's king to be publicly acknowledged, little could be left to chance. A quick look at Salma's face, her background, and her résumé suggest why she was considered the ideal partner for the king. Such a match is rarely accomplished through a love-at-first-sight formula, yet the romantic narrative of the way the orphan became a princess steers us strategically to notice not only Salma's resilient and feminine qualities but also those of the king who displayed such fine judgment as to fall in love with her.

The royal wedding allowed the king a chance to demonstrate his own qualities and capacity to rule. Whereas it would have seemed illogical for a king, whose office claims its legitimacy through ancestral links to the prophet Mohammed and ultimately to God as the Commander of the Faithful (*amir al mouminin*), to advertise his curriculum vitae in the media, his marriage to Salma, a simple girl of the people, allowed him the opportunity to do just that.[9] In addition to giving the king occasion to publicize his academic achievements and accomplishments, their marriage led to new political opportunities to absorb her qualifications into his, thereby entangling the process of ordering and judging power and politics. To advertise a monarch's academic accomplishments without such an event might be crass, but to publish them in parallel with those of his wife implies a certain kind of equality. Associating his image with hers allows him to publicize his ability to measure up according to impersonal measures such as diplomas. To move beyond the mere recognition of the revolutionary nature of viewing Morocco's king as part of a couple, we need to notice the different yet coexisting ways in which the image of Salma and her husband are projected. By reading the wedding by distinguishing three coexisting worlds of judgment of proximity, rationality, and celebrity, we can derive an understanding of how making Salma visible as a princess led to a particular incarnation of the royal couple, with specific implications for the image of the king and his kingdom.

The model of three worlds is an effort to move beyond binary oppositions that have shaped our understanding of the contemporary world in terms of oppositions of modernity and the global with tradition, locality, or personalism. This model recognizes contradiction as a part of the way in which power works through the world at large, and it identifies sites of friction not between classes or cultures but in terms of the varying degrees and situations in which certain worlds are put forth as dominant by an individual or entity such as a state. This model is derived from ethnographic work, and I have drawn out elsewhere the ways in which particular kinds of interactions lead people to learn about their distinctive manners of conceptualizing the world.[10] A short account of proximate, rational-legal, and celebrity worlds is in order.

Proximity stands for a world of face-to-face interaction where the opinions or actions of particular individuals have more weight than others, perhaps due to their age, gender, or reputation. We might associate this world with sites of social interaction where "regulars" exchange news and opinions. This world of proximity must be distinguished from a second world of *legal-rationality*, where individuals are assumed to be equal. In this realm, achievements lead to the valorization of individuals according to measurable skills, which include quantifiable standards ranging from test scores to dress sizes. Worlds of *celebrity*, on the other hand, not only involve us as audiences for global media reports of famous singers or politicians but also link us in our daily lives to charismatic figures we actually know, be they high school prom queens or college football stars. We judge these individuals in terms of their radiance as centers of fame and prestige, and thus this world works on the notion of aura that cannot be measured yet shines out for all to see.

By paying attention to how each of these worlds can be mobilized in the media, or in action, we come to appreciate how modern power structures are composed by playing on several kinds of justification, each of which might involve different people. While a single image or article might involve references to several discrete worlds, not each reference will be understood by everyone. Gendered life experiences determine access to the experiences that teach people to reason and act according to the criteria of each world. For instance, it is likely that a woman who is illiterate and lives in a poor quarter of Rabat might have more opportunities to engage with the criteria of face-to-face relations and fewer with those of the legal-rational worlds that tend to dominate institutions such as schools or large factories. Similarly, a woman in another part of the city might strive to promote "equal" hiring practices in her office, regardless of social background or gender. She might focus on people's academic qualifications, because she herself has had the opportunity to attend school and to get ahead due to measurable accomplishments. The point is that worlds collide, and hence there is a layering and selective application of these various criteria of measurement, proximity, and interactional contact. This leads to the construction of barriers between public and private spaces and constitutes relationships which are defined according to the dominance of particular worlds.

Particular institutions can encourage certain hierarchies among these worlds. State policies regarding geographic and social mobility condition access to each way of knowing the worlds. It is important to note that for those who have equal access to all of these worlds, it is the way of deciding which set of criteria to favor that is often perceived as problematic. When the worlds appear to be harmonized, when a decision or a person seems to pass from one to another with ease, only then do the actual contradictions among these worlds with their very different criteria of judgment seem to disappear. It is this apparent calm that might be seen as the sign of a successful political rhetoric or advertising campaign, whereby a political figure, idea, or product seems to appeal simultaneously to the criteria of each of the three worlds, thereby not only reaching groups of people but also covering different ways in which a single individual might choose to judge a candidate, issue, or commodity.

When Mohammed VI became engaged to Salma, it provided an opportunity to be publicly judged according to criteria of face-to-face and rational worlds that played no part in a political system legitimized by dynastic succession and charismatic connections to the prophet. Salma's own accomplishments were undeniable according to the standards of rational measurement, which were reinforced by her academic success in the fields of mathematics and computer science. Her achievements associated her presence with a world of equality and openness. Her position as first in her class in a world of men only added to the perception that she could compete for a place in the "open market" with anyone, any time, any place. Although her husband had also earned diplomas and learned important linguistic and diplomatic skills as a young man, the innate contradiction between his dynastic position and the world of legal rationality made it difficult to focus closely on his academic or professional record without undermining the charismatic basis of the very regime that put him into power. His marriage to Salma allowed him to publicize his own successes by printing them alongside those of his soon-to-be wife. The emotional and sexually charged process of selecting a wife was informed by the paradigm of rational choice and priorities of the state. His choice of Salma underscored his ability to show his own measurable accomplishments.

In addition to the soon-to-be princess being an outstanding student, the press also offered interviews with people who knew her as a young girl and a student. They vouched for her observable good conduct, confirming after careful scrutiny of her school attendance records that she missed only one day of high school, because she was ill. Neighbors confirmed that she returned home right after classes, intimating that she did not hang out with a bad crowd in public places. She thus passed the scrutiny of proximate judgment. For the king, showing his good reputation in the day-to-day world of proximate interactions was another story. Although his image was broadcast across the country from the time he was a child, royal protocol tightly controls media reports about the life of the royal family. Rumors are rife, yet it is dangerous to try to prove allegations about royals' behavior, as a number of bloggers and print journalists have recently been reminded.[11] What was publicized as Salma's "ordinariness" and the fact that she had a life in the neighborhood and at school that predated her being a part of the royal couple allowed the king some measure of association with the everyday world of proximity. Meanwhile, Salma obviously gained prominence in the world of celebrity through her association with the king. Salma may have had some small notoriety as the valedictorian of her class, and her family may have frequented royal circles, but her inclusion into royalty obviously transformed her position in measures of celebrity. From obscurity, on the very edge of the royal circle, her marriage brought her onto the front pages of magazines and newspapers worldwide.

As the princess's prominence in worlds of celebrity increased, her ability to act outside the royal circle was curtailed. She underwent a process of restriction of access to face-to-face and rational worlds in her day-to-day life, reflecting the curious ways in which fame and power dictate social life. The king's unique position in the world of celebrity is underscored daily in the media. Photographs of the monarch displayed in shops and offices throughout the kingdom might portray him as an "ordinary" guy, but this only underscores his special status. Royalty may involve struggles for the kingship, but its charismatic logic cannot admit the kind of abstract accounting of accomplishments and virtues associated with modernity. Becoming associated with a woman who did more than equal his measureable successes allowed the king to represent himself as one among many, and as a father among fathers. His marriage to someone with clearer associations to rational and proximate worlds allowed him to demonstrate his own ability to work in each world. Political and social analysis can be refined if we draw on the three-worlds model to notice how restriction of access and participation in any of the worlds has important consequences for the empowerment of the subject. In accounting for the next phase of Princess Salma's media journey, the details of her academic training and her day-to-day life are obscured as her image is developed not only in relation to her husband, the king, but also with respect to those of other princesses, queens, and first ladies.

Celebrity Worlds

> In the last six years Princess Lalla Salma has made her mark as a gracious and dignified member of the Moroccan Royal family and one with a world class sense [of] taste in fashion who can represent her country on the world stage.[12]

Media reports and online discussions about first ladies display a variety of opinions about how these privileged spouses should carry out their roles. The recent discussions about how an Ivy League–educated lawyer such as Michelle Obama will inhabit the role of first lady are indicative of a broader perception of the difficulties associated with assuming this position for women who have been successful professionals in their own right.[13] A first lady might be criticized for overstepping the bounds of her position, as Hillary Clinton was during the first years of the Clinton presidency in the United States. However, that the first lady ought to have public presence seems to go unquestioned. Although writers point to the ways in which playing the role of the spouse of the president or prime minister might be changing, noting for instance that Cherie Blair continued to work in her profession while her husband was in office, there is still a perceived need to fill out the image of the leader with multiple family portraits and accounts of his wife's comportment and clothing that are absent in narratives of first husbands.[14] Although the women inhabiting these positions are increasingly well-trained and experienced professionals, when their professional activity is recounted in the domain of celebrity, it turns these into stylish accessories or dwells on aspects of their work that brought them closer to centers of fame and glamour. Thus, even when first ladies deploy their skills and knowledge in the running of day-to-day affairs, and although media narratives do account for this work, in worlds of celebrity, it is the symbolic branding of them as graduates of Harvard, Oxford, or Yale that adds to their luster. A dress marked by a designer and a degree bearing the seal of a famous university function in the same way when it comes to celebrity evaluations. Men and women are equally able to act as centers for the constellations of fame. A well-known female politician might very well shine on her own merit, as Benazir Bhutto did. But it would be worth devoting further study to the tendency of the abstract criteria of rational worlds to be represented as signs of celebrity when it comes to female leaders such as Bhutto, whose Ivy League education was often highlighted in the media. However, when a woman's very position as a celebrity is the result of her relationship with a man who has chosen her as his bride, her own qualities become proof of his good judgment. Of course, this assumes that he has indeed chosen her.

The case of Morocco's Princess Salma is interesting, in this regard, in that it illustrates these trends while contrasting the position of women who gain positions through marriage with those who participate in global media celebrity because of inherited position. While marrying allowed the Moroccan king to show how he was in some ways more like his own people than was his father, simply deciding to give Salma the title of princess did not solve the problem of finding a place for her in the royal family. Until the king married, his sisters presented the feminine face of the monarchy. Under the present king's father, and still today, the sisters attend charity events, inaugurate hospitals on the national news, and appear in international fashion magazines as signs of the modernity and glamour of their country. With the introduction of Princess Salma to the family, gossip in the Moroccan capital rapidly took hold of the apparently inevitable conflict between the new princess and those who preceded her. Leaving any attempt to know the "real" relationship of the women aside, it is clear that finding a place for the new princess that was more than "the mother of his children" would be a problem. Would the new princess be shown only as a consort to the king, or might her picture show up individually? Salma had the disadvantage of being a neophyte, a newcomer to a formerly nonexistent role. Yet, as detailed earlier, she also had the advantage of having had a life that made possible public perusal of her day-to-day activities, her quantifiable achievements, which she could wear on her sleeve in ways that were as difficult for her sisters-in-law as they were for her husband. Her husband and, indeed, the national image could draw on her individually demonstrated strengths in ways that resembled the process by which first ladies in democratic nations add to their husband's charismatic powers. Like the ill-fated, but fabulously successful, Diana, Princess of Wales, Salma was distinct from anyone who had inherited his or her royal position. In 2007, *Gala* magazine praised Princess Salma by writing that she had "become a first lady."[15] By then, she had given birth to an heir to the throne, consolidating her preeminence among Moroccan royalty through her reproductive capacities and the photo opportunities they enabled. Having demonstrated her ability to be an appropriate consort to the king and the mother of his children, the princess began to appear more frequently at important international meetings both with her husband and individually. This placed her ever more firmly in the world of celebrity, leading her to be compared to the wives of other leaders, particularly those of other Arab countries. The criteria associated with proximate and rational worlds were set aside; elements of local style or lines on a résumé did not disappear, but they became elements of performances aimed at enabling the princess to shine on the world stage.

Women in the Middle

> Now I wish MORE of our Middle Eastern Princesses at least wore hijab on their hair but I am in love with Princess Lalla's gorgeous caftan and soft make-up. And she looks so happy playing with her husband and their children.[16]

Although dynastic succession worldwide has been profoundly influenced by European norms since the colonial period, the visibility of royal spouses has not always been evident.[17] The lack of a royal wife that prevailed under Morocco's Hassan II continues to inform the play of visibility and power in Arab nations such as Saudi Arabia. We do see images of the wives of presidents of Arab nations in both global and Arab media, and yet the most prominent on the international stage have been wives of monarchs, led by the successive queens of Jordan. Following narratives of progressive visibility of women, it could be stereotypically assumed that in a region where religion is assumed to cover female bodies, as indicated by the frequency with which pictures of women in *hijab* are used to connote Islam, royal wives might shy away from internationally dictated fashions or adopt *muhajiba* fashion styles. Yet neither Salma nor the Jordanian queen, who have been so visible in the international media, don scarves except for expressly religious events or occasions. Just like the decision to wear a little black dress or a caftan, wearing a scarf is an orchestrated performance.

I have suggested that Princess Salma scripted the new position she married into by working on international standards in worlds of celebrity in ways that took advantage of her ordinary background and scholastic excellence. But her image is also made up in ways that situate her positively by placing her fame as somehow both representative of progressive women and living up to the expectations for pious behavior that are often associated with wearing the *hijab*. While the idea that all Muslim women should cover their hair might be upheld when it comes to a certain reading of Islamic law, in the quotation that begins this section, even a devout *muhajiba* who would prefer that "middle eastern Princesses at least wore hijab" adores the princess's "gorgeous caftans and soft make-up." These online accounts and statements were echoed in conversations I had with women in Morocco in the course of my fieldwork. Other *muhajibat* made a point of the fact that Salma might not have the same positive reception internationally if she covered her hair and forsook her stylish clothes, and thus they decided that it is after all a part of her job to appear as she does.

A resolutely modern princess—this is the image that is painted by these accounts I gathered from online chat rooms and interviews. It is important to note that some veiled women were very pragmatic when asked if the princess should wear the *hijab*. "It's a personal choice," admitted an activist from the Justice and Development Party, an Islamist party represented in the Moroccan parliament. "I would like it if she wore the veil, since she is the wife of the Commander of the Faithful. But I know that's too much to ask of her." "That would be putting Morocco at a disadvantage internationally," responded one woman. Other *muhajibat* proposed that she might consider wearing a discreet, modern scarf that let some of her hair show. "There are some really nice models from haute couture," a well-off veiled Casablanca woman noted.[18]

These reactions demonstrate how the princess gently pushes evaluation of her image toward celebrity frames of reference. She cannot be judged, as others are, for she occupies a special place, a particular role. And yet attending to the ways in which these images are crafted cannot make sense without taking note of the distance and movement between the pictures of the princess and the static images of unidentified women in ample dress and covered with various kinds of veils that connote Islam in the international arena. Is she or isn't she an Arab, Muslim princess? And is it her royal stature that frees her from the implications of these identities? The pictures of the princess seem to answer these questions in ways consonant with what I have called earlier "the epic of opening"—the master narrative linking unveiling with women's modernity and liberation.[19] Her presence with the mane of flowing hair pointedly rejects the image of covered Arab and Muslim women. In fact, there is not even a hint of the hair-covering middle ground adopted by such figures as Benazir Bhutto, with her slippery transparent headscarf. Instead of a hybrid image that "blends" traits associated with the West and the East, this princess has made the Moroccan caftan an important element of her signature style. Commenting on Princess Salma, a blogger wrote,

> She is frequently seen at state functions and royal banquets in sumptuously embroidered caftans. On other official occasions she dons beautifully constructed

Chanel and Valentino suits. She tends to go for more classic pieces that are altered slightly (the lengthening of a skirt hem or covering of the shoulders) to adhere to Islamic customs modesty. . . . Often eclipsing the women in western dress, she attended a dinner at Versailles in an embroidered silk and chiffon caftan; in a Valentino couture coat, fall 2004.[20]

In this regard, it is interesting to note how the sartorial practices of Princess Salma are regularly contrasted with those of Jordan's Rania, who as the more established royal wife and mother tends to serve as the model for modern, educated, stylish Arab royalty. Commentators have compared the two women's distinctive ways of dressing at events where they appeared together: "Official duties over, the two couples dined together amid the gilded surroundings of the royal palace. Hostess Lalla Salma had donned an intricately decorated Moroccan costume in fuchsia pink, while ever-chic Rania kept it simple by opting for a classic little black dress."[21] Another writer, Marion, writing on a women's forum, took a more opinionated position when she noted, "Salma not only has exceptional academic qualifications," but "she wears the typical Moroccan caftan" and "doesn't play the fashion victim, unlike Rania of Jordan."[22]

What this narrative fails to mention is that the alternating of garments deemed Western and Moroccan is typical of the practices of many Moroccan women. Indeed, as Hassan Rachik has noted, well-to-do Moroccan homes tend to have two dining rooms, one with a low, round Moroccan table and the other with a European-style dining table and chairs. This is reflective of a much more generalized notion of *art de vivre*, in which the appropriate juxtapositioning of such elements of style and grace is appreciated and, indeed, expected of someone who represents the nation.[23] Caftan styles change, and Moroccan "nouvelle cuisine" is flourishing far beyond the kingdom's borders. For Moroccans and those familiar with the country, Salma's attire is not revolutionary or individualistic; it could indeed be seen as rather conservative. She might stand for a brand of nationalist pride in Moroccans' ability to shift gracefully among aesthetic or linguistic repertoires without challenging their status as Muslims, Arabs, Berbers, Africans, or inhabitants of the Mediterranean region.[24] One might thus interpret the way that the image of the princess has been developed as following the way photographs have been used by the royal family. The variety of these images show a nation that is not so much a mosaic or patchwork of various elements as it is a proposition for learning to work with each of them in turn. Images are worked not dynamically but serially. Each picture is judged successful if it retains its semiological unity. Politics works not only by arranging and distributing images but also by instituting environments that follow their norms.

The portrayal of Queen Rania of Jordan as an active, modern leader reiterates the split between modernity and tradition by projecting clothing choices as pivotal to the enlightenment or liberation narrative. Designer clothing goes along with being a celebrity, but knowing how to elegantly select and wear Western clothing appears, in this case, to be indicative of modernity as well. The way that particular head coverings or types of clothing have been taken as a sign of social progress in the Middle East tends to encourage this interpretation. Yet when Princess Salma decides to wear a caftan to a state dinner, she does not stand for tradition. Her choice of attire reflects the practices of many women across the country. Their collective movement among types of clothing or daily practices that derive from varied cultural repertoires might be understood as questioning both the notion that modernity draws on particular modes of European dress and the fact that Islam associates piety with the *hijab*. Salma engages in a diplomacy-of-the-image that eschews the polarities of covered to undressed, veiled to unveiled, and repositions these oppositions in terms of particular places and appropriate times and situations. It is neither a kind of hybridized mixing of old and new nor a recovering of tradition that her caftan effects: instead, it leads away from associating her with any given picture, focusing instead on her taste and ability to calibrate her appearance in response to different social situations. Her autopoesis plays on established images and their conventional associations to develop the visual presence of her nation as a vibrant meeting place where Arab, Muslim, or European realms come together. Knowing how to appear is shown to be a dynamic process of moving among several worlds.

NOTES

1. Arjun Appadurai, *Modernity at Large: Cultural Dimensions of Globalization* (Minneapolis: University of Minnesota Press, 1996); Zygmunt Bauman, *Liquid Modernity* (Cambridge, UK: Polity, 2000).

2. I am referring to initiatives against gay marriage here, but once might also view this phrase with respect to the question of polygamy. On the ways in which the nuclear family was ensconced into the very building of modern Moroccan cities, see Paul Rabinow, *French Modern: Norms and Forms of the Social Environment* (Cambridge, MA: MIT Press, 1989).

3. For more on first ladies in the United States, see, for instance, Robert P. Watson, *The Presidents' Wives: Reassessing the Office of the First Lady* (Boulder, CO: Lynne Rienner, 2000).

4. Susan Ossman, *Picturing Casablanca: Portraits of Power in a Modern City* (Berkeley: University of California Press, 1994).

5. For more on reactions to the wedding in the Moroccan press, see Susan Ossman, "Cinderella, CV's and Neighborhood Nemima Morocco's Royal Wedding," in "Mediated Politics in the Middle East," special issue, *Comparative Studies of South Asia, Africa and the Middle East* 27 (2007): 525–535.

6. Jürgen Habermas, *The Theory of Communicative Action*, vol. 1 (Boston: Beacon, 1984).

7. See Susan Ossman, *Three Faces of Beauty: Casablanca, Paris, Cairo* (Durham, NC: Duke University Press, 2002).

8. These comments were gleaned from chat rooms on Moroccan politics and international royalty and magazines such as *Gala* that specialize in reporting on the lives of celebrities. These chat rooms were overwhelmingly visited by women.

9. Ossman, "Cinderella, CV's and Neighborhood Nemima Morocco's Royal Wedding."

10. Ossman, *Three Faces of Beauty.*

11. For instances of how bloggers and journalists have been pursued in Morocco when they have been seen as overstepping the bounds of reporting on royalty, see Mike Nizza, "Moroccan Bloggers Protest Jailing for Facebook Prank," *New York Times* (February 26, 2008), http://thelede.blogs.nytimes.com/2008/02/26/a-moroccan-blogger-react-to-jailing-of-facebook-prankster/.

12. "Morocco's Princess Lalla Salma," *The View from Fez* (September 8, 2008), http://riad-zany.blogspot.com/2008/09/moroccos-princess-lalla-salma.html (accessed September 8, 2008).

13. See, for instance, Rachel L. Swarns, "From Home and Away, Advice for a First Lady," *New York Times* (November 23, 2008), http://www.nytimes.com/2008/11/24/us/politics/24advice.html?_r=1&scp=8&sq=swarns&st=nyt.

14. This is not confined to the Muslim world. One might also examine the way that German Prime Minister Andrea Merkel's husband is presented (or not).

15. See "La First Lady Marocaine," *Gala.fr*, http://www.gala.fr/le_gotha/les_icones/lalla_salma_du_maroc_52073 (accessed June 25, 2008).

16. Posted by Pixie, "Princess Series: Lalla Salma of Morocco," *Beautiful Muslimah* blog (June 25, 2008), http://beautifulmuslimah.blogspot.com/2008/06/princess-series-lalla-salma-of-morroco.html (accessed June 25, 2008).

17. In precolonial times, the principle of primogeniture was not followed in Morocco. Since independence in 1956, it has been assumed that the eldest son of the monarch would assume the throne.

18. Author's translation of Oumayma, "Comment les Marocaines se représentent-elles Lalla Salma?" in "Lalla Salma: Les marocaines donnent leur avis," *Telle Quelle* (March 9, 2007), http://www.yabiladi.com/forum/read-2-1714586.html (accessed March 9, 2007).

19. For more on this subject, see Ossman, *Three Faces of Beauty*, chapter 1.

20. "How They Wear It: Queen Lalla Salma of Morocco," *The Polyglot* blog (December 25, 2007), http://the-polyglot.blogspot.com/2007/12/how-they-wear-it-queen-lalla-salma-of.html (accessed December 27, 2007).

21. Agence France Presse, "Lalla Salma Welcomes Fellow Humanitarian Rania to Morocco," *Hellomagazine.com* (January 17, 2008), http://www.hellomagazine.com/royalty/2008/01/17/rania-lalla-salma/. *Hello* magazine specializes in news about celebrities and royalty. Its readership is international.

22. These comments appear on the chat room of the "Society" section of an online magazine based in Canada. Participants came from a variety of Francophone countries, with a large representation of women from Morocco and the Maghreb. Author's translation of "Que Pensez Vous de la Princesse Lalla Salma du Maroc," *Aufeminin.com* (July 6, 2003), http://forum.aufeminin.com/forum/actu1/__f13219_actu1-Que-pensez-vous-de-la-princesse-lalla-salma-du-maroc.html (accessed December 29, 2007).

23. Hassan Rachik, "Roumi et beldi: Réflexions sur la perception de l'occidental a travers une dichotomie locale," *Egypte/Monde Arabe* 30–31 (2eme et 3eme trimestre 1997): 293–302.

24. Fatima Badry, "Positioning the Self, Identity, and Language: Moroccan Women on the Move," in Susan Ossman, ed., *The Places We Share: Migration, Subjectivity, and Global Mobility* (Lanham, MD: Lexington, 2007), 173–186.

2 Constructing Transnational Divas

Gendered Productions of Balkan Turbo-folk Music

Zala Volčič and Karmen Erjavec

If you were wounded, I'd give you my blood
If you were blind, I'd give you both of my eyes
—Ceca, a Serbian singer, from song lyrics of "Kad bi
 Bio Ranjen" (If You Were Wounded)

The same year in which former Serbian president Slobodan Milosevic was on trial for war crimes at The Hague, the wife of one of his former henchmen held a concert in the Serbian part of Bosnia—a country deeply scarred by the violence of the 1990s. Ceca, a Balkan superstar in her own right, a well-known Serbian nationalist, and by that time a widow, took the opportunity to showcase "turbo-folk" music along with her unique blend of performance and politics. In the wake of the global censure of Serbia, Ceca incited the crowd's virulent opposition to the international court and its sense of victimization. As the crowd invoked her dead husband, Ceca responded, "Let's sing! Let's sing so they don't send us all to The Hague."[1] For audiences in countries where politics is studiously dissociated from popular culture, this might have seemed a strange spectacle. All the elements of pop-kitsch glamour stood out—the skimpy dress stretched tightly across Ceca's surgically enhanced curves, the pounding of overamplified music, and the audience of teenage girls enthralled by the sentimental love lyrics. However, this cultural energy was harnessed to a different kind of idol—the lingering patriarchal fantasy of a strong Balkan woman steeped in patriotic love of the homeland but willing to leave the sphere of the political to men. It is this image of contradictions that Ceca strategically cultivates in her concert—strong but lovelorn, powerful yet submissive, both politically charged and allegedly apolitical. Ceca has managed to claim regional success despite her close identification with some of the more controversial figures of Serb nationalism during the wars of the 1990s. In her public interviews, Ceca tends to portray both sides of this image, highlighting both aggressive ambition and submissive sex appeal. As she put it, "I am a very ambitious woman. Even when I was a child I knew that I was going to become the biggest star in the Balkans. . . . I'm happy that I'm earning the fruits of my effort and struggle. I like to show my femininity. And I also have very strong sex appeal."[2]

35

This chapter explores the trajectory of Ceca's ascent as a pop icon despite her clearly nationalist identification and political commitments. Ceca is a locally positioned star who manages both to exploit and to disavow her political entanglements, including the fact that she was arrested (and later released uncharged) in connection with the assassination of former Serb prime minister Zoran Djindic. The disintegration of Yugoslavia in the 1990s transformed what had once been a national culture into a transnational one and significantly altered the broader cultural and social scene of the region. Mediated forms of popular culture, including music, movies, and television, that had previously been organized by the guiding hand of the state were now being influenced and shaped by new forms of nationalisms driven by market forces. Especially after the wars and the subsequent fall of Serbian president Slobodan Milosevic in 2000, new cross-border cultural relations and practices emerged between the seven resulting states (Slovenia, Croatia, Bosnia-Herzegovina, Serbia, Montenegro, Macedonia, and Kosovo). In this new cultural scenario, turbo-folk music and Ceca, its iconic singer, stand out as illustrative of the new and emergent transnational ethos.

Turbo-folk, a hybrid musical form comprising Balkan folk, the popular music of Serbian and Roma brass bands, Middle Eastern beats, and contemporary electro-pop-dance music, rose to popularity in the 1990s.[3] It was around the same time that Serbia lost four wars, endured widespread poverty and violence, was bombed by NATO, and was threatened by international isolation. Turbo-folk music combines a militaristic Serbian nationalism with a kitschy aesthetic that features provocatively dressed female performers, pumped full of silicon, singing about death, love, passion, emotions, blood, and patriotic sacrifice.[4] This genre has been directly linked to a wartime culture of violence, crime, nationalism, and war profiteering as it helped legitimize the ideal of a Greater Serbia as a hegemonic force in the region.[5]

In this light, it is perhaps ironic that after the former Yugoslav wars, turbo-folk and its most visible performer, Ceca,[6] have been gaining great popularity in former Yugoslav nations.[7] In a transnational media environment, characterized by the cross-border movement of people, cultural artifacts, and ideas, Ceca emerges as a borderless celebrity with iconic standing in all the former Yugoslav countries. Despite the fact that her musical career is perceived to be caught up in the corruption, ethnic cleansing, and destruction wrought by Serbian nationalism, Ceca is still able to invoke a sense of Serbian national belonging and simultaneously reach beyond to a transnational audience by establishing her popularity in the whole Balkan region.[8] From an almost mythical stance, her music invokes themes of exoticism, passion, tradition, freedom, justice, sexuality, and modernity. But Ceca is insistent that she is neither a political figure nor a politically motivated artist. She claims that her songs are a part of a shared regional popular culture and common spirit, not anthems for the vision of a Greater Serbia.[9]

Since the 1990s, with the rise of commercial media, the nexus of politics and popular culture has opened up a dynamic site for performers such as Ceca to strategically combine patriotism and nationalism with show business. Ceca is variously portrayed as vulgar, attractive, the embodiment of a *real* Serbian woman, a sexy diva, a divinely seductive siren of emotional songs, a loving mother, and the widow of a Serbian warlord. Ceca's appeal as a "Balkan diva" emerges against the background of the violent Yugoslav wars that resulted in an estimated three hundred thousand deaths and millions of refugees.[10] The transition to capitalist democracy in the region has been accompanied by the increasing economic instability and stratification of society.[11] The "triumph" of the (neo)liberal marketplace, which has led to trade liberalization, privatization, reduction of state-supported social services, and lowering of wages, has transformed social conditions in the region and complicated the very concept of social collectivity.[12] While anything "collective" is questioned, individualism is both encouraged and expected of all citizens.

This chapter examines how Ceca, through her music and image management, mediates between a violent past and a transnationally intertwined present and future. Ceca's global transformation provides a compelling case study of the ways in which Balkan turbo-folk singers are both produced and consumed in a transnationally networked, mediatized environment. What are the conditions that facilitate Ceca's phenomenal success in postwar Yugoslavia? How do we explain the admiration and repulsion that she evokes? The ambivalence represented by Ceca is mirrored in the reception of turbo-folk music itself, which is celebrated yet dismissed as frivolous and not deserving of critical attention. Using textual analysis of Ceca's public appearances (including media coverage of her concerts and her published interviews) combined with interviews, we explore the mediated transformation of Ceca's public image from nationalist icon to transnational pop star.

In order to map this transformation, we situate turbo-folk culture and Ceca within the sociohistorical context of Serbia and offer a critique of her music as an amalgamation of high camp, kitsch, and Serbian nationalism. In the final section, we draw on our interviews conducted in the region to show how Ceca's appeal carries over to a media-savvy new generation.

Turbo-folk and the New National Aesthetic: 1990–2000

In the decade of the nineties, Serbian mainstream media supported the production of a populist war culture through turbo-folk entertainment, thereby upholding nationalist versions of Serbian tradition, history, myths, and culture.[13] New commercial television stations, such as Palma and Pink TV, helped to legitimize an emergent cultural practice in which paramilitary war criminals and gangsters were celebrated[14] in both entertainment programming and (nationalistic) turbo-folk music video spots. The refrain of one famous turbo-folk song captures this version of the world: "Coca-Cola, Marlboro, Suzuki/Discotheques/That's life, that's not an ad/Nobody has it better than us."[15] Goran Tarlac writes that despite turbo-folk's self-proclaimed apolitical stand, its music videos emphasize intense emotions and national belonging, reinforcing a war culture that supported the expansionist and nationalist politics of the Serbian regime.[16] Turbo-folk invokes an aggressive, overtly sexual aesthetic and also promotes Serbian militarism fueled by a combined sense of patriotism and victimhood. The songs are full of tales of devotion to the nation and/or a man that lead to either victory or destruction.[17] Turbo-folk singers, including Ceca, became celebrities of the gangland era of war profiteering and its culture of criminal activities, which involved a stereotypical mob lifestyle complete with excessive drinking, spending, sex, and violence.

The decadent themes of this genre can be written off as being both excessive and even ludicrous. It is easy to be dismissive of this music, especially since its worn-out tropes of femininity and kitschy quality invite criticism about its lack of seriousness or artistic merit. However, these songs attempt to legitimize the idea that the version of patriotism and love they convey are *a real* reflection of *the authentic* voice of the people.[18] The Milosevic government supported the music, since turbo-folk largely promoted the alleged superiority of the Serbian nation even during an era of wars, violence, poverty, and hyperinflation. Turbo-folk was able to deflect attention and offer a nationalistic drone in the background. In the battlefields in Croatia and Bosnia, the strains of turbo-folk served as tools of nationalist propaganda and motivation.[19]

Ceca: The Production of a Diva

Ceca has been received by critics and the public as a quintessential Balkan diva—a universal figure along the lines of a female Don Juan or a Faust.[20] Known for her seductive beauty and her association with a violent and fatal past, she looms as a paradigmatically female mythological figure. Her sensational return to the stage in 2003, after her husband's death, escalated her popularity in the region. Ceca both embraces and exploits the fact that she has come to be known as the Balkan diva. How do we explain her popularity as a media phenomenon in the context of Balkan nationalisms and emerging patterns of transnational publicity set into motion by new technologies and media systems?

Fig. 2.1. Ceca, turbo-folk superstar. (Ljubo Vukelic/Delo, Slovenia)

Ceca successfully combines three essential aesthetic ingredients that have come to characterize her status as turbo-folk diva: beauty, rural origins, and urban style. As you can see in the photograph in figure 2.1, Ceca's image is a carefully crafted one—fine-tuned to capitalize on the well-established synergies between the music industry, celebrity media coverage, and public-relations management. Unlike many contemporary Western celebrities, she is able to combine a highly controversial political presence with a carefully managed show-business persona. Ceca renegotiates a postcommunist space through the mobilizing of memory, transnational media, and current local conditions.

To understand the way in which Ceca assumed the role of the diva of Serbian nationalism, it is helpful to consider some of the details of her history. Born in

1973, in the small Serbian village of Prokuplje, she recorded her first album at the age of fourteen and rose from local to national celebrity.[21] From the beginning, her songs were sentimental and dramatic love stories, about relationships and love for the homeland. Her best known hit, "Kukavica" (Cuckoo), describes the suffering of a young woman falling in love with a married man, trying to survive in this desperate emotional state of mind. Ceca's records have sold over ten million copies, mainly in the Balkan countries. Some samples of the themes of her work are reflected in the titles of her various albums: *What's Going through Your Veins* (1993), *I Still Sleep in Your T-shirt* (1994), *Fatal Love* (1996), and *Emotionally Crazy* (1996). She was also one of the first female Balkan singers to pose in a military uniform.[22]

In 1995 she married Zeljko Arkan, a notorious gangster and warlord who built his fortune as a smuggler and a war profiteer. In 1992, he established his own political party, the Party of Serbian Unity, and led a paramilitary army called the Serbian Voluntary Guard. Ceca and Arkan's political love story started in 1993 in a military camp in Erdut, where Arkan trained future soldiers for his paramilitary unit. Ceca was invited to sing and inspire his troops. The paramilitary unit that he commanded, known also as the Tigers, was accused of being responsible for ethnic cleansing in Croatia, Bosnia, and Kosovo. The Tigers were widely recognized as murderers, gangsters, and organized criminals. Arkan was reportedly responsible for some of the worst killings of non-Serbs in the wars in Croatia and Bosnia, and charges were brought against him by the International Criminal Tribunal for the Former Yugoslavia in The Hague.[23]

Ceca and Arkan's glamorous wedding in February 1995 was a public spectacle organized as a media event for national consumption. Both the ceremony and reception were broadcast live on national television and radio and sold on videotapes across the country. With this publicity and media presence, Ceca's audience grew, which in turn extended her political reach. It was after the (in)famous wedding that she consciously started to produce herself as a celebrity and increase her purchase on the public imagination, first in Serbia and later across the region. She employed professionals from the celebrity industry to help craft her image as an international star. As Graeme Turner argues, one of the defining characteristics of celebrity is the capacity to sustain public interest in one's private life.[24] As a publicity strategy, Ceca keeps her audience actively engaged and suspended with curiosity about her personal life.

According to some scholars, the marriage between Ceca and Arkan symbolized the connection between turbo-folk music and the paramilitary nationalist project, especially because of their respective positions.[25] For many observers, Ceca, her music, and her aesthetics epitomize all that was wrong with Serbia under Milosevic, when wars, ethnic cleansing, and international economic sanctions helped the Serbian criminal underground gain significant economic and political power.[26] In 1999, after Arkan's death, Ceca went into mourning for two years and withdrew from public life, leading to much rumor and public speculation. She emerged, after this hiatus from her performing career, as the tragic figure of Serbian womanhood, loyal to her dead husband and to her children, a patriot and an activist fighting against injustice. Ceca portrays herself as a strong, yet sad, mysterious, and suffering woman. As she claims, "I am fragile and emotional. . . . What doesn't kill me makes me stronger. . . . I'm a victim, . . . a victim of my name and my huge popularity, and of my great love, . . . that I was married to Zeljko. I'm not a criminal. I'm not a Mafioso. I'm just a woman who's fighting her way through life."[27] Ceca, supported and produced by consumer culture, is able to erase the memory and complexity of historical forces. She triggers emotions that connect her with a particular type of public persona—the strong woman who lives only to give of herself in many ways. As the Balkan diva, she offers herself up for destruction at the hands of a lover, the nation, or the law.

Even after Milosevic's fall in 2000, Ceca invokes, albeit in indirect ways, her ties with Milosevic's nationalism and his paramilitary group, the Tigers. In 2002 she appeared in a television advertisement for a brand of coffee called Coffee C, posing in a seductive way, surrounded by tigers—a direct reference to the Tigers. When she was a guest of a Pink TV show called *Klopka*, the host asked for her thoughts about the war-crimes tribunal in The Hague, and she responded, "God help us in burning down the Hague Tribunal."[28] She also frequently expresses her love for the homeland: "I am a huge patriot, and no one has the right to take it away from me. I love my nation, and my country."[29] And yet Ceca also disputes the critics who say turbo-folk was the soundtrack for Milosevic's nationalistic regime: "I don't know what they're talking about. I don't sing songs about nationalism. I only sing about love. And besides, Milosevic has been gone for four years, and I'm still here."[30] She actively dissociates herself from the way her music circulated during the Milosevic years by now masking that influence with romantic compositions, as a softer way of marketing to the diverse audiences in former Yugoslav countries.

Commercial media and a globally savvy publicity machinery strategically market Ceca both as a transnational diva for the Balkans and as a national diva for Serbian audiences.[31] Thanks to new technologies, including the Internet and satellite television, Balkan diasporic and national spaces are developing new, interlinked forms of transnational connections through cultural production. Ceca has become popular not only among the fans in the region but also among former Yugoslav diasporic communities living in the United States, western Europe, and Australia who have crafted hybrid forms of identity and cultural practices, balancing their homelands and new locations.[32] At the same time, Ceca is not

Fig. 2.2. Ceca's predominant fan base of young girls at a concert. (Ljubo Vukelic/Delo, Slovenia)

welcome in Croatia, is forbidden from entering many countries in the European Union, and was denied visas to enter both Canada and Australia. However, almost every year she holds numerous concerts in former Yugoslav sites ranging from Ljubljana, Slovenia, to Banja Luka in Bosnia-Herzegovina, where she often pays politically controversial tributes to her husband, Arkan.

The media representations of Ceca fall within a set of formulaic scripts that typically include exoticism, transgressive sexuality and seduction. In addition, Ceca seems to invite the politicomythical twist to accommodate the public drama of her political life. Asked in an interview about her husband, Arkan, and his connections with violence and crime, Ceca replied, "Do I look like someone who, being a young woman, being fragile, can be with someone who is a criminal and murderer to you? I think I don't look like that."[33] Using the question as an opportunity to project her own image, Ceca is able to promote her career by transcending both the question and the war itself, and she skillfully leverages the contradictions.

We now turn to examine how Ceca's music and image, which exceeds national boundaries, are interpreted at the level of the everyday by her fans.

Neoliberal Variations

To understand Ceca's enduring popularity, we conducted field interviews with a diverse group of young women. As seen in the illustration in figure 2.2, this demographic represents an important segment of Ceca's fan base.[34] Our interviews revealed how Ceca's appeal is embedded within a very transnational frame of meaning that spans the Balkan region.[35] During the interviews, the fans talked about how they connected with Ceca and perceived her popularity. The interviews confirmed that even those respondents who did not necessarily listen to Ceca's music still admired her and considered her a diva. An analysis of the responses reveals that there are four dominant and sometimes overlapping readings of Ceca.

Ceca as a Mythical Hero

To our respondents from Serbia, Bosnia-Herzegovina, Croatia, and Slovenia, Ceca is deeply or integrally connected to the myth of a greater Serbia, in which the Serbs are positioned both as victims and as strong and proud agents of history. This connection elevates Ceca to mythic proportions in the eyes of her fans. According to Olivera, a Serbian respondent, "To me, Ceca is a Serbian hero. I connect with her, her music, and her history." Some Serbian respondents, no matter where they were from, went a step further and constructed Ceca as a female victim of anti-Serbian politics. They often defined her as "Ceca Nacionale" (Zorana, a Serb), "Ceca, a real Serbian" (Željka, a Macedonian Serb), or "Ceca, a Serbian woman hero" (Goga, a Slovene Serb). Applying the Serbian myth of victimhood to Ceca, they concluded that Ceca is oppressed by those who continue to fight against the Serbian *way of life*—the same politics responsible for the death of her husband. Such sentiments are exemplified, for example, in the following statement: "Ceca just rules. . . . She has used her own life to help to shape Serbia. It's, however, clear she is a victim of anti-Serbian politics. . . . Not just Western interest, also local ones are sometimes used against her. . . . They've killed her husband and arrested her, the mother of two children!" (Nataša, a Serb).

These comments illustrate how nation and woman are superimposed, even as the woman is constructed as both victim and martyr. Ceca herself, while remaining an active participant in national, economic, political, and military struggles, continues to mobilize her own image as oppressed by anti-Serbian politics and as an embodiment of Serbian suffering. In the process, Ceca succeeds in using the power of the media and publicity to strip history of controversy and clear space for her celebrity power to hold sway. According to some of the respondents, the death of her husband at the hands of enemies of Serbia places her grief alongside the larger image of Serbs as an oppressed people who suffer because of the tragedy of warfare, the death of heroes, and most recently, the traumatic loss of Kosovo. As one respondent mentioned, "When I listen to Ceca, I feel the pain that I think only the Serbs can feel. Ceca lost the most precious gift—her husband—and we also lost one of the most precious things, which is the cradle of Serbia, Kosovo. First, we were expelled from Croatia, then, from Kosovo. We suffer as a nation, as she suffers as a woman" (Tea, a Serb, in Bosnia-Herzegovina).

On the other hand, the same respondents framed Ceca as a strong and a proud woman who always fights back, since she embodies the power and passion of the Serbs. According to Dragana, a Bosnian Serb, "It is the fact that she is a Serbian lily—she is very proud and strong. I admire her: she has everything, and she could easily withdraw from public life, but she wants to encourage the Serbian nation. . . . She wants to give us the energy and spirit to live on. . . . I really respect that. And the older she gets, the better she looks!"

To Dragana, Ceca emerges not only as a mythic hero but a Serbian embodiment of the American dream: "You can do anything, achieve anything, only if you work hard or if you marry a rich and influential man." This response mirrors the global transformations in the region, which have progressively redefined the realm of social relations through privatization of the means of production, rationalization of time, and intensification of class distinctions. As societies in the Balkans are becoming more "Western" (i.e., capitalist) in their outlook, the pattern of consumption practices has also followed in step with the West. It is against this neoliberal backdrop that Ceca successfully manages her politics, commercial appeal, and popularity as a transnational diva.

Ceca Depoliticized and Reinvented

There is a general consensus that "neoliberal" forms of economic and political restructuring in the Balkan region are accelerating an active form of depoliticization, in conformity with an imagined ideal of perfectly working markets spread as wide and deep as possible.[36] These neoliberal changes were echoed in the second narrative that emerged from the interviews, a narrative in which politicians are covered by the media as celebrities, and in turn, stars from the world of entertainment are invited to comment on the political. Moreover, it is a context in which nationalism appears not so much as a top-down political configuration but as a market-based arrangement. Nationalism, in the neoliberal context, is no longer a form of political identification but a mode of consumption increasingly oriented toward the sentimental and kitschy aesthetics of commercially produced cultural spectacles.

The porous border between politics and entertainment also contributes to the ambiguity and mystique about Ceca. Despite her explicitly articulated nationalistic sentiments and sometimes overtly political activities,[37] many respondents, regardless of their national belonging, repeatedly doubted or denied Ceca's political involvement. In these responses, Ceca is paradoxically positioned as an apolitical figure, and the focus is shifted to other aspects of her celebrity presence, including glamour, beauty, and lifestyle. Ceca is reinvented by her audience as first and foremost a musician and a performer, as this comment from Maja, a Slovene, reveals: "She is just a musician. She has no political interests really."

This response came not only from Serbian students but also from Slovene, Bosnian, and Croatian respondents. These are students from nations that were at war with the Serbs and who are likely to find Ceca's politics antithetical to their own political views. Their responses enable them to justify Ceca's popularity through a denial of her nationalistic discourse and political connections. Ceca powerfully invokes political history for the mobilization of her Serbian audiences, but she also suppresses it in strategic ways for other audiences. Furthermore, Ceca has been successful in presenting herself as an ordinary woman, since many respondents feel that "she is just like" them. This allows them to more easily identify with Ceca at the level of the everyday and to sidestep both her politics and her commercial success.

In the unfolding of celebrity culture, audiences identify with the star through emulation and a fantasy of intimacy.[38] To a young fan from Macedonia, Ceca becomes a gateway to talk about the nation: "I can identify with her and her life story, you know. It's intense, dramatic—that's how we live here." Remarks such as "no one helped her" or "she was all alone" were often made by the respondents to highlight Ceca's determination and drive. What is forgotten, of course, is that Ceca's success is closely dependent on the fact of her marriage to a powerful, well-connected Serbian military leader who espoused highly nationalistic views. These facts fade into the background in responses such as the following: "I admire her as a woman. . . . She is very independent. She is our role model here. She is strong and independent. . . . She fought for her own status, by herself, with her own hands, and no one has ever helped her" (Zerina, Kosovo Albanian).

To these respondents, Ceca is a romantic figure and a widow who continues to unconditionally love and adore her husband even after his death. By focusing on her through the frames of romance and domesticity, the fans effectively disconnect Ceca from her sociopolitical context and disregard her husband Arkan's political actions, even though most of the respondents seemed to know about Arkan's past and his violent death. The use of the words *exclusively, only,* or *extremely* seems to suggest that the respondents deliberately depoliticize Ceca. Consider the following quote from Ivana, a Croat: "I do not listen to Ceca, because this style of music is not my favorite. I do respect her, however, as a person, since her success and beauty are both the result of her strong personality. Look, her husband has died, but she still loves only him. Ceca is an extremely strong personality, she is unique; you cannot deny this."

Some respondents have defined Ceca as a Balkan diva only on the basis of her voice and overlook the political context. This type of political erasure by Dina, a Muslim from Bosnia, is telling: "I listen to her because of her voice. . . . She is the Balkan diva, sure; it is about her voice. Her voice has colors in it. I get hit by it, as soon as I hear it." Ceca's fame as a diva is explained only through recourse to her love songs, with almost no acknowledgment that many of her songs are nationalistic and are characterized by expressions of love for Serbia.[39] For example, according to Vladka, a Croat, "I love her because of her texts; these are new, . . . rich lyrics. Her texts are full of love for Arkan." Some respondents, such as Senada, a Muslim Bosnian, explicitly noted that Ceca's success is about turbo-folk rhythm and appeal: "She's not a politician; she is a musician. I think we need to make a difference here. Her fans respond to the rhythm of her songs and not her politics. At parties, we listen to turbo-folk music, and when we drink, . . . I get emotional, like everyone else, and I love the rhythm of her music then."

While Ceca's fans see her mainly as a successful entertainer and performer, her seemingly apolitical style is in fact politically significant, insofar as it serves as both alibi for and distraction from recent tragedies. It comes as no surprise that our respondents, like their peers, were largely uninterested in historical or political knowledge. Local scholars point out that compared to previous generations, contemporary youth of the region are generally not interested in historical knowledge and devote less of their attention to social problems.[40] Comments such as "I really do not care anymore about the past and all the wars" were frequently made, demonstrating the lack of interest in remembering the troubled past.

Ceca as the Balkan Other

Distinct forms and practices of Othering take place within the Balkans, casting some nations (in particular, Slovenia and Croatia) as more civilized, Western, and democratic and positioning those in the south as Balkan or Byzantine, hence boorish yet passionate.[41] However, Ceca consciously represents herself as being steeped in the authentic and passionate cultural space of the Balkans. Ceca personifies the converted stigma of the Balkans as an Eastern pleasure dome—the locus of joyful fulfillment of those desires that are discouraged and repressed by European values, rules, and tastes. Locating Ceca in the context of neoliberal transformations in the Balkans, it seems clear that multiple versions of modernity are simultaneously being contested and negotiated.

While our respondents perceived the Balkans through a stereotypical Orientalist frame, ironically, they also saw these characteristics as trendy and desirable. So the sensory association of Balkan bodies as uncouth is now resignified as playful and spontaneous. These new associations can be understood as an alternative take on modernity—a new construction of an imaginary Balkans, where enjoyment and emotions prevail over work and rationality. Through Ceca's image management in a hypermediated environment, she scripts an alternative modernity that has a transnational appeal. In reframing Balkan identity, the respondents celebrated Ceca as representing a kind of a voluntary regression into the Balkan world of authentically passionate and emotional music, away from the "overly rational and boring" European lifestyle. For the majority of Slovene and Croatian respondents, the Balkans and Ceca work as a cultural replacement for the enjoyment and passion that the West clearly lacks.

For Slovene students, Ceca stands for a life of passion and enjoyment. The respondents referred to the lack of emotions and the routinization of their own reality, since most of the time they are expected to conform to what they see as European mainstream modes of behavior:

> I listen to turbo-folk music in general, and I like Ceca a lot, . . . since she clearly knows what life is. And she lives it. She has emotions, she feels pain and love . . . till the end. You can feel it. It's not fake. It's a real thing. She expresses her feelings regardless of consequences. One can see it on her face, how she enjoys love, life, and pain. . . . One cannot see these passionate expressions living in Slovenia, since we are forced to live in a controlled way. We became the robots. (Nina, a Slovene)

Despite the fact that the young students from Slovenia do not have clear memories about life in former Yugoslavia, they position Ceca in the context of a Slovene framework, where the dominant political discourses constantly stress a sense of belonging to western Europe. However, the respondents long to be less "European" and more "Balkan," like Ceca. Through the strategic use of the very technologies of globalization, Ceca dissociates her image from war and instead forges an alternative script that reclaims new and appealing ways of being. Maja, a Slovenian respondent told us, "Now, when we have proven to the world how European we are, we can open ourselves to the Balkan way of life again. We are allowed to enjoy again that Balkan spirit that was prohibited for a long time here."

For the majority of Croatian and Macedonian young women, Ceca is a diva because she inspires a sense of regional unity. According to Despina, a Macedonian, "Ceca connects us all in the Balkans. . . . Her music unites us. After the wars, that's very important. She is successful in going beyond nationalisms, because she is authentically Balkan." Ceca, to a younger generation of Slovenes and Croats, serves as a symbolic "Other"—a personification of authenticity, joyfulness, passion, and entertainment. These are precisely the attributes of everyday life that many people in the Balkans feel have been or will have to be sacrificed in order to conform to the West and what is considered a more European, rational, regulated way of life.

"Ceca is a living proof that we also have Hollywood icons here, who are sexy, successful, and rich. I think she is kind of artificial, but she is famous." To young Serbian fans such as Dada, who made this comment, Ceca represents a Balkan version of a Hollywood diva. As a typical megastar, Ceca continually invents herself and sustains her appeal to her large and growing audience base, who claim her as their own Balkan icon. During the 1990s, Ceca mainly addressed a homogeneous (Serbian) audience, but now her audience extends beyond national borders. In addition, Ceca has amassed a commodity trail to follow her, with CDs, films, calendars, and photographs which promote her presence as a sexy, independent, rich, and successful woman, yet with an everyday appeal.

Her body becomes a focal point of her appeal, especially to the respondents who cited her makeup, fitness, and unusual fashion sense; her cosmetic surgery is interpreted as a sign of her independence and success. According to Lindita, a Kosovo Albanian, "So what if she has silicone in her breasts?! All the rich people do. . . . She can; she has the money. If I would have it, I would enlarge my breasts as well." Ceca achieves the status of a Hollywood diva through the power of silicone. Her attempt both to embrace and to exaggerate Western standards of beauty seems to be widely admired and lies at the heart of our respondents' desire to be "modern."

Although Ceca is seen widely as a subversive figure, her appeal is still primarily rooted in her appearance, physical beauty, and sex appeal. Many respondents commented on her visual appearance and "sexy" body, as did Milivoja (a Macedonian): "I would like to look like her. That's all—just to look like her. She has it: good looks and sex appeal." Respondents celebrated her Madonna (Ciccione)–like ability to update herself constantly, both in appearance and style: "Ceca transforms herself all the time. She changes her image—she can be sexy or more businesslike, . . . mysterious. . . . She fulfills the desires of many different people" (Lucija, a Croatian).

Most of the respondents are also fascinated by Ceca's celebrity lifestyle, which both catapults her into the ranks of global celebrity and encourages a form of adulation—a staple of celebrity culture. Mojca, a Slovenian student remarked, "I don't really like her music, but I surely would love to live like she does! To be rich and not worry about the money, to be beautiful and sexy. . . . I wouldn't mind having a house with a swimming pool, expensive cars." As a fetish, she is celebrated and imitated, and often the respondents buy her products. Vildana, a Macedonian student, claimed, "She is my hero. . . . I have all her CDs, I attend her concerts, read her interviews, buy the same cosmetics she uses." Regardless of their national belonging, our respondents got excited when they talked about

Ceca's lifestyle and her presence as a strong, independent woman. Propped by emerging forms of entrepreneurialism in the region and crony capitalism, Ceca provides her fans an escape from reality into joyful consumption, romance, and entertainment. Here are the words of Ilinka, a Macedonian:

> I adore her, especially because I can switch off while listening to her. She is familiar yet strange to me at the same time. I escape into Ceca-land—and forget about my troubles. Pure joy. I fantasize about being in some other world that is full of richness, shopping, entertainment, . . . yes, and love and passion. If I wouldn't have this, I would probably go crazy. Really—she just gives me energy.

Conclusion

It is precisely Ceca's ascent as a global turbo-folk pop icon, transcending her ties to Serbian nationalism, that makes her an interesting case study. Her star trajectory crosses spatial and temporal zones in a series of paradoxical and unexpected moves. Despite the fact that she sang nationalistic songs, performed for Serbian soldiers in Bosnia-Herzegovina, and was married to a Serbian war criminal, she is popular in Bosnia and Croatia alike. Ceca's entertainment trajectory reveals that even as the sense of national belonging is handed over to the machinations of the marketplace, nationalist sentiments are commercialized, with all the trappings of manipulative sentimentality. It is an aesthetics into which Ceca's own music and style fits neatly, and it enables her to adopt specific strategies of performing history.

In addition, the analysis shows that our respondents ignore Ceca's political connection and represent her as a strong woman who suffers but is able to overcome all her personal grief and trauma. More significantly, Ceca succeeds in installing herself as a Balkan diva, through strategic linking of the new opportunities opened by commercial media, the neoliberal economy, and the strains of an older nationalism. The shifting societal values of postcommunist Yugoslavia due to political and economic changes have also contributed to Ceca's rise and popularity. Ceca does not provoke or challenge dominant ways of thinking or being. By imitating and reproducing familiar global trends in popular culture, she contributes to the consolidation of political shifts and reaffirms national interests through a transnational media presence.

It is not simply a question of asserting that those who are fascinated with Ceca's music or celebrity story are ideological dupes. Rather, we have tried to trace the elements of her appeal against the background of the contradictions and political tensions that characterize everyday life, especially for young people in the neoliberal climate of postsocialist capitalism in former Yugoslavia. On the one hand, it is a society that now seems more politically and economically free;

yet, on the other, we see a society of new forms of constraints, imposed by the culture of the marketplace and circulated by media technologies. It is a society that invokes the ideology of capitalist individualism even while practicing older social forms, remnants from an earlier time of socialism, such as cronyism, networking, and favoritism. These anxieties open a commercial space of success for Ceca where she, as well as her fans, can gloss over ideological contradictions through the creation of a new mythology. The celebration of the autonomous self-fashioning subject is presented not through the lens of political citizenship but rather through the lens of commercial success and the injunction to have fun, to enjoy, and to consume. Simultaneously, Ceca's mythology works to distance the commercial world from the political and military violence that have taken such a toll on the region. Cultural practices, linking communities across national borders, are embedded in complex asymmetries of nationalism, sexism, and class conflict. As the example of Ceca demonstrates, the transnational flow of capital and media enables the staging of new malleable identities which are both defined by the nation and exceed its boundaries.

NOTES

The authors would like to thank Radha S. Hegde and Graeme Turner for their help and feedback on this chapter.

1. Miladin Mihajlovic, "Ne treba mi Zapad, dovoljni su mi Srbi," *Patriot OnLine* (February 2003), http://www.patriotmagazin.com/arhiva/0021/media/007.htm (accessed April 19, 2009).

2. Teja Tomic, *Neofolk kultura v Srbiji; Studij primera: Svetlana Raznatovic-Ceca* (Ljubljana, Slovenia: Fakulteta za družbene vede, 2006).

3. Andrej Nikolaidis, *Balkanska rabsodija* (Sarajevo, Bosnia-Herzegovina: Pres-sing, 2007), 22.

4. Ivana Kronja, *Smrtonosni sjaj: Masovna psihologija i estetika turbo-folka* (Belgrade, Serbia: Tehnokratia, 2001); Catherine Baker, "The Politics of Performance: Transnationalism and Its Limits in Former Yugoslav Popular Music, 1999–2004," *Ethnopolitics* 5, no. 3 (2006): 275–293.

5. Kronja, *Smrtonosni sjaj*; Baker, "The Politics of Performance." Also see Alexei Monroe, "Balkan Hardcore," *Central Europe Review* 24 (February 2000), http://www.ce-review.org/00/24/monroe24.html.

6. Nikolaidis, *Balkanska rabsodija*, 4.

7. In Macedonia, Croatia, Slovenia, and Montenegro alike, contemporary popular female singers, such as Slovene Natalija Verboten, Croatian Maja Suput, and Serbian Jelena Karleusa, all imitate and recycle the aesthetic and musical techniques of turbo-folk music.

8. Kronja, *Smrtonosni sjaj*, 70.

9. Ibid.

10. Eric Gordy, *The Culture of Power in Serbia: Nationalism and the Destruction of Alternatives* (University Park: Pennsylvania State University Press, 1999), 22.

11. Ali H. Zerdin, "Spremembe v notranjem krogu omrezja slovenske ekonomske elite v letih 2004–2006," *Druzboslovne razprave* 23 (September 2007): 7–25.

12. Anthony Giddens, *The Third Way: The Renewal of Social Democracy* (Cambridge, UK: Polity, 1998).

13. Lazar Lalic, *Tri TV Godine u Srbiji: Godina Prva* (Belgrade, Serbia: Nezavisni Sindikat Medija, 1995), 31; Dusan Reljic, *Killing Screens: Media in Times of Conflict* (Skopje, Republic of Macedonia: CER, European Institute for the Media, 2001), 23; Kronja, *Smrtonosni sjaj*, 21.

14. Milica Dragicevic-Sesic, *Neofolk kultura: Publika i njene zvezde* (Sremski Karlovci and Novi Sad, Serbia: Izdavačka knjižarnica Zorana Stojanovića, 1994), 19–21.

15. Nikolaidis, *Balkanska rabsodija*, 33.

16. Goran Tarlac, "Vojaski in Politicni Turbo-folk," *Mladina* 12 (March 21, 2003), http://www.mladina.si/dnevnik/21-03-2003-vojaski_in_politicni_turbo_folk/ (accessed April 19, 2009).

17. Another turbo-folk song says, "I don't know what I'll do/All Europe is fascist, it's sad but true/I can hear their barking sound/They want to knock Serbia to the ground." Tomic, *Neofolk Kultura v Srbiji*, 23.

18. Ivan Colovic, *Bordel ratnika: Folklor, politika i rat* (Belgrade, Serbia: Slovograf, 1994), 83–93.

19. Tarlac, "Vojaski in Politicni Turbo-folk," 31.

20. Charles Bernheimer, *Decadent Subjects: The Idea of Decadence in Art, Literature, Philosophy, and the Culture of the Fin de Siècle in Europe* (Baltimore: Johns Hopkins University Press, 2002), 44.

21. Marko Lopusina, *Ceca, Izmedu Ljubavi I Mrznje* (Belgrade, Serbia: Evro, 2003).

22. Ibid., 76.

23. Ibid.

24. Graeme Turner, *Understanding Celebrities* (London: Sage, 2004).

25. Dina Iordanova, *Balkan Wedding Revisited* (Vienna: Center for Austrian Studies, 1998), 98.

26. Nikolaidis, *Balkanska rabsodija*, 37; Tarlac, "Vojaski in politicni turbo-folk," 39; Tomic, *Neofolk kultura v Srbiji*, 60.

27. Adam Higginbotham, "The Beauty and the Beast," *Observer* (January 4, 2004), http://observer.guardian.co.uk/magazine/story/0,11913,1115508,00.html (accessed April 19, 2009).

28. Lopusina, *Ceca, Izmedu Ljubavi I Mrznje*, 199–200.

29. Mihajlovic, "Ne treba mi Zapad, dovoljni su mi Srbi."

30. Matt Prodger, "Serbs Rally to 'Turbo-folk' Music," *BBC News* (January 11, 2005), http://news.bbc.co.uk/2/hi/europe/4165831.stm (accessed May 5, 2005).

31. Especially in Slovenia and Croatia, the media cover her extensively.

32. Zala Volčič, *Mediji in Identiteta* [Media and Identity] (Maribor, Slovenia: University of Maribor Press, 2008).

33. Matthew Price, "Ceca: Serbia's Singing Heroine," *BBC News* (June 16, 2002), http://news.bbc.co.uk/2/low/entertainment/2043291.stm (accessed June 24, 2002).

34. Kronja, *Smrtonosni sjaj*; Nikolaidis, *Balkanska rabsodija*; Lopusina, *Ceca, Izmedu Ljubavi I Mrznje*.

35. We interviewed ninety-three female students aged eighteen to twenty-five, in twelve focus groups composed of Slovene, Croatian, Bosnian Serb, Bosnian Muslim, Macedonian, Kosovo Albanian, and Serbian participants. We focused on this demographic group precisely because of Ceca's popularity within it. The research was conducted during the spring of 2008. We held interviews with female students from diverse ethnic, class, and religious backgrounds, coming from both urban and rural areas (including small towns) and different fields of study.

36. Nikolas Rose, "The Politics of Life Itself," *Theory, Culture and Society* 18 (December 2001): 1–30.

37. Nikolaidis, *Balkanska rabsodija*, 93.

38. P. David Marshall, *Celebrity and Power: Fame in Contemporary Culture* (Minneapolis: University of Minnesota Press, 1997), 158.

39. Ibid.

40. Mirjana Ule, "Mladi in družbene spremembe," *IB revija* (Ljubljana: Zavod SR Slovenije za družbeno planiranje) 41 (April 2007): 62–69.

41. See more on this subject in Milica Bakic-Hayden, "Nesting Orientalism: The Case of Former Yugoslavia," *Slavic Review* (Stanford, CA: American Association for the Advancement of Slavic Studies) 54 (December 1995): 917–931.

3   The Gendered Face of Latinidad

Global Circulation of Hybridity

Angharad N. Valdivia

This chapter examines the gendered face of Latinidad as it is transported, manipulated, and articulated by popular media networks under the contemporary conditions of globality. *Latinidad*, the process of being, becoming, and/or performing belonging within a Latina/o diaspora, challenges many popular and academic categories of ethnicity, location, and culture. As a cultural and conceptual framework, Latinidad enables a more nuanced reading of the disjuncture between the lived realities and commodified constructions of hybridity. Focusing on three sites of mobile popular culture—girl culture, global television, and celebrity bodies—I explore how gender and hybrid cultures of Latina/os are reproduced and normalized in a complex mediated global environment. The foregrounding of female characters, whether in television, mediated doll lines, or celebrity culture, demonstrates a strategic deployment of sexualized femininity. In none of these three areas is there a male counterpart, suggesting that it is Latinas who are stereotypically amenable in the marketplace to the production of a commodified ethnic sexuality. The transnational Latina/o diasporic community is made visible in the global context through particular articulations of gender and sexuality that are deployed by consumer culture and transported by mediated images.

The global presence and mobility of the Latina/o population has led to significant reconfiguration of the U.S. national imaginary with regard to race, gender, ethnicity, and sexuality. In particular, the heterogeneity of the Latina/o population has unsettled a deeply entrenched black and white racial system which is embedded in various types of institutional and social discourses.[1] Although the category of Latina/os was originally articulated in the context of U.S. ethnic politics, the transnational lives and cultural hybridity of Latina/os and Latinidad exceed national boundaries and disrupt conventional categorizations of race. In an era of global media production, distribution, and circulation, nation-bound notions of Latinidad can no longer be sustained. With a population whose contours refuse conventional representations, difference continues to be policed in a manner in which certain bodies, skin tones, accents, and shapes are more visible or desirable than others. The repercussions are evident in the terrain of cultural production and everyday life. Diasporic mobility and the circulation of these new discourses of race and ethnicity through media and markets transnationalize the discourse of race and ethnicity. More recently, market forces and media institutions have recognized the economic power and consumer potential of the Latina/o diasporic community. The aura of what is understood as Latina/o is embedded into a range of consumer products and cultural programming, making Latina/os both the target and the resource for global popular culture.

The wide-ranging influence of the ways in which media circulates gendered discourses globally is undeniable, and old repressive patterns of representation continue to be reproduced.[2] The inclusion of transnationalism, hybridity, and Latinidad shifts the discussion of media discourses into a terrain that is flexible and indeterminate. Though not providing solutions or easy answers, what Marwan Kraidy calls "hybridity without guarantees,"[3] this essay argues for a more textured understanding of gendered meanings and cultural hybridity.

Global Face of Latinidad

The transnational movement of people and cultures generates hybrid formations that demand deep contextualization. The ways in which these transnational cultures are made visible in circuits of global distribution and circulation speak to the logics by which difference is articulated and reproduced in global popular culture. The diversity and hybridity that characterize Latina/o communities complicate discrete and separate ethnic categorizations which are typically contained within national boundaries. Elsewhere I have argued that Latina/os demonstrate a radical hybridity which has reshuffled the national imaginary by expanding the ethnic register to a fluid spectrum and highlighting the fact that there are no rigid borders between vectors of difference.[4]

While many scholars still reject the use of hybridity as implicated in an effort to secure and reproduce a racist and hierarchical global regime,[5] others have taken this concept and applied it to contemporary cultural formations.[6] Kraidy argues for specificity in the use of the term *hybridity*, lest we fall into the trap of claiming that everything is hybrid and thus lose any theoretical and methodological value that the term might offer.[7] We need to explore the gains and losses incurred in cultural and population mixtures rather than acritically celebrate mixture, as commodity culture urges us to do.[8] Distinguishing hybridity from syncretism, Hamid Naficy writes that the latter is a more stable, longer lasting, and less ambivalent condition than hybridity, in which cultures blend and shift in an indeterminate array of positions.[9] Extending the distinction to Latinidad, Elana Levine argues that contemporary mainstream cultures constructs a syncretic Latina/o identity.[10] While Latinidad signals a dynamic multiplicity and plurality of voices, media and the marketplace stabilize and flatten hybridity in the name of multiculturalism. Media and popular culture move not only faster but often independently of the populations that create and produce them. Transnational cultural products, favored by global capital, receive greater welcome than the culturally marked bodies of Others.[11] In this chapter, I examine the constellations of power within the circuits of global popular culture that syncretize the enactments and embodiments of hybridity, especially through gendered tropes.

Transnational cultural practices of Latina/o communities are rapidly redefining the lived realities of transnational Latina/o hybrid cultures on the ground. The manipulation of sexualized bodies on mediated sites of popular culture offers a way to examine how particular scripts of hybridity are mobilized in order to construct normative notions of the category *Latino/a*. Looking at a range of sites such as the global circulation of television, girl culture, and celebrity stars also reveals the work of the cultural imaginary in relation to a new Latinidad. The hybridity of everyday life is paralleled by the genre blending generated by technological convergence, which has blurred the boundaries between various types of media products and markets. Globalization and media convergence have made it profitable to produce across media platforms by reworking content into multiple formats and marketing to a wide-ranging global audience.[12]

In order to explore the global circulation of a hybrid Latinidad through the travel of form, artifacts, and actors, I focus on the television show *Ugly Betty*, mediated Latina doll lines, and the polysemic and spectacular visibility of Latina celebrities. Although seemingly divergent, these three sites are linked by the implicit and explicit inclusion of hybrid Latinidad, its transportation across the globe, and its resulting challenge to narratives of purity or binary racial regimes, albeit deterritorialized from its original U.S. ethnic politics. The popularity of all three chosen sites, their global portability, and their foregrounding of sexualized bodies attest to the current value of a gendered Latinidad as a hybrid resource of commodification in the global context.

Hybrid Travels and Gendered Destinations: Global Television Flows

I now turn to a recent example of the global deployment of hybridity through U.S. Latinidad—the popular television show *Ugly Betty*.[13] While media scholars have written about the global resonance of melodramatic serials,[14] *Ugly Betty* succeeds in hybridizing genre, representation, and ethnicity. Originally a Colombian hit named *Betty la Fea*, the show proved so popular, profitable, and irresistible that many countries have spun off versions: from Russia's *Ne Rodis' Krasivoy* (Не родись красивой; Russian for "be not born beautiful"), Spain's *Yo Soy Bea* (Spanish for "I am Bea"—itself a hybrid name for Betty la Fea), and the U.S. version, *Ugly Betty*. The latter turns the Colombian telenovela into a hybrid genre of soap opera and comedy—known as dramedy—and infuses the narrative with the hybrid representation of Betty as a working-class Mexican American Latina working in the mostly white upper-middle-class world of New York City fashion magazines. In turn, U.S. *Ugly Betty* is marketed to dozens of countries, thus globally transporting a gendered and classed face of Latinidad.

Circulating globally, the U.S. version of *Ugly Betty* is the most successful retelling and, as such, often competes with local versions. In Spain, the introduction of *Ugly Betty* coincided with the resolution of the local *Yo Soy Bea*. The Spanish main characters married, and Bea's beauty finally shone through. In a sense, the narrative and thus the series of local versions of *Ugly Betty* were resolved so U.S. *Ugly Betty* could take over in local television. The national version ceded to the slick U.S. version gone transnational.

The many forms that *Ugly Betty* takes throughout the globe speak to the global adaptations of the popular theme of the Ugly Duckling.[15] U.S. *Ugly Betty* incorporates the Latina/o difference centrally into the narrative in a way that could not happen in Colombia, where Latinidad does not stand out as a marker of difference. Latin American telenovelas include a class dimension as a regional marker of difference. In the United States, Betty is both Latina and working class, thus reiterating, as noted by Latina/o studies scholars, the collapse of class and ethnic categories.[16] Moreover, as the hybrid symbol of the tale of the Ugly Duckling, Betty's body and style embodies in various ways the shifting contact zone between cultures. U.S. Betty originally commutes from Queens to Manhattan, though in a later season, she is able to move out on her own into a small apartment in Manhattan, only to have to return home to help take care of her ailing father. Her appearance, family, and food choices code her ethnic and class difference. Her blue braces have become the most prominent sign of "ugliness," though they gain meaning in concert with her hairstyle, clothing, and lunch items. Betty's difference also applies to her moral standards, her ethical outlook, and her "innocence," which often helps to unmask other characters' subterfuge. While she is the "ugly" one at *Mode* magazine, where she works, and her co-workers recognize her work ethic and problem-solving abilities, she is the smart and upwardly mobile one at home. Nonetheless, scholars such as Madeleine Shufeldt Esch note that in the final instance, her ugly coding reinscribes traditional ideals of beauty.[17] Betty's sister, Hilda Suarez, plays a foil character, the loose, hot, single-mother Latina whose occupational choices are limited in relation to Betty's decidedly more straight-laced approach to sexuality and her investment in her education and therefore a more mainstream path.

Ugly Betty not only represents contemporary gendered Latinidad but also reflects the national identity crisis as the United States comes to terms with the heterogeneity of its newer immigrant population. It is no coincidence that Betty is the ironic ugly one in an ethnically and sexually diverse workplace full of double-faced characters. Her difference checks in as "ugly" in a symbolic economy in which Anglo-European ethnicities are coded as superiorly beautiful yet morally compromised. Unsurprisingly, an immigration narrative of criminality is written into the show—Betty's dad, Ignacio, not only has problems with immigration but also has a criminal background, having killed a former boss. Ignacio's character neatly combines the discursive construction of the male Latino immigrant as both illegal and lawless. Locating that element in a distant past cleanses his present situation as an innocuous father. Gender types in terms of beauty and scheming are borne out by the women of color, while criminal threat seems the domain of Latino men. There is a stereotypical pattern in the representation of queerness. The Suarez family is shown as being supportive of Justin, Betty's gay nephew. However, within both the Suarez family and the Mode environment, there is a normalization of queerness. In the microcosm of Betty's Mexican American world, we are introduced to a particular type of resistant difference—one of the competing narratives of Latinidad. The extended patriarchal Mexican American family is portrayed as belonging to an unassimilable working-class ethnic community. In this setting, Betty, the hybrid character, is the only one who has elements of upward mobility and potentiality to participate in the dominant culture written into her ethnic character.

The identifiable Latinidad in the United States cannot be assumed to be decipherable in other countries, where Betty might just sign in as "ugly." The show has an international fan base, and these scripts of race and hybridity run the risk of being further flattened, as they are multiply interpreted around the globe.[18] It is likely that the racial and sexual diversity in the workplace might fade into a general aesthetic of high comedy. Betty's family poverty might be interpreted as the traditional class divisions routinely seen in a generic telenovela. The overriding fact is that Betty remains one of the more prominent Latinas in mainstream television, with the power of conglomerate capital to transport her around the world, and as such, she becomes a vehicle for the transaction and accommodation of global difference.

Mediated Doll Lines

The script of hybridity together with an exaggerated Latinidad is globally circulated through the highly profitable mediated doll lines of American Girl, Dora the Explorer, and Bratz.[19] Mediated doll brands as a category focuses on the analysis of the multiple media channels of television, film, books, and online chat rooms that constitute a discursive formation of gender and ethnic identity that in turn circulates transnationally. Thus, the analysis focuses on media circulation rather than on the dolls themselves. Unsettling Barbie's five-decade reign, the three new mediated doll lines challenge the narrative and the profit line of Barbie, the doll who exemplified suburban whiteness and whose femininity reigned supreme in the U.S. marketplace. Barbie was distributed globally in her original form as well as in national versions such as Spanish, Greek, and Puerto Rican Barbie—all of whom were traditionally dressed in national costume. Of the three contemporary doll lines, American Girl began as media and doll simultaneously; Dora the Explorer began as a television show and branched out into other media and a huge range of products; and Bratz began as dolls, in the Barbie model, and branched out into media through television, movies, and books, as well as into a generalized range of products. The three mediated doll lines were hugely successful, and all but one, American Girl,[20] is marketed globally. Examining the marketing and narrative approach of these doll lines provides some insight into the possibilities and limits of girl culture hybridity in the global market.

The original American Girls were white and firmly ensconced within Eurocentric histories—the marketing approach being one of releasing a doll with an accompanying book that described the historical period. The girl/doll was the agent of that historical period. The mediated doll line thus combined a pedagogically grounded history with an upscale target audience, as each doll cost nearly one hundred dollars, with accessories for the dolls and its girl owner potentially adding up to over a thousand dollars. In 1992, Addy, an African American girl, was introduced, and in 1997, Josefina, a Mexican girl, joined the other American Girls. Of note is that unlike the other American Girls, Josefina was the only one whose history located her outside the U.S. national space, thus reiterating the characterization of U.S. Latina/os as eternal outsiders.[21] American Girl has a number of other doll lines, among them Girl of the Year, which changes annually and whose accessories are retired, thus becoming more valuable on marketing sites such as eBay. American Girl weathered the controversy in the Latina/o community following the introduction in 2005 of Girl of the Year Marisol Luna, whose narrative had her moving out of her undesirably coded Pilsen neighborhood, which is home to a large Latina/o community in Chicago. American Girl did not directly answer the resulting outcry from a number of Latina/o organizations, although subsequent Girls of the Year have remained white. The only hybrid Girl of the Year, Jessie of 2006, was of Japanese and Irish American background. Her adventure year spent in an archaeological dig in Belize among ancient Mayan ruins seems to have externalized difference while simultaneously transitioning away from the more ethnically coded and potentially problematic Marisol to the safe whiteness of most of the other American Girls. Both Marisol and Josefina, the Latina American Girls, represent the traditional Mexican American discourse. Josefina is more static than her contemporary counterpart, Marisol, who, as politically incorrect as her narrative was found to be, moves out of her Pilsen neigh-

Fig. 3.1. A multiracial mediated line of Dora the Explorer dolls

borhood in a quest for upward mobility. Unlike the other mediated doll brands, American Girl exhibits nation-specific coding. Whereas Dora the Explorer and Bratz are globally known and distributed brands, American Girl is marketed only nationally, an anomaly in an economy in which global expansion is the norm. Hybridity was only attempted on the transition back to a safe whiteness after Marisol ushered in a wave of Latina/o outcry. The other Latina doll, Josefina, remains safely encoded in the historical past, outside the nation space. American Girl's history impels us to engage with the conditions under which hybridity is possible or the way hybridity can be performed, either exploding outside the nationally contained space or being confined within it. Does an upscale narrowcasting implicitly draw on nationalist rhetoric? Does a global marketing approach dilute the class exclusivity of the nationalist strategy?

A different marketing and ethnic coding strategy is exemplified by Dora the Explorer, which began as a television show in 1999 in the Nickelodeon children's cable television network, and was also shown in over-the-air broadcasts by CBS television, and quickly expanded to other media as well as a huge range of products ranging from clothing to furniture, food, toys, linens, and draperies. Whereas the American Girls are nationally encoded into traditional paradigms of ethnicity, albeit foregrounding gendered agency, Dora is ambiguously encoded within

Latinidad in terms of national origin but unambiguously portrays a Latina body. Dora resides in a deterritorialized island with elements from the Mexican American and tropical narratives of Latinidad. The latter paradigm features island life and vegetation such as palm trees, monkeys, coconuts, and beaches. The tropical often includes its own set of nearly combustible colors in neon-bright hues as well as more movement in concert with upward-mobility narratives that represent assimilating smaller families and single people. Dora's island contains both a Mayan-looking pyramid and tropical palm trees. Background music tends to be tropical salsa, yet the monkey reminds us of Frida Kahlo's pet, a Mexican reference. Moreover, Dora plays with a squirrel and walks by an oak tree, neither of which are elements of a Mexican nor a tropical setting. These mixed-up signifiers, within Latinidad, have generated heated discussion on online chat rooms,[22] but it is doubtful whether many non-Latina/os notice the incongruousness of Dora's setting. Because cartoons are supposed to be about fantasy, audience complaints about their construction often fall on deaf ears. This is also the case with Dora, although the virulence of online chat rooms demonstrates the burden of underrepresentation. Since Dora is one of the few little Latinas widely visible in contemporary commodity culture, her construction bears the burden of representing the heterogeneity within Latinidad. Nonetheless, Dora has been highly successful, as her longevity, branding, ability to generate spinoffs, and growing up as a character attest. She is globally distributed, but her U.S. Latinidad has to be recast in other settings.[23]

> In Israel, Dora's "foreign" language is not Spanish but English. To me this is a very interesting twist, because learning English is "aiming up," rather than "aiming down." What I mean by this is that while in the U.S. Dora is trying to raise the status of Spanish to its rightful position, in Israel English is already very highly valued and is looked up at as a high-status and upper-mobility language. For Dora to have the same effect as it has in the U.S. with Spanish, it should have taught in Israel, for example, Russian—a language of a huge group of immigrants (about 15 percent of the population), which is perceived as a minority language of lower status. . . . So I think that, culturally, Russian in Israel would have been the equivalent of Spanish in the U.S. English is not.[24]

Dora's difference in the United States is not reproduced in the same valence elsewhere. Viewers abroad do not necessarily recognize her Latinidad; however, a program that promotes active learning through difference represented by an innocuous brown girl seems to be globally alluring.

Bratz, the third mediated doll line, is intrinsically hybrid, containing such subtle ambiguous Latinidad that it can be harnessed to represent any, all, or no difference. Introduced in 2001 by MGA Entertainment, Bratz dolls were meant to compete with Barbie, with an updated all-around aesthetic. Bratz have huge heads, large lips, lots of hair, and small torsos and hips, and (slightly unnervingly) they have feet that snap on and off at the ankle, with painted-on shoes or boots. Bratz look more like Beyoncé and Jennifer Lopez than the Grace Kelly look of Barbie. Their marketing logo is "girls with a passion for fashion," thus co-opting hip hop's social-justice impetus toward a consumerist goal ensconced in the language of girls and consumerism. Their staging forms a bridge between *Ugly Betty* and Jennifer Lopez. They muddle difference but remain inescapably different and brown. They bring in new styles, which are coded as hip and contemporary rather than ugly and foreign. Bratz are a reaction to and rejection of Barbie. As an illustration of the recoding at work within this brand, a Bratz original accessory was a chunk of a brick graffiti wall. What used to signify urban, antisocial youth is recast in Bratz as the epitome of fashion. Much like Disney princesses of color,[25] Bratz hair is huge and takes a life of its own. These poster girls of post-feminism exhibit highly independent attitude, or rather *brattitude*, with subtle racial hybridity. The *radical hybridity*—that is, hybridity of more than one element within a category and across categories—of these dolls in nonetheless attached to familiar ethnic identities as the mediated doll line crosses over into mainstream Hollywood film. For instance, Jade, one of the original dolls, performs her Latinidad in *The Bratz* movie (2007) through her proclivity for dance and the fact that she appears to have a mariachi band living in her kitchen.[26] The ethnic brownness of most dolls renders them potentially Latina. The Hollywood film reveals the extent that Bratz is willing to push ethnic registers. The dolls' website and their transition into feature-length-movie stardom have morphed their look into straight hair and almond-shaped eyes, making them very similar to each other, all of them possibly and ambiguously Latina. Those subtle signifiers of difference may not resonate with their target audience. Like Dora, Bratz are marketed globally. They are not constrained by the nation-specific narrative of American Girl and tap into the global force and potential of hip hop music and culture. Bratz, like the other two mediated doll lines, expose internal contradictions, commodifying and sexualizing increasingly younger girls. Much of the reaction to Bratz focuses on their sexuality and generates a moral panic. Still their *brattitude* coincides with the representation in other mainstream media of ethnic girls, including Latinas, as physical and pushy. Whereas assertiveness can be coded as positive, its slippage into *brattitude* places it within the racialized realm of behavioral problems. These hybrid girls are tamed when they cross into Hollywood film, made more assimilable, and therefore made more commodifiable for a mainstream audience.

Hybridity as Star Power

Another area to explore concepts of hybridity and transnationalism as they overlap with gender and Latinidad is the highly sensationalized coverage of Latina celebrities. In the United States, a Latin boom in the late nineties translated into the celebrity status of a wide range of women who are covered as Latina/os. Deeper inspection of these celebrities reveals that they embody hybridity and transnationality. We can begin with Shakira,[27] whose global visibility and popularity as a star rests on her identity as a hybrid transnational subject. Shakira, who is of Colombian and Lebanese descent, after immigrating to the United States began to identify herself as a Latina. Her crossover process, managed by the Estefans, included blonding the hair, shedding some weight, and learning English. Yet she shakes her hips in a manner informed more by Middle Eastern dancing than any form of salsa or cumbia—a commodified cosmopolitanism writ large on her body.[28] She is claimed by a number of nationalities and ethnicities as their own. Shakira's transnationalism cannot be confined to a U.S.-Colombia nexus but rather stems from Lebanese, Spanish, and Colombian roots and then fans out globally, transnationally. Her fluid appeal and presence carries different meanings across settings. While in the United States she is predominantly coded as Latina since she hails from Colombia, elsewhere, both in Europe and the Middle East, her Lebanese background is recognized. Her music circulates globally in both Spanish and English. Her musical genres refuse a simplistic reductionism to "Latin pop" but remain rooted in rock, with tinges of Middle Eastern components. Shakira is difficult to contain within a single nation space.

Salma Hayek, another celebrity star, resembles Shakira in that she is a recent immigrant to the United States, though unlike Shakira, her Mexican origin is also recent. Whereas Shakira hails from a longstanding Lebanese community in Colombia, Salma is first-generation Mexican. They share Lebanese roots yet are recoded in the U.S. space as Latinas. Isabel Molina Guzmán connects the transnational flows into Latin America and the United States of both Shakira and Salma.[29] As Salma Hayek reinterpreted Frida Kahlo in the movie *Frida* (2002), she reinscribed the iconic artist within Latinidad and Latin Americanism, though Frida herself was of recent Mexican provenance. The fact that the U.S. Post Office released a Frida stamp as a tribute to Latinas attests to the United States as a nation officially accepting Frida, a first-generation Mexican, as a U.S. Latina, despite the fact that she never changed her citizenship and, but for a brief stay in the United States, lived and died in Mexico. Frida, therefore, was allowed a posthumous border crossing. Furthermore, the transnational circulation of Frida's art and image escapes the ability of Frida's heirs and of U.S. Latina/os to contain her Mexicanidad and Latinidad. Finally, neither "Salma" nor "Hayek" nor "Frida" are commonplace Spanish names, unless one includes the considerable and complex history and presence of Middle Eastern and Eastern European flows into Spain and the Americas.

A third hybrid Latina star is Celia Cruz. Unmistakably part of the Latina/o diaspora, she also represents transnational flows that cannot be contained by the Cuba-U.S. nexus.[30] Her African roots and the global circulation and resonance of her musical and visual material affirm to that. Her tropicalized circulation—with regard to music, style, and location of origin—expands beyond Cuba and the United States. Moreover, her Cubanidad is written out of contemporary U.S. narratives that continue to erase Cuba as a sovereign nation.[31] With regard to her own construction of self, Celia had to consciously think through issues of gender and race in relation to music and geopolitics.[32] The negative reaction on the part of some Cuban Americans to a Smithsonian exhibit of her clothes, shoes, and wigs highlighted the tensions that during her life Celia tried to assuage.[33] Her coding within the Latin Grammies further speaks to her liminal location within Latin America and U.S. Latinidad. Her global stature outside of the U.S. anti-Cuban discourse speaks to the flow of music culture independent of particular national and ideological proclivities. Celia, known as "The Queen of Salsa," embodied not only that musical hybrid of hybrids but the unsettled meaning of a musical star whose ethnicity did not match dominant discourses of Latinidad—she was too dark—and whose provenance does not match ideologically acceptable national origins—Cuba as the unmentionable thorn to U.S. regional hegemony.

The reigning U.S. Latina celebrity remains Jennifer Lopez, a Nuyorican by birth—a person of Puerto Rican parents born and raised in New York. Lopez crossed over into mainstream celebrity attention through her role as Selena in the movie that represented the Tejana star's posthumous crossover into mainstream popular music.[34] Through a sophisticated deployment of self, Jennifer Lopez has parlayed her original role as a dancer "Fly Girl" in *In Living Color* into a branded multimedia and multiproduct enterprise that includes acting and producing roles in movies, performance of popular music, two clothing lines, two perfumes, and other products. Whereas Salma was deemed by Mexican audiences as an inauthentic Frida,[35] Jennifer was seen as inauthentic by U.S. Mexican American audiences because she represented their beloved Selena. The casting call for that role was the largest in U.S. film history, and many Mexican American actors hoped to break into the mainstream through Selena. That Jennifer Lopez was cast is consistent with a long history of Puerto Ricans playing Mexican Americans and not vice versa.[36] Jennifer Lopez, her movies, her music, and her products reach a global audience and set of consumers. While in the United States, she is mostly recognized as the quintessential Latina, especially after she married "Latin" heart-throb Marc Anthony, that legacy does not necessarily follow her abroad. Given that she is a very light Latina and therefore can play ethnically ambiguous roles in movies and in real life, and that as a New Yorker she speaks English as a native, her transnational deployment can be accomplished without much translation. Her hybridity is loud enough to appeal to national ethnic audiences yet subtle enough to pass as "American" abroad.

Shakira, Salma Hayek, Frida Kahlo, Celia Cruz, and Jennifer Lopez represent different locations in the U.S. Latina celebrity continuum. The nature, the ease or difficulty, of their transnational crossovers illustrates their positions within a hybrid Latinidad. Although some scholars hold that Latinidad flattens difference within this ethnic category, these celebrity Latinas and their differential hybridity result in disparate transnational paths. Within the United States, Celia's racialized persona resulted in less visibility, though arguably she is the most talented of the three musical stars. Shakira and Salma are less unambiguous, because although they are quite light skinned, their accents are noticeable and therefore noted within U.S. popular culture. Nonetheless, as they circulate globally, those accents become less important than other components of their identity. Jennifer Lopez, being both light and a native English speaker, experiences the easiest national and transnational success and flow and greater success in commodification. Their hybridities demonstrate that while mixture is endemic, certain mixtures are more powerful, commodifiable, and therefore transnationally circulated. All of their trajectories challenge a nation-bound conceptualization of U.S. Latina/o studies. Simultaneously their foregrounding reiterates the gendered face of U.S. Latinidad. While Latina stars are celebrated for their beauty and Latinidad, there is no male counterpart in this cohort, just as there is no male action figure in the world of mediated dolls. The success and transnational deployment of Latinidad remains mostly female.

Conclusion

The transnational staging of hybrid Latinidad provokes some interesting mediated consequences as national U.S. ethnic categories are disrupted in their global travel. The ethnically ambiguous light-skinned Latina represents the safe and preferred way of representing difference. One can hardly expect audiences in Europe, South Africa, or Israel who are consuming these media products to have the racial context to understand the operation of this racial ambiguity embodied in the presence of the light Latina. *Ugly Betty*, Dora the Explorer, and Salma Hayek represent the national identity crisis of a nation that until recently had thought of itself in two color tones, black and white. Within the United States, the ethnic community remains suspended between the flattening of difference within Latinidad and the exoticization of difference through the light-brown

Latina body. The United States is exporting not Latinidad but, rather, media that foregrounds females as signifiers of slight difference who nevertheless are firmly contained within traditional patterns of femininity.

Bratz is the most complex example in the terrain of mediated doll lines and the other examples of hybridity discussed in this chapter. Unsurprisingly, they generated the broadest range of reactions, including the legal decision within U.S. courts to pull them off the shelves due to intellectual property violation.[37] However, even this line, when it crossed over from the doll and television lives into mainstream Hollywood film, began to resemble the light, ambiguous ethnics founds elsewhere in popular culture.

The three examples discussed in this chapter demonstrate how a commodified version of gendered Latinidad is taking shape within a global imaginary. A market-driven sexualized Latina presence is reproduced and inserted into the circuits of transnational popular culture through technological convergence that layers cultural forms, genres, and markets. Clearly, as these representations and products circulate, more research remains to be done to understand global audiences' interpretations of hybrid Latinas. However, at this point the acknowledgment of hybridity, while generating a range of different representations, has tended to be harnessed into a commodifiable difference as it spans out into the globally dispersed locations of popular culture.

NOTES

1. See Angharad Valdivia, *Latina/os and the Media* (Malden, MA: Polity, 2009).

2. Radha S. Hegde, "A View from Elsewhere: Locating Difference and the Politics of Representation from a Transnational Feminist Perspective," *Communication Theory* 8, no. 3 (1998): 271–297; and Angharad Valdivia, ed., *Feminism, Multiculturalism, and the Media: Global Diversities* (Newbury Park, CA: Sage, 1995).

3. Marwan Kraidy, *Hybridity or the Cultural Logic of Globalization* (Philadelphia: Temple University Press, 2005), xii.

4. Angharad Valdivia, "Latina/os as the Paradigmatic Transnational Post-culture," in David Muggleton and Rupert Weinzieri, eds., *The Post-subcultures Reader* (London: Berg, 2003), 151–167.

5. Robert J. C. Young, *Colonial Desire: Hybridity in Theory, Culture, and Race* (London: Routledge, 1995).

6. John Kraniauskas, "Hybridity in a Transnational Frame: Latin Americanist and Postcolonial Perspectives on Cultural Studies," in Avtar Brah and Annie Coombes, eds., *Hybridity and Its Discontents: Politics, Science, Culture* (London: Routledge, 2000); Marwan Kraidy, "Hybridity in Cultural Globalization," *Communication Theory* 12, no. 3 (2002): 316–339.

7. Kraidy, *Hybridity or the Cultural Logic of Globalization.*

8. Marilyn Halter, *Shopping for Identity: The Marketing of Ethnicity* (New York: Schocken Books, 2000).

9. Hamid Naficy, *The Making of Exile Cultures: Iranian Television in Los Angeles* (Minneapolis: University of Minnesota Press, 1993).

10. Elana Levine, "Constructing a Market, Constructing an Ethnicity: U.S. Spanish-Language Media and the Formation of a Syncretic Latino/a Identity," *Studies in Latin American Popular Culture* 20 (2001): 33–50.

11. Coco Fusco, *English Is Broken Here: Notes on Cultural Fusion in the Americas* (New York: New Press, 1995).

12. See Gillian Doyle, *Media Ownership* (Thousand Oaks, CA: Sage, 2002).

13. In January 2010, the network announced that the show would not be renewed for the 2011–2012 season.

14. Tamar Liebes and Elihu Katz, *The Export of Meaning: Cross-Cultural Readings of* Dallas (Oxford, UK: Polity, 1990).

15. The fact that successful versions of this show were popular in all the global regions in a wide range of countries points to the universality of this theme.

16. Angharad Valdivia, *A Latina in the Land of Hollywood and Other Essays on Media Culture* (Tucson: University of Arizona Press, 2000).

17. Madeline Shufeldt Esch, "Rearticulating Ugliness, Repurposing Content: Ugly Betty Finds the Beauty in Ugly," *Journal of Communication Inquiry* 34, no. 2 (April 2010): 168–183.

18. Work on *Ugly Betty* includes the following, in addition to the previously mentioned article by Madeline Shufeldt Esch: Kim Akass and Janet McCabe, "Not So Ugly: Local Production, Global Franchise, Discursive Femininities, and the Ugly Betty Phenomenon," *Flow TV* (January 26, 2007), http://flowtv.org/?p=74 (accessed February 21, 2009); Daniel Mato, "The Transnationalization of the Telenovela Industry, Territorial References, and the Production of Markets and Representations of Transnational Identities," *Television and New Media* 6, no. 4 (November 2005): 423–444; Yeidy Rivero, "The Performance and Reception of Televisual 'Ugliness' in Yo Soy Betty la Fea," *Feminist Media Studies* 3, no. 1 (March 2003): 65–81; Mary Beltrán, "Rooting for Betty," *Flow TV* (December 1, 2006), http://flowtv.org/?p=92 (accessed February 21, 2009); "Betty Expands Scope with Online Series," *UPI.com* (November 29, 2006), http://www.upi.com/Entertainment_News/2006/11/29/Betty-expands-scope-with-online-series/UPI-15441164843511/ (accessed February 1, 2009).

19. The dolls were withdrawn from U.S. shelves in early 2009, after Mattel scored a legal victory asserting intellectual property rights.

20. Based on anecdotal evidence, the American Girl popularity has begun to spread abroad to the highly mobile upper middle classes. I met women in Chile, Argentina, and Brazil whose girls had begun collecting American Girl dolls.

21. Carolina Acosta-Alzuru and Peggy J. Kreshel, "'I'm an American Girl . . . Whatever That Means': Girls Consuming Pleasant Company's American Girl Identity," *Journal of Communication* 52, no. 1 (January 2006): 139–161; Carolina Acosta-Alzuru and Elizabeth P. Lester Roushanzamir, "Everything We Do Is a Celebration of You! Pleasant Company Constructs American Girlhood," *Communication Review* 6, no. 1 (January 2003): 45–69.

22. Susan J. Harewood and Angharad N. Valdivia, "Exploring Dora: Re-embodied Latinidad on the Web," in Sharon Mazzarella, ed., *Girl Wide Web: Girls, the Internet, and the Negotiation of Identity* (New York: Peter Lang, 2005), 85–105.

23. Nicole Guidotti-Hernández, "*Dora the Explorer,* Constructing 'LATINIDADES' and the Politics of Global Citizenship," *Latino Studies* 5 (Summer 2007): 209–232.

24. Dafna Lemish, Professor of Communication, Southern Illinois University Carbondale, personal communication (January 22, 2008).

25. Celeste Lacroix, "Images of Animated Others: The Orientalization of Disney's Cartoon Heroines from the Little Mermaid to the Hunchback of Notre Dame," *Popular Communication* 2, no. 4 (November 2004): 213–229.

26. Claudia Puig, "'Bratz' Movie Totally Cliché," *USA Today* (August 2, 2007), http://www.usatoday.com/life/movies/reviews/2007-08-02-bratz_N.htm (accessed September 5, 2007).

27. Maria Elena Cepeda, *Musical ImagiNation: U.S.-Colombian Identity and the Latin Music Boom* (New York: New York University Press, 2010).

28. I am indebted to Radha Hegde for this astute observation.

29. Isabel Molina Guzmán, "Mediating Frida: Negotiating Discourses of Latina/o Authenticity in Global Media Representations of Ethnic Identity," *Critical Studies in Media Communication* 23, no. 3 (August 2006): 232–251; and Isabel Molina Guzmán, "Salma Hayek's Frida: Transnational Latina Bodies in Popular Culture," in Myra Mendible, ed., *From Bananas to Buttocks: The Latina in Popular Film and Culture* (Austin: University of Texas Press, 2007).

30. Frances R. Aparicio, *Listening to Salsa: Gender, Latin Popular Music, and Puerto Rican Cultures* (Hanover, NH: University Press of New England, 1998).

31. Katynka Z. Martinez, "American Idols with Caribbean Soul: Cubanidad and the Latin Grammys," *Latino Studies* 4 (December 2006): 381–400.

32. Frances Negrón-Muntaner, "Jennifer's Butt," *Aztlán* 22, no. 2 (Fall 1997): 181–194.

33. Ibid.

34. Deborah R. Vargas, "Bidi Bidi Bom Bom: Selena and Tejano Music in the Making of Tejas," in Mary Romero and Michelle Habell-Pallan, eds., *Latino/a Popular Culture* (New York: New York University Press, 2002), 117–126.

35. Isabel Molina Guzmán, "Gendering Latinidad through the Elian News Discourse about Cuban Women," *Latino Studies* 3 (July 2005): 179–204.

36. Marc Zimmerman, "Erasure, Imposition and Crossover of Puerto Rican and Chicanos in U.S. Film and Music Culture," *Latino Studies* 1, no. 1 (March 2003): 115–122.

37. See Angharad Valdivia, "Living in a Hybrid Material World: Girls, Ethnicity and Doll Products," *Girlhood Studies: An Interdisciplinary Journal* 2, no. 1 (Summer 2009): 73–93; and Matthew P. McAllister "'Girls with a Passion for Fashion': The Bratz Brand as Integrated Spectacular Consumption," *Journal of Children and Media* 1, no. 3 (October 2007): 244–258.

4 E-Race-ing Color

Gender and Transnational Visual Economies of Beauty in India

Radhika Parameswaran

News Release

Pond's Launches White Beauty Detox Range

July 11, 2007, New Delhi

Dia Mirza, the beauty from Bollywood was recently in the capital to launch "White Beauty," the new range of skin lightening products from the house of Pond's.

Enriched with detoxifying vitamins, White Beauty is not only popular for whitening the skin, but to neutralize the effects of darkness causing elements in today's harsh environment. The range consists of White Beauty Detox Cleanser, White Beauty Detox Toner, White Beauty Skin-Lightening Cream and White Beauty Detox Lotion, to give you the radiance you've always wanted.[1]

Pond's proposition:

White = Beautiful/Recoverable Purity

Dark = Ugly/Accumulated Poison

Pond's = Cure/Detoxifying Agent

Pond's medicalized and mystical representation of the Indian female body in this news release as filled with dark poison that can be extracted in order to restore white purity belongs in a larger constellation of proliferating discourses on beauty in globalizing India. Extending Pond's equation of whitening with purifying to *Newsweek's* March 2006 cover portrait, a slim and light-skinned Padma Lakshmi (international supermodel and celebrity chef) captures the glowing purity of "The New India," a promising emerging-market nation that is detoxifying itself of the poison of an undesirable socialist "third world" past. Bathed in golden yellow light, Padma Lakshmi's Orientalized costume—deep-red sequined fabric wrapped around her torso and floating high above her shoulder—and her hands folded in the signature Indian "namaste" gesture insert her light-skinned body within the semiotics of non-Western "brown" ethnic tradition. In contrast to her pale luminosity in *Newsweek*, the very same Padma Lakshmi displays a tanned and darker-skinned body on the cover of *Nirvana*, a fashion magazine for "affluent, dynamic, and upscale Indian-American women."[2] The aesthetics of global high fashion's primitive "African queen"—black wooden bangles on her raised forearms, strips of cloth decorating her bare shoulders,

Inside the cover image:

Newsweek

March 6, 2006: $3.95

newsweek.msnbc.com

THE NEW
INDIA

Asia's Other
Powerhouse
Steps Out
By Fareed Zakaria

America,
India and My
Generation
By Jhumpa Lahiri

Actress Padma Lakshmi

Fig. 4.1. Global celebrity Padma Lakshmi represents the transformed global
nation. (*Newsweek*, March 6, 2006, cover photo)

and her direct bold stare—darken Padma Lakshmi's body even further for the
whitened gaze of upper-class Indian American consumers.

The unstable epidermal surfaces of morphing white, light, fair, olive, dusky,
tanned, wheatish brown, dark, and black bodies that populate India's transforming semio-sphere of the past decade bear the forensic traces of competing and
colluding signifying forces—racism, individualism, nationalism, cosmopolitanism, and commodity feminism.[3] This chapter's critique of beauty's supple visual
economy tracks the polysemic meanings of corporeal lightness and darkness that
circulate in India's recently altered public sphere, meanings that are always articulated within and against historical and transnational matrices of power. While
foregrounding the orchestration of gendered meanings and subject positions that

unfolds in the cultural terrain of India, the chapter's analytic circuit takes seriously Radha Hegde's imperative in the introduction to deploy the transnational as a frame to engage the "dynamic interrelationality" of seemingly disparate media worlds and "capture the layering of social, political, economic, and mediated processes that exceed conventional boundaries."[4] The empirical and narrative architecture of the chapter thus works against methodological purity and conceptions of pristine or hermetic national spaces, media technologies, aesthetic genres, and gendered subjectivities.

Dipping into and migrating across economic, ethnographic, and visual-textual data, I trace the genealogy of beauty's troubled relations with the epidermis in entangled geographic spaces that speak to each other, even as I stage India as the main protagonist. Cultural representations of the body in film, television, print, and online texts inhabit the media ecosystem I reconstruct here in order to deconstruct fantasies of the body's mutability. I sometimes take unexpected detours that shadow ethnographic moments, as in the analytic route I follow from a young woman in India to stories of her celebrity idol, Michael Jackson. Mining visual configurations of femininity and masculinity and positioning them alongside unequal global material relations, the chapter juxtaposes, connects, and disconnects chains of epidermal significations, thus illuminating the "scattered hegemonies"[5] that regulate cultural and economic imaginations of the body.

The Physiognomy of Transformation

Madhur Bhandarkar's award-winning 2007 film *Traffic Signal* takes viewers into the intriguing underworld of poverty and profit that has sprung up along one of Mumbai's busy streets. As scores of the city's commuters are rendered immobile at one traffic signal, an itinerant workforce of poor street-side hawkers routinely descends upon this captive market to hawk flowers, clothing, candy, cigarettes, and other trinkets. Damber, a cheerful and dimpled young boy, who sells newspapers and magazines at this signal, longs to be light-skinned and spends most of his hard-earned money on skin-lightening creams.

> *Scene 1:* Damber stands mesmerized in front of a billboard that advertises a tube of Fair Fast. He asks the dark-skinned male worker installing the billboard if the cream would really make his face lighter in four weeks. The worker shrugs and says, "Who knows? They say it will."
>
> *Scene 2:* Damber stops at a small store and asks if he can purchase a fairness cream. The amused storeowner hands over a small packet and asks the boy to give him Rs. 22.50.
>
> *Scene 3:* Viewers see Damber's glowing silhouette framed against complete darkness.

Squeezing the tube of Fair Fast, Damber applies the cream to his face and then rubs it in with a frenzied passion.

When projected onto the collective desires of Indian citizens witnessing their mobilization as consumers, Damber's quest to alter his skin color turns into powerful psychic fuel for the global beauty industry's engines. By the year 2000, fairness or skin-lightening cosmetics had surged far ahead of competing skin-care products to claim the largest market share in India's beauty market.[6] More recently, a 2007 *New York Times* report, which describes skin-lightening cosmetics as the "most popular product in India's fast-growing skin care market," notes that the "$318 million market for skin care has grown by 42.7 percent since 2001."[7] Spreading its tentacles across India's deeply divided socioeconomic spectrum, the skin-lightening cosmetics industry targets low-income consumers whose lives resemble *Traffic Signal*'s Damber as well as the new Indian high-tech consumer class residing in exclusive gated communities.

Pigment and Profit, Magic and Makeovers

The fictional Fair Fast cream that Damber purchases in *Traffic Signal* has a dizzying array of siblings in India's booming skin-lightening cosmetics sector that includes creams and lotions, massage oil, bleaches, talcum powders, face washes, face packs, body oils, under-eye cream, and exfoliators. Scores of Indian beauty companies as well as multinationals compete for the attention of Indian women who have joined the burgeoning workforce in the past decade. Facing increased domestic and international competition, reigning cosmetics leader Hindustan Lever has pursued a two-pronged strategy to retain its dominance. On the one hand, Lever launched its premium product line, Perfect Radiance, to appeal to the expanding demographic of professional upper- and upper-middle-class women consumers. On the other hand, the company also extended the dreams of its signature cream, Fair & Lovely, to poor women. Although Fair & Lovely's standard tube, priced at Rs. 24, makes it affordable for lower-middle-class women, Lever's introduction of small sachets priced at Rs. 10 and sold at small grocery stores and street-side stalls targets daily wage laborers and women working in the urban economy's informal sector. Lever's investment in these low-priced sachets has been hailed as innovative retailing that can mold uninitiated poor Asian and African citizens into new markets for "luxury" products such as cosmetics: "Smaller unit packages, enough for a single immediate use, enable poor consumers to buy a product they could otherwise not afford, thus unlocking their purchasing power."[8]

A thriving libidinal economy of media and advertising images that trains emerging-market consumers to desire mobility both secures and spawns the

Fig. 4.2. Range of skin-lightening products in India's marketplace. (Author's photograph)

material economy of beauty products and retailing practices. Advertising's therapeutic images map magical "before and after" stories of young women's cyclical shedding of their dark skin. A two-page magazine advertisement anchors the temporal evacuation of dark pigment in the model's face to the awakening sensations of pleasure and fulfillment that lie dormant in her body. The caption, "Six weeks to a fairness like never before" (translated from Telugu), explains a pictorial canvas that bears six faces of the same wholesome woman, with each new face enlarging and changing color as the reader's eyes move from left to right. The first unsmiling and downcast "dark" face of the model morphs into a beaming and wide-eyed lighter-skinned face, a visible progression that offers proof of Fair & Lovely's power to subdue the body's unruly production of excess melanin.

Television commercials for cheaper skin-lightening cosmetics offer similar but more elaborate variations of such empirical maps of the body's changing skin color. A concerned (and light-skinned) mother in a Tamil commercial for All Fair cream begs her sulky and desperate younger daughter to end her futile pursuit of light-skinned beauty. She tells the young woman to get advice from her pretty and "glowing" older sister. The protagonist borrows her sister's All Fair cream, and then cascading close-up shots of the model's face calibrate alterations in her skin color. Embedded simultaneously within discourses of narcissistic anxiety, patriarchal capitalist surveillance, and empowered consumer agency, these pedagogic images of the body's visible transformation assume that new markets of uninitiated working-class and poor Indian women need lessons on the labor and money they have to invest in order to earn returns on beauty. In contrast to these didactic stories of magical transformation, high-end skin-lightening-cream advertisements in magazines dispense with beauty demonstrations and instead showcase the product itself as an object of high art—magnified jars and tubes of Clinique, Perfect Radiance, and Avon's PT White, set against pastel backgrounds, invite readers to self-consciously fetishize the pleasures of viewing the image itself as part of an upper-class lifestyle.

Tracking Agency, Traveling Colorism: The Epidermis as Transnational Tissue

I am sorting through a pile of skin-lightening cosmetics, taking inventory of prices and packaging, at the dinner table in my sister's house in New Delhi, India. My six-year-old niece walks in and wants to help. She begins reading the names of the cosmetics but stops as she holds a sachet of Fair & Lovely and then calls out to her nanny, "Sushmita Didi, please come here. I have your cream." Sushmita, a young woman who had migrated to Delhi from a village in Bihar, appears at the table and inquires, "Are you taking all these back with you?" My niece interjects and explains as she imitates what I had said to her mother a few days before, "Yes, this is all for a 'project.' It's all going on the plane with her." Sushmita looks at me and responds, "But these creams don't work. I don't think any of them really do." Without disputing her claim, I ask Sushmita, "Why do you buy them?" Sushmita retorts with a smile, "Because I have some extra money now, and I think if there is even a small chance it may work, why not?" Affirming Sushmita's negotiated (undecided and down-to-earth) response to the beauty that skin-lightening creams promise to excavate, Shanti, a municipal sweeper interviewed by Anita Anand in her book *The Beauty Game*, also expresses a similar nuanced pragmatism about Fair & Lovely: "I use it when I go out. People say, your face looks clean, your complexion looks bright (as we live with dirt)."[9]

After much giggling in response to my request, a group of women child-care workers living in the suburbs of Delhi agree to watch a television commercial for Fair & Lovely's cheapest package, a sachet of cream that costs Rs. 5. The commercial's unvarnished and none-too-subtle story, centering on arranged marriage, endows women's light-skinned beauty the power to win a good husband. An anxious father in this commercial tells his wife that a sought-after groom with an excellent job has agreed to "view" their daughter, but this hard-to-please man had reportedly rejected three women already. When the father expresses concern over his daughter's dark skin, the confident mother raises her right palm, with all five fingers distinctly separated, in front of her husband's face as though to

Fig. 4.3. An advertisement for Fair & Lovely that illustrates gradual changes in the model's facial skin color. (*Femina*, March 2005)

stem his flow of verbal anxiety. The father is puzzled, but viewers soon learn from the next scene that the mother's five fingers stand in for the economical price of the product. The next few scenes show the wedding celebration, in which the prized groom admires his beautiful bride, who has been growing "more radiant every day." The parents and the bride exchange smug smiles in acknowledgment of their success. At the end of the commercial, one of the oldest women in the group says, "I've seen that before. I wish it were so easy to be happy! But I do buy those sachets for my daughter, and she says the cream smells good. I think *malai* [cream] from milk works better." Another, younger woman chimes in, anger lacing her voice, "But it's true: I think men and everyone value beauty on the surface like white skin. All the film heroes call the heroine 'gori' [light-skinned girl], don't they? I do get these creams to put on for *shaadis* [weddings] and *pujas* [religious rituals]. . . . Am not sure they work, but many others get them too. I also put *malai* and *haldi* [turmeric powder] on my face though."

Women's ambivalent responses to this commercial's peddling of beauty as a route to conjugal bliss foregrounds the complexity of their agency, the fine line they walk between capitulation to and resistance against advertising's patriarchal and formulaic tales of physical perfection, success, and happiness. Although the commercial's linear cause-and-effect narrative constructs its viewing subjects—

the demographic of low-income women consumers—as simple-minded and credulous, these women's skepticism toward instantaneous makeovers even as they patronize manufactured skin-lightening creams alongside traditional beauty rituals constrains scholars from *pathologizing* the links between poverty and capitalist beauty regimes' racialized promises of upward mobility. As Ammina Mire reminds us, it is often the "terribly damaged" faces of poor African women that have become the visual signposts for warning the public about the dangers of skin whitening.[10] These pathologized spectacles of African women's suffering disavow the historical ways in which white women have been and continue to be sutured to the ideological fabric of skin whitening. While manufacturers of skin-bleaching solutions in the United States targeted racially white eastern and southern European women in the late nineteenth century, as Mire notes, today skin whitening has a lucrative life as an antiaging therapy that promises to bleach out dark discoloration in the aging skins of white women. Taking an inventory of Indian women's flickering agency and skin whitening's global incarnations does not diminish capitalism's exploitation of social hierarchies, but it does point to beauty's asymmetrical relations with differently raced bodies.

While Indian advertising sells the feminine body's obedience to normative beauty, a global black male celebrity's pale skin color provokes reflections on cross-cultural hierarchies of whiteness. I show one young Indian woman, a college-educated marketing executive, an advertisement for Emami's Naturally Fair cream—this image displayed a female model whose cumulatively lightening face, encased in pearl-like bubbles, illustrated the cream's power to imbue women with the "shimmering fairness of pearls in four weeks." Aditi examines the model in the ad and says, "She's so pale already, she does not need the cream! I prefer a light brown color like the actress Nandita Das. I buy this cream because it forms a good base to apply my face powder, not because it works." Continuing her comments, she gets a bit emotional: "Several men rejected my mother because she's dark-skinned. Finally, my father saw her beauty and grace, but she's still angry. We don't talk about this problem in our country enough. Look how much they criticized Michael Jackson in America. So many people thought he was strange." Turning the tables on me, she begins to reel off a list of questions: "What do they say over there in America? Why do you think Americans said that Michael Jackson *should not* have pretended to be *gora* [white]?"

Traveling to America, as Aditi directed me, to follow her instructive citation of Michael Jackson's epidermal troubles, we find that race, skin color, and beauty are woven into a much more politicized and historical fabric of civil-rights and post-civil-rights discourses. Whereas antiracist activism in the sixties challenged the equation of whiteness with ideal beauty (black is beautiful), a more recent stream of research has gone beyond the racism of the black/white divide to define "colorism" as an insidious form of internal discrimination that penalizes dark-skinned black men and women.[11] Colorism enables the preferential treatment of light-skinned blacks both within and outside their community, and it presents even greater barriers for dark-skinned black women to overcome racism, sexism, and classism. Yet, complicating colorism's uneven ideological patterning of skin color even further, charges (emanating from black nationalism) that light-skinned blacks are not authentic racial insiders also police the boundaries of affirmative racial identity. Debates over racism and colorism percolated into popular discourse and converged at the site of Michael Jackson's pale skin, leaving their historical registers on audiences' interpretations of his motives for whitening his body.

A January 2007 YouTube video narrative titled "Michael Jackson Face Transformation" bears a striking resemblance to the commercial "before and after" discourses of skin-lightening cosmetics that peddle images of Indian women shedding their dark skin.[12] This video collage of the celebrity singer's controversial metamorphosis—whitening along with changing facial features—showcases Jackson's changing physiognomy and his evolution from childhood to adolescence to adulthood. As each of the celebrity's darker faces melts progressively into the next lighter one (along with alterations from cosmetic surgery), viewers witness Jackson's alleged exhibition of internalized racism. A provocative epilogue—"If this is what's happening outside, what's going on inside?"—featured at the end of the collage cues viewers to speculate on the racialized pathologies of skin lightening and cosmetic surgery.

Opposing such indictments of Jackson as a racial traitor, another YouTube video, posted a month later, attempts to clear the celebrity of all blame. Proposing knowledge and critical thinking as antidotes to prejudice, this producer's sympathetic video testimony declares her mission to redeem Jackson: "Because prejudice is ignorance, no one asks what happened to him without judging him. . . . Knowledge grants us the possibility of love. . . . 'Before you judge me, try hard to love me,' Michael Jackson sings."[13] Articulating a postmodern argument on fluid and overlapping social identities to build homologies between the "deviant" Jackson and his "normal" critics and voyeurs, the video artist "Acucena" states that "everyone changes during their lives with or without surgery," because manipulations of light, emotions, clothing, and photographic techniques generate multiple iterations of the same person. Toward the end of the video, this producer's defense, soaked in the rhetoric of public-health campaigns and anticolonial race scholarship, exonerates Jackson of all charges of racial betrayal because he has a disease called vitiligo, which destroys the substance that gives color to the skin. Michael Jackson himself, when interviewed on *The Oprah Winfrey Show* in 2007, stated emphatically that he was very comfortable in his racial identity but suffered from an uncontrollable "skin disorder that destroys pigmentation."[14]

I am back at work in the United States. Aditi, the young woman in India who had inquired about Michael Jackson six months earlier, has sent me an e-mail message with the subject "Colorism in India." She writes, "Radhika-aunty, please see this flyer for a discussion at my old college. We had invited many parents of small children too. Thank you for telling me about this word colorism and its history, makes it so much easier to publicize this event when I can call this problem something. Please also read the news report on protests against Fair & Lovely in India. (Michael Jackson is still the best!)."[15] The text on Aditi's flyer, printed against the background of a *Fair & Lovely* face wash advertisement showing a before (dark) and after (light) face reads, "Colorism, Why is fair the same as lovely and dark the same as ugly? Attend speech and discussions afterward." A passenger with the name *colorism*, carrying historical baggage from America that could provoke debates on skin color, caste, colonialism, patriarchy, and consumer culture, had crossed several borders to land safely at one venue in India.

Technowhiteness Meets Ethnonationalist Brownness

Usha Zacharias writes that India's transition from frugal socialism to expansive capitalism was predicated on the cultural production of a "consumer class that is in the permanent process of racial passage from brown to white, and which may be unwilling, or even helpless to reverse the material destiny of an upwardly mobile trajectory of signification."[16] Zooming her critical lenses onto Crown TV's advertising image of *Mona Lisa* gracing a television screen that has a remote control's operations superimposed on it, she argues that this iconic white woman metaphorically embodies "ideologies of cultural nationalism wrapped in whiteness."[17] If the mnemonics of a remote control pasted onto a legendary European beauty—*Mona Lisa*'s visage—captures the messy collisions between colonial pasts and global futures, contemporary visual configurations of Indian celebrity whiteness—Aishwarya Rai and Rajinikanth—offer distinct yet overlapping versions of the nomadic Indian body's gendered and classed currency in transnational, national, and regional spaces.

The celebrity allure of legendary Indian beauty Aishwarya Rai (global supermodel, Bollywood actress, and former Miss World) in L'Oreal's advertisement for the skin-lightening product White Perfect crystallizes the ongoing marriage of technocapitalist whiteness with ethnonationalist brownness. Rai's "international face," authorized by her ambiguous racial coding, graces a glossy two-page L'Oreal ad in the Indian women's magazine *Femina*. Similar L'Oreal advertisements in Europe and Asia have transported the green-eyed and light-skinned Rai well beyond India to affix her seductive and amorphous ethnic appeal to a host of other L'Oreal products including hair color. In the *Femina* magazine ad for L'Oreal's White Perfect, Rai's wide-eyed face, exuding the luster of her global currency, serves as a soft companion to a hypertechnomedicalized lexicon that legitimizes the product's tested labor of skin whitening. The headlines "Dermo-expertise" and "Breakthrough Melanin-Block Technology" in the ad anchor a step-by-step outline of the luminosity that "L'Oreal patented-Mexoryl SX" and "L'Oreal patented-BHA" can induce in women's faces with a 90 percent guarantee of effectiveness. Magnified pictures of the dermis and epidermis augment the scientific credibility of the product's claims to destroy melanin and release whiteness from the recesses of consumers' bodies. L'Oreal's brand of technopharmaceutical whitened modernity flows through an archive of other such commercial discourses—Clinique's Active White Light Powder, Elizabeth Arden's Whitening Capsules, Avon's PT White Fairness cream—to construct women's dark skin as a disease that can be diagnosed and controlled.

Although imperceptible on the surface, Rai's sterile technocelebrity whiteness in the multinational advertisement is sutured simultaneously to the bright postcolonial green, white, and orange colors (the colors of the Indian flag) of her ethnonational loyalties, her indisputably Indian essence. The supermodel's alliances with her national citizenship emerge from her own public performances and from discourses of nationalism that authenticate her success not merely as a famed transnational celebrity figure but also as a global *Indian* whose beauty has conquered both domestic and foreign territories. Such cultural compositions of aseptic, imperial technoproficient whiteness alloyed with seemingly resistant postcolonial nonwhiteness index the reimagining of an *Indian transnational modernity* that has radiated from sites within and outside India in the midst of sweeping economic reforms. Unpacking representations of whiteness in the Chinese television film *Sunset at Long Chao Li*, Kathleen Erwin argues that technomediated images of white women in China—as in the crafting of *Sunset's* Margie, a wealthy American woman whose devotion to her Chinese husband signals her submission to Chinese culture—do not merely signify Western imperialism; instead, they also bolster the Chinese nation's claims to transcendence over Western domination.[18] My case study of Aishwarya Rai's whiteness/Indianness differs from Erwin's analysis of a Chinese television hero's relations with his white American wife; nevertheless, Rai's celebrity profile bears similar inscriptions of nationalist modernity that can absorb the West in a new transnational economic order marked by Asia's rapid ascendance.

The currency of former Miss World and Bollywood superstar Rai's traveling whiteness, as evidenced by her passage into international/Hollywood cinema and global advertising (L'Oreal, Coca-Cola, and DeBeer), earned her a spot on CBS's *60 Minutes* and NBC's *Oprah Winfrey Show* as the most beautiful woman in the world. Bob Simon's interview for *60 Minutes*, enacted through the erotics of white, heterosexual male appreciation, portrays a cosmopolitan Rai, garbed in a two-piece suit with well-groomed shoulder-length hair, straddling the globe in her Westernized avatar even as she claims the resilience of her Indian traditions.[19] Moving beyond oft-cited paradigms of fused East-West hybrid identity, Rai's public performance, combined with *60 Minutes'* visual footage, fabricates a whitened Indian transnational modernity, a discourse of dominant Indianness that gets stored within a portable global epidermis.

Interviewing Rai on location in a studio in Mumbai, Simon begins the segment by installing his subject, a beautiful Indian woman with seventeen thousand fan websites and Julia Roberts's endorsement, in a pantheon of classic global *white* celebrity beauty that includes Ingrid Bergman, Audrey Hepburn, Grace Kelly, and Elizabeth Taylor. Sitting close to Rai within the intimate setting of a living room, Simon asks her, "Are men intimidated by you?" as the camera lingers on Rai's well-groomed face. Rai then responds with her own question as she draws attention to Simon's sexuality: "Are you?" Taken aback by the unexpected infusion of sexual chemistry in a televised journalistic interview, Simon says, "No, not really," but when Rai interjects with "I guess not then" to indicate that she has no effect on men, Simon, no longer a seasoned professional, rushes to reassure her that he is indeed impressed. He gestures with one hand toward her face and body as he struggles to express his admiration, and Rai, taking charge of the interview again, points to Simon's reddening face color with the accusation, "You're blushing." The interaction between Simon, the *gora* (generic Hindi term for a white male foreigner) journalist, and Rai, her beautiful light body encased in Western designer clothing, speaking English fluently, and flirting subtly with an older, authoritative white man, crystallizes this Indian celebrity's proficiency in enacting upper-class whiteness. After the first quarter, however, in the remainder of the interview, viewers also witness the robust Indianness that fills Rai's body, lying close to her thin outer armor of epidermal and performative whiteness. As Simon asserts, the Indian Rai, unlike some of her counterparts in Hollywood (symbols of degenerate white femininity), acts in "squeaky clean" Bollywood films and is "innocent, wholesome, and deeply religious." He explains that Rai still lives with her parents even though she is thirty years old, because she believes in the sanctity of family. He then says that on Rai's insistence, they visited a Ganesh temple in Mumbai. Visual footage of a pious and traditional national ambassador Rai worshiping at the altar—wearing Indian clothing, a bindi on her forehead, and hair braided with a string of jasmine flowers—ensures that Simon and his viewers are given glimpses of the global Indian celebrity's deep allegiance to her Hindu Indianness. Describing the crowds of fans who had gathered to watch Rai, Simon lets audiences know that "Rai attracted more worshipers than Ganesh" and that people had lined up to see her as though she were a goddess herself.

Rai's brand of whitened transnational Indian modernity is manifested with equal strength on *The Oprah Winfrey Show*, where she is again presented as a "global goddess" whose "international face" sells a range of commodities.[20] After affirming Rai's beauty with a collage of still-photo displays, Oprah tells her largely white female studio audience that "Ash," as she is known in India, is a wholesome woman who "like most single Indian women follows tradition and lives at home with her parents." When questioned about the recent escalation in the commerce of skin lightening in India, where "Indians spend over a hundred million dollars on skin lightening cosmetics," Rai, classified as among the most light-skinned celebrities in India, repudiates colorism and calls for a celebration of the diverse plurality of Indian men and women's bodies. In the second half of this interview, Rai dresses Oprah in a sari, the quintessential symbol of Indian tradition, and finally a sari-clad Oprah sashaying onstage declares that the lovely "red carpet" sari makes her feel sensual. These interviews are drenched in the colonial discourses of Orientalism; however, they also project an image of the successful whitened Indian female celebrity who has managed to exceed Western standards of beauty while she also protects her Indianness from the contaminating influences of Western commodity and entertainment culture. Such television performances that showcase Rai's fidelity to Indian traditions *and* her physical desirability in the West construct technovisual articulations of whiteness within the ethnonational spaces of Indian transnational modernity.

Digital Whiteness and Divine Masculine Modernity

If Aishwarya Rai's cosmopolitan currency enjoys a good conversion rate in the West, particularly in Europe and the United States, another Indian male celebrity's spectacular performance in the Tamil blockbuster film *Sivaji—The Boss* radiates a masculine technowhiteness that shores up vernacular regional patriotism. Press releases and news stories on *Sivaji—The Boss*, reputed to be the highest-budget Indian film of the past two decades, enumerate the production costs for the film, ranging from expenses incurred for high-end artistic talent and hair to "break-through technology . . . that has rewritten the rules of celluloid history."[21] Publicity discourses on the film also valorize the cutting-edge digital technology and painstaking technical labor that enabled the hero Sivaji's (well-known actor Rajinikanth) dramatic change in skin color from a wheatish-brown Indian complexion to a Caucasian skin tone and color for the famed song-and-dance sequence "Oru Koodai Sunlight" (One Basket of Sunlight). Taking up the theme of a divided globalizing nation in which poor citizens continue to struggle for basic amenities amid the sweep of middle-class economic prosperity, *Sivaji—The Boss* narrates a familiar tale of the accomplished and patriotic global Indian male, who returns to his homeland—and his ethnic Tamil community—to implement a noble program of social and economic justice. *Sivaji—The Boss* is only one film among scores of Kollywood films, the prolific South Indian Tamil film industry (parallel to Mumbai's Bollywood films) based in the Kodambakkam district of Chennai, in which Rajinikanth has acted. Unlike the seemingly polished Aishwarya Rai, whose linguistic and bodily ethnowhiteness enables her to occupy a spectrum of national and Euro-American spaces, Rajiniknath's earthy performances have earned him a firm foothold in a more bounded but equally profitable regional, classed, and diasporic Tamil space. Hailed as the authentic vernacular hero of poor and working-class male audiences, Rajinikanth, whose Tamil films are popular in Malaysia, Indonesia, and Japan, has earned the reputation of being South India's greatest star.

Mapping colorism's discriminatory practices onto the male rather than the female body, the film initially creates a comic narrative of epidermal suffering that undermines the far greater penalties that Indian women have incurred for violating normative beauty conventions. On Sivaji's return to his home state from the United States, he discovers that his parents are determined to find a bride for their eligible son. Rejecting all the inappropriately Westernized (immodest, immoral, and secular) women who offer themselves to him, Sivaji instead covets the wholesome and religious light-skinned Tamil woman he spots at an old temple in the city. After a series of events, including troubling episodes of blatant colorism in which he recoils at the sight of two dark-skinned prospective brides, Sivaji gets engaged to the beautiful object of his desire, Tamil Selvi. Even though Tamil Selvi loves Sivaji, she decides to distance herself from him because an astrologer informs her that their doomed union would result in Sivaji's death. When Sivaji visits Tamil Selvi, she lays her hand next to his hand as she draws attention to his dark skin color, and then she announces that they can no longer be engaged because she finds his dark skin repulsive. In the ensuing scenes that feature canned background laughter, viewers follow Sivaji's tragic theatrical quest to lighten his skin color—he covers his entire body with Fair & Lovely cream, immerses himself in tubs of clay, and then tries his mother's messy and painful home remedies. In the midst of this patriarchal parody of feminine skin lightening, Sivaji enters an extravagantly surreal realm of technofantasy—the "Sunlight" song-and-dance sequence—where he turns into a white male, thus signifying the "infinite possibilities of transformation and mobility to the socially ascending postcolonial viewer."[22]

Publicity stories on Sivaji's transformation juxtapose the magical powers of Western technomodernity or "digital skin grafting" with the seductive possibilities of a transgressive marriage between authentic white European femininity and the fake technowhitened surface of the Tamil male body.[23] A graphic artist in one news story explains that the film's deployment of high-end digital technology methods to whiten Rajinikanth required twenty-five dedicated CG technicians. This artist claims that simple digital color correction of the hero's skin could not achieve the authentic whiteness that the film's director had demanded of his technicians. He then clarifies that a complicated series of photographic and digital techniques were deployed to graft the skin color of a real white woman—London-based Jacky—onto Rajinikanth: "After the final edit all the 630 hero shots and 630 girl [Jacky] shots were scanned in 4K resolution. Each of the 9000 scanned frames was rotoscoped to separate body parts (face, hands, legs, etc.). The white lady's skin was mapped onto the Superstar's image using Eyeon 'Digital Fusion' software."[24] Illustrating the technological transposition of white European femininity onto Sivaji's body, several fan websites post side-by-side images of actor Rajinikanth and a white woman whose body language imitates the actor's poses in frozen stills captured from the movie during the song "Oru Koodai Sunlight."

Surrounded by the off-screen publicity aura of technological innovation, the "Oru Koodai Sunlight" song-and-dance performance showcases the homespun, provincial hero's mutation into a slick global avatar. Rajinikanth's theatrical masquerade as a whitened Sivaji with glistening blond hair unlocks the porous Tamil nation's abilities to absorb European racial whiteness, multicolored visions of ethnoracial diversity, and sexualized discourses of territorial conquest. In contrast to the film's introductory song, set in the pastoral utopia of a lush green village, Sivaji's energetic dance as a white man in "Oru Koodai Sunlight" takes viewers in and out of hypermodern, avant-garde architectural spaces that simulate the towering constructions of New York, Sydney, Hong Kong, and Dubai. The choreography of white Sivaji's dance with a white Tamil Selvi, who worships his body's exuberant calisthenics, and a multicultural supporting ensemble of Black and Latina dancers enacts the reimagination of the virile Tamil nation's transcendence over Western domination. The lyrics of the chorus—"a basket of sunlight and a basket of moonlight were mixed to produce a white Tamilian"—that accompany this spectacular visual rendition of epidermal mutation project Sivaji's persona as a potent reincarnation of Tamil whiteness. The film returns to the symbolic hues of patriotic technowhiteness when the formerly white Tamil hero, standing atop a building in New York, uses his laptop computer to convert all the illegitimate "black money" circulating in India into legitimate "white money." Sivaji's whitened currency fulfills the utopian vision of a bygone postcolonial era of Nehruvian socialist modernity. Signaling a triumphant Tamil masculinity's conquest of geographic, digital, and racialized territories, Sivaji's gleaming clinics and schools empower poor citizens left behind by the failed Indian state and a selfish Indian consumer elite.

Conclusion: The Transnational Epidermis and Its Fluctuating Semiotics

I am visiting a close friend in Hyderabad in South India. She has taped a Fair & Lovely commercial for me, one whose blatant colorism has made her quite angry. In contrast to *Sivaji's* recuperation of the nation's potential greatness, this commercial's double-edged discourse on arranged marriage casts the nation as both an agent of women's patriarchal oppression and a source of their empowerment. Wedding technowhiteness with ethnoreligious imagery, the commercial proposes that market nationalism can liberate women from a primitive patriarchy's humiliating practices of colorism. A young female model hiding behind a pillar surveys a depressing scene in the courtyard of her home. Her father appears relieved that he may have finally found an eligible groom for his dark-skinned daughter, but a picture of the unattractive groom's acne-scarred face with a large nose tells a more pessimistic story. In a spirited act of resistance, the young woman, who decides to take charge of her destiny, turns the yellowing pages of an ancient Ayurvedic text that contains long-forgotten remedies for skin lightening. In the next few scenes, viewers witness a technoreligious nationalist spectacle of traditional Indian science's authentic skin-lightening power. As melodious devotional music invokes religious sentimentality, an intricately carved mortar and pestle appears, and saffron, rose petals, turmeric, and sandalwood begin to rain down from the skies into the mortar. After the woman uses Fair & Lovely's Ayurvedic cream, she walks through a shopping mall, where an attractive young man, thoroughly distracted by her light-skinned beauty, bumps into her. When the woman and the man smile at each other, the happy father exclaims, "The perfect match has been made!"

The fluctuating meanings of the epidermis in globalizing India do not imply a free-floating universe in which whiteness and nonwhiteness always share parallel and equally affirmative spheres of meaning. The tide in the semiotics of skin color in India's visual economy of mobile and cross-cutting magazine, television, Internet, and film images ebbs and flows between the binaristic opposing poles of "whiteness/lightness/fairness is generally positive" and "blackness/darkness/brownness is generally negative." My own childhood recollections of the sociolinguistic architecture of skin color in the Tamil language spoken within the social circles of family and friends highlights the stigma associated with dark skin. The varied terminology for skin color in Tamil included (in translation) "rosy," "red," "little color," "lots of color," "no color," "shining," and the occasional "black" or "lots of black," which unlike the other words were often whispered in public or uttered within tightly knit groups of women. Yet I also heard my light-skinned grandmother, fiercely protective of her dark-skinned granddaughters, insist that light skin color without any grace, charm, or intelligence could not make any woman beautiful. Her comment, while reassuring when I was a small child, also made me wonder why she felt the need to defend our dark skin tone in these particular ways.

In globalizing India's shifting ethnoscapes, fluctuations in skin color are also tied to the greater velocity of the traffic in white and Indian female bodies that are moving across borders through new channels of mediated culture. A *Washington Post* report documents the recent dramatic increase in Caucasian female models in advertisements for products and services, originating from India, that are seeking to establish themselves as global brands.[25] White models wearing Indian clothes in these advertisements embody both the demands of "glocality" and the desire for an equal cultural exchange in which "India's economic self-confidence" becomes visible.[26] Revealing the uneven cleavages that litter the epidermal fields of whiteness and brownness, the reporter notes that eastern European models in India whose faces "stare out from billboards, from the facades of glitzy glass-fronted malls, and from fashion magazines" earn far less than the local Indian advertising celebrities, namely, cricket and Bollywood superstars and Indian supermodels.[27] At the same time as India begins to emulate postwar Japan's fascination with white models, dark-skinned Indian models whose bodies are Photoshopped to become lighter in the Indian advertising industry earn praise for their natural body color as exotic when they work for clients in Europe. Across the border in China, the recent barrage of tanned white male bodies in the media has led to the trend of tanning among the upper-class Chinese male elite in a country where skin-lightening cosmetics make up half the cosmetics market.[28]

Finally, the cultural politics of the epidermis in India also haunts the visual field of postcolonial national state politics, an arena that presents ripe opportunities for future work. The Italian politician Sonia Gandhi, president of the Indian National Congress party and wife of former prime minister Rajiv Gandhi (son of Indira Gandhi and grandson of Jawaharlal Nehru), offers a compelling case study of white femininity's accommodation to the demands of authentic political identity in a non-Western postcolonial nation. Sonia Gandhi's Italian-Indianness has had to grapple with the pressures of dynastic rule in a democracy, the legacy of anticolonial activism, the burdens of being a public daughter-in-law and wife, and the maternal desire to preserve power for her children. Sonia Gandhi's practices of ethnic disguise—covering her foreign whiteness in the sartorial modesty of saris and learning to speak Hindi—along with this chapter's discussions of advertising, ethnographic data, and celebrity discourses illustrate the densely textured historical complexion of the fluctuating epidermis, an organ whose coloration and discoloration in the global representational realm waxes and wanes in tandem with constructs of nation, gender, ethnicity, class, sexuality, and race.

The author is indebted to Sunitha Chitrapu, Sara Friedman, and Radha Hegde for their insightful contributions to this chapter. She thanks Kavitha Cardoza and Purnima Bose for their support, and she is grateful to her family members—Nivedita Raju and Bala Raju—for their hospitality in India.

1. "Ponds Launches White Beauty Detox Range," *Models N Trends* (July 11, 2007), http://modelsntrends.com/view_story.php?id=116 (accessed July 13, 2008).

2. "Fashion Portal," Nirvana Woman website, http://www.nirvanawoman.net/html/fashion_portal.php (accessed August 4, 2008).

3. For a full explanation of forensic analysis, see John Hartley, *Popular Reality: Journalism, Modernity, Popular Culture* (New York: St. Martin's, 1996).

4. See Radha S. Hegde, introduction to this volume, p. 8.

5. This term is borrowed from Inderpal Grewal and Caren Kaplan, *Scattered Hegemonies: Postmodernity and Transnational Feminist Practices* (Minneapolis: University of Minnesota Press, 1994).

6. Nirmala Sinha, "Skin Care: Fair and Growing," *India Today* (December 6, 2000): 48.

7. Heather Timmons, "Telling India's Modern Women They Have Power, Even over Their Skin Tone," *New York Times* (May 30, 2007), http://www.nytimes.com/gst/fullpage.html?res=9C02EEDB1430F933A05756C0A9619C8B63&sec=&spon=&pagewanted=all (accessed October 31, 2007).

8. Allen L. Hammond and C. K. Prahalad, "Selling to the Poor," *Foreign Policy* (May–June 2004), http://www.foreignpolicy.com/articles/2004/05/01/selling_to_the_poor (accessed May 31, 2007).

9. Anita Anand, *The Beauty Game* (New Delhi: Penguin Books, 2002), 149.

10. Ammina Mire, "Pigmentation and Empire," *Counterpunch* (July 28, 2000), http://www.counterpunch.org/mire07282005.html (accessed May 7, 2007).

11. For example, see T. Banks, "Colorism: A Darker Shade of Pale," *UCLA Law Review* 47, no. 6 (2000): 1705–1746; A. Celious and D. Oyserman, "Race from the Inside: An Emerging Heterogeneous Race Model," *Journal of Social Science* 57, no. 1 (2001): 149–165; J. Falconer and H. Neville, "African-American College Women's Body Image: An Examination of Body Mass, African Self-Consciousness, and Skin Color Satisfaction," *Psychology of Women Quarterly* 24, no. 3 (2000): 236–243; Margaret Hunter, "If You're Light, You're Alright: Light Skin Color as Social Capital for Women of Color," *Gender and Society* 16, no. 2 (2002): 175–193.

12. Videostar3001, "Michael Jackson Face Transformation," *YouTube* (January 2, 2007), http://www.youtube.com/watch?v=ri6ilBfMBu0 (accessed October 8, 2008).

13. Acucena, "Michael Jackson-Documentary: 'Changes,'" *YouTube* (February 20, 2007), http://www.youtube.com/watch?v=uNUfIuOXLLE&feature=related (accessed October 8, 2008).

14. TheMJtheory, "Black or White, Episode 2," *YouTube* (April 1, 2008), http://www.youtube.com/watch?v=vqmwls5FRjA (accessed October 8, 2008).

15. Aditi Mishra, "Colorism in India," e-mail communication (July 18, 2007).

16. Usha Zacharias, "The Smile of Mona Lisa: Postcolonial Desires, Nationalist Families, and the Birth of Television in India," *Critical Studies in Media Communication* 20, no. 4 (2003): 389.

17. Ibid.

18. Kathleen Erwin, "White Women, Male Desires: A Televisual Fantasy of the Transnational Chinese Family," in Mayfair Mei-Hiu Yang, ed., *Spaces of Their Own: Women's Public Sphere in Transnational China* (Minneapolis: University of Minnesota Press, 1999), 232–257.

19. ChocolateDove71, "Aishwarya Rai 60 Minutes Interview Part 1," *YouTube* (February 21, 2008), http://www.youtube.com/watch?v=aUfElxbqPgE&feature=related (accessed August 28, 2008).

20. "Aishwarya Interview with Oprah Winfrey," *Google Videos* (December 28, 2006), http://video.google.com/videoplay?docid=-2278044500626117388&q=Oprah+Winfrey# (accessed August 28, 2008).

21. Kishore Singh, "Rajini: The Man with the Midas Touch" *Rediff India Abroad* (June 19, 2007), http://www.rediff.com/movies/2007/jun/19rajni.htm (accessed September 2, 2008).

22. Zacharias, "The Smile of Mona Lisa," 396.

23. Dyankayn, "Digital Skin Grafting," *Vfxtalk.com* (June 25, 2007), http://www.vfxtalk.com/forum/sitemap/digital-skin-grafting (accessed September 2, 2008).

24. Ibid.

25. Rama Lakshmi, "In India's Huge Marketplace, Advertisers Find Fair Skin Sells," *Washingtonpost.com* (January 27, 2008), http://www.washingtonpost.com/wp-dyn/content/article/2008/01/26/AR2008012601057.html (accessed August 22, 2008).

26. Ibid.

27. Ibid.

28. Quentin Sommerville, "China's Changing Skin Colour," *BBC.com* (February 13, 2007), http://news.bbc.co.uk/2/hi/asia-pacific/6357439.stm (accessed August 23, 2007).

II Contesting Ideologies

5 Gendered Blueprints

Transnational Masculinities in Muslim Televangelist Cultures

Nabil Echchaibi

The tragic shooting in the Texas military base of Fort Hood has reanimated an extant post-9/11 debate about Muslim men as culturally confused, excessively pious, and intrinsically violent. American media coverage initially—and briefly—steered explanations in their conflicted attempt to avoid anti-Muslim bigotry, but a linear link between Muslim men and ideologically induced violence was clearly the underlying subtext informing much of the ensuing coverage of this incident. Major Nidal Malik Hasan, the Muslim Palestinian American behind the shooting rampage, readily became the subject of disjointed and muddled speculations by pundits and journalists linking him to al-Qaeda and questioning the loyalty of Muslims in the U.S. military. CNN's Wolf Blitzer made sure his viewers understood that the name of the suspect was Arab as he was revealing it for the first time, plastering in the process the neat portrait of a Muslim/Arab terrorist male over a complex situation. The incessant replays of a surveillance video showing Hasan buying coffee at a store wearing a long white kameez (identified loosely by various media reports as "Middle Eastern traditional garb") hours before the shooting also served as a potent visual cue to cement this easy association. At one point, this video appeared on CNN and MSNBC on one half of the screen, while the other half showed Dr. Zuhdi Jasser, an American-born secular Muslim and former Navy officer, dressed in a suit and tie (read as modern attire) as he was denouncing the terror of Hasan's actions, as if the shooter's traditional garb could help us rationalize the irrational and safely find a religious and cultural explanation to this tragedy.

What is striking about this type of coverage is not only its spurious logic as more information flows but also and more importantly its consistency in invoking predictable images and narratives to explain anything "Muslim." This Orientalist trope of the culturally rigid Muslim man continues unabated in these accounts, joining other immanent frames that see Islam as an intransigent orthopraxy, allowing Muslims no self-reflexivity. Following this putative logic, Nidal Hasan is nothing but an invariant extension of the destructively dangerous Muslim male, like 9/11 hijacker Mohamed Atta or the 7/7 London bomber Mohammed Siddique Khan or the 3/11 Madrid bomber Jamal Zougam or the many other men waiting to follow in their footsteps.[1] Their propensity to jihad and death is not limited to disturbed individuals but is usually considered a reflection of the immutability of Muslim cultures and the lack of discursive deliberation in Islam as a whole.[2]

Inherent in such cultural frames, of course, is a longstanding Western claim that secular humanism, with its emphasis on freedom and individual agency, is the only antidote against the fundamentalism of Islam and the uncritical submissiveness of its followers.[3] This Islam-versus-the-West binary, however, has so dominated our view of Islam that we fail to imagine Muslims contesting and negotiating their faith and its place in their daily lives. Instead, we see an unyielding emphasis on angry Muslims on the margins of "modern" global culture resisting and denouncing the homogenizing forces of secular modernity. Following this rather linear evolution of Muslim identities in a post-9/11 context, Muslim men become inevitably vulnerable to political radicalism and even terrorism because they are culturally disaffected and politically disenfranchised. A variety of theories are put forth to rationalize the luring effects of radical and aggressive dissent among young Muslim men both in Muslim-majority countries and in Western societies: high unemployment and lack of social mobility render young Muslim men more bitter and vulnerable to incendiary rhetorics; women outperform men in education, causing men to feel emasculated; dislocated young men turn to a literal interpretation of their religion as a stable marker for their identity in a context of fragmentation born out of living as minorities under constant scrutiny; or even theories with shoddy sociological accuracy, such as the lack of public displays of affection between parents and their children in Muslim cultures, which purportedly explains their proclivity to brutality. Muslim men, as a portrait solidifies around these narratives, suffer from a crisis of masculinity which becomes pertinent only in the context of geopolitical security, augmenting their threat and effectively denying them any form of self-reflexive autonomy.

A number of scholars have written about the importance of countering the jarring logic of the recent rhetoric about Islam which sees in its resurgence in public life only blind subordination and patriarchal violence.[4] These scholars have been rightly dismayed by the obsession with veiling in discussions of Islam and the implications it has had on producing thin descriptions of other sociocultural dynamics in Muslim societies, and the role religious discourse plays in shaping them. This chapter is an attempt to render our perceptions of Muslim masculinities more complex and to move them beyond our preoccupation with security and religious extremism. It does so by examining what I call *transnational Muslim masculinity* and tracing its cultural reproduction through specific media narratives on satellite Islamic television. It demonstrates how Muslim televangelists draw on historical memory, scriptural texts, and local/global cultural experiences to generate new discursive sites around the various roles of men in society, such as in the family, in the workplace, in religious communities, and in social relationships. For many years, Muslim conceptualization of gender roles followed a traditional pattern that assigned men and women to separate spaces of public versus private. Arguably, the discourse embraced by these televangelists challenges the binarism of more traditionalist views on masculinity and femininity and reinscribes gender roles within the larger project of religious and social revivalism.

In recent years Middle Eastern satellite television has prominently featured a new generation of media personalities who, in the face of a crisis of authority in Islam and a climate of semantic disarray, are creating public deliberative spaces to revalorize their religion and redirect individual energies in the service of an Islamic revivalism that is concerned less with the militancy of political Islam than with the Islamicization of modernity. This is indeed the face of a rising popular Islam that uses the oratorical passion of sermonizing to encourage public participation and civic engagement and that eventually asks Muslims to shed the sternness of punitive religious discourse and to embrace the permissiveness of a forgiving and life-relevant Islam. What is striking about this emerging culture of media proselytizing is the gendered nature of the discourse it promotes and its implications for the construction of masculinities in transnational spaces such as the pan-Arab world. Indeed, most of these Muslim televangelists are young men who capitalize on their privileged gendered position in society and use it to promote an arguably progressive religious discourse while reinscribing normative gender values. Aided by a dynamic transnational television culture, their media performances cross national boundaries and increasingly target what they perceive as a homogeneous Arab Muslim audience.

By focusing on the programs of Amr Khaled and Moez Masoud, two of the most popular televangelists on Islamic television, this chapter will analyze how masculinity is constructed and negotiated in what is largely promoted and perceived as an alternative form of liberation piety. Both Masoud and Khaled represent a major shift from the politicized masculinity of Islamic extremists and potentially provide a blueprint for a less essentialized notion of gender norms. The goal here is to evaluate whether this new mediated religious discourse has spurred a critical and transformative public debate about gender roles in Muslim societies or whether the charismatic aura of these religious celebrities ultimately obfuscates social change along gender lines and reappropriates a traditionalist patriarchal discourse.

Mediatizing Islam on Television

"The Islamic media was so poor, so traditional. It wasn't television. It was televised radio, a man in front of a camera speaking for hours and hours about obscure religious texts with no appeal. . . . Words with nothing connected to life."[5] This is how Ahmed Abu Haiba, an Egyptian television producer and the mastermind behind contemporary Islamic entertainment media,[6] describes older forms of religious broadcasting. He recently launched 4Shbab, the first twenty-four-hour Islamic music-video television channel, as a way to counter what he says is the West's secular message and its seeping effects into Arab Muslim culture.[7] 4Shbab is the latest in a series of bold television initiatives that seek to make religion a debatable topic and to groom "cooler" role models based on Islamic ethos. In fact, until a few years ago, Islam on Arab transnational television was limited to sporadic programs of stern-faced imams who thought of television studios as an extension of their mosque pulpits but offered no alternative message. Today, there are thirty Islamic channels available on satellite across the Arab world, western Europe, and North America, and programming ranges from fatwa call-in shows, Quran recitation (*tajweed*) contests, and motivational shows run by superstar televangelists to a spate of sleek reality television shows with an Islamic tinge.[8]

This shift in religious broadcasting occurred in 2000, when, with the help of television producer Ahmed Abu Haiba, Amr Khaled, an Egyptian accountant turned television preacher, started his show, *Words from the Heart*, on the Saudi-owned Iqra' channel. Khaled had been an underground celebrity as a preacher in middle- and upper-class social clubs in Cairo. Audio- as well as videotapes of his engaging lectures on how to pursue a spiritual journey became instantly popular in the streets of Egypt and Arab Gulf states. His oratory skills coupled with an emotional delivery; his use of colloquial Egyptian Arabic (largely understood by most Arabs); his clean-shaven style, polo shirts, and designer suits; his multimedia arsenal, with a very popular website,[9] self-help books, and DVDs; and his ease in addressing anything from relationships, veiling, drugs, and banking to intergenerational problems—all have pushed the boundaries of Islamic preaching largely beyond the modest circles of the mosque. Since then, Amr Khaled has built an impressive media empire unparalleled on Arab television and the Internet, with numerous television shows on multiple stations and a strategic position as the director of programming at Al-Resalah, the most popular Islamic television channel, which is based in Cairo with studios in Dubai. Many preachers have followed in Khaled's footsteps, populating television grids with an array of shows inspired by his style and mode of delivery.[10]

At the core of this mediatization of religion is not merely the transportation of the religious message across the airwaves but a long-term reconfiguration of modes of social interaction, political deliberation, and community, hitherto controlled by formal institutions. By widely opening the religious field to debate, these media owners, producers, and hosts automatically create and nurture a new public of religion which is less and less dependent on formal religious authorities for its understanding of Islam and the applicability of religious teachings in a context of ever-expanding horizons. These new religious media personalities command increasing powers in shaping the political and religious contours of contemporary Arab Muslim identities. Such an authority is acquired not solely by their ability to address topics considered taboo in religious and secular circles but also by their emphasis on personal piety—not Islamist polity—and their revalorization of the role of the individual in the ambitious project of Islamic *Nahda* (revivalism).

The appeal of this kind of religious rhetoric lies in the fact that figures such as Amr Khaled provide an arguably convincing alternative to the putative failure of political Islam and the religious and cultural stagnation in Arab societies. Their emphasis, in a solipsistic fashion, on personal virtue and correcting the ethical foundation of Muslim individuals is seen by their public as a more effective path to changing entire Muslim societies and maybe indirectly nations-states, even if this mode of preaching, as Assef Bayat describes it, "is scripturally rich but politically thin."[11] But what is interesting about the tangle of discourse that these religious celebrities have generated through television, the Internet, and scores of self-help books is the new corpus of behavioral ethics they think must regiment the actions of what they call the "modern Muslim." Self-help religious guides existed across the Muslim world before the popularization of Islamic media,[12] but never were they as available and as all encompassing as they are today.[13] This ethical therapeutics, which unlike its predecessor is not merely devoted to helping the individual fight earthly temptations, is deeply invested in the material world, with its logic of consumption and self-fulfillment. Spiritual advice in this modern form of preaching proscribes rules of individual success and encourages its followers, as Turner describes, to adopt new tastes and aspirations:

> Piety movements are culturally creative. They typically involve the destruction or overcoming of many traditional or taken-for-granted ways of practicing religion. They involve either a new emphasis on religious practices or the invention of practices that are then claimed to be orthodox, or more exactly orthoprax. Piety tends to have a radical impact on the everyday world of believers by encouraging devotees to change their habits or in the language of modern sociology to transform their habitus or their dispositions and tastes towards the material world. Piety is about the construction of definite and distinctive life styles of new religious tastes and preferences.[14]

As for tastes and preferences, Khaled and this new generation of preachers offer plenty, ranging from the kind of music to listen to, the kind of clothes to wear, and the type of films to watch to the kind of social project to invest in. Increasingly, the shows of these preachers become for their followers more like blueprints for good Islamic behavior and guides for social action. However, in acting as spiritual therapists, televangelists are also impacting social and cultural norms such as gender, relationship to authority, and sexuality in unprecedented ways. An interesting question that follows from the rising popularity of this new television institution is how much of its discourse is changing some of these norms and how much remains the same and is simply presented in a modern garb.

Islamic Televangelists and the Making of the Modern Muslim Man

In 2004, Amr Khaled introduced a new genre of television programming which enjoyed a huge following among Muslims across the Arab world and in western Europe. His show, *Sunaa al-Hayat* (*LifeMakers*), was not merely a *da'wa* (invitation to proper Muslim practice) program but an ambitious project of social and economic revival based on concrete actions such as collecting food and clothing for the poor, organizing antidrug campaigns, and fighting unemployment by starting new businesses. Khaled's creatively delivered message of personal and economic "development through faith" (*attanmiyya bil iman*) was a fresh alternative to swaths of Muslim youth who he says have been mired in a culture of laziness and passivity. The following excerpt is from the *LifeMakers'* first episode, in which Khaled urges young Muslims to "shatter the shackles" that hold them back:

> The Arab youth are like a sad young man, feeling depressed, and sitting in a cramped, depressing room, with cobwebs covering the walls. A prayer mat is draped carelessly on a sofa very close by, and on his desk there is a copy of the Holy Qur'an, covered with dust. Outside this room it is sunny and bright. We asked him, "Why don't you come out of the room, into the light?" He answered, "There's no way I can come out." We then said, "But it is possible." His body started twitching in an attempt to move, but he could not manage. He felt that his body was shackled to the ground. A shackle was binding his left arm. On it was written the word "passivity." A shackle was binding his right arm. On it was written the word "laziness." A shackle was binding his neck. On it was written the word "ignorance." Shackles bound his feet. On them was written "no aim in life." We told him, "In order for you to get up you must unshackle yourself first. We will help you to achieve that." Step by step, he started to learn. He started to learn how to build his will power, how to identify his target and how to develop his knowledge. He started putting it all into practice, and he kept practicing, until one day, we came and opened the door of the room. He tried to get up, and he managed to get up smoothly. As he finally left the room, he held onto two things: he had the Holy Qur'an in his right hand, and the key to life making in his left hand.[15]

After diagnosing the ailment of Arab youth using an elaborate graphic that details unemployment rates, registered patents, income levels, and the number of doctors, engineers, daily newspapers, and published and translated books in the Arab world, Khaled unveils his zealous project over the course of a few months and asks his devoted viewers to change their approach to life. In a series of episodes divided into three stages (1—breaking off the shackles, 2—taking off, 3—projects of renaissance), he tells vivid stories of great Muslim minds such as Imam Bukhari, Ibn Khaldoun, and Ibn Battouta. His point is that in order to renew with the glorious past of Islam, Muslim societies need "selfless people who are concerned about the welfare of their countries, people empowered by the word 'us,' not the word 'I' and people toiling, not for their own good, but for Allah and their religion."[16]

In presenting this rather detailed and prescriptive outline, Khaled is also acting as an alternative role model for what a pious Muslim man can be. He is not the punitive mufti who proscribes everything *haram* (illicit) or the renegade bin Laden who uses religious fervor to foment violence. Neither is Khaled the anti-modern devout Muslim who sees in Western culture only moral decadence and excessive materialism or the pious Muslim whose faith is expressed only through the observance of religious rituals or else the victim Muslim who blames the state of cultural and intellectual stagnation on Western imperialism and colonialism. In fact, much of what Khaled and other televangelists' message has come to represent for their followers is cogently suggested through a comparison with the kind of stale piety they fight against. They are first and foremost pragmatic: not simply preachy, compassionate, and inclusive, not punitive and exclusive, and critically embracing—not squarely denouncing the material world. The modern Muslim man, accordingly, is someone who takes initiatives even if the odds are working against him, because his faith is not only his rallying cry but the source of his creativity. In one episode of *LifeMakers*, Khaled bemoans the fact that men spend hours in cafes smoking and toiling around aimlessly. He then calculates the hours that could be saved each day by avoiding unproductive activities and the amount of constructive work that could be achieved instead. If his audience is short on ideas to become productive, Khaled is always resourceful in providing concrete examples and charting out specific strategies which he introduces on air and develops further on his highly interactive website. In an episode entitled "Culture, Art, Media and Making Life," Khaled invites his audience not to stop at simply denouncing music videos on Arab satellite television which objectify women's bodies. On his website, he explains that

> the problem with video clips is not only the dissolute words and movements, but the biggest problem is, in fact, the importation of something that has nothing to do with our own culture. The picture is Western and the voice is ours, what would the clip look like? It is useless and aimless. In that way, it is not art that will exalt the soul; it is directed to desire and lust; this is the result of blind imitation. . . . I ask all those

who are with us today, please don't accept the obliteration of the identity of our nation, preserve our culture and our arts.[17]

He then urges everyone to write a letter to artists and television channels and complain about the overt sexualization of women and their denigration. A few days later, it was reported that some of these channels received thousands of letters from across the Arab world. Khaled's action does not stop there; in what is becoming a typical fashion in his shows, he likes to provide examples of the kind of change he advocates. On the question of art and music, he has invited Sami Yusuf, a young British Muslim singer and composer of Azeri origins whose Western/Oriental music and videos praise the Prophet and God and creatively teach Muslims to be proud of their religion and identities. Since that appearance, Yusuf has been leading a new wave of what is loosely labeled *al-fan al-hadef* (purposeful art), and a number of Arab and non-Arab Muslims have followed in his footsteps, creating a vibrant scene of Islamic music videos on which the 4shbab channel is currently seeking to capitalize. This comes as a major departure from traditionalist religious leaders who have denounced art as shameful and immoral. Khaled and Masoud see art as a critical tool in the edification of the Muslim *Ummah* (larger Muslim community) and urge Muslim artists to reorient their talents for a higher cause.[18]

Another distinctive trait of the modern Muslim man in satellite and new media televangelism is his transnational consciousness and his cosmopolitan ease in navigating different cultural lifeworlds. Besides touring the world on speaking engagements, Khaled's and Masoud's shows are set in Dubai, Cairo, Berlin, and London, both giving their viewers a sense of their global reach and forging affective ties to the *Ummah*. In the wake of the Danish cartoons controversy, both Khaled and Masoud traveled to Copenhagen and organized a conference on Muslim-West dialogue, signaling again to their followers that Muslims need to engage different viewpoints, even when they are hurtful and demeaning. Khaled is also proud to showcase the transnational impact of his *LifeMakers* project by frequently reporting on the more than twelve thousand LifeMakers clubs that have sprouted worldwide since the launch of his show in 2004. Many of these clubs in the Arab world and in countries such as England, France, Italy, the United States, and Australia are currently carrying out several projects, ranging from collecting winter clothing and food for the poor to other charitable and entrepreneurial initiatives.

This emphasis on social activism is critical in popularizing Khaled's project of development through faith. The centrality of community in the discourse of religious leaders is not new, but the revalorization of the role of the individual in building a stronger Muslim community, coupled with a detailed prescription of how that role could be carried out, is quite new. The modernist project of Islamic revivalism at the turn of the twentieth century had been calling for openness to science and art and a better deployment of youth energies toward a moderniza-tion of Muslim mentalities, but that approach had a top-down impact on intel-lectuals and political leaders without affecting the masses. Contemporary tel-evangelists, particularly Khaled, offer a concrete social program with well-defined goals inspired by lived social realities.

The realism of televangelist discourse is an important dimension in building authority and credibility. Both Khaled and Masoud eagerly remind their viewers of their prior indulgence in life's temptations before God brought them back to the right path. Recounting elaborate stories of once enjoying drugs, alcohol, and the company of women helps project an image not only of fallible men but also of men who have experienced life to its fullest and can therefore speak from a much more life-informed position. In contrast, traditionalist religious leaders are often perceived as paragons of virtue, untouched by life impulses and the weaknesses of the body. This contrast helps bring televangelists such as Khaled and Masoud closer to their audience, because following a ritualized mediated experience, their characters are constantly dramatized through the telling of their own life stories and the exaltation of their personas as television megastars.

Consistent with the importance of the mediation of this religious discourse, Khaled and Masoud opt for a Westernized dress style, with polo shirts and trendy suits. Neither has a beard, considered by some Muslims to be essential for devout Muslim men, and both relate their aesthetic choices to the kind of progressive message they advocate. When Khaled was asked about why he has no beard, he said that his look is a critical extension of his message of change and a cautious choice that enables him to relate more effectively to his audience of young, middle- and upper-class Muslims.

Despite the popularity of these televangelists and the changes they have brought to the centrality of religion in personal and economic development, it is important to note that their approach remains heavily scripturalist and lacks historical or critical reasoning in interpreting the texts. Their positive message of empowerment can also be undercut by their rigidity in dealing with issues such as femininity and gender relations.

Femininity and Modesty in Televangelist Discourse

One of the major points of appeal of the new Muslim televangelist discourse has been the proactive nature of its message, but I argue that its most significant con-tribution is not the core of this message but the innovation of its rhetoric and style of delivery. Much like the cassette sermons in Charles Hirschkind's study of the ethical soundscapes in Egypt, televangelism also provides "one of the means by which Islamic ethical traditions have been recalibrated to a new political and technological order, to its rhythms, noise, its forms of pleasure and boredom, but also to its political incitements, its call to citizenly participation."[19] But the recalibration of tradition in the televangelist discourse is at times only superficial and lacks a historicized reading of the texts. This is particularly evident in the way Amr Khaled has approached the controversial topic of veiling.

Khaled argues in his 2005 lecture on women's veiling that the Quran is unequivocal about the need for women to wear the veil as a condition for them to preserve their modesty but also, and most importantly in this case, as a requirement that prevents men from falling into the trap of women's sexuality and carnal desire:

> If I ask you, sister, a question: If you have something precious, will you protect it? If a woman has a pearl, for instance, will she put it in a safe place away from danger? I do believe every woman will. The more this pearl is precious, the more the woman will keep it aloof of others. She will keep it away from any treacherous eyesight. A pearl is preserved in an oyster, which is not beautiful at all. Nevertheless, the oyster is badly needed for the protection of the pearl. The same applies to hijab, which is indispensable for women's protection. What is the most precious possession of a woman? Isn't it her modesty? Doesn't that deserve even higher protection? In this respect, some people might broach a question: "Why were women ordered to put on the veil, and not men? Was this a restriction imposed just upon women?" Our answer is that a hundred men cannot make one woman infatuated with them unless she allows it intentionally, but one woman can make a hundred men infatuated with her. For that reason, the veil has been imposed as an obligation (or ordinance) enjoined upon women because they are the source (springhead) of stimulation.[20]

As this quotation exemplifies, Khaled's discourse on veiling is direct, unapologetic, and uncompromising: women's modesty and morality can be guaranteed only by a proper form of veiling (what he calls "the Perfect Veil"), one that does not reveal the contours of the female body while, at the same time, preserving women's femininity.[21] Khaled justifies his adamant position on veiling by referring to Sura 24:31 of the Quran, which reads, "And tell the believing women to subdue their eyes and maintain their chastity. They shall not reveal any parts of their bodies except that which is necessary. They shall cover their chests, and shall not relax their code in presence of other than their husbands, their fathers." Khaled's approach to the sacred texts reveals a literal and strict reading, which leaves no room for interpretations or contextualizations.

Khaled's lecture on veiling is rich with reminders and admonitions to women who might object to the prescription to veil; this is clearly not an ontological departure from what a traditional Azharite[22] scholar would advocate. Khaled's rhetoric is, however, different from his more traditional counterparts, because he connects women's chastity to his grand plan of Islamic revivalism, while reminding women of the urgency to veil as a necessary step toward modesty and success in the Muslim *Ummah*. In fact, both women's and men's active and successful involvement in civic and religious life is strongly linked to women's decision to veil: women who wear the "perfect veil," Khaled argues, not only will display their piety and religiosity, but their behavior will also provide the necessary moral climate for men's righteous actions in the service of Islamic revivalism.

In this logic, the desexualization of the female body is perceived as an imperative condition for the resurgence of the modern, transnational *Ummah*. Khaled's views on veiling are often couched in imploring and supplicatory terms toward women, who are *asked* (not forced) to wear the veil to support his revivalist project. Yet his seemingly empowering discourse is embedded in a patriarchal system that masks a scheme of power relations in which women's agency is clearly at the margins. In Khaled's lecture, women are encouraged to watch over each other's shoulders and remind their unveiled "sisters" of the individual and societal consequences that their rejection of the hijab can have. Khaled's carefully crafted rhetoric advocates a system of subtle self-surveillance on veiling that is reminiscent of Foucault's notion of panopticism, a central regulatory characteristic of modern societies that guarantees the effective functioning of a disciplined community. Unlike in earlier times, when social norms and behaviors were rigidly enforced by state apparatuses, Khaled's focus on individual agency within the *Ummah* decentralizes authority, but the kind of power vested in the individual in this case is inscribed within an existing and resilient power structure which privileges the gendered and classed vantage point from which Khaled speaks. It is worth noting here that Khaled's celebrity, acquired through the performative act of televangelism, augments the perceived value of his message and renders him more credible. In a clear contrast with the traditional television religious show, which consisted of a single, unchanging camera angle, Khaled's televisual aesthetics are more elaborate, with multiple camera angles and frequent reactive shots from his audience, thus ritualizing the viewing act and creating an experience of communion.

Clearly, Khaled does not rely solely on the verbal content of his messages, but he also, and at times more strategically, resourcefully uses performative strategies, including facial expressions, pitch variations, camera editing, and dress. In this context, dress should be understood as what Bourdieu calls an "embodied practice" that is neither the result of a free act of choice nor the forceful imposition dictated by social norms but, rather, is a practice developed within an "acquired system of schemes."[23] In the case of Khaled's performance, his sartorial choices become even more pivotal to understand the relationship between the body and the dress and the normative gender roles he endorses. As Joanne Entwistle explains, "The study of dress as situated practice requires moving between, on the one hand, the discursive and representational aspects of dress, and the way the body/dress is caught up in relations of power, and on the other, the embodied experience of dress and the use of dress as a means by which individuals orientate themselves to the social world."[24] Khaled consistently capitalizes on the instrumental role of dress as an agent of modern masculinity and, at the same time, of bounded femininity.

Conclusion

Much of the Western discourse on Islam in general and Muslim masculinities in particular has focused on issues of security, safety, and integration in an emerging field that Bryan Turner labels "the management of Muslims."[25] Examining the discursive politics of Islamic televangelism is an attempt to write against this obsession with these geopolitical concerns, which minimizes our understanding of various sociocultural dynamics within Muslim societies. The point in this chapter has not been not to draw an uncritical portrait of this emerging television institution and its impact on its public. Rather, the aim has been to locate rich discursive spaces as viable loci for the study of how religious/gendered identities are constructed and negotiated.

Islamic televangelism has taken advantage of an arid public sphere in the Arab world which has devalued intellectualism and the role of young Muslims in the project of personal development. Khaled Abou El Fadl and others have argued that Islamic extremism is a bitter result of this kind of "intellectual dissonance," which has produced no real answer to the challenge of modernity in the Muslim world.[26] Unlike the bin Laden strand of Islamic revival, a nihilistic type of activism meant, as Abou El Fadl explains, "to protest against modernity by destroying its symbols, to deconstruct what exists without much thought for what can be constructed in its place,"[27] Amr Khaled's proactive motivational discourse not only generates discussions but also imagines a world defined by an Islamic modernity, even if it remains inimical to historical critical inquiry. The curious appeal of this kind of discourse, albeit much invested in a direct dialectic with modernity, lies precisely in its timidity in critically engaging the Islamic doctrine and its creative and emotional deployment of piety in building an Islamic modernization. Both Muslim men and women are entrusted with an active role in this project, with a reminder that anyone is qualified to speak on behalf of Islam, but they are quickly discouraged from using that epistemological freedom to deconstruct sacred texts and objectify the Islamic tradition.

1. In a controversial *Forbes* column, New York University professor Tunku Varadarajan coined the phrase "going Muslim," borrowing it from the "piquant" phrase "going postal," to explain the rage of Major Nidal Malik Hasan at Fort Hood: "This phrase would describe the turn of events where a seemingly integrated Muslim-American—a friendly donut vendor in New York, say, or an officer in the U.S. Army at Fort Hood—discards his apparent integration into American society and elects to vindicate his religion in an act of messianic violence against his fellow Americans. This would appear to be what happened in the case of Maj. Hasan." Tunku Varadarjan, "Going Muslim," *Forbes* (November 9, 2009), http://www.forbes.com/2009/11/08/fort-hood-nidal-malik-hasan-muslims-opinions-columnists-tunku-varadarajan.html.

2. See Daniel Varisco, "Words Matter: The Linguistic Damage of Going Muslim," *Religious Dispatches* (November 17, 2009), http://www.religiondispatches.org/archive/politics/2039/words_matter%3A_the_linguistic_damage_of_"going_muslim"_/ (accessed December 1, 2009).

3. See Saba Mahmood, *Politics of Piety: The Islamic Revival and the Feminist Subject* (Princeton, NJ: Princeton University Press, 2005).

4. See Leila Abu Lughod, *Dramas of Nationhood: The Politics of Television in Egypt* (Chicago: University of Chicago Press, 2004); Leila Ahmed, *Women and Gender in Islam: Historical Roots of a Modern Debate* (New Haven, CT: Yale University Press, 1993); and Fadwa El-Giundy, "Veiling Infitah with Muslim Ethic Egypt's Contemporary Islamic Movement," *Social Problems* 28, no. 4 (1981): 465–485.

5. Jeffrey Fleishman, "Fighting Fire with Fire," *Los Angeles Times* (April 6, 2008), http://articles.latimes.com/2008/apr/06/world/fg-eastwest6 (accessed August 12, 2009).

6. Ahmed Abu-Haiba was also a bureau chief at the popular Islamic channel Al-Risalah before he raised millions of dollars from Saudi investors to start his 4Shbab satellite channel. He is considered by many observers as the mastermind behind the popularization of Islam in entertainment media.

7. Ibid.

8. Reality television on Islamic television has become a well-established genre, with shows stressing Islamic values such as almsgiving (*zakat*) and charity. Since the first Islamic reality program, *Green Light*, a show that featured four young Muslim men as they devised marketing plans for the best philanthropic project, a number of shows have aired, claiming a loyal following across the region. For more on religious broadcasting, see Lindsay Wise, "Whose Reality Is Real? Ethical Reality TV Trend Offers 'Culturally Authentic' Alternative to Western Formats," *Transnational Broadcasting Journal* 15 (2006), http://www.tbsjournal.com/Archives/Fall05/Wise.html (accessed August 12, 2009).

9. Khaled's website has consistently ranked among the top five hundred most popular sites on the Web. In twenty languages, Khaled's website offers lecture transcripts, "educational" jokes, songs, music videos, and discussion groups, with the latter accounting for 36 percent of the site's traffic.

10. Other preachers such as Moez Masoud, Khaled El-Giundy, and Mostafa Hosni have become household names in the Middle East and North Africa, and Khaled recently hosted a reality show in which young men were learning how to become good modern preachers.

11. Assef Bayat, "From Amr Diab to Amr Khaled," *Al-Ahram Weekly* (May 22–28, 2003), http://weekly.ahram.org.eg/2003/639/fe1.htm (accessed August 15, 2009).

12. See Charles Hirschkind, *The Ethical Soundscape: Cassette Sermons and Islamic Counterpublics* (New York: Columbia University Press, 2006).

13. See Nabil Echchaibi, "From Audiotapes to Videoblogs: The Delocalization of Authority in Islam," *Nations and Nationalism* 17, no. 1 (2011): 1–20.

14. Bryan Turner, "Introduction: The Price of Piety," *Contemporary Islam* 2, no. 1 (2008): 3.

15. To read the entire transcript of this episode, see Khaled's website, "Episode 1: Introduction—Part 1," http://amrkhaled.net/articles/articles62.html (accessed August 17, 2009).

16. Ibid.

17. To read the entire transcript of this episode, see Khaled's website, "Episode 28: Culture, Art, Media . . . and Making Life," http://amrkhaled.net/articles/articles406.html (accessed August, 18, 2009).

18. Jessica Winegar, "Purposeful Art between Television Preachers and the State," *ISIM Review* 2 (2008): 28–30.

19. Charles Hirschkind, *The Ethical Soundscape: Cassette Sermons and Islamic Counterpublics* (New York: Columbia University Press, 2006), 11.

20. To read the entire transcript of this episode, see Khaled's website, "Al-Hijab," http://amrkhaled.net/articles/articles498.html (accessed August 14, 2009).

21. On his website, Khaled writes,

The scholars mentioned some conditions for a Muslim woman's hijab:

1. It should not give a representation of a woman's figure nor give an outlining of her body. It should be loose. If the garment depicts any part of your body, then it contradicts the specifics of the Islamic manner of dressing.

2. It should not be transparent.

3. It should cover the whole body.

4. It should be different from men's way of dressing.

5. It should not be perfumed (redolent with scent).

We have been dealing hitherto with bashfulness and modesty as a significant part of woman's ethics. The veil is the most important manifestation of woman's bashfulness.

Ibid.

22. Consistent with the teachings of Al-Azhar University in Cairo, an important center of Sunni Islam.

23. Pierre Bourdieu, *Outline of a Theory of Practice* (Cambridge: Cambridge University Press, 1977), 95.

24. Joanne Entwistle, *The Fashioned Body: Fashion, Dress and Modern Social Theory* (Cambridge, UK: Polity, 2000).

25. Bryan Turner, "Religious Authority and the New Media," *Theory, Culture and Society* 24 (2007): 117–134.

26. Khaled Abou El Fadl, "The Ugly Modern and the Modern Ugly," in Omid Safi, ed., *Progressive Muslims: On Justice, Gender, and Pluralism* (Oxford, UK: Oneworld, 2003), 33–77.

27. Khaled Abou El Fadl, "The Orphans of Modernity and the Clash of Civilizations," *Global Dialogue* 4, no. 2 (2002): 16.

Abolishing the "New Slave Trade" or the New Nativism?

Felicity Schaeffer-Grabiel

Government websites, television, films, documentaries, news channels, and other media depictions equate sex trafficking with what is popularly labeled the "New Slave Trade." While various political parties and organizations are divided over how to address migration, the branding of sex trafficking as modern-day slavery strategically galvanizes these very same politically divergent constituencies.[1] Bipartisan support and popular consensus against trafficking is evident in the outpour of funds for this cause. The administration of George W. Bush announced that from 2000 to 2008, the federal government spent $295 million in tax dollars toward the fight against sex trafficking in the United States and a total of half a billion dollars globally.[2] A significant amount of resources earmarked for media campaigns in the United States and around the world educate the public on the severity of sex trafficking and how best to combat it. This chapter focuses on media campaigns during President Bush's tenure from 2000 and 2008 that saturated the public with images of horrific sexualized exploitation and regurgitated statistics circulated by government officials and documents. In a vicious cycle of misinformation recently proven to be grossly overestimated, the government relied on sensationalist media accounts to profess alarming statistics.[3] Since 2000, state officials claimed that from fifty to eighty thousand people are trafficked to the United States each year and six hundred to eight hundred thousand globally. In fact, the administration only identified 1,362 victims of human trafficking during Bush's presidency. Scholars and journalists, in contrast, assert that trafficking is being blown out of proportion and that most women know what they are getting into but have few choices for livable jobs in their home and destination countries.[4] These statistics do not capture the nuances for defining and distinguishing those who are exploited "against their will" from other "undocumented" migrants.

So the question remains, what purpose does this glut of government and media attention on sex trafficking serve if these funds are not actually helpful in improving the lives of women and children and in preventing trafficking? There are true victims of sex trafficking who lack the most basic of human rights. Yet a media campaign to invigorate public outrage and manpower in capturing the "criminal networks" obfuscates the structural inequalities and global desires fueling women's entrance into sex work. The spectacle of enslaved bodies repeated in media accounts more broadly creates national panic over the movement of people across borders. This anxiety generates collective support for an increase in state power and in the state's budget (in militarizing the border, building more prison detention centers, and deporting more immigrants), in order to apprehend and return subjects at the border. By raising fears over women's mobility through images of sexualized violence, the media works in tandem with heightened border surveillance to slow down or halt migration rather than opening up safe avenues for women to find employment.

Trafficking is defined in a United Nations protocol as the movement of bodies across borders and the lack of choice: "the recruitment, transportation, transfer, harbouring or receipts of persons" by "the threat or use of force or other forms of coercion, of abduction, of fraud, of deception, of the abuse of power or of a position of vulnerability."[5] Wendy Chapkis argues that the emphasis on sex trafficking elides the fact that the U.S. Trafficking Victim Protection Act (TVPA) of 2000 protects few "innocent women" while criminalizing the broader masses of migrants who presumably "choose" to break the law by crossing "illegally" into the United States.[6] Only the innocent are worthy of legal protection from criminal charges or immediate detention and deportation. At stake in eradicating trafficking is the protection of innocent women and children and, by extension, the nation from the onslaught of "barbaric" forms of slavery and violence, perpetrated by organized crime, that subvert the hegemony of the law and modernity.

Trafficking debates, while supposedly not targeted against migrants, stir up national anxieties over just how detrimental certain forms of difference are to modern nation-states. Transnational media depictions of gender and race (and specifically, the treatment of women) are critical in calibrating a nation's alignment with or distance from modernity and its other, slavery. To be sexually enslaved is depicted as the most grotesque form of "otherness," the underside of capitalist profit and the modern nation. In fact, the status of women (whether they are "enslaved" or "free") becomes an important symbol of national order in an increasingly transnational space. Trafficking campaigns inadvertently shift the focus from the masses of migrants who are exploited every day as cheap laborers to saving "duped" female migrants shuttled into the commerce of underground prostitution.[7] The focus on the innocent and moral victims perpetuates neoliberal immigration policies that judge migrants' (sexual) morality as the basis for citizenship.[8] Mainstream feminist notions of freedom and slavery are summoned in ways that hijack human rights debates from questions of labor exploitation to feminist concerns with agency or women's ability to freely *consent* to their movement and the labor of their bodies.[9] In fact, as President Bush defined it, prostitution is inherently degrading and hence must be forced.[10] The abolition of trafficking is encased within an individual and neoliberal framework that projects the nation as the modern savior, while severing past and present transnational practices that configure the state and corporate profit at the center of trafficking logic.[11]

Numerous accounts of trafficking cases by corporate and state actors fall out of the focus on sex trafficking.[12] For example, managers of the meatpacking corporation Tyson Foods were acquitted even after it was proven that they hired recruiters to import Latin American workers whom they submitted to inhuman labor practices. Even U.S. defense contractors hired by the Pentagon in 2005 deflected charges after they trafficked workers into Iraq and then confiscated their passports to further exploit their labor.[13] By focusing on the most egregious cases, these horrific accounts of feminized abuse shift our attention from the nation to the foreign. The media's reporting of extreme cases of gendered enslavement normalizes the lack of rights and criminalization attached to other migrant workers and situates this calamity in non-Western regions and peoples, rather than identifying it as a practice at the heart of state sovereignty and capitalist profit. In this chapter, by critically examining global sex-trafficking campaigns, I hope to foreground the power of the media as a leading force in shaping transnational policies, perception, and public sentiment against migrants, even when the focus is elsewhere.

In order to understand the media's role in redistributing symbolic and material power from the transnational to the national, I analyze antitrafficking media campaigns that have appeared in a variety of media formats—film documentaries, art exhibits, and campaigns by nongovernmental organizations (NGOs)—funded by the United Nations and launched in the United States, Britain, and Brazil. I argue that UN media campaigns traffic transnational metaphors of slavery to foment gendered social panics that reinvigorate national boundaries and exclusions, sovereignty, and exceptionalism. In other words, the transnational sphere—especially notions of gender, time, and space—is a critical fiction dramatized in the media to bolster the nation-state's global moral authority. How, I ask, does the media not only enlist citizens' support for heightened state power but also demand everyday civic participation in more invasive forms of surveillance against migrants, sex workers, and traffickers? The broad scope of media outlets, from the United States to Britain to Brazil, opens up three areas of inquiry: First, the media preserves the image of the West as the modern endpoint, the saving force that can turn victims into progressive subjects of the future. Simultaneously, certain "foreign" bodies are rendered incompatible with Western modernity and must be expunged from the nation. And lastly, I turn to Brazilian NGO campaigns, to compare how media campaigns similarly arrest the movement of women through fears of sexualized violence, but I also redirect the media gaze to the West, rather than the Global South, as the source of violent practices of slave labor and exploitation.

Sex Trafficking as the "New Slave Trade"

Contemporary discourses against sex trafficking as the "New Slave Trade" today resonate with the social anxieties expressed over the "white slavery trade" at the turn of the nineteenth century. During a time of economic decline in Europe, the number of European migrants entering the United States became a major concern, especially when it was discovered that many of these migrants were single women who came to find a better life, although oftentimes this meant working as a prostitute.[14] Similar to today, media attention to sex trafficking corresponded to a time when the migration of women from non-Western countries was on the rise.[15] Mark P. Lagon, ambassador and director of the State Department's Office to Monitor and Combat Trafficking in Persons (TIP), stated that 80 percent of all contemporary trafficking cases involve women.[16] Yet, unlike the "white slavery" crisis (that many historians argue was also exaggerated by the media), the group of women in need of rescue has changed. Today, the majority of female migrants targeted are not French, Italian, Swedish, or (Russian) Jewish but are from Asia, India, Russia, and Latin America. Despite the fact that migrant women came from many countries in the early 1900s, only certain bodies were depicted as worthy of being saved from the "slave trade." Morality and innocence, defined within a transnational context of gender and race, determined which bodies were in need of reform and, ultimately, citizenship. At the turn of the twentieth century, Chinese immigrant women were popularly imagined as "natural" slaves because of their projected lack of value back in China. Both Japanese and Chinese women were considered naturally "wayward" girls who voluntarily sought prostitution, in contrast to the "sympathetic images of naïve ethnic European women tricked or seduced into prostitution."[17] Only the true victims—white women equated with morality and innocence who could not possibly choose prostitution—deserved the protection of the law. Dierdra M. Moloney argues that Mexican migrant prostitutes during this time, considered contingent labor, were not as threatening as European women, who were considered permanent migrants and future citizens. Furthermore, Mexican migrant prostitutes serviced their own communities, unlike European prostitutes, who were imagined to threaten Anglo families and communities.[18]

It is striking that both panics emphasize the slavery of innocent women. The focus on slavery shifts attention from the exploitation and victimization of racialized bodies—African slaves and racialized migrants—to white women and, by extension, the nation. The abuse of white women's bodies is seen as particularly abhorrent, ranking worse than slavery, thus erasing the humanity of blacks as well as the sexual exploitation of black women.[19] The abolitionist stance in the 1900s and today configure sex trafficking to be the most pressing form of slavery, deserving immediate moral attention. Though less visible than the campaigns against the slavery of blacks in the nineteenth century or the exploitation of migrant labor today, today's antislavery movement, predicated on protecting "the innocent," has ignited Christian activism and media campaigns meant to expose the hidden evils of such a crime against humanity.[20] Both panics also focus attention on empowering the state in an attempt to bring about order during a time of great changes in the movement of people and capital.

Contemporary policies against sex trafficking, beginning with the 2000 TVPA, stimulate popular support through campaigns that define sex trafficking as an archaic form of slavery. So heinous a crime is sex trafficking that the website of the United Nations' Global Initiative to Fight Human Trafficking (UN.GIFT) brands this phenomenon in bold black letters stretched across the yellow tape that one would find at the scene of a crime: "Human Trafficking: Crime That Shames Us All."[21] Sex trafficking is reinforced as a morally shameful act. Even the use of "shame," a moral technique that relies on social surveillance, normalizes one's sense of outrage and disgust against sex trafficking, foreshadowing the dramatic tone that sets this crime at a tenor above the rest. It is the toxic mixture of sex and slavery that is meant to moralize and educate the viewer-as-patriot to take necessary action to end this form of exploitation that is encroaching across U.S. borders and seeping into cities and neighborhoods. The boundaries between "us" and "them" are clear, although the line threatens to collapse in the event of apathy. Thus, the range of media campaigns targeted toward eradicating sex trafficking educate the viewer as to how trafficking works, how to determine who is involved, and how to do something about it. Everyday viewers are implored not only to participate in an ideological battle over migration but also to actively engage in the apprehension and surveillance of migrants.

To associate sexual exploitation with trafficking presumes that this new form of human slavery is imported from elsewhere, that migrants who come to the United States threaten to demolish "our" way of life.[22] The association of trafficking with slavery invokes a precapitalist era of highly exploitative labor conditions that wreak havoc on the national fantasy that slavery can be contained to the past, rather than being recognized as a practice and ideology at the heart of capitalist expansion. Furthermore, the reference to slavery is necessary in order to isolate capitalism within a progressive and democratic trajectory born in the West, while locating barbaric practices of authoritarian rule elsewhere.[23] TIP ambassador Mark P. Lagon defends the absence of the United States from the "Special Watch List" of countries and its status in fighting trafficking: "You know, the United

States is not only in a position to point fingers. We need to say we had our legacy of slavery, we had our legacy of segregation, we had our legacy of discrimination. Serious democracies have evolved."[24] Slavery, segregation, and discrimination are relegated to the past. As the moral leader in this fight, the West is racially polluted by the infiltration of sex trafficking, it is tainted with exploitation, and its modern status is threatened. Since slavery coincides with the precapitalist past, it must be purged as incompatible with current forms of capitalism and democracy. For example, during a statement to a group in Florida on efforts to combat sex trafficking, former president George W. Bush justified the eradication of socialism and the transition to democracy in Cuba by critiquing Cuba's dictator, Fidel Castro, who has refused to participate in the global fight against sex trafficking. Bush accused Castro of abetting the enslavement of women in Cuba in his welcoming statement to sex tourists: "Cuba has one of the cleanest and most educated prostitutes in the world."[25] The status of women, especially their sexual exploitation via prostitution, represents a nation's alignment with, or inability to achieve, sovereignty and democracy, as well as its modern status in fighting for the human rights of women. Within the transnational space of Miami and the nation at large, the status of women marks the barometer of disorder across global flows but also serves as the anchor for reestablishing national order.

In order to protect the integrity of democracy and modernity in the United States, documentaries, films, and television reenactments reinforce viewer consent in expunging this modern form of enslaved prostitution from U.S. cities and borders. In the beginning of Michael Corey Davis's documentary film *Cargo: Innocence Lost*, reenacted scenes of forced sex with minors are mysteriously set in black-and-white film-noir style that dramatizes "real events," in contrast to the rational documentary-style interviews with various experts including detectives, police officers, psychologists, lawyers, NGO workers, and agents from the U.S. Department of Health and Human Services. The fictional black-and-white dramatic scenes, suspended in slow motion, contrast with the real-time, full-color frames of documentary-style interviews with victims and experts. The tension here between the fictive world of violence and the veracity of expert testimony authorizes a desire to purge the scenes of racialized violence, of fiction, of the unknown, and to enter the verifiable present of rational time and space of the nation, of modernity, and of whiteness. Given the difficulty of tracking evidence of sex trafficking, fiction fills the gaps between what is known and what is unknown and, through repetition, becomes truth or part of the repertoire of cultural knowledge. The only way to access the "other" is to become swallowed in the horror and pain of suffering. The desire to rid exploitation is entangled in the longing to purge the scene (and by extension, the nation) of suffering and, therefore, of the racialized subjects attached to pain.[26] Suffering must also be rehabilitated into Western values of happiness, success, and individual achievement. Freedom, in contrast to slavelike conditions, entails absolving the nation of suffering.

The film informs and disturbs our desire to know and uncover the underworld of sex trafficking. From the outset, we are led to understand that this is no longer simply a "foreign affliction" but an aberration that strikes "Anytowns" in the United States.[27] Scenes depicting domestic cases of sexual abuse are framed by a roving camera that scans neighborhoods "littered" with images of massage parlors and the neon signs advertising to an Asian and Latino clientele. All commercialized sexuality is rendered exploitative, and these markets and acts are mapped onto the bodies of migrants of color. In addition, trafficking is characterized as a form of barbarian violence and authoritarian rule imported by international illegal migrant crime syndicates. The film draws heavily from interviews with coordinators of the Polaris Project (an NGO funded by the United Nations and supported by Mark P. Lagon, who accepted the position as executive director in February 2009). One of the coordinators outlines the "coercive chart" used by criminal networks today that resonates with the method of control wielded by fascist regimes and gulags, or Russian penal-labor camps. The psychological profile of criminal syndicates today and in the past is the same: perpetrators isolate victims from support networks to break their will, which is necessary for individuals to allow themselves to be penetrated. The use of psychology to understand the motivations of traffickers and victims blames individuals and a culture of absolute power that thrives outside the law and thus outside the nation.

To protect the innocent, the state must move deviant sexuality from the shadows and into visibility, to know all the dark contours of its secrets.[28] The film authorizes the experts, who assure viewers that once we know all the contours of this deviant sexuality, we can eradicate it. The metaphors of light and darkness simplify the problem as a patriotic fight of good against evil, rendering invisible how structures of poverty make sex work an inevitable option.[29] That women would choose sex work as an avenue toward economic mobility becomes incomprehensible, further stigmatizing those who do so. In fact, in various news editorials, we are led to many cases in which women return to their traffickers or other sites of sex work for lack of other options.[30]

The state's moral authority in this "battle" is so fierce that an attorney (and father of two girls) from Houston, Texas, portrayed in the film *Cargo*, finds this crime to be so barbaric that any man found in this situation "should be strung up in town square and hung up by his testicles." The reference here to public lynching is historically chilling and a sober reminder of the moral ground that justifies counterviolence against traffickers and clients alike. Slavery can hardly be contained to the past as it continues to demarcate legal versus criminal parameters and continues to discipline African Americans and all others who step out of line. Not even the law, however, is sufficient to punish this caliber of brutality against the most innocent. One is reminded of the violence against and rationale for imprisoning newly freed black slaves, who were imagined to threaten the purity of white women. These fantasies of revenge against the villain who tortures innocent women are deeply ingrained in U.S. popular culture, sanctioning sentiments of national victimization and counterviolence. These Western (cowboy) plots validate and normalize a state of exception similar to authoritarian regimes that empower heightened governmentality, including authorizing everyday citizens to take the law into their own hands.[31]

Media Activism, Patriotism, and Surveillance

The challenge today (similar to the 1900s) is how to distinguish the innocent victims from those who knowingly break the law. One of the U.S. government's strategies in saving victims and catching traffickers has been to pay one of the largest global public-relations corporations operating in over fifty countries, Ketchum, to launch an advertising campaign to spread knowledge of this impending crisis and to purify the image of the United States around the world. In collaboration with the United Nations and the Ricky Martin Foundation, this global corporation commenced an ad campaign around the world based on their motto: "Look Beneath the Surface: Rescue & Restore Victims of Human Trafficking."[32] Ketchum spread sex-trafficking campaigns to nearly two hundred million media impressions on prime-time television networks, newspapers, and radio networks in the United States and around the world. Part of Ketchum's strategy for global distribution involves the use of globally recognizable Hollywood figures to achieve transnational visibility, marketability, and translation.

Ketchum's main website ad depicts a young, attractive Latina looking down toward her handcuffed hands folded in front of her mouth as if in prayer. She is voiceless and in need of rescue. Under the photo, a caption reads, "The next prostitute, stripper, illegal immigrant, runaway youth, domestic servant, or migrant worker you encounter or take into custody may be a victim of human trafficking" (see figure 6.1). Each ad depicts Latina, Asian, or young white (Russian) women in scenes of bondage, either crouched down in the dark corner of a room or in prisonlike surroundings. It is not their undocumented, and thus hidden, labor that is the cause for their potential exploitation; it is their potential for sexualized abuse that is of concern. Beneath the 1-800 number is the following text: "Helping trafficking victims can help you shut down the real criminals." These misrecognized feminized figures are not the "true" culprits but are victims of traffickers lurking in the dark spaces beyond the frame. It is precisely the instability

Fig. 6.1. Ketchum's ad campaign focused on depicting the victims of human trafficking as modern-day slaves.

of visual cues—the hidden force of this crime and the difficulty of relying on bodily cues—that challenges antitrafficking strategies. In the absence of clues on the culprits, the ads rely on already formulated knowledge of the typology of the criminal that haunts the framing of the innocent victim. The profile of the victim comes into focus via photos of young, mostly Latina, Asian, and white migrant women cast as immobile and helpless.

Ketchum designed posters, videos, pamphlets, and PowerPoint presentations to train and unify the efforts of three primary groups: health providers (including the U.S. Department of Health and Human Services); police, FBI, and immigration officers; NGOs and faith-based communities. In the police documents, there is a clear desire to unite local citizens as well as county and state police units with federal agencies. A video describes the need for police officials to meticulously document all suspicious behavior and to submit this documentation to the FBI and the U.S. Immigration and Customs Enforcement (ICE). While cross-border movements are the jurisdiction of the federal government, they also need local officials to dismantle international trafficking rings that bypass the border and proliferate across state boundaries. Everyday individuals, too, are offered guidelines in Ketchum's pamphlets and websites on how to detect victims: "A person who is trafficked may look like many of the people you see daily, but asking the right questions and looking for small clues will help you identify those people who have been *forced or coerced* into a life of sexual exploitation or forced labor."[33] Questions they suggest asking when faced with suspicious migrants include whether they are forced to work; whether they speak English; whether they were recently brought from eastern Europe, Asia, Latin America, Canada, Africa, or India; whether they lack a passport or other immigration or identification documentation; and whether they are held against their will.

Even though the line between "undocumented" migrants and those who are trafficked is difficult, if not impossible, to determine, the adoption of these forms of civic surveillance coincided with the increase in immigrant deportation raids since the INS was taken over by the Department of Homeland Security after the events of September 11. Congress implemented the Illegal Immigration Reform and Immigrant Responsibility Act in 1996, resulting in the deportation of more than five hundred thousand people to more than 160 countries around the world.[34] In the name of national security, the Bush administration transformed its policy of "catch and release" to "catch and return." Rather than return Mexican nationals and Latinos to the border, where they merely crossed back into the United States, many are dumped off into the interior of Mexico or as far as Guatemala or El Salvador. The majority of deportees become displaced persons, as they have no family or social ties to the locations to which they are sent, thus generating great instability in Mexico, Latin America, and ultimately back in the United States.[35] These policies fail to consider the cost to Latin American governments, which lack the time, infrastructure, and resources to handle this influx of displaced populations. To survive without the help of one's family, one's community, or the government, some of the deportees turn to the underground economy, such as the smuggling and sex-trafficking trades.[36] Despite actual corporate, or in this case state, complicity in migrant trafficking, carefully crafted media campaigns play a powerful role in protecting the moral reputation of those companies or states that apparently fight against sex trafficking, even when the evidence suggests otherwise.

The majority of UN trafficking campaigns, including Ketchum's, display the trafficking hotline number for everyday citizens to call if they witness behavior that may be a case of trafficking, similar to the hotline number used to turn in "undocumented" migrants. Citizenship is enacted through everyday participation in an increasingly wider scope of issues related to national security. One of the many consequences of the conflation of neoliberal notions of private property, citizenship, and the protection of state borders exploded in the lawless practices engaged in by vigilante groups along the southern U.S. border.[37]

Dramatizations of Sex Trafficking: Human Value and Human Rights

Much of the success of media activism against trafficking has been the passionate outreach by various actors and actresses such as Emma Thompson, Ricky Martin, Michael Corey Davis, and Daryl Hannah, who have used their global media cachet to raise public awareness against trafficking. Celebrities prop up a neoliberal order reliant on the global appeal and power of individuals to elicit change. Most of the campaigns depend on the innocence of women and children to humanize the victims and to ignite broad public sentiment and activism against trafficking. Especially relevant are the exhibition and documentaries by British actress Emma Thompson. Thompson worked closely with a team of curators on an interactive art exhibition, "Journey," that premiered in Trafalgar Square in London 2007 and then again at the UN Global Trafficking Conference in Vienna in 2008.

"Journey," similar to media campaigns on trafficking, demands more than pure spectatorship. This interactive, clunky exhibit of seven shipping containers is spray-painted with colorful graffiti images of prostitutes in chains, again emphasizing the enslavement of women. Reminiscent of the forced passage of African slaves, this journey from eastern Europe to Great Britain is also, curiously, an inner voyage that metaphorically takes one through a forced rite of passage from innocence to maturity, from the primordial womb to the marketplace of sex and adulthood. One is led through seven thematic cargo containers that reflect the experiences of Thompson's coproducer, a Moldovan woman named Elena who was trafficked into the sex trade at the age of eighteen. The first container, "Hope," initiates the viewer into the sex worker's life back home when she was a child to set the scene for her transformation from innocent to destitute. One peers through a keyhole to see the life this woman led as a child back home in eastern Europe. Written on the child's bedroom walls are the words, "I dreamed that I could be someone special. I just wanted to go to school." To become a citizen-subject is to have the freedom to strive for the future, in opposition to being a mechanized object that is stuck in a repetitive motion that objectifies and absolves the subject of personhood and value. This becomes clear later as one moves through a colorful curtain of condoms to enter a foul-smelling bedroom

Fig. 6.2. Graffiti art image of a prostitute's chained ankle, part of the "Journey" art exhibition.

where a rickety bed simulates the up-and-down movement of mechanical sex, sex devoid of emotion. Exploitation is defined by repetitive sexual penetration and forced movement. Whether or not one takes the journey, the media coverage of the exhibit provides the outlet to direct the collective gaze toward what we learn to be the most heinous abuse of women's most intimate human rights. It is in the shift in gaze from Elena's exterior to her interior, the universality of her inner being, that she becomes human. The masses of bodies used up by mechanization, as in the case of factory workers, stand apart from Elena, an appropriate neoliberal feminist figure who aspires to be more. Only the private features of her life are made visible within a transnational terrain, while the economic inequalities across nations do not fit this story of individual heroism.

There is nothing sexy or familiar about this exhibit. Rather than lead us through a voyeuristic tour of women's sexualized bodies, another container invites spectatorship through an oval hole carved to fit the face. At the moment of peering into a hole to find the "other," one's mirror image is reflected back on the sex worker's body. Not only is the "other" reflected back as "you," but the bodies are slumped over in chairs or depicted with flesh protruding out of tightly fitted skirts. The easy slippage between the self and the other is reinforced by the description of the circumstances that lead some women to trafficking: "When her father died, the family's income dried up and Elena was easily seduced, like many other girls with few other options, into sex work." That the "other" could easily become "us" leads us into the deep anxieties of the fall of the West. Elena's tragedy reflects that of the former Soviet Union, and viewers are asked to momentarily imagine a bleak future as "their" present. Immigration similarly brings these anxieties to the forefront as Thompson explains her motive for organizing the exhibit: "Londoners are already uncomfortable in their own city, because they are uncomfortable with the number of strangers and the strange languages they hear. We are showing them what the reality of the lives of some of these women is like—the women who are sold into slavery and tortured." Popular sympathy, important in humanizing bodies that are imagined as "other," however, can only be imagined for the most extreme cases of sexualized female exploitation. While the focus here is on sex-trafficking victims, the underlying anxiety assuaged is that of difference and the threat migrants pose to the stability of British culture and ethnicity. Elena, we discover, is not so different after all, and thus she is one of the "exceptional" migrants who deserves citizenship.

Structures of gazing and the desire to know are entangled in dehumanizing the female body but also in setting her free. In "Journey," the pleasure of looking is consciously denied in order to break the violence of eroticization and female objectification.[38] The intent is not simply to blame individual clients but rather to question collective complicity in this inhuman exploitation. The exhibit questions the categorization of certain bodies as nonhuman, or as exploitable, and reroutes empathy for women in the hope of ending sexualized violence.

Destabilizing the social gaze from these women's bodies and onto the viewer has the potential to elicit empathy for devalued foreign bodies. The end of the exhibit demands more than sympathy. Knowledge of these acts or crimes against humanity burdens one to act. Upon the visitor's exiting the tour, there are petitions to sign that would bring about more legislation to protect the women caught up in sex work. Rather than advocating for the deportation or detention of the women, as was done in the early years of the TVPA, Thompson has been active in advocating for laws that support the rehabilitation and needs of the women. Yet, rather than demand rights or citizenship status, Thompson's activism, like most NGO approaches to trafficking, deploys empathy for the human dignity of women regardless of race, class, or national status in the form of protection and rehabilitation.[39]

There is a success story at the end of the exhibit. Elena is currently a UK-based lawyer fighting for other trafficked victims. The celebration of the individual who makes it against all odds is seductive, but it raises a question about the use of exceptional cases of individual success as a barometer to normalize the good life. There is a Western neoliberal feminist vision at play here that stimulates middle-class dreams of transforming women from victims, or sexualized objects, to powerful subjects in high-powered suits. While there is potential for Elena to transform the British legal system, the implication is that capitalism and the marketplace will save the day and must be revived as a myth that will, ironically, continue to draw more migrants to the West. There is little need for rights when the market proves able to rectify inequalities.

At stake in these dramatizations of sex trafficking are universal notions of human rights and the distribution of value. A short film clip on the Helen Bamber Foundation's website shows Thompson enacting a violent rape scene of a woman in chains. The culprit is again invisible, as the camera sharpens on Thompson's reenactment of this woman's inner metamorphosis, symbolized by her name change from Elena to Maria. Maria exudes death as she becomes numb after her transformation from human to a machine, an object of pleasure devoid of feelings, without a future trajectory, stuck in a present of repetitive motion and penetrated by an invisible, masculinized foreign body. Maria is forced to have sex with more than forty clients a day. The use of ethnic names here is striking, as Elena's transformation from subject to object, from human to devalued commodity suggests her shift from the (almost) white body of Elena to the racialized body of Maria. While both are common names in eastern Europe and Mexico, Elena symbolizes the possibility of whiteness as the only form of subjectivity that can embody value. Her white body symbolizes the nation, while Maria represents England's anxious transformation from innocence into a country enslaved by the penetration of foreign bodies. To be enslaved is to become racialized, to occupy the time of the past, the space of the foreign, to become a figure of tragedy and loss, and to become a victim of capitalist use and waste.[40] These media forms work through a culture of repetition through which Western nations embody the time and space of modernity, which must be quarantined from other gendered bodies that reproduce scenes of lack, suffering, and death.

NGOs and International Media Campaigns

Public service announcements displayed on the UN website, *telenovelas,* and billboard advertisements launched by Ketchum have flooded Asia, Russia, and Latin America with a similar message: women who migrate abroad are likely to be sexually abused or trafficked into the sex trade and, thus, should remain at home. Although funds funneled into NGOs for combating sex trafficking can be seen as a positive step in empowering local agencies in rehabilitating victims, many NGOs have shifted their scope from migrant abuse cases more broadly to solely targeting sex-trafficking victims.[41] Not only has the government attempted to attack the problem of unwanted migration and specifically sex trafficking from the U.S. side, but President Bush and the United Nations have channeled funds into international NGOs and media campaigns to halt the flow of female migrants even before they reach the border.

Projeto Trama (or Project Trama), a Brazilian NGO, worked with UN.GIFT to splatter airports with a passport ad campaign that associates feminized mobility with sexualized danger, the loss of innocence, and death.[42] Ads repeat images of women in transit with pain and suffering. For example, on one passport photo ad we see a woman turned away, with only her bare neck exposed (see figure 6.3). She rubs her neck as she looks down, in an obvious gesture of pain and humiliation. This series of ads asks the potential female viewer to choose one of two choices that, in actuality, are the same: One is *"Ser explorada em un pais estranho"* (To be exploited in a foreign country). If you travel abroad, in other words, you leave yourself no option but to choose exploitation. The other choice is *"Ser explorada sexualmente dia e noite"* (To be sexually exploited day and night).[43] Although accounts of men are rampant in sex-trafficking cases, these campaigns make evident the gendered consequences of trafficking. Male migrants are also dissuaded from migrating via images of field workers: *"Trabalhar sem descanso e sem salário até o fim do dia"* (To work until the end of the day without rest and without pay). In contrast to President Lulu's statement to TIP that Brazil suffers from slavery, a confessional demanded by the TIP report if nations such as Brazil want to continue trade relations, Projeto Trama's campaign shifts the media gaze to the West as the breeding ground for barbaric labor practices.[44] Although these campaigns equate feminized mobility or transit with sexualized trauma, Brazilian women are not naturalized as the harbinger of pain and death. The ads function on two levels: to keep women from migrating and to shift the gaze on the West as a violent and contaminating force.

Another goal of Projeto Trama has been to educate women as to how to avoid trafficking scams. A mock newspaper ad targeting young professional women seeking exciting and high-paying international jobs included listings for dancers,

Fig. 6.3. Projeto Trama's ad campaigns included passport images such as this one to depict the pain, suffering, and humiliation of sexual exploitation.

models, personal assistants, manicurists, and secretaries. Next to a picture of three young smiling women are catchy phrases typical of these ads: "*Independencia financeira. Sucesso profissional. Qualidade de vida. E o melhor: recebendo em dolar ou euro!*" (Financial independence. Professional success. Quality of life. And the best part: we pay in dollars or euros!). These ads, Projeto Trama states, lure aspiring women to wealthy nations. The profile of "at risk" populations includes women who seek to improve their lives and realize their dreams of traveling, buying their own home, finding success, marrying, and achieving Western imported models of "happiness." These Western dreams, Projeto Trama counters, are traps that lure women into sex trafficking and reduce women "*a uma mercadoria*" (into merchandise).

Almost all forms of feminized migration and mobility (with the notable exception of domestic work) are constructed as high risk.[45] Even as the demand for domestic workers is on the rise, more restrictions, such as those regarding vocational training, language, and education, have been placed on women seeking marriage visas, as well as entertainment, modeling, and dancer visas.[46] Not only does the media powerfully discipline gendered behavior across transnational terrains, but foregrounding sexualized exploitation in regard to gendered mobility has material consequences for collapsing important migration avenues for women, rather than opening up new ways to ensure women's access to safe and secure routes.

Conclusion

By focusing on the global media outreach against trafficking, this chapter has demonstrated the extent to which nation-state power and sovereignty are reliant on mediating global gendered panics, through which the state can assert itself as the moral global force protecting the human rights of the most vulnerable, in this case, innocent women. Even when the evidence of trafficking cases suggests a more complex picture, these moral dramas extend and expand the power of the state to an array of actors, including individuals, to purge the nation of "foreign" male bodies, often portrayed as migrants. The global scope of the problem is pulled into a hierarchical cartographic mapping by the media, which continues to purge the nation of memory, history, and suffering and thus of the problem's transnational origins. Media campaigns, while global in scope, blind us by what they make visible in relation to what remains hidden. Ketchum's media campaign, UN websites, and media productions by global celebrities transform the transnational image of the United States and other states from the perpetrator of aggressive displacement of populations to the heroic force paving the way in the global fight for human rights.

The focus on individual "culprits" and nations also functions to elide the transnational structural forces that make sex work and migration, on the one hand, and trafficking networks, on the other, necessary gendered strategies of survival by populations displaced by Western-led trade agreements, deportation tactics, corporate demand for cheap labor, and consumer demand for sexual pleasure. While we are called into action as concerned patriots and nationals, we must be ever more alert to the misleading force of the media in pitching the problem, its scope, and its solution within neoliberal values that may function to enact even more widespread violence against the masses of exploited laborers who do not fit the "exceptional" category of the "innocent victim." At the same time, the focus on saving individual "victims" makes it possible for a national feminist political vision to emerge in support of undocumented women such as Elena to obtain citizenship, so she can move from the dark shadows of sex trafficking and climb the legal scaffolding of British society as a lawyer. Yet even focusing on bringing people from out of the shadows of the law and into legal structures forgets, again, how closely embedded legal structures are within hegemonic constructions of the nation as an innocent, sexually pure, and moral body.

1. Some of the groups actively fighting sex trafficking include abolitionist women's organizations such as the Coalition Against Trafficking in Women (CATW) and Equality Now, Christian organizations including the National Association of Evangelicals, Concerned Women for America, the Salvation Army, Focus on the Family, and thousands of local and international nongovernmental organizations.

2. These funds have trickled down to forty-two Justice Department task forces, the HHS (Health and Human Services), domestic and international nongovernmental organizations (NGOs), Christian and Catholic organizations, and feminist abolitionist NGOs.

3. These statistics have been repeated in media news coverage, newspapers, and documentaries on sex trafficking. See the White House Office of the Press Secretary, "President Announces Initiatives to Combat Human Trafficking" (July 16, 2004), http://georgewbush-whitehouse. archives.gov/news/releases/2004/07/20040716-11.html (accessed August 8, 2010).

4. Jerry Markon, "Human Trafficking Evokes Outrage, Little Evidence," *Washington Post* (September 23, 2007): A01; Debbie Nathan, "Oversexed," *Nation* (August 29, 2005): 27–30. Also see Laura María Agustín, *Sex at the Margins: Migration, Labour Markets and the Rescue Industry* (London: Zed Books, 2007).

5. United Nations Protocol to Prevent, Suppress and Punish Trafficking in Persons, Especially Women and Children (2000), Article 3.

6. Wendy Chapkis, "Soft Glove, Punishing Fist: The Trafficking Victims Protection Act of 2000," in Elizabeth Bernstein and Laurie Schaffner, eds., *Regulating Sex: The Politics of Intimacy and Identity* (New York: Routledge, 2005).

7. Nathan, "Oversexed."

8. See Eithne Luibhéid's *Entry Denied: Controlling Sexuality at the Border* (Minneapolis: University of Minnesota Press, 2002) and the book she edited with Lionel Cantú, *Queer Migrations: Sexuality, U.S. Citizenship, and Border Crossings* (Minneapolis: University of Minnesota Press, 2005).

9. For some scholars such as Ronald Weitzer, heightened attention to women's trafficking through the sex trade has authorized what Weitzer calls a "moral crusade" against prostitution as the most grotesque form of exploitation against women. Ronald Weitzer, "The Social Construction of Sex Trafficking: Ideology and Institutionalization of a Moral Crusade," *Politics and Society* 35, no. 3 (September 2007): 447–475. NGO groups run by radical feminists, such as the Coalition Against Trafficking in Women, envision prostitution as encapsulating a broad framework of male domination—whether women enter into it voluntarily or not, whether legal or illegal. Laura María Agustín, *Sex at the Margins: Migration, Labour Markets and the Rescue Industry* (New York: Zed Books, 2007), 33. Others, such as Kamala Kempadoo, have intervened in the debate by arguing that prostitution should be considered a form of labor, a shift from questions of morality to the need to protect women's rights as laborers. Kamala Kempadoo and Jo Doezema, eds., *Global Sex Workers: Rights, Resistance, and Redefinition* (New York: Routledge, 1998).

10. The White House Office of the Press Secretary, "Trafficking in Persons National Security Presidential Directive" (February 25, 2003), http://georgewbush-whitehouse.archives.gov/news/releases/2003/02/20030225.html (accessed on August 8, 2010).

11. Various feminist scholars have critiqued the platform of "saving" women and children to justify military aggression and war. See Saba Mahmood, "Feminism, the Taliban and Politics of

Counter-Insurgency," *Anthropological Quarterly* 75, no. 2 (Spring 2002): 339–354; Cynthia Enloe, *The Curious Feminist: Searching for Women in a New Age of Empire* (Berkeley: University of California Press, 2004).

12. Mark P. Lagon entreats corporations to participate in antitrafficking as philanthropists. See the statement from April 14, 2008, "Ambassador Lagon Discusses How to Combat Human Trafficking," on the America.gov website: http://www.america.gov/st/washfile-english/2008/April/20080414142804xjsnommiso.6027033.html (accessed June 12, 2008).

13. See Stephanie E. Tanger, "Enforcing Corporate Responsibility for Violations of Workplace Immigration Laws: The Case of Meatpacking," *Harvard Latino Law Review* 9 (2006): 59–89. For the role of the state in an obvious form of trafficking, see Cam Simpson, "US: Pentagon Stalls on Banning Contractors from Using Forced Labor," *Chicago Tribune* (December 27, 2005): 1.

14. See Donna J. Guy, "'White Slavery': Citizenship and Nationality in Argentina," in Andrew Parker, Mary Russo, Doris Sommer, and Patricia Yaeger, eds., *Nationalisms and Sexualities* (New York: Routledge, 1992), 201–217.

15. Between 1900 and 1910, women made up about 30 percent of all new arrivals, and that percentage increased over the following decades, to 43 percent in 1915 and 46 percent in 1925; women were the majority by 1930. See Martha Gardner, *The Qualities of a Citizen: Women, Immigration, and Citizenship, 1870–1965* (Princeton, NJ: Princeton University Press, 2005).

16. "Ambassador Lagon Discusses How to Combat Human Trafficking."

17. Gardner, *The Qualities of a Citizen*, 56.

18. Deirdre M. Moloney, "Women, Sexual Morality, and Economic Dependency in Early U.S. Deportation Policy," *Journal of Women's History* 18, no. 2 (2006): 105.

19. See Mary Ann Irwin, "'White Slavery' as Metaphor: Anatomy of a Moral Panic," *Ex Post Facto: The History Journal* (San Francisco: History Department, San Francisco State University) 5 (1996).

20. Ibid. Also see the website for Concerned Women for America: Brenda Zurita, "Christians Shine the Light on Sex Trafficking," http://www.cwfa.org/familyvoice/2005-07/sextrafficking_july_august.pdf.

21. UN.GIFT home page, http://www.ungift.org/ (accessed July 6, 2008).

22. Migrants have been depicted alongside various threats to the nation as (1) an invasion, through feminized discourses of fertility (see Leo Chavez, *Covering Immigration: Popular Images and the Politics of the Nation* [Berkeley: University of California Press, 2001]), and (2) as a health threat (Alexandra Minha Stern, "Buildings, Boundaries, and Blood: Medicalization and Nation-Building on the U.S.-Mexico Border, 1910–1930," *Hispanic American Historical Review* 79, no. 1 [February 1999]: 41–81; and Jonathan Xavier Inda, "The Value of Immigrant Life," in Denise Segura and Patricia Zavella, eds., *Women and Migration in the U.S-Mexico Borderland: A Reader* [Durham, NC: Duke University Press, 2007]).

23. For example, Kamala Kempadoo identifies the neocolonialist framework of sex trafficking in Kathleen Barry's book *The Prostitution of Sexuality: The Global Exploitation of Women* (New York: New York University Press, 1995). Barry situates the trafficking of women in anachronistic time and space as it "prevails in pre-industrial and feudal societies that are primarily agricultural and where women are excluded from the public sphere" and where women, she states, are the exclusive property of men. At the other end she places the "post-industrial, developed societies feature women who "achieve the potential for economic independence." Kamala Kempadoo, "Introduction: Globalizing Sex Workers' Rights," in Kempadoo and Doezema, *Global Sex Workers*, 11.

24. U.S. Department of State, "Release of the Seventh Annual Trafficking in Persons Report, Ambassador Mark P. Lagon, Senior Advisor on Trafficking in Persons" (June 12, 2007), http://www.state.gov/g/tip/rls/rm/07/86306.htm (accessed July 6, 2008).

25. White House Office of the Press Secretary, "President Announces Initiatives to Combat Human Trafficking." Bush also signed the Protect Act, making it a crime for U.S. men to engage in prostitution in other countries.

26. Lauren Berlant, "The Subject of True Feeling: Pain, Privacy, and Politics," in Sara Ahmed, ed., *Transformations: Thinking through Feminism* (New York: Routledge, 2000).

27. The reference to "Anytown" was made in Peter Landsman's lengthy article about Mexican nationals without documentation who were found in a middle-class U.S. home with squalid conditions that he compares to a nineteenth-century slave ship. See Peter Landsman, "The Girls Next Door," *New York Times* (January 25, 2004), http://query.nytimes.com/gst/fullpage.html?res=9B04EEDA1439F936A15752C0A9629C8B63 (accessed June 14, 2007).

28. In the *History of Sexuality*, Foucault argues that sexuality is far from repressed but in actuality is produced through state discourses. See Michel Foucault, *The History of Sexuality, Volume 1: An Introduction*, trans. Robert Hurley (New York: Vintage Books, 1990).

29. During media accounting of the "white slave trade" in the early 1900s, state power was authorized, argues Mary Ann Irwin, through metaphors of light. The state was equated with godly powers from above, shining a light into the unknown and cleansing and purifying the nation from the forces of evil. Irwin, "'White Slavery' as Metaphor."

30. William Finnegan, "The Countertraffickers: Rescuing the Victims of the Global Sex Trade," *New Yorker* (May 5, 2008): 44–59.

31. Ashley Dawson and Malini Johar Schueleer, eds., *Exceptional State: Contemporary U.S. Culture and the New Imperialism* (Durham, NC: Duke University Press, 2007).

32. For the array of posters in English, Spanish, and various Asian languages, see U.S. Department of Health and Human Services, Administration for Families and Children, "Campaign Fact Sheets," http://www.acf.hhs.gov/trafficking/about/posters.html (accessed August 8, 2008).

33. See U.S. Department of Health and Human Services, Administration for Families and Children, "Resources: Identifying and Interacting with Victims of Human Trafficking" (emphasis added), www.acf.hhs.gov/trafficking/campaign_kits/tool_kit_law/identfy_victims.pdf (accessed August 8, 2008).

34. In addition, roughly 13,350 Mexican nationals are serving time in California state prisons, and 20,000 are in the federal penitentiary system; all of them will be deported at the end of their sentences. See Salvador A. Cicero-Domínguez, "Assessing the U.S.-Mexico Fight against Human Trafficking and Smuggling: Unintended Results of U.S. Immigration Policy," *Northwestern Journal of International Human Rights* 4, no. 2 (Fall 2005): 319.

35. Gang activity in Honduras and El Salvador has grown exponentially due to the deportation of young boys who often grew up in the United States. See Tom Hayden, "When Deportation Is a Death Sentence," *Los Angeles Times* (June 28, 2004), available at http://www.commondreams.org/views04/0628-06.htm.

36. See Kit R. Roane, "Gangs Turn to New Trade: Young Prostitutes," *New York Times* (July 11, 1999), available at http://psych.colorado.edu/~blechman/Th3-6.html; and "Crack Blamed for Rise in Central American Child Prostitution," *Miami Herald* (November 22, 1999), available at http://www.latinamericanstudies.org/guatemala/crack.htm.

37. See Roxanne Lynn Doty, "States of Exception on the Mexico-U.S. Border: Security, 'Decisions,' and Civilian Border Patrol," *International Political Sociology* 1 (June 2007): 113–137.

38. Teresa De Lauretis, *Technologies of Gender: Essays on Gender, Images, and Rights* (New York: Routledge, 2000). Also see Laura Mulvey, "Visual Pleasure and Narrative Cinema" (1975), in Amelia Jones, ed., *The Feminism and Visual Culture Reader* (New York: Routledge, 2003), 44–52.

39. Aihwa Ong makes a similar argument for NGO activism in Asia for foreign maids. See Aihwa Ong, *Neoliberalism as Exception: Mutations in Citizenship and Sovereignty* (Durham, NC: Duke University Press, 2006).

40. For debates about the construction of identity with pain and suffering, see Elaine Scarry, *The Body in Pain: The Making and Unmaking of the World* (Oxford: Oxford University Press, 1985); Wendy Brown, *States of Injury: Power and Freedom in Late Modernity* (Princeton, NJ: Princeton University Press, 1995); and Berlant, "The Subject of True Feeling."

41. For example, in the 1990s, the NGO Polaris Project served exploited migrant workers, before concentrating primarily on trafficking after 2000. The same has been the case for international NGOs funded to support solely trafficking victims. And less visible is the stringent abolitionist stance that is imposed on organizations for them to qualify for funding. Especially noteworthy are organizations' complaints that their funding may be withdrawn if they engage in activities that purportedly advocate prostitution, such as handing out condoms. This antiprostitution angle reflects the position of many Christian and Catholic organizations that are heavily funded through these programs. See Ronald Weitzer, "Moral Crusade against Prostitution," *Society* (March–April 2006): 33–38. On January 23, 2009, President Barack Obama overturned the "gag rule" prohibiting the United States from funding groups that provide abortions or abortion counseling overseas.

42. During the "white slave" trade, leaflets and posters at railway stations warned girls from traveling abroad or to the city. See Jo Doezema, "Loose Women or Lost Women? The Re-emergence of the Myth of White Slavery in Contemporary Discourses of Trafficking in Women," *Gender Issues* 18, no. 1 (Winter 2000): 23–50.

43. UN.GIFT, "Iniciativa Global da ONU contra o Tráfico de Pessoas—UN.GIFT," http://www.ungift.org/brazil/ (accessed July 6, 2008).

44. In the 2008 TIP report, Mark P. Lagon documented Brazil's continued practices of slavery on sugar plantations, as their production of ethanol, a biofuel, is becoming a growing national export.

45. For a discussion of the separation between domestic workers and sex workers in UN public service announcements, see Julietta Hua and Kasturi Ray, "The 'Practice of Humanity': Neoliberal Constructions of Domestic Workers and 'Sex Slaves,'" *Feminist Media Studies* 10, no. 3 (2010): 253–267.

46. See Rhacel Parreñas, "The U.S. War on Trafficking and the Moral Disciplining of Migrant Women," chap. 6 in *The Force of Domesticity: Filipina Migrants and Globalization* (New York: New York University Press, 2008); and Felicity Schaeffer-Grabiel, "The Erotics of Citizenship: Cyber-Marriage, Transnational Imaginaries, and Migration across the Américas," unpublished manuscript.

"Recycling" Heroines in France

Coutured Identities and Invisible Transitions

Julie Thomas

Museum exhibitions often present significant, if rarely analyzed, examples of framing group identities and masking cultural divides by presenting culturally hegemonic definitions of identity. In the contemporary mediated space of the museum, technologies of display may be manipulated in service to a variety of goals: mediation between cultures, naturalization of the nation, presentation of difference as spectacle, or promotion of cultural diversity. In a critique of museums, Tony Bennett argues that museums are civic laboratories where distinctive forms of cultural objecthood are produced and social relations regulated. They are "machineries implicated in the shaping of civic capacities."[1] Since museums, as James Clifford writes, "work the borderlands between different worlds, histories, and cosmologies,"[2] these mediated spaces have gained renewed importance in the context of migration and transnational identities. Museums not only serve as custodians of national culture and regulate populations, but they also reveal how and to what extent the culture defines itself as open or closed to transnational mobility.

Exhibitions are thus beginning to be recognized as important communicative media,[3] contributing to contemporary national and international mediascapes, which

> are exploited by nation-states to pacify separatists or even the potential fissiparousness of all ideas of difference. Typically, contemporary nation-states do this by exercising taxonomic control over difference, by creating various kinds of international spectacle to domesticate difference, and by seducing small groups with the fantasy of self-display on some sort of global or cosmopolitan stage.[4]

The visual display of museums, as a national archive, particularly lends itself to a reproduction or evocation of conventional images of national or ethnic identity, which remain active in the hierarchical ordering of culture and ways of being especially when "others" are the focus of attention. The objects of the gaze of the museum spectator are reduced and deprived of agency even as they are framed by the mediation of the exhibitionary display, managed by the operative cultural narrative, and removed from the world of privilege inhabited by the active viewer. Commenting on the photographs of the *National Geographic*, Catherine Lutz and Jane Collins note that production of cultural difference is often visualized as dependent on whether or not "individuals or groups . . . hold on to their own culture or decide to go modern"—modernity in this case being defined as "associated with valuing money and Western commodities, and accumulating goods."[5] In the context of global consumerism, appropriate culture(s) are similarly commodified and are transformed into goods to be valued and acquired.

In France, cultural policy actively envisions the role of national museums as media to preserve and propagate the *patrimoine*—the national heritage—as cultural model. The official website of the Ministry of Culture and Communication explicitly states that this is one of its essential missions and that since the 1970s policy has aimed to place culture at the heart of the life of people, while guaranteeing to all the right of access to *la culture*.[6] The importance of the role of the Ministry of Culture and Communication lies in its power to conflate French identity, citizenship, and participation in the national culture and also in its evocation of a right to access an established definition of culture, rather than a right to express cultural identity. As Catherine Ballé has pointed out, this right of access manifests itself in a policy that appears on the surface to be one of democratization:

> Cultural democratization is an explicit objective of the Ministry of Culture and Communication. As for the museums, most of them have developed strategies addressed to the entire population. With such a goal, every social category is taken into account and, in a marketing approach, becomes a "target group" liable to become the object of a specific action.[7]

From June 29 to August 19, 2007, the Petit Palais (Museum of Fine Arts of the City of Paris) mounted an exhibition entitled "L'Etoffe des héroines" (The Stuff, or Material of Heroines), which presented the successful completion of the cultural project of the designer Sakina M'sa, undertaken in cooperation with the Petit Palais. This project was described in the text displayed at the entrance to the exhibition as a "workshop of insertion through fashion and the creation of clothing."[8] The thirteen women who volunteered to participate in this project were identified as members of various disenfranchised and marginal publics from diasporic communities dealing with issues of immigration, or perhaps excluded from the mainstream by age rather than cultural affiliation or identity, thus, to rephrase Lowenthal, making age rather than the past "a foreign country."[9] The women were trained in couture practice and encouraged to design and customize garments by recycling and using old secondhand clothing donated by the charitable association Emmaus. This customization was defined in the "Communiqué de Presse" as "the action of personalizing and transforming a garment with the goal of making it unique. It does not mean inventing garments, but reinventing them so they may be reborn to a new life."[10]

The artistic collections of the museum set the creative standards against which the creations of the participants were judged. At the entrance to the exhibition, the role of the museum was extolled in the text: "The Petit Palais affirms itself as a site of life and exchange, open onto the world." Sakina's project, on the other hand, was defined as a "project of cultural development with a social aim . . . conforming to the political mission of the city [of Paris]." Indeed, the "Communiqué de Presse" issued by the Petit Palais in June 2007 echoes the official policy of the Ministry of Culture and Communication by confirming that the Petit Palais has, for the past fifteen years, been concerned with organizing access to a public distanced from cultural offerings.

Through a discourse analysis of the intended and alternative readings of the visual and verbal museum text,[11] this chapter analyzes how couture is socially constructed as the entrance to culture for these marginalized women, whose transnational identities seem to matter only insofar as they prove a transitional step in the process of being recycled. Like the garments that they produce, these women are portrayed in the mediascape of the museum as sewing for themselves the "right stuff" of accomplished French heroines from the raw material of their old identities. The national, global, and, indeed, transnational museum audience (French visitors, tourists, and the very culturally disparate and transnational public of Paris residents) is thus led to the conclusion that the proof of the marginalized women's ability to recycle culture(s) in the production of appropriately coutured identities now entitles them to become full consumers of the stuff of culture. Ironically, the participants also act as mirrors to confirm and reinforce a neoliberal version of modernity as consumption of commodified culture. Ultimately, the representation of the recycled identities is in turn meant to reflect the spectators' own successfully cultivated identities.

Citizenship as Spectatorship

According to the press releases for the exhibition, as well as the texts that greet the viewer at the entrance to the exhibition, the Petit Palais, first constructed in 1900 for the International Exhibition to represent French national and cultural identity to the world, is continuing its mission as an active cultural institution. This mission is undertaken in cooperation with the Mission of Integration of the City of Paris, which aims to "integrate French citizens of foreign origins[12] into the life of Paris by giving value to their cultural origins, promoting their access to their rights, and fighting against racial or ethnic discrimination."[13]

The couture workshop, the focus of the exhibition, required a commitment from the volunteer participants of attendance once a week for six months, beginning November 2006. The participants, described in the press release as "for the most part, immigrants," were encouraged through lectures and discussions on various works of art in the collection of the Petit Palais to consider four aesthetic themes which would aid them in the customization of their own garments: Materials and Contrasts, Motifs and Colours, Silhouettes and Representations of the Body, and The Displayed and The Hidden.

The text of the press release clearly captures the benevolent stance of the nation toward its immigrants. The press release states that the women will be led to develop their faculties of perception and analysis and their mastery of language and self-expression through attending the lectures in the museum. They would also acquire some of the history and social customs of their host country and would experience the *liberty* of *circulating* in the museum, a space and history which would otherwise have been foreign to them. This experience is equated to the freedom of being at liberty in the city itself, which had hitherto represented a *restricted* zone and experience for them[14]—the assumption being that, given their marginal status, the women have not felt at ease culturally in the public space of the nation.

The way in which the immigrant women were brought into visibility in the Petit Palais was a comment on the very meaning of citizenship in a context of global mobility. As Ursula Huws notes, the term *citizen* comes to stand in for concepts such as participation, equality, and democracy.[15] Embedded in the concept of citizenship is also the normalized civilizational superiority of the West in contrast to its Other. Thus, the implication that these women had not previously enjoyed the *freedom* of the city reinforces the impression that until their participation in the project, they had not truly been citizens in any functional sense, whatever their legal status might have been. In fact, they had been foreigners until they became accustomed to circulating in the museum. Learning through spatial stories is a characteristic feature of the medium of the museum, but it is also what constitutes familiarity, as de Certeau shows:

> The opacity of the body in movement, gesticulating, walking, taking its pleasure, is what indefinitely organizes a *here* in relation to an *abroad*, a "familiarity" in relation to a "foreignness." A spatial story is in its minimal degree a *spoken* language, that is, a linguistic system that distributes place insofar as it is *articulated* by an "enunciatory focalization," by an act of practicing it. . . . Space appears once more as a *practiced* place.[16]

Further, the project in its design reduces the experiences of the women participants to the fact of their sex rather than taking into account the totality of their experience. This removes them from the collectivity both existentially and politically and, as Nira Yuval-Davis writes, results in women being set apart from the body politic and hence retained in an *object* rather than a *subject* position.[17] For the imagined global audience of French and foreign visitors to the exhibition, the "transnational" identities of these women is easily submerged in their "otherness" as women and the commodification of both their ethnicity and the gendered body. This results in a manipulation that masks the production of global hierarchies, which are simultaneously gendered and racialized.[18]

The ability to be at ease with *circulation* or *free movement*, acquired over weeks of practice during the project by the participants, is exactly the quality which the visitors to the exhibition exude as they navigate through the space of the displays. The spectators become both models for and witnesses of the women's transformation and can engage in a self-congratulatory vicarious journey themselves. More interestingly, the new citizens, through the *time lag* between completing the project and the exhibition, are now emplaced to be the spectators of their own transformation and to trace their own initiation into spectatorship. Citizenship thus becomes equated not only with freedom of movement but also with the informed spectatorship necessary if the museum audience is to consume culture appropriately.

Ella Shohat and Robert Stam identify *multiple registers* necessary to any comprehensive and historically situated ethnography of spectatorship: the spectator as fashioned by the text, by the technical apparatuses, by the institutional contexts of spectatorship, and by ambient discourses and ideologies and the spectator as "embodied, raced, gendered, and historically situated."[19] Although the participants, now spectators, satisfy the first four of these conditions as they are fashioned during the course of the exhibition, they only become embodied once they have satisfactorily completed the journey from the invisibility of being foreign to the visibility that arises as a result of familiarity, of cultural citizenship.

Couture and Culture: Visible and Invisible

The creator of the project, Sakina M'sa, is herself a member of a diasporic community, having come to Marseilles as a child with her family from the Comoros Islands. She emphasizes the need for garments to express the individual identity of the wearer, to communicate history and a sense of place; she sews a label with the "birth date" of the garment on each one of her creations and expresses dislike of conventional "designer labels."[20] The garments themselves thus acquire agency and identity, and this concept is in fact crucial to the narrative of the exhibition. Previously M'sa has worked with the transformative powers of couture in several senses: the transformation of garments in terms of function and design (the use of recycled materials, for example, or remaking dresses into trousers) and also the ability of couture to transform human lives, as in the project she began more than ten years ago in which she runs workshops with the marginalized and disenfranchised as a method of offering self-esteem and possibly the opportunity of a new profession.[21] Daika, the association founded to promote couture as a tool of integration, is based on the principle that clothing and fashion today are vehicles of reinvention and adaptation. The official press release of the exhibition emphasizes Sakina M'sa's commitment to encourage diversity in society.[22]

These platforms prove problematic when considering the project as mediated by the Petit Palais in the exhibition—the diversity of the participants remains for the most part hardly identified and certainly unexplored. Rather than avoiding any stereotyping of the individuals, which was perhaps what was intended, this absence has the effect of reducing the participants to an amorphous whole representing *immigrants* or *marginalized women* or even *diversity*—diversity as otherness, an otherness foreign to the French culture into which they are being initiated. Couture is definitely presented as an agent of transformation and an active *terrain* of culture—certainly an affirmation of French culture. Indeed, the display of couture in the Fine Arts Museum of the Petit Palais confirms the status of haute couture as an integral and *active* element in the constitution of postmodern French cultural identity, an identity which is, of course, being commodified and sold to the many foreign tourists and visitors to the exhibition as well as to the local French audience. The familiarity with the museum which has been acquired throughout the project and which has become the sign of the participants' citizenship is embodied in the garments, which they have constructed during this time in the public space of the museum. As signifiers, the garments acquire a form of agency that is for the most part denied to the women themselves, who are reified as objects to be worked on in the process of transformation and initiation into full French cultural citizenship, rather than as active subjects.

The museum becomes a space of visual discipline prescribing cultural conformity to those who are outside on the margins of the nation. Commenting on the phenomenon of cultural security, Alison Beale writes that the use of culture as a tool is being increasingly used in Europe for a variety of government projects designed for the absorption of refugee and immigrant populations and mitigating conflict between these groups and native populations. This cultural surveillance, echoed in the project described here, indicates a return to assimilationist policies which have significant impact on further marginalizing the status of women.[23] The affirmation of French culture represented by the exhibition is accomplished through these women, rather than by them—their participation in the project has merely granted them the faceless freedom of strolling or roaming in the city of culture, not a role in its shaping.

There is also another social project and campaign in which Sakina M'sa is actively involved and which was included in and publicized by the exhibition—the "Appel des 93." This campaign, led by ninety-three *personalities*, was mobilized to change the public image of the Seine-Saint-Denis area—a suburb with the postal code 93 and the reputation of being an immigrant enclave marked by poverty, violence, and civil unrest. This project was motivated by the statement of young students that being from "93" was a cultural label which, no matter how hard they tried, could not be removed, giving rise to the "Remove the Label" campaign.[24] Young members of this campaign, residents of Seine-Saint-Denis, were invited to pose in their chosen "special" places of the neighborhood, wearing some of the garments created as part of the project or some of the garments from Sakina M'sa's own autumn/winter 2007 collection. The resulting photographs, taken by Benoit Peverelli, with the accompanying commentaries of the young models, were displayed in one of the rooms of the exhibition.

Diana Crane, commenting on women's performance of dress at the end of the nineteenth and the beginning of the twentieth centuries, relates that working women were often allowed to wear male-gendered (and thus inappropriate) clothing when in the workplace (such as factories) because they were considered invisible.[25] The factory was not public space but *liminal* space. Immigrant and marginalized women today are often equally invisible because they work in positions such as domestic help or child-care providers or engage in housework—in private space. Sweatshop work is perhaps one of the most notorious and extreme examples of this invisibility. Emphasis on sweatshop work also demonstrates the very class-informed assumption that skills and/or interest in sewing are possessed by most women from so-called traditional cultures across a wide range of ethnic and national origins. The bourgeois and upper-class manifestation of this stereotype is the unquestioned commonplace that women everywhere share an interest in fashion and the consumption and performance of clothing. One of the most overarching globalized and heavily mediated myths of modernity is that, cultural diversity and class aside, all women share involvement in couture: however, even if this myth is accepted at face value, immigrant and marginalized women are often relegated to performing their involvement invisibly, through the actual practice of sewing in the liminal space of the workshop or the private, domestic space of the home, whereas the public performance of fashion is the practice of fully fledged, visible members of the community—citizens, as it were.

An interesting feature of the "Stuff of Heroines" project is that the participants not only attended lectures at the Petit Palais but also had their workshop in the Petit Palais, thus bringing their previously invisible practice out into public space and confirming their newly acquired status as partakers of the culture which grants them visibility. However, it was not for them to dignify their creations through the actual performance of wearing/introducing the clothing which they had created in the public sphere—this task was reserved for young people, the youth who are the most visible in contemporary consumer society and whose imprimatur is necessary to validate any transformation.

Further, these youth also embodied the physical movement from the periphery, or margin, to the center—their photographs wearing the garments placed them and the garments firmly in the marginalized area of Seine-Saint-Denis, but these photographs were displayed in the central cultural sphere of the museum, dignifying both their role in the project and the garments created by the female participants. Here is another level of enactment, but one which illustrates the circularity and complexity of the center-periphery flow of cultural relations in terms of gender, race, citizenship (and age) in the commodification of diversity and marginalization. First, appearing here as models are both young men and women who are not being asked to sew couture to acquire their place in the center of culture but simply to perform their ease of mobility in the mainstream. As youth, the young models may validate the transformative nature of the garments, but the garments validate the presence of the marginalized community of the youth of 93—and the presence of the images of their accustomed marginalized home space of the *banlieu* (the suburb)—in the central public space of culture that is the museum. It is not only in production but also in the consumption of what is produced that the right of those on the margins to claim and access centrality is proven. As Inderpal Grewal and Caren Kaplan note, cultural flows are not necessarily one way—they are multifaceted in their ability to accommodate collaboration of all kinds.[26]

The narrative of this exhibition in terms of couture, culture, diversity, and the creation of community may be compared with the approach of another exhibition "Fil de Trois" (Thread of Three), also held in 2007, at the Centre de Création Contemporaine 2angles in Flers, Normandy. This gallery and arts center sponsors residences for artists particularly having to do with the themes of urbanism and cultural diversity.[27] In July 2007, the artist Danielle Lebreton, one of the three female artists whose project was documented and exhibited in the "Fil de Trois" exhibition, conceived and carried out a project entitled "2angles fillette" (Little Girl), in which women from the many diverse cultural and ethnic communities of the industrial town of Flers were asked to participate. The women from this economically depressed town were asked to create dresses for all the schoolgirls of Flers between the ages of five and six, who would then each wear and take away a dress at the end of the exhibition. In this project, the conflation of women and couture was used to create a community consciousness, which capitalized rather than effaced the transnational identities of the participants. It must be noted that the dresses that were created conformed to the traditional French image of an appropriate dress for a little girl, rather than expressing the cultural diversity of the participants, thus confirming the primacy of the French place/space in the creation of community. This results in an ironic construction of couture as an avenue to building alternate community awareness, as opposed to the more hegemonic cultural reinforcements offered by haute couture. Lebreton, in the statement of purpose that defines the vision behind her artistic practice of the past fifteen years, emphasized,

> It has to do with shaping the space of lived experience into a logic which is neither economic nor aesthetic, but which puts the artistic action in a very close relation with daily or practical life, so that it may be confused with life itself and may reveal another, eccentric point of view which has now been integrated and granted its own role and function.[28]

The Stuff of Heroines: Viewing the Exhibition

It is now time to become the spectators and to assume the role of the media audience for the exhibition in order to follow the thread of this *stuff* and examine how these heroines have been constructed. First it should be remembered that as spectators in the social space of a museum exhibition, we follow what Henri Lefebvre identifies as a "logic of visualization," which seems to merge with a logic of "constant metaphorization."[29]

The very title of the exhibition, "L'Etoffe des Héroines"—aside from the pun on *l'etoffe* ("stuff," "material"), as fabric as well as spiritual or cultural content—has added resonance for the French audience, as *L'Etoffe des Héros* was the French title of the 1983 American film *The Right Stuff.* Thus, associations of courage, astronauts aiming for the stars, and embodiment of cultural values of patriotism and loyalty are reinforced.

At the beginning of the exhibition, we find ourselves in a darkened room, greeted on one side by a long formal white dress on which is scrawled in pencil-like handwriting the word *disobedience,* followed by the phrase "Centre of great/grand ambitions." The writing on the dress itself is primary proof of "disobedience"; however, as this dress is evocative of the wedding dress which traditionally closes couture runway shows, some further forms of reversal or "disobedience" of the rules is immediately evident. Here the dress is opening the "show" and setting the tone, which is reinforced by a later wall text telling us that these women, in customizing their own garments and reworking/transforming the secondhand clothing supplied by Emmaus, have integrated elements of their own cultures and learned how to cross the boundaries of traditional codes by following this principle of "disobedience."

We are not, however, given further evidence of how they have integrated their own cultures or details about how they have actually crossed the boundaries of traditional codes in everyday life, as promised by the organizers. The conversion of dress styles requiring the women to convert, for example, trousers into skirts is hardly subversive. Clearly the mere fact of being immigrants circulating in a museum is made to stand in for the crossing of boundaries. Here resistance is being evoked and enacted as a tool for inclusion, and the crossing over to the *center of culture* for the marginalized women both represents the fulfillment of a *grand ambition* and confirms the preconception that ambitions are only to be realized and fulfilled at the center of European modernity.

But what are the distinct cultures that the women, as we are told, have integrated into their work? And who are these women? On the opposite wall, we see a bulletin board which resembles a school bulletin board, with schoolwork. On closer inspection, we see these are the letters of the thirteen participants, written at the beginning of the project in answer to Sakina M'sa's question, "Et toi, comment la robe est arrivée dans ta vie?" or, literally, "How did 'dress' first enter your life?" The use of the familiar second-person pronoun *toi* here emphasizes the easy familiarity and equality of the workshop—but all children are also addressed as *toi*. The presumed familiarity along the visual resonance of the school-like bulletin board and the fact that most of the letters, because of the inflection of the question, involve reminiscences of childhood infantilize the participants and make them emerge childlike, as beginners in their education process. This effect is reinforced by the fact that although Sakina M'sa herself has written a letter, her essay letter is longer and thus more visible than the others—she is the teacher, the leader. Further, as these reminiscences for the most part are rooted in the participants' individual non-French cultural and ethnic pasts, these "pasts" also become, by association, a "sign" of their cultural childhood—a childhood that will be educated and elevated through contact with French culture during the project. This appeal to individual memory and feelings of personal nostalgia is juxtaposed later in the exhibition with images of works of art in the museum collection, thus equating and in some measure replacing individual memory with what Andreas Huyssen might term the "public media memory" of the museum.[30]

The emphasis on "education" is even more significant if we recall that in *The Field of Cultural Production*, Bourdieu argues that for culture to fulfill its ideological function of class cooptation, the link between culture and education, "which is simultaneously obvious and hidden, [must] be forgotten, disguised and denied."[31] However, here education is being highlighted rather than disguised as an important element of culture. The underpinnings of the power—the cultural capital—which education confers is being exposed because the spectators, in the process of knowing that such culture did not in fact come naturally to the participants, will be reassured in the possession of their own cultural knowledge. Having acquired their culture openly through education, the participants may become citizens, but they will never be perceived as equal; they will remain as the Other—transformed but still other. So who are these *others* who are about to be educated? Although their letters are signed, it is only after a close reading that we learn some details about the individual women, and only in a few cases are the reminiscences located in places such as Senegal or Haiti, for example. Will the spectator spend the time to read these letters? And, even if so, will the audience wonder if this is a satisfactory way of removing the labels? The individual backgrounds and transnational identities of the participants become blurred.

Turning away from the bulletin board, we notice a large table in the middle of the entry room, on which a collage of images has been pasted. These images consist of photographs from fashion magazines and advertising which, obeying the rule of "questioning" and "disobedience" of contemporary cultural standards of publicity, have been cut up, taken apart, and reassembled to create new, more subversive images. This display echoes the school-like, ludic effect of the bulletin board, foreshadows the reworking of the actual garments to create new images, and it hints at the simultaneous reworking of identity—the goal of the project. Once again, superficial subversion is used in service to eventual conformity within an accepted hegemonic framework.

Walking into the exhibition down the long hall, a series of displays shows us the range of secondhand clothing that has been used—the raw material of the *before*—grouped with the tools of couture used in transformation and supported by an audio background of the disembodied voices of the women talking, laughing, and discussing their work. An aural space is created where we cannot see the women but can only hear them; we feel surrounded by them and momentarily become part of their community. It is at this point that the two levels of spectatorship mentioned earlier begin to operate—we are with the women, being faceless spectators at their own transformation. In a photograph, we see some of the women seated before a painting in a gallery of the Petit Palais, listening to a lecture, but their backs are to the camera and their faces are hidden. They remain raw material, an amorphous group, in the process of being transformed and not yet fit or ready to be seen as individuated citizens. A wall text informs us that none of the women was accustomed to going to museums, but they had been socialized into the practice by the workshop. The aesthetic diversity of the museum is also praised as a source of inspiration, but the ethnic diversity and indeed the possible diversity of aesthetic values of the participants themselves is not mentioned.

Now, in the next displays, the results of the "recycling" appear—the garments which the women have constructed are exhibited. On the level of couture, the garments demonstrate that a certain transformation has been successfully accomplished; here, once again, the garments stand in for the women and suggest the existence of their culturally acceptable bodies, which have not yet appeared. The display of these completed garments terminates the first half of the exhibition and prepares us for a pause, or break, in the narrative, accentuated by the physical movement necessary in order to complete the visit.

We exit onto a staircase and cross the landing to enter a room of transition in which a story entitled "The Swan"[32] can be listened to with earphones. A storyteller also participated in the workshop, and we read that this use of storytelling serves the function of an "Open Sesame" in the museum interface, to open the door for participants to connect the narrative of "The Swan" with their work—and with their own transformations. This use of storytelling reminds the spectator of the ludic, schoolroom atmosphere of the introduction to the exhibition, as well as providing a link with the fantasy, fairy-tale quality of the project.

At this point, the "rebirth" of these heroines is assured; yet they still exist as an unseen collective, their recycled garments standing in for their presumably recycled identities. The faces that *are* seen at the end of this room are the faces of the young models of Seine-Saint-Denis, whose photographs wearing the garments, together with their comments on "93," provide a crucial element in the rationale of the exhibition. The garments are validated through being accepted and worn by the youth of Seine-Saint-Denis, just as the collective identity of the "93" is broadened and enriched through the garments, which in turn acquire further significance. The garments do more than simply stand for the "reconstructed" identities of the participants; they serve as active facilitators of identity and transformation. In fact, instead of remaining as just symbols of transition, the garments acquire a life of their own, apart from their creators, confirming the success and worth of the project and of the museum itself.

But Where Are the Heroines?

In the last section of the exhibition, we finally see the faces of the women in a video in which the women talk about their work. However, their testimony is interspersed with images of works in the galleries of the Petit Palais. Have they also become part of the valued *collection* of the museum? They have, after all, been *created* for the exhibition and now can be seen to inhabit the freedom of the public space of the museum and Paris. In fact, as mediated images, they exist as a documentation of their project; they have taken on their true form as testifying witnesses to the power and the implicit hegemonies of culture.

As the visitor exits the exhibition, framed photographs of twelve of the women line the walls, and underneath the portraits, each one has signed her first name in chalk, reminding the visitor of the original school bulletin board. The names—the unframed raw material—have now become the framed face, transformed by and endowed with French cultural capital, finding full identity visually only after being "recycled." Their names, which reflect their origins and their diverse individual, ethnic, and cultural identities, are the only remaining infantilized clues of their history and former selves.

At the exit, the obligatory small exhibition shop sells examples of Sakina M'sa's couture products. Here a final wall text informs the visitor how the participants have benefited from the project. Three of the participants, we learn, have been permanently hired by the association Daika. In addition, we are told that "the discovery of paintings, the acquisition of knowledge about couture, the discovery of their creative capacities have given confidence to the participants. They have looked for work, enlarged their network, signed up for further training, taken their children to museums." The spectator should now not only welcome these women to the freedom of the center of French culture but should even identify with them. At this stage, the women, like the visitor, have participated in the ritual of museumgoing and have become familiar with the traditional ritual site of museum space, which "is carefully marked off and culturally designated as special, reserved for a particular kind of contemplation and learning experience."[33]

The French visitor might also remember that André Malraux remarked in *Museum without Walls* (*Le Musée Imaginaire*) that "the museum was an affirmation"[34]—in contrast to the "museum without walls," which is an interrogation. Although we are now in postmodern, rather than in Malraux's modern, France, the museum continues to affirm rather than to interrogate. The multicultural diasporic communities represented by the women taking part in this project are literally invisible, as are their own identities. The women only acquire faces once they, like their raw material of secondhand garments, have been recycled and are appropriate representatives of integration with the national culture. Now that they have acquired confidence and self-esteem, they no longer feel they are in a restricted zone when they navigate as citizens in the public space of the museum that contains the treasure of French culture.

The transnational does not speak in this narrative. The fluidity of immigrant cultures which straddle nations has been diverted to flow into an all-encompassing reservoir of acceptability. The museum of colonialism, which highlighted difference in order to establish and justify cultural superiority, has morphed into the contemporary museum, in which the shifting qualities of the transnational are tamed in service to the goal of cultural assimilation. Cultural institutions such as museums in France follow the official policy of the Ministry of Culture and Communication, which guarantees citizens the right to have access to the cultural *patrimoine* of France. This places the expression of transnational cultural identities as secondary and subservient, often depicted only in order to confirm the dominant power of the *patrimoine*, a culture which has been commodified for public consumption. The museum both offers a cultural commodity and produces citizens who have been educated in the proper way to consume it—citizens who are not only comfortable as spectators but are themselves "fit to be seen," at ease in the public spaces of the nation.

As noted earlier, this public visibility as offered to the participants of "L'Etoffe des Heroines" is both part of the process of their integration and a crucial sign of their successful assimilation. Further, as women, their gendered bodies serve to mask their ethnicities and their dual otherness, conflated and more easily manipulated in service to the triumph of the dominant cultural values. At the same time, they themselves are reduced and objectified in the final video by being juxtaposed with images of works from the collection of the Petit Palais. The fact that the designer Sakina M'sa is herself an immigrant lends authenticity and rectitude to the narrative of the exhibition and raises issues about the appropriation by the dominant culture of the successfully integrated other.[35] Her own ethnicity is here commodified to lend credibility to the cultural work of mediating and perpetuating the myth of modernity. To become modern, one has to be the recipient of a civilizing education, which here implies a replacement of previous practices in favor of appropriate forms of consumption. Behavior, like the garments that are featured in the exhibition, must be customized, reinvented, so that the participants "may be reborn to a new life."[36] The message of these heroines suggests otherwise—integration for marginalized women in France demands the invisibility of the transnational.

NOTES

1. Tony Bennett, "Civic Laboratories: Museums, Cultural Objecthood, and the Governance of the Social," Working Paper No. 2, CRESC Working Paper Series (Milton Keynes: Centre for Research on Socio-Cultural Change, Open University, 2005).

2. James Clifford, "Museums as Contact Zones," in David Boswell and Jessica Evans, eds., *Representing the Nation* (London: Routledge, 1999), 451.

3. Flora Kaplan, "Exhibitions as Communicative Media," in Eilean Hooper-Greenhill, ed., *Museum, Media, Message* (London: Routledge, 1999), 37–58.

4. Arjun Appadurai, *Modernity at Large: Cultural Dimensions of Globalization* (Minneapolis: University of Minnesota Press, 1996), 39.

5. Catherine Lutz and Jane Collins, *Reading National Geographic* (Chicago: University of Chicago Press, 1993), 240–241.

6. "Depuis sa création, l'une des missions essentielles du ministère de la Culture est de rendre accessibles au plus grand nombre le patrimoine architectural et artistique ainsi que les œuvres de création contemporaine . . . Dès le début des années 70, apparaît la notion de développement culturel pour nommer une politique destinée à mettre la culture au cœur de la vie des gens, répondant aussi à l'obligation de l'État d'assurer à chacun l'exercice de son droit à la culture." Ministère de la Culture et de la Communication, "Développement culturel," www.culture.gouv.fr/culture/politique-culturelle/accueil.htm (accessed January 28, 2009). See also Dominique Pou-

lot, *Patrimoine et Musées* (Paris: Hachette, 2001); and Catherine Ballé and Dominique Poulot, *Musées en Europe* (Paris: La Documentation Française, 2004).

7. Catherine Ballé, "Democratization and Institutional Change: A Challenge for Modern Museums," in Diana Crane, Nobuko Kawashima, and Ken'ichi Kawasaki, eds., *Global Culture: Media, Arts, Policy, and Globalization* (New York: Routledge, 2002), 142.

8. All texts displayed at the exhibition and cited here and throughout the chapter were in French. The texts were transcribed by the author in a visit to the exhibition in August 2007 and then translated by the author.

9. David Lowenthal, *The Past Is a Foreign Country* (Cambridge: Cambridge University Press, 1985).

10. Petit Palais, Musée des Beaux-Arts de la Ville de Paris. "Communiqué de Presse," June 4, 2007. Translation by the author. "Depuis une quinzaine d'années, par le biais de son Service éducatif et cultural, le Petit Palais a eu à cœur d'organiser l'accès et l'accompagnement des publics eloignés de l'offre culturelle. . . . La customisation est l'action de personnaliser et transformer un vetement dans le but de le rendre unique. Elle permet non pas d'inventer des vetements, mais de les réinventer et de les faire renaitre pour une nouvelle vie."

11. Here, the exhibition is considered as separate from the project itself, but as defining the project for the public.

12. "Foreign" is defined here as not coming from European Union member states.

13. Dossier de presse, "L'Etoffe des Héroines" (Service éducatif et culturel du Petit Palais, Musée des Beaux-Arts de la Ville de Paris, 2007). Translation by the author.

14. Ibid.

15. Ursula Huws, "Women, Participation, and Democracy in the Information Society," in Katharine Sarikakis and Leslie Regan Shade, eds., *Feminist Interventions in International Communication: Minding the Gap* (Lanham, MD: Rowman and Littlefield, 2008), 45.

16. Michel de Certeau, *The Practice of Everyday Life*, trans. Steven Rendall (Berkeley: University of California Press, 1988), 130.

17. Nira Yuval-Davis, *Gender and Nation* (London: Sage, 1997), 47.

18. Radha Hegde, "Feminist Media Studies—Transnational," in Wolfgang Donsbach, ed., *The International Encyclopedia of Communication* (Oxford, UK: Wiley Blackwell, 2008), 1794–1799.

19. Ella Shohat and Robert Stam, *Unthinking Eurocentrism: Multiculturalism and the Media* (London: Routledge, 1994), 350.

20. Severine Maublanc, "Sakina M'sa, Créatrice Capitale," *Latences* (Paris) 2 (Summer 2007). Translation by the author.

21. Ibid.

22. Dossier de presse, "L'Etoffe des Héroines."

23. Alison Beale, "The Expediency of Women," in Katharine Sarikakis and Leslie Regan Shade, eds., *Feminist Interventions in International Communications: Minding the Gap* (Lanham, MD: Rowman and Littlefield, 2008), 68.

24. L'Appel des 93, http://www.appeldes93.fr/ (accessed July 8, 2008). Also see B.S., "Expo cet été au Petit Palais," *Le Parisien* (May 24, 2007); and J.D., "La Seine-Saint Denis ou l'éloge de la diversité," *Metro* (November 15, 2006).

25. Diana Crane, *Fashion and Its Social Agendas: Class, Gender, and Identity in Clothing* (Chicago: University of Chicago Press, 2000), 199–231.

26. Inderpal Grewal and Caren Kaplan, "Introduction: Transnational Feminist Practices and Questions of Postmodernity," in Inderpal Grewal and Caren Kaplan, eds., *Scattered Hegemonies* (Minneapolis: University of Minnesota Press, 2006), 1–33. For further remarks on the inad-

equacy of the center-periphery model, see also Inderpal Grewal and Caren Kaplan, "Warrior Marks: Global Womanism's Neo-Colonial Discourse in a Multicultural Context," in Ella Shohat and Robert Stam, eds., *Multiculturalism, Postcoloniality, and Transnational Media* (New Brunswick, NJ: Rutgers University Press, 2003), 256–278.

27. 2angles, "Filles de Trois," http://www.2angles.org/expositions/2007-2008/fil de trois/trois.htm (accessed July 8, 2008).

28. Danielle Lebreton, "2anglesfillette," in *Fil de Trois* (Flers: Editions 2angles, 2007). Translation by the author.

29. Henri Lefebvre, *The Production of Space*, trans. Donald Nicholson-Smith (Oxford, UK: Blackwell, 1991), 98.

30. Andreas Huyssen, "Present Pasts: Media, Politics, Amnesia," in Arjun Appadurai, ed., *Globalization* (Durham, NC: Duke University Press, 2001), 57–77.

31. Pierre Bourdieu, *The Field of Cultural Production*, trans. Randal Johnson (Oxford, UK: Polity/Blackwell, 1993), 235.

32. A narrative with an ugly-duckling motif.

33. Carol Duncan, "Museums and Citizenship," in Ivan Karp and Steven D. Levine, eds., *Exhibiting Cultures* (Washington, DC: Smithsonian Institution Press, 1991), 91. For further work on museums as "civilizing rituals," see Carol Duncan, *Civilizing Rituals: Inside Public Art Museums* (London: Routledge, 1995).

34. André Malraux, *Museum without Walls*, trans. Stuart Gilbert and Francis Price (London: Secker & Warburg, 1967), 62.

35. The project itself, as considered separately from the mediating exhibition, raises other interesting issues and prompts further questions; however, the author's attempt to interview Sakina M'sa about the project and exhibition was not successful.

36. Petit Palais, Musée des Beaux-Arts de la Ville de Paris. "Communiqué de Presse."

8 Celebrity Travels

Media Spectacles and the Construction of a Transnational Politics of Care

Spring-Serenity Duvall

A long history of celebrity involvement in politics and humanitarian efforts has contributed to the production of *celebrity activism* as an influential media phenomenon that now permeates popular culture. Such A-list celebrities as Bono, Angelina Jolie, Madonna, David Beckham, Brad Pitt, Paul Newman, Bruce Springsteen, and Robert Redford are well recognized for creating almost second careers out of political and social activism.[1] The travels of Western celebrities to third world spaces on humanitarian and awareness-raising campaigns generate compelling narratives in mainstream U.S. media. Media coverage of actress and Goodwill Ambassador for the United Nations High Council on Refugees Angelina Jolie offers a dynamic site from which to critically examine neoliberal, neocolonial, and postfeminist discourses that intersect in constructing a transnational agenda for humanitarian intervention.

Celebrity activism is framed within a media space that privileges neoliberal ideologies of individualism and accentuates discourses about the agency of powerful Western women traveling to "save" women of the Global South. In the spectaclization of the strong celebrity heroine that follows, local women of the area are either marginalized or overlooked in the mediasphere. I focus on Jolie's celebrity activism as promoting a style of engagement in a politics marked as noncontroversial and as capitalizing on the pervasive power and transnational appeal of Western celebrity culture. Examining the mediated spectacles of celebrity activism, I argue that these social and political celebrity interventions reproduce old colonial dynamics and promote a version of American exceptionalism intact with its racial and gendered scripts. Mapping the travel of celebrity icons reveals how humanitarian causes come into transnational visibility coded in racial and gendered terms.

Celebrity activism is a distinctly global neoliberal phenomenon that has to be situated within a globally saturated and networked transnational environment. John Street argues that the extent to which celebrities gain legitimacy for their political activities depends on the type of media coverage they receive, the attention they gain from institutions, and the willingness of audiences to accept them as activists.[2] While celebrities such as Jolie gain cultural currency and political legitimacy through activism, others such as Richard Gere who advance controversial positions receive much less media attention for their political activities or, as in the case of Madonna, receive primarily negative media coverage that represents their political involvement as misguided or self-serving publicity stunts. At the same time, institutions such as the United Nations have long sought celebrity popularity to circulate their mission and message around the world. So what follows is a dramatic intersection of celebrities with popularity and good intentions, a networked media gaze waiting for spectacle, and institutions hoping to use the powerful commodity of celebrity status. The resultant visual and discursive contest is over who exerts the power to set an agenda for humanitarian intervention.

In this chapter, I examine how scripts of sexuality are interwoven into the narratives of celebrity activism. Extending Street's ideas, I argue that media coverage typically privileges celebrity activism that adheres to traditional gender norms. Western movie stars such as Jolie, Gere, Madonna, and others share a status as sex symbol first and as activist second in the public arena. Intense media concern with their bodies and personal relationships is inextricably linked to coverage of their activist undertakings. Jolie's and Madonna's have been most visible for their political actions and family "building," and this has contributed to both the derision and deification of celebrities who advocate on behalf of and adopt children from third world nations. Jolie, in particular, embodies a postfeminist figure whose individual achievements are offered as evidence of a Western feminine empowerment that assumes both the success of feminism and its current irrelevance.[3] Jolie is the ultimate example of one of the "ideal girls, subjects *par excellence,* and also subjects of excellence" who McRobbie argues represent the depoliticization of feminism.[4] Jolie and Madonna are represented as postfeminist icons who appear not only to have achieved great professional success but also to have conquered gender inequality in their personal lives. In other words, the complex politics of sexuality and motherhood is bypassed as the media discourse remains firmly focused on normalizing heterosexual social and family values. I turn to a wide range of media texts in order to unravel these issues and understand the contestation underlying the construction of a transnational politics of care.

Media Production of Star Benevolence

Jolie's image as a global power-player is dependent on the creation and maintenance of her media role as the "perfect" woman. She did not always fit the part, but her image has been molded into a perfection frame over the past decade. The progression of Jolie's image over time reveals the scripted nature of her production as a media spectacle on the global scene. Jolie's early career as an actress was highlighted by media reports of her "freakish" behavior, such as wearing a vial of her husband's blood and being sexually radical. After being an Academy Award–winning subject of celebrity gossip that focused largely on her sexual practices and partners, in the past several years Jolie's media profile has changed dramatically to that of loving mother, representative of a respectable clothing line, and UN ambassador who visits refugee camps and cancer centers. Jolie stands alone in the mediasphere for her stark conversion "from wild child to worldly humanitarian, from provocative hellcat to dazzling glamour-puss" and therefore offers an even more compelling tale of compliance with hegemonic norms because she seems to have tried alternatives before embracing those norms.[5]

Jolie's linear "transformation" is reported to have taken place as a result of her decision to adopt a Cambodian boy, whom she named Maddox Chivan Jolie in 2002. In discussing the importance of Cambodia in opening her eyes to third world countries, Jolie described it this way: "First place I learned about land mines and refugees but most of all tolerance. All they have suffered, and they remain smiling. I will watch with pride as Maddox discovers his ancestry."[6] Any personal growth aside, media coverage of Jolie shifted from casting her as a rebel Hollywood outsider to granting her a position of legitimacy based on her newly acquired role as mother.

As a young woman who flaunted sexual and social conventions by openly discussing her sexual exploits and traversing the globe as a single mother of an adopted nonwhite child, Jolie was represented as the embodiment of assertive femininity. Her openness and her position as a sex symbol also prompt media coverage that sexualizes virtually every aspect of her body and behavior. One image of Jolie sitting close to her son Maddox carries a caption that sexualizes his nearness to her breasts: "Maddox, resting comfortably, is no doubt the envy of his little bro Pax—not to mention every other red-blooded male."[7] Images of Jolie as a mother of a multiracial family further accentuate her own racialized presence as a powerful white woman. Emphasis on her children's status as adopted, though, paired with intense attention to her heterosexual relationship with Brad Pitt (also a humanitarian celebrity) and their three biological children, complies with a script that highlights heterosexuality, motherhood, and benevolence over other "radical" aspects of her life.

Jolie's appearance is specifically noted as an aspect of her conversion in the mainstream, because "in the process she has abandoned her vampy look in favor of the three S's: subdued, soft and smoky."[8] Jolie attracts both deification as a "goddess" and media policing of her body as a site of social control. Websites and tabloid coverage devoted to chronicling her tattoos and critiquing her body size and her fertility contribute to a discourse that minimizes her political voice.[9] Jolie's media metamorphosis had become complete as of May 2006, when *People* magazine named "Angie" (as she is often called) the "most beautiful person in the world." The article, which credits humanitarian work and motherhood as the reasons for her transformation, emphasizes that it is Jolie's embodied presence that sets her apart:

> Her beauty lies in her work.... "She looks the most beautiful when she is in the field—natural, no makeup, nothing," says [friend Wyclef] Jean. "Because you see Angelina, the angel. It doesn't get any better than that." ... Still, it's yet another role that reveals the actress at her most breathtaking. Expecting her first child with [Brad] Pitt any day, the mom-to-be "glows," says Rebecca Matthias, head of the maternity-wear retailer A Pea in the Pod, where Jolie stocked up on spring cashmeres and designer denim. "She's probably more beautiful than we've ever seen her."[10]

Jolie is cast as fully embracing her femininity by performing the ultimately reproductive task of bearing a child, which seems to add an extra dimension of feminine beauty beyond that of already being a mother of two adopted children. In both of these physical alterations, from changing her makeup and clothes to carrying a child, the belief that Jolie is at her most beautiful when she is "natural" (read: makeup free) and pregnant reinforces the perception that feminine beauty, inner beauty, and childbearing fluidly merge into one another in Jolie's persona. The narrative that Brad had sexually conquered Angelina by convincing her to have biological children is also strongly evident in some media coverage. Having submitted to Brad's desire for biological children, Angelina pronounces that his appreciation of her postpregnancy body gives her confidence. "I'm with a man who is evolved enough to look at my body and see it as more beautiful, because of the journey it has taken and what it has created. He genuinely sees it that way. So I genuinely feel even sexier."[11] In addition, Angelina's maternal body is glorified through Brad's gaze in published photographs that he took of her for the same cover story. Carrying the headline "Exclusive: Brad Pitt's Private Photos of Angelina Jolie," the twenty-one black-and-white images inside the magazine feature closeups of her lips, her bare body in silhouette, and her interactions with their children. The story offers a compelling example of her being framed as submissive through his gaze, while he is masculinized as dominant through her words. Interestingly, while Brad's photos of Angelina may appear at first glance to be candid family photographs, the list of credits for clothes, accessories, styling, hair and makeup, and a "fashion assistant" shows that the photo shoot was a highly planned production and an example of the couple manipulating media coverage by displaying her maternal body through the perspective of his gaze.

The narrative of Jolie's transformation from "freak" to "most beautiful," her shift from marginality to mainstream prominence, provides a storyline to consumers that justifies conformity and reinforces hegemonic norms. The description of moving from a radical outsider who challenges gender norms by openly displaying her aggression and sexuality to a more conservative figure who embodies mainstream norms of heterosexual femininity and beauty serves as an allegory that structures media coverage of Jolie's motherhood and her work for the United Nations.

Motherhood as Global Activism

Jolie's claim to political legitimacy, and the media's support of that legitimacy, is based in large part on her subject position as a mother, specifically the mother she became after leaving her wild ways behind. For example, a *People* magazine article entitled "Ambassador Mom" reported Jolie's address to the National Press Club by focusing on her role as mother: "'The best education I can give [son Maddox] is to show him the world,' says Jolie, who was promoting her new legal-aid project, the National Center for Refugee and Immigrant Children. Jolie adopted Maddox from a Cambodian orphanage in 2002 and takes him everywhere."[12] While she may not have control over the way *People* frames her, Jolie's repeated assertions that her activism is an extension of her motherhood shapes the ways in which she is represented.

Participating in a 2002 humanitarian mission in Sierra Leone, Jolie, who met with high-profile politicians and victims of the violent civil war, asserted, "I'm here as a woman. As a mom."[13] Her emphasis on mothering in her humanitarian work also leads to references to Mother Teresa, as in one photo of Jolie in a flak jacket meeting with an elderly Iraqi refugee (see figure 8.1). Though the Iraqi woman in the foreground of the image wears a headscarf and may visually resemble Mother Teresa, it is the youthful Jolie who is dubbed "Mother Angelina" in the photo caption. Here, Jolie is cast again in the role of rescuer and caretaker of an unnamed, nonwhite woman who becomes a collective symbol of all refugees that Jolie "mothers."[14]

Jolie's image as an iconic mother figure is reinforced by speculation that she will continue to adopt more children in the future: "Will Jolie adopt again? 'Yes, absolutely,' she says. 'Almost any country I go to I'm prepared to adopt.'"[15] In addition, magazine articles about Jolie's career, personal life, and activism sometimes feature breakout boxes devoted to explaining the plight of orphans in countries that Jolie visits.[16] The emphasis on adoption in narratives about Jolie is compelling because it situates aid to foreign countries as rooted in individual adoptions of underprivileged children rather than in other forms of political activism.

The various strands of this media commentary on Jolie's family-planning choices coalesce in one 2006 *People* magazine article. Jolie's depiction on the magazine cover as the "most beautiful person in the world" moved on to capture her as part of the "most beautiful family."

> He's a two-time Sexiest Man Alive. She's the world's most beautiful woman. Together they are building a multiracial brood that transcends continents and boasts the

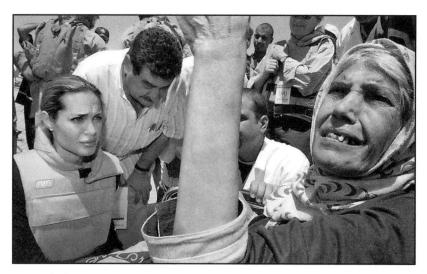

Fig. 8.1. Jolie during a visit to Al Waleed refugee camp in Iraq with an unnamed woman. (Morris Bernard and UNHCR, August 2007)

> two cutest kids ever to sport a Mohawk and a kerchief. Is it any wonder, then, that Brad Pitt and Angelina Jolie—who await the arrival of their first child together any moment now—preside over what might only be deemed the World's Most Beautiful Family? . . . Even the windswept splendor of the sub-Saharan desert can't upstage this family's combined gene pool.[17]

This statement not only defines the ideal family but at the same time polishes the Orientalist lens through which Westerners view Africa. Jolie and Pitt's family, built through childbearing and multiracial adoption, is held up as the ideal cosmopolitan family of today. The notion of "building" the ideal family and the emphasis on the "gene pool" rhetoric echoes current discourse on designer babies. Underlying this global family is the reality that such a multiracial family can only exist when two white, heterosexual, wealthy people adopt or "rescue" disadvantaged children from the Global South. Additionally, the journalist commends the couple for strategically "building" the ideal family that seems to transcend nations as deliberately as one might stack a football team with the best players from around the world.

It is the emphasis on not only the multiracial but also the multinational nature of the Jolie-Pitt family that illuminates a final interesting aspect of this last remark. Jolie's individual choice to adopt children from three different cultures exemplifies an American multiculturalism in which liberal ideology elevates the individual and privileges the role of choice in being able to adopt any hyphenated or nationalistic identity.[18] In this case, multiculturalism is achieved through the choice to adopt children who represent different cultures into one family that serves as a metaphor for world harmony. Jolie says, "For me, our family is just what America is—a melting pot, a mixture of many different races and nations,"[19] and U.S. media point to the Jolie-Pitt family as proof that people of all races and nationalities share essential qualities that enable them to blend seamlessly as families and should therefore inspire institutions and governments to follow suit. In addition, the reporter reinforces colonial stereotypes by setting the Jolie-Pitt family against a backdrop of "the windswept splendor of the sub-Saharan desert,"[20] which serves as a primal backdrop for the spectacle of the wealthy, cosmopolitan Western family.

Gendering of Cosmopolitanism

Jolie's sexualization as a beatific Madonna figure shapes the way that she conducts her UN work, not from the position as a knowledgeable activist but specifically as a concerned mother.[21] Jolie's role as a Goodwill Ambassador for the United Nations High Council on Refugees has shaped her activism and led her to meet refugees in over twenty countries and become a fixture at international summits on war, land mines, hunger, health crises, and, specifically, the future of Cambodia, Africa, Afghanistan, and other formerly colonized countries. The UN influences, structures, and lends institutional legitimacy to Jolie's activism as well as grants her entrée into the privileged circle of world leaders. In considering Jolie's association with the United Nations, it is noteworthy that there has been a long history of UN recruitment of famous names and faces to spread its message and gain support for its causes. Since 1954, Western celebrities actively involved with the United Nations have included Audrey Hepburn, David Beckham, Mia Farrow, and Whoopi Goldberg. More recently, celebrities from non-Western countries have become vocal advocates for UN campaigns on behalf of children and human rights, but it is unsurprising that UN ambassadors from India, Africa, and South America do not garner the overwhelming attention of Western or international media that is commanded by prominent U.S. and UK stars. "Celebrities attract attention, so they are in a position to focus the world's eyes on the needs of children, both in their own countries and by visiting field projects and emergency programmes abroad. They can make direct representations to those with the power to effect change."[22]

This phenomenon of celebrity ambassadors reflects how the United Nations as an international organization reinforces hegemonic norms and values.[23] While discussing the role of the United States as the "world's only remaining superpower," Donald Puchala notes that "the United Nations is largely an American creation."[24] The claim that the United Nations functions as a purveyor of U.S.

hegemony is compelling because even though the specific geopolitical ambitions of the United States may clash with the United Nations at times, the values of liberalism, democracy, and Judeo-Christian ideology are prominent in the political and humanitarian actions of the United Nations. In addition, after interviewing members of the United Nations and describing the heavy presence of U.S. representatives on the UN council, Puchala concludes that "the predominant impression within the Secretariat and among many member state delegations is that almost everything the United Nations does or does not do is conditioned by the will, whims, and resources of the United States."[25]

If we understand the United Nations as an international organization that is subject to and reinforces Western (specifically U.S.) hegemony, how does Jolie's work operate within that institutional structure? What impact does being associated with the United Nations have on Jolie's life and work? To what extent does Jolie's choice to work within the United Nations, as opposed to taking an activist stance "outside" of or "against" states and institutions, shape her message and her work? According to Jolie, her activism and personal behavior have come to conform to some extent to the mold of UN policies and the rules of working within systems: in a 2005 *Nightline* interview, she noted the restrictions that this association entails, because "they have to be neutral": "So it's really difficult. And working with the UN, I've learned that. And it's tough because part of you just wants to get angry."[26]

By presenting her personal emotions as secondary to institutional processes, Jolie strengthens the power that institutions have not only over her work but also over the politics and policies that contribute to the construction of a transnational space where Western institutional power reigns. Jolie's quoted desire to subdue her "natural" impulses also relates to her newfound acknowledgment of herself as an iconic of mainstream femininity. Not only has she come to embody the ideals of womanly beauty and motherhood, but she has also taken on the traditionally feminine quality of being beatific and calm. Ironically, as a postfeminist icon, Jolie's ability to critique is silenced as a price for her power. Indeed, her voice is provisionally "granted" by the United Nations (and the U.S. mainstream media) on the condition of her submission to existing hegemonic rules of global politics.

In the process of forming a Western-centric transnational politics of care, Jolie's submission to the United Nations and her promotion of a feminine politics of care also contribute to a gendering of U.S. cosmopolitanism. On the global stage, the U.S. nation is masculinized by an emphasis on its military might, autonomy, and patriarchal role in war and diplomacy.[27] The politics of care promoted by Jolie and others, however, serve to soften U.S. cosmopolitanism by emphasizing motherly images, collective solutions, and interdependence between the United States and international humanitarian organizations. Even male celebrity activists such as George Clooney, Brad Pitt, and Richard Gere advance humanitarian intervention strategies that are internationally cooperative and offer alternatives to the traditionally masculine nationalistic displays of military force. This feminine ethic of care may be seen as a valuable alternative to the traditionally masculine U.S. national identity, yet it exists in its present form not in opposition to but as submissive to and supportive of U.S. masculine institutions.

Spectacles of Benevolence

Identifying the public personality as a peculiarly modern phenomenon, David Marshall writes that celebrity as "a concept of the individual moves effortlessly in a celebration of democratic capitalism."[28] The presence and popularity of celebrity activists in today's global media environment stands at this potent conjuncture of the ideology of individualism, globalization, and neoliberal capitalism. Even when celebrity activists seek to highlight communal solutions to social problems, media coverage promotes an excessive focus on the individual, celebrity personae rather than their political messages. A cover story for *Esquire* reporting Jolie's efforts to create a UN Millennium Village in Cambodia, where she funds a 230-square-mile conservation project, devotes more time to characterizing Jolie as an independently powerful individual—"the best woman in the world, in terms of her generosity, her dedication, and her courage."[29] Jolie, Richard Gere, Madonna, Susan Sarandon, and many other U.S. celebrity activists advocate a variety of collective actions, yet the media highlight their star status as charismatic individuals over their political messages.[30]

Reflecting this liberal ideology, journalists such as George Stephanopoulos and Ann Curry cast Jolie as a unique, lone crusader who is single-handedly changing the world through her activism.[31] Jolie becomes the face of American individualism and benevolence in a troubled global order that needs humanitarian intervention. In covering Jolie, Stephanopoulos and Curry both reproduce these hegemonic values and discourses of liberal white power and American exceptionalism. While elevating Jolie to the role of heroine, media coverage also obscures the extent of its own role in framing celebrity activists. By constructing Jolie as a powerful agent, the media absolves itself of playing a role in setting the larger agenda for humanitarian issues, as journalists plead objectivity and even victimhood at the hands of the Jolie-Pitts. Journalists have accused Jolie of favoritism in her decisions of when and to whom she grant interviews; they argue that by limiting access to herself and her family, she undermines journalistic integrity to report legitimate news.[32]

Several pivotal moments have defined the ongoing struggle between the media and the Jolie-Pitts over control of their media image and activism. In spring 2006,

Angelina Jolie and Brad Pitt moved their family to the African nation of Namibia to await the birth of their first biological child. While there, they worked closely with Namibian authorities to maintain their privacy, which included Namibia's deporting or refusing entry to journalists and paparazzi who did not have the couple's approval.

> We were in this little hospital in Africa when Shi was born, [Jolie said]. I don't think there was anybody else in the hospital. It was just a little cottage, the three of us. It ended up being the greatest thing. We had wonderful doctors and nurses. It was lovely, very personal, all three in this sweet room. We had an American doctor with us, who had met the Namibian doctors, and they worked in tandem because it was a C-section and my first and we didn't know the country. He spent a few weeks with us. There was only one pediatrician in town, and one anesthesiologist, who had to come in for that—you have to plan it.[33]

Jolie and Pitt's decision to move their family to Namibia set in motion a media and political spectacle that prompted British journalist Brenden O'Neill to describe their actions as "celebrity colonialism."[34] O'Neill attributes celebrity colonialism to the individual nihilism of celebrities and to a celebrity culture in which a privileged few enjoy limitless power. Jolie and Pitt argued that their presence in Namibia actually forced media to focus on the health and education crises facing the African nation.

The United Nations High Commissioner for Refugees posits that "celebrities use their privileged access to mass media and other resources to give a voice to refugees, who are often victims of forgotten humanitarian crises and who often suffer from uninformed negative stereotyping."[35] Here, Jolie's duties are specifically to travel and to compel media to follow her to places of "humanitarian crisis" such as Namibia, rather than to trail her around Beverly Hills. However, the restrictions placed on reporters in Namibia resulted in harsh criticism of Jolie and Pitt, and media outlets cried First Amendment foul when Jolie requested that reporters sign an agreement not to ask questions about her personal life during one film-promotion press conference.

When the couple sold exclusive photographs of Jolie's children to *People* from 2006 to 2008 and donated the fees to their humanitarian organization, they argued that there is a "price on their heads" because paparazzi stalk them and that they were grasping power back from the press by deciding to publish photos and use the money for their own purposes.

> The Jolie-Pitts have proven adept at slyly commandeering the celebrity gossip mill to further their own philanthropic goals. Regarding the $14 million fee paid this summer by *People* and *Hello!* for rights to the first pictures of the newborn twins (the couple donated the entire sum to their foundation), Jolie acknowledges that the figure is astounding: "There's nothing to say other than it's bizarre. But we're happy

that we have our hands on it to distribute it to people we think are worthy, rather than some paparazzi."[36]

Jolie and Pitt's candid comments on their efforts to "force" media to cover them in a way that focuses on their activism contribute to an ongoing feud of sorts that is playing out in the public sphere. In a moment of casting media as victim, the *New York Times* claimed that Jolie "dictates terms to celebrity magazines involving their coverage of her and her family, editors say, creating an awkward situation for publications that try to abide by strict journalistic standards."[37] Pitt also argued that Jolie is "savvy" about utilizing the media glare in which she stands. Jolie and Pitt's claims of utilizing their fame to manipulate media attention lays bare the tug-of-war between them and U.S. media outlets over who can wield power to set the agenda for humanitarian issues and how.

Yet, to the extent that Jolie has been successful in turning the media gaze where she wants, the media focus remains on the privileged individual celebrity heroines and sustains hegemonic stereotyping that reinforces the very liberal, colonial hierarchies that celebrity activists claim to break down. As Radhika Parameswaran notes, stereotypical representations of third world peoples in U.S. media persist at least in part because of the influence of existing stereotypical representations on journalists.[38] Jolie may have forced cameras to follow her to Namibia, but the lens remained steadfastly focused on her pregnancy, her relationship with Pitt, and her heroine identity. The direction of the gaze, as always, remains fixed on the celebrity in a neocolonialist stance.

Media Continuums of Global Care

Another way in which media outlets continue to determine Jolie's image and to construct celebrity activism more broadly is by creating false dichotomies between Jolie and other celebrity activists. Jolie's image as mother and savior is produced in opposition to other celebrities, who are framed as not measuring up to her, including, ironically, Madonna. Despite the two celebrities' shared goals, similar activities, common friends, and public statements of support for each other, media discourse pitted Jolie and Madonna against each other in the summer of 2006. Following directly on the heels of Shiloh Jolie-Pitt's birth in Namibia, Madonna, long recognized as the queen of shock, made headlines again with her adoption of a thirteen-month-old Malawian boy she named David.[39] Why did her role as adoptive mother and humanitarian garner the same type of public outrage as her sexual and religious exploits? As U.S. news media reported, Madonna's sensational antics have become almost expected, but her decision to adopt and her efforts to harness her star power to bring visibility and aid to the

underprivileged African nation of Malawi caused even staunch Madonna supporters to denounce the "material Mom."[40]

While Angelina is routinely framed as a savior of abandoned children, one
of the persistent criticisms lobbied at Madonna is that she had shopped for a
baby as if he were nothing more than the latest accessory.[41] Madonna has been
accused of "plucking an African child out of poverty and out of the arms of the
boy's father," suggesting that she is a home wrecker more than a humanitarian.[42]
Despite writing a children's book and having two biological children, Madonna
does not conform to the ideal image of motherhood, in part because of the juxtaposition of her mothering against her controversial performing career.[43] The criticism of Madonna's adoption served to heighten the perception of Angelina Jolie
as a knowledgeable, committed long-term activist and not an opportunist. Angelina repeatedly illustrates the myth that motherhood changes one completely and
children become the center of one's life, but Madonna refuses to alter her professional choices and so appears to break the mold of the ideal mother.

Whereas Angelina Jolie's shift from whore to virgin has been somewhat
accepted, her transformation hinges on a clear, linear development over time.
Madonna, however, shows no clear redemption and does not seem to have
left behind her bad-girl image; rather, she has added the mother image to the
mix. Journalists were skeptical about whether Madonna could be trusted. One
talk-show host compared Madonna with other celebrity activists, arguing, "Let
me ask you this: is it really about Africa? I believe it with George Clooney and
Darfur. He's been there a billion times. I believe it with Angelina Jolie. She lived
it. Madonna, come on."[44] This media-generated opposition between Jolie and
Madonna reproduces conventional ideologies of motherhood that Jolie is made
to fulfill and enables a public division of women who might otherwise represent
a common cause. The two women are individualized as postfeminist figures who
exemplify feminine archetypes in opposition to one another; difference is maintained at the expense of even the appearance of cooperation.

Also contributing to the media's ability to shape the agenda of celebrity
activism is its positive coverage of certain interventions at the expense of others. Media accounts insist that certain kinds of political involvement are detrimental to celebrity careers, and, Hollywood's liberal tendencies notwithstanding,
the consequences for celebrities speaking out on controversial issues can be swift
and negative. Particularly when criticizing U.S. foreign policy, celebrities such as
Susan Sarandon and Sean Penn have been harshly criticized as anti-American
or have had their efforts pointedly ignored. Richard Gere received a lifetime ban
from presenting at the Academy Awards after using the stage to advocate for the
freeing of Tibet from Chinese rule. His efforts to raise awareness of Chinese

human rights violations went largely unreported in the media frenzy surrounding the Beijing Olympics. George Clooney and Mia Farrow both received somewhat more, and more positive, media attention for their calls-to-arms regarding the genocide in Darfur, but in both cases, the focus remained on the celebrity-as-savior to nameless, faceless people in the third world.

In many cases there is audience backlash against celebrities who become involved in hot-button issues such as war protesting, immigration, feminism, or electoral politics. When audience criticism of celebrity activism does take place, it often carries gendered and nationalist overtones. Letters to the editor and some media commentary have criticized Jolie through racialized and sexualized rubrics that mock her decision to adopt nonwhite, non-Western children rather than white, U.S. "natives."[45] Likewise, Oprah was criticized for opening a girls' academy in South Africa rather than in the United States, suggesting that U.S. children deserve first priority in humanitarian efforts.[46] Those celebrities who receive positive media coverage for their activism tend to work within institutions to address issues, such as aid to children, that do not trigger criticism. Even Jolie's most recent opinion columns, calling for greater support of Iraqi refugees, do not contradict U.S. policy but merely call for existing policy to be better enforced. In the *Washington Post*, Jolie discussed her support for a continued U.S. presence in Iraq to address humanitarian needs, writing,

> As for the question of whether the surge is working, I can only state what I witnessed: U.N. staff and those of non-governmental organizations seem to feel they have the right set of circumstances to attempt to scale up their programs. And when I asked the troops if they wanted to go home as soon as possible, they said that they miss home but feel invested in Iraq. They have lost many friends and want to be a part of the humanitarian progress they now feel is possible.[47]

Conclusion

Celebrity activism is both sustained and constituted by the contemporary media environment that sustains celebrity culture and, with it, a politics of difference. While Western institutions such as the United Nations play a role in determining priorities for humanitarian intervention and engage in many behind-the-scenes intervention efforts, their partnership with A-list celebrities and dependence on publicity underscores the power that media wield in calling the shots for what to care about and how to respond to crises. The transnational humanitarian ethics of care that has emerged in the global media culture today is one rooted in the West and characterized by an engagement with relatively noncontroversial issues, which mainly involve assistance to third world women and children on behalf of Western institutions. In one sense, celebrity activism operates as a feminine global politics of care framed as complementary to, yet separate from, the masculine official endeavors of war and state politics, from which women and humanitarian interests have historically and contemporarily been excluded. Besides, in concert with media and international organization, the promotion of old cultural hierarchies and selective agendas have also succeeded in positioning humanitarian work within a neoliberal and postfeminist model.

The travel of white celebrity activists such as Jolie in the Global South further strengthens the image of American exceptionalism and highlights the United States as a site of progressive sexual politics, agency, and a specific form of gendered cosmopolitanism. Old patterns of silencing emerge from new mediated locations such as the apparent magnanimity of movie stars and performers. The very act of trying to speak for women in the third world echoes older colonial discourses of benevolence that treat people in the third world as victims in need of rescue. Jolie's postfeminist image as a fully realized woman is predicated on her contrast with an imagined third world woman mired in traditionalism. Chandra Mohanty's argument speaks to this relational hierarchy in which the agency of Western white woman exists in relation to an implicit third world nonwhite woman: "Without the overdetermined discourse that creates the third world, there would be no (singular and privileged) first world. Without the 'third world woman,' the particular self-presentation of Western women mentioned above [Western women as secular, liberated, having control over their lives] would be problematical."[48] Celebrity support of Western institutions and media framing of their activism as supporting neoliberal, neocolonial strategies for aiding third world nations not only marginalizes the aid recipients of the Global South but also produces a U.S.-determined form of transnational exchange. Though Jolie and other celebrities claim strong global alliances, "the nation" continues to be evoked to regulate and hierarchize transnational space. The United States emerges as powerful and benevolent, while third world nations are infantilized in comparison. Thus, transnational space is articulated as an extension of the national space—ordered, managed, and civilized through a traditional and gendered deployment of motherhood and the hegemonic centers of the national.

Ultimately, the transnational humanitarian efforts of celebrities such as Jolie are dependent on mainstream media and are propped up by a neoliberal consumerist worldview that privileges individual celebrity heroism and reinforces neocolonial sexual and racial hierarchies. While Jolie is the subject par excellence and focuses her political efforts on the plight of women and children, the media coverage that constructs the agenda of transnational humanitarianism produces a postfeminist discourse that evacuates the political and the possibilities for democratic global dialogue. The lengths to which media go to situate Jolie as a powerful agent also succeed in obscuring media's own role in constructing transnational space and determining the culture and the politics of care possible in that space.

NOTES

1. A number of scholars have analyzed the relationship of celebrity and politics/activism. See, for example, A. Conley and D. Schultz, "Jesse Ventura™ and the Brave New World of Politainer Politics," *Journal of American and Comparative Cultures* 23, no. 3 (2000): 49–59; Jaideep Mukherjee, "Celebrity, Media and Politics: An Indian Perspective," *Parliamentary Affairs* 57, no. 1 (2004): 80–92.; John Street, "Bob, Bono and Tony B: The Popular Artist as Politician," *Media, Culture and Society* 24 (2002): 433–441.

2. John Street, "Celebrity Politicians: Popular Culture and Political Representation," *British Journal of Politics and International Relations* 6 (2004): 435–452.

3. Tom Junod, "Angelina Jolie Dies for Our Sins," *Esquire* (July 2007): 134.

4. Angela McRobbie, "Post-feminism and Popular Culture," *Feminist Media Studies* 2, no. 2 (2004): 257.

5. Suzanne Zuckerman. "Angelina Jolie," *In Style* (June 2005): 49.

6. "Brad & Angelina One World, One Family," *People* (December 26, 2005): 77.

7. "Celebrity Photos: The Big Picture, Angelina Jolie and Brad Pitt," *E!online*, http://www.eonline.com/photos/gallery.jsp?galleryUUID=6#2730 (accessed May, 2008).

8. Polly Blitzer, "Jolie Good!" *In Style* (March 2005): 416.

9. Media coverage heralds Jolie as a global citizen whose multiculturalism is literally inscribed on her body with tattoos of the five different longitude/latitude coordinates for the birthplaces of her children and with figures and words from around the world. At the same time, an obsessive policing of her body size, body shape, fertility, and sensuality distracts from her political actions and positions her as an object for consumption. In one example, Jolie's body is visually dissected into pieces, with her lips, tattoos, and eyes being dubbed her "best body parts." "Angelina Jolie's Best Body Parts: Our Top 9," *E!online* (June 25, 2008), http://www.eonline.com/uberblog/b2304_angelina_jolies_best_body_parts_our_top.html (accessed June 25, 2008). Though Jolie is undeniably a sex symbol for male audiences, this and many other images of Jolie that appear in women's celebrity media outlets indicate her position as an object of female gaze as well.

10. "World's Most Beautiful," *People* (May 8, 2006): 68.

11. Christopher Bagley, "One Week: Brad & Angelina," *W Magazine* (November 2008): 230–263.

12. Olivia Abel, "Ambassador Mom," *People* (March 21, 2005): 28.

13. Ibid.

14. This is reminiscent of recent images of women in Afghanistan. See Shahira Fahmy, "Picturing Afghan Women: A Content Analysis of AP Wire Photographs during the Talban Regime and after the Fall of the Taliban Regime," *Gazette* 66, no. 2 (2004): 91–112.

15. Abel, "Ambassador Mom," 28.

16. Michelle Tauber, "And Baby Makes Three," *People* (July 18, 2005): 58.

17. "World's Most Beautiful," 73.

18. Inderpal Grewal, "Transnational America: Race, Gender and Citizenship after 9/11." *Social Identities* 9, no. 4 (2003): 535–561.

19. "Angelina Jolie: 'Obama Would Be Great for My Family," *Huffington Post* (October 10, 2008), http://www.huffingtonpost.com/2008/10/10/angelina-jolie-obama-woul_n_133705.html (accessed October 2008).

20. "World's Most Beautiful," 73.

21. Michelle Tauber, "Angelina's World: From Motherhood to Brad to Saving the Globe; The Truth about the Mysterious Ms. Jolie," *People* (February 7, 2005): 71.

22. UNICEF, "Goodwill Ambassadors and Advocates" (2006), http://www.unicef.org/people/people_ambassadors.html (accessed May 2008).

23. Donald J. Puchala, "World Hegemony and the United Nations," *International Studies Review* 7 (2005): 572.

24. Ibid., 573

25. Ibid., 574.

26. "Ms. Jolie Goes to Washington," *Nightline* (March 9, 2005), ABC News transcripts.

27. Lisa Brooten, "The Feminization of Democracy under Siege: The Media, the 'Lady of Burma,' and U.S. Foreign Policy." *NWSA Journal* 17, no. 3 (2005): 134–156.

28. P. David Marshall, *Celebrity and Power: Fame in Contemporary Culture* (Minneapolis: University of Minnesota Press, 1997), 4.

29. Tom Junod, "Angelina Jolie Dies for Our Sins," *Esquire* (July 2007): 78–85, 134.

30. Lauren Berlant, *The Queen of America Goes to Washington City: Essays on Sex and Citizenship* (Durham, NC: Duke University Press, 2002).

31. "Teach the Children," *Dateline* (March 30, 2006), NBC broadcast.

32. While promoting the film *A Mighty Heart*, Jolie held a press conference at which journalists were asked to sign a contract agreeing not to ask her personal questions. After several news outlets refused to sign and reported on the contract, Jolie and Paramount Vantage (which released the film) stated that lawyers had drawn up the contract and that Jolie had actually raised concerns about those limiting clauses. Regardless of the details, news outlets reported the incident as evidence of Jolie's disregard for journalism and her self-serving image control. Steven Zeitchik and Addie Morfoot, "Press Junket Turns into 'Mighty' Spin," *Variety* (June 18–24, 2007): 3.

33. Rich Cohen, "Woman in Full," *Vanity Fair* (July 2008), 133.

34. Brendan O'Neill, "Brad, Angelina and the Rise of 'Celebrity Colonialism,'" *Spiked* (May 30, 2006), www.spiked-online.com/index.php?/site/printable/327/ (accessed June 2006).

35. Statement appearing on the website UNHCR.org (accessed May 2008).

36. Bagley, "One Week."

37. Brooks Barnes, "Story behind the Cover Story: Angelina Jolie and Her Image," *New York Times* (November 21, 2008): A1.

38. Radhika Parameswaran, "Coverage of 'Bride Burning' in the *Dallas Observer*: A Cultural Analysis of 'Other,'" *Frontiers* 16, nos. 2–3 (1996): 69–100.

39. "Madonna Appears on 'Oprah Winfrey Show,' Blames Media for Controversy Surrounding Boy She's Adopting from Africa," *CBS Morning News* (October 26, 2006).

40. "Hi, Madonna? Can We Speak with You for a Second?" *Project Gay* (November 6, 2006), http://projectgay.blogspot.com/2006/11/hi-madonna-can-we-speak-with-you-for.html (accessed November 2006).

41. "Madonna and Child," *Showbiz Tonight*, CNN (October 25, 2006).

42. "Madonna Appears on 'Oprah Winfrey Show.'"

43. In contrast to Angelina's linearly constructed tale of transformation, Madonna's entire career has been characterized by a simultaneous deployment of both virgin and whore images. See Susan Bordo, *Unbearable Weight: Feminism, Western Culture, and the Body* (Berkeley: University of California Press, 1995); John Fiske, *Reading the Popular* (Boston: Unwin Hyman, 1989).

44. "Madonna: Adoption or Accessory?" *Glenn Beck Show*, CNN (October 18, 2006).

45. "Mailbag," *People* (August 8, 2005): 8; "Mailbag," *People* (September 26, 2005): 10.

46. Allison Samuels, "Oprah Goes to School," *Newsweek* (January 8, 2007).

47. "Activist Celebrities Mum on Immigration Issue," *NewsMax.com* (April 24, 2006). http://archive.newsmax.com/archives/ic/2006/4/14/123402.shtml (accessed May 2008).

48. Chandra Mohanty, "Under Western Eyes: Feminist Scholarship and Colonial Discourses," *Feminist Review* 30 (1988): 82.

III Capital Trails

9   Objects of Knowledge, Subjects of Consumption

Persian Carpets and the Gendered Politics of Transnational Knowledge

Minoo Moallem

Connoisseur books, as a genre of knowledge production, have been crucial sites for the formation and transformation of material culture and for the production of racial and gendered differences, especially in the modern structure of empire. The genre has led to the creation of a decontextualized knowledge in which commodities such as the Persian carpet are disconnected from the circuits of labor and complex hybrid trajectories of cultural meaning. This chapter examines the ways in which connoisseur books have mediated and mediatized Oriental carpets in general and the Persian carpet in particular as a commodity. Connoisseur discourses have invested in mediating the meaning and exchange value of the Persian carpet and have mediatized it through the circulation of the carpet as a commodity via photography, advertisement, museum exhibitions, and books. Connoisseur knowledge has been supplemented by a visual and textual intertextual discourse[1] (of journalism, travelogues, anthropology, and feminism) regarding the conditions and pain involved in the labor of carpet weavers. However, this discourse, which is both constitutive and constituted by gendered subjects positions, mostly serves the moral economy of consumerism by uniting pain and pleasure in the commodity in order to influence consumer affect and desires. The transnational circulation of the commodity relies on the discourse of difference in order to produce both subjects of production and consumption. The connoisseur text's interweaving of the tribal female carpet weaver's labor with the sensory and exotic appeal of Orientalia transforms the carpet into a sublime and mobile object. This enables the texts to circulate an aesthetic education which prepares subjects of consumption with the affect and civilizational optic of empire. This process of mediatization produces the Oriental and Persian carpet as a highly mobile object of desire that attaches social subjects to particular notions of time and space regardless of their location or dislocation within the territorial boundaries of the nation or the empire. The world of carpets and connoisseur literature provides a rich intersection to examine the significance of knowledge production for the transnational circulation of commodities and also the importance of the politics of mediation in the global marketplace.

Fig. 9.1. "The most enjoyable and gratifying rugs to own are endlessly enigmatic: there is great pleasure in discovering a hidden motif or a pleasuring color pattern—even after you've owned the rug for sometime. Look for a rug that speaks to your soul." (Quotation from John B. Gregorian, *Oriental Rugs of the Silk Route* [New York: Rizzoli, 2000], 151. Photograph by the author taken at a carpet exhibition in the Carpet Museum of Tehran in 2008.)

Subjects of Knowledge, Objects of Consumption

From a luxury item in the Safavid courts of the sixteenth century, the Persian carpet has now joined the assemblage of modern commodities—"things with a particular type of social potential."[2] The importing boom for Oriental carpets began in the late nineteenth century,[3] just around the time when a systematic form of knowledge of Oriental carpets in general and Persian carpets in particular emerged. This knowledge industry, located mainly in France, England, and Germany, brought together academic and nonacademic writing (travelogues, trade guidelines, collectors' books, exhibition catalogues) in producing the connoisseur book—a particular genre of publication which offered a lush combination of words, pictures, and plates on the exotic appeal of the Persian carpet. This space for cultural and aesthetic knowledge was filled by a vast group of male and white specialists, traders, and experts who created the profession of specialized research. Oriental and Persian carpets and connoisseur books are a powerful example of how desire and demand for commodity production are created through value and the politics of knowledge.

Connoisseur books are first an important site of the "visualization of knowledge,"[4] which relies on both Eurocentric and masculinist epistemic assumptions. Indeed, as argued by Barbara Stafford, this process of opticalization and visualization remains invested in logocentrism and the devaluation of sensory, affective, and kinetic forms of communication.[5] Second, the sheer quantity of connoisseur discourses has over the years created "the empire of merchandise."[6] Third, these mediated discourses, carried mostly over print culture to now newer virtual formats, have enabled the complicity of the nation and empire within the context of a free-market economy and aided the expansion of consumer capitalism beyond the territorial boundaries of nation-states.

Based on my examination of over three hundred books, travelogues, and museum or trade catalogues in this genre of writing in English and French (including a number of works translated from German to either French or English), I elaborate on the convergence of empire and nation in creating pedagogic and affective relations to material objects that are targeted to exhibit total mastery of the Other's culture. Focusing on late-nineteenth- and early-twentieth-century connoisseur texts, I present a genealogy of the carpet in a Foucauldian sense—an evolution of the carpet as a commodity constructed and circulated by these specialized texts. The commodification of carpets, as Abdul JanMohamed has argued in the case of other commodities, cannot be separated from the fetishization of the Other and the transmutation of difference and specificity into magical essence.[7]

The connoisseur's discourses on the Oriental carpet and the Persian carpet function through what Edward Said calls "the citationary practices,"[8] referring to a large and varied body of writing that functions by referring back and forth within itself. Here, I examine not only the constitution of connoisseur expertise but also the technologies within which such expert knowledge could examine, judge, and compare the carpet within the larger frame of knowledge and commodity production. These systems and technologies of organization of the carpet have created a transnational expert knowledge base that links image, information, and experience. This mediation relies extensively on transnational politics of gender and the fetishization of the Other. An examination of the relationship between knowledge and power is crucial for both our understanding of the production of desire for an object and the context within which a commodity is produced and exchanged. Questions of exploitation and the feminization of labor are an integral part of the apparatus of the politics of knowledge.

In the sections that follow, I trace the shaping of colonial knowledge production and aesthetic education that construct the Persian carpet as a decontextualized cosmopolitan product. Through an examination of connoisseur books, I elaborate on the ways in which gendered subaltern subjects and their labor are embedded and reproduced in the flow of this discourse.

Commercial Imperialism and the Material Culture

While the study of the modern operation of empire through territorial and political claims to power has been central to a critical postcolonial perspective, the story of what Mark Crinson calls "informal imperialism,"[9] which includes the complicity of the nation and the empire in entertainment, consumerism, and the military-industrial complex, still needs to be told. This imperialism is mostly established through networks of peaceful means of free trade, consumerism, and economic integration, as well as modes of knowledge production. For example, as argued by Carol Bier, the modern production of the Persian carpet cannot be separated from the commercial rivalry of Europeans and Russians in Iran:

> The commercial rivalry between England and Russia grew particularly strong, each evolving a political sphere of influence in Iran. In spite of the complaints of Iranian merchants, European imports reached a peak in Iran in the middle of the nineteenth century. But the decline of textile manufacturing in Iran was difficult to reverse. The most effective effort, however, was that attempted by foreign capitalists who sought to commercialize rug weaving to suit the new demands of the European market. Towards the end of the nineteenth century, investment and capitalization of local and foreign firms in Iran instigated development of the Persian carpet industry. Income from the sale of carpets supplanted that once derived from the export of silk.[10]

The history of commodities is not separate from particular temporal and spatial formations and specific modes of economic exchange. Literacy and numeracy[11] have been crucial both in investing value in certain objects as commodities and in making them visible in a regime of calculation, as they are circulated through the old and new media and communication technologies. The study of the material culture calls for what Peter Pets calls "a recognition of materiality in social process, by systematically treating materiality as a quality of relationships rather than things."[12] What is specific about connoisseur books is the ways in which they construct the materiality of human interaction and the object in terms of the aesthetic and "the material process of mediation of knowledge through the senses."[13] In the connoisseur books, the visualization of knowledge is regarded as crucial to the life of the commodity. Visual literacy includes the optical training and education of sight in order to shape particular ways of seeing. This process has been influenced by the discourse of commodity as a historical object, the discourse of civilizational and cultural difference, and finally the discourse of Orientalism.

I argue that what I have elsewhere called "the scopic economy"[14] is mediated through the creation of regimes of curiosity as well as modes of surveillance, producing both attachment to and detachment from the object being looked at. Indeed, the scopic economy functions as a modus operandi that constitutes social practices related to the production, exchange, and consumption of commodities. Here, I show how connoisseurs' texts, academic writing, and advertisements, among other items, mediate the politics of value. The concept of scopic economy is crucial for tracing those regimes of visibility which have enabled the construction of a commercial empire and the creation of transnational, imperial, and national networks, bringing to the fore the historical traffic between Europe, the United States, and the so-called Orient through the juxtaposition of taste, desire, consumerism, and commodity fetishism.[15]

Connoisseurs, Curiosity, and Culture

I now turn to the regimes of curiosity that produce knowledge by participating in the consumption, circulation, and production of certain narratives, images, signs, tropes, and signifiers. These regimes do not define knowledge either by itself or by opposing it to ignorance but as "a whole cycle of accumulation: how to bring things back to a place for someone to see it for the first time so that others might be sent again to bring other things back. How to be familiar with things, people and events, which are *distant*."[16] Through the mediation of experts who signal a stylized form of discourse and networks of actors who are connected to these forms of consumption and production, connoisseur discourses forge links between the desire to see and know and practices of belonging.[17] It is this regime of curiosity that makes an object desired, preferred, chosen, and performed which, in turn, can result in the way an object is linked to the flow of value, either through commodification or decommodification. Connoisseurs enable the development of business practices and change everyday practices of consumerism through affective modes of knowledge, which demand active participation in trade, from collecting objects and traveling to becoming a full-fledged connoisseur.

For example, in a catalogue of the Herr R. G. Hubel Exhibition, *Oriental Carpets*, we come across such citations as the following:

> The wish to collect artistic objects may be regarded as one of the most attractive human passions. The collector of Oriental carpets combines in his person the hunter, the digger for hidden treasure, the adventurer, and the dedicated researcher. The hunt is exciting until the booty is safely got home. The consequent cherishing, restoring, and preserving of the treasure is a creative activity, which exceeds the mere sentimental contemplation of beautiful objects.[18]

The connoisseur's knowledge is a particular form of knowledge in both its pedagogical directions and its bonding with the object of the trade. C. J. Delabère May regards this knowledge as crucial for every consumer of Persian carpets, claiming,

> With regard to this subject we cannot too strongly urge upon our readers that they must learn to know the rugs themselves before they can really learn to know their values; nor can we over-emphasize the fact that in achieving the ability to correctly identify and classify specimens they will have acquired the chief essential of successful and accurate rug valuation.[19]

Connoisseurs' mediation between consumptive production and productive consumption also generates symbolic capital, which lends both credibility and visibility to the imperial project. The connoisseur knowledge links image, experience, and information through the simultaneous release and confinement of the Other in the pathways of transnational circulation. The relationship between the collector and the trade transcends mere interest in the objects; rather, collectors are portrayed partaking passionately in the space of connoisseurship. Thus, the connoisseur's affective relationship to the object both elevates the carpet as commodity and completes both the cultural and economic circle of meaning.

The Carpet as a Mobile Commodity and a Historical Object

> Shopping for a Persian rug can be like taking a journey through history. Not only is your rug purchase a fine investment, but in some cultures it is a form of currency!

> Certainly it will be a keepsake to hand down from generation to generation. The element of luxury with which Persian rugs are associated today provides a marked contrast with its humble beginning among the nomadic tribes that wandered the great expanses of Persia.[20]

The carpet as both a sign and a commodity is produced through a historical narrative with a coherent sense of the past, the present, and the future. The connoisseur books include illustrations of various carpet designs along with the carpet-weaving tools and random pictures of carpet workshops, weavers, and unnamed villages where carpets are produced. The illustrations typically serve as visual supplements to the text without any specific caption. The carpet's status in the present becomes legible through its identification as an object with a historical and an almost mythical aura.

As noted by David Sylvester in a gallery catalogue on Islamic carpets, "Scholarly collecting—collecting governed by a sense of history—entered the field in the 1870s. Till then, however cherished carpets may have been, little was known about their origins."[21] Indeed, irrespective of the historical fact, connoisseur books depend on such narratives of conjecture. Once the carpet is constructed as a sign, a historical object, and a commodity, it also becomes a site of differentiation of cultures and civilizations.

In this body of knowledge, the carpet and the people who produce them are both conjoined and separated in terms of their cultural capital. The carpet is considered a primitive craft but one that has the potential for being included in civilized life due to its long history and the mystery of being intertwined with an Orientalist aura and religious faith.[22] Cecil Edwards, one the most well-known connoisseurs of the Oriental and Persian carpet remarks, "The Persian people are by nature skilled and artistic craftsmen. Such a people would not for long remain content to cover their tent floors—like Eskimos or Red Indians—with the skin of beasts. The urge to fashion something closer to the need, more varied and above all more colorful, was there."[23] The historical narrative follows modern anthropological and racist notions of civilized and primitive material production as sequences in the history of progress. For example, in one of the earliest connoisseur books, *Rugs of the Orient*, published in 1911, C. R. Clifford writes,

> Simple design has been inspired always by primitive thought in so many remote countries that it discourages any logical analysis. In some cases it seems as though these varying geometrical shapes sprung from the extraordinary mosaics in Byzantine, but a child can take a square or octagon and by drawing from various points intersecting lines evolve innumerable designs. It is primitive world thought.[24]

A linear progression from simple to complex, child to adult, primitive to civilized in terms of artistic and material production serves as a basic assumption in the formation of technical knowledge on the Oriental and Persian carpet. In the connoisseur's modes of knowledge production, the focus is on three areas: the construction of the Oriental carpet as an object of domestic Orientalia and home design, distinct from the carpet as an antique object; the carpet as a commodity displaying cultural difference located within an evolutionary path from primitiveness to civilization; and the detailed description of carpet-weaving technologies including various tools that depict the technologies as an extension of nature, radically distinct from modern technological evolutions. Each connoisseur book repeats either the technical details or a descriptive account of the carpet: the wrap, the floral motif, the decoration of the border. The fascination with the techniques and technologies of carpet weaving—the loom, the raw materials, the colorants, the knots, wefts, and wrap—conceals the collective work involved in carpet weaving, including the collaboration between various forms of labor and networks of sociability and solidarity. In this context, carpet weaving is reduced to a set of technical knowledge, dissociated from the embodied experience of the community of producers—weavers, designers, and traders. The exoticized commodity is distanced from the everyday world of women weavers who make it possible for each other to pursue this difficult labor, which requires high levels of concentration, while taking care of their domestic work, child rearing, cooking, and taking care of older people.

The association with the primitive also relegates carpet weaving to an older temporal order, hence incapable of connecting to modern technologies.[25] Fortifying this view is the main argument advanced by connoisseur texts that the weavers follow tradition without understanding the design. E. Gans-Ruedin, an eminent connoisseur, writes, "Indeed, the description of the motifs is as complete as possible, but it is often very difficult to obtain from the rug makers themselves the explanation of the designs; they use such and such motif in accordance with tradition, but they are no longer aware of its original meaning."[26] Since the labor to produce the carpet is separated from the symbolic capital, the savoir faire becomes the natural function of the traditional bodies. Through this move to detach the labor from its symbolic value, the commodity as fetish turns out to be the raison d'être of the symbolic production altogether.

Instructing the Eye

> Merely glancing at an object does not enhance one's understanding of it. Only by looking again and again can one develop that degree of contemplation that leads to meditation and final involvement.[27]

According to the connoisseur texts, in order to appreciate a carpet and learn how to estimate its value, one needs to learn how to look at it and train the eye through aesthetic education backed by technical knowledge. C. J. Delabère May instructs readers that rather than merely looking at and enjoying carpets, "in achieving the ability to correctly identify and classify specimens they will have acquired the chief essential of successful and accurate rug valuation."[28] The more one knows of connoisseurs' knowledge, the better one can appreciate the carpet and estimate its value.

One of the important sites of Orientalia and the instruction of the eye was painting.[29] Carpets became an important motif in Oriental painting in the seventeenth and eighteenth centuries. According to Delacroix, they were the most beautiful pictures he had ever seen.[30] In Orientalist painting, carpet is represented as either a luxury item and a component of aristocratic life or an exotic object displayed in Oriental markets. After the invention of the power loom in Europe, carpet weavers in Kidderminster mimicked the famous Hunting carpet,[31] which impressed the Duke of York, who made a speech in which he said, "After what you have shown me, I am at a loss to understand why the public are inclined to prefer modern Oriental carpets when they can obtain such beautiful ones made by British labour."[32] The attempt to commodify such a luxury item to make it possible for the middle classes to own it led to a short-lived attempt to produce them in Europe. The focus soon shifted from attempts to produce locally to imperial export of raw materials to the Middle East, the exploitation of the cheap labor force in Iran and other parts of the Middle East and South Asia, and the import of the carpet to England, France, and Germany. It also resulted in a new division of labor between what was produced for consumption in the public sphere by power looms in Europe and Oriental carpets imported mostly for domestic use.

A focus on the visual education of the eye as part of the connoisseurs' culture was crucial in the spectacularization of Orientalia and commercial capitalism. As argued by Thomas Richards, the Great Exhibition of 1851 was essential for the spectacle of the commodities, in which "spectacle and capitalism became indivisible, a world produced, a world distributed, a world consumed, a world still too much with us."[33] In connoisseur books, the reader or the viewer is invited to learn about a scientific mode of viewing, which is defined by modern modes of differentiation and binaries of nature/culture, tradition/modernity, primitive/civilized, East/West, and women/men. The connoisseur's intervention becomes a necessity for understanding the carpet. While Westerners need to learn about the Oriental carpet, the connoisseur's knowledge is equally important for Orientals since they, too, need to learn how to understand and appreciate the carpet. According to Fernand Windels,

> The Oriental does not make a green or blue carpet because these colors please him, but because they represent this or that idea necessary to remind of the circumstance or the place where the work is realized. Once again, an Oriental carpet reads, it does

not judge itself in an Occidental way; one needs to be initiated to understand it and to appreciate it.[34]

For Windels, the weaver of Oriental carpets does not use particular colors because of his or her pleasure but because they are necessary.

It is also through the mediation of the Persian carpet, as an otherness domesticated and displayed in the private sphere as a commodity, that the site of the European home becomes a unit of consumption rather than production. In René Huyghes's view,

> It is in the art of the carpet that the Orient has developed the sense of the curve and the winding, carried by him so high, which contrasts or complement the Occident. This opposition reveals a fundamental division of the history of forms, linked to civilizations: the agricultural people, who are at the origin of the Occident, and the nomadic people, who are at the origin of the Orient.[35]

In this passage, carpet stands as a marker of a radical civilizational divide between agrarian and tribal societies, one ingrained in the Occident and the other in the Orient.

While novelty is crucial for consumerism, I believe Orientalia created a form of consumerism which relied on a linear and fixed history of a highly mobile object such as the Persian carpet. In an age when innovation is key to both production and consumption, such a historical narrative enables the production and reproduction of Oriental carpets without a concomitant need for innovation and change. The consumptive production of the Oriental carpet and the need for mass production, which relied on repetition of the same design, assigned the carpet to a liminal space somewhere between art and commodity. This ambiguous position of carpet as art, commodity, or craft continues, and therefore it remains resistant to modern forms of artistic differentiation.

Domesticating the Carpet

The Oriental carpets, once described as luxury objects covering palaces and mosques, became an element of the bourgeois household in European private spaces in the twentieth century. With its extraordinary power to display the eternal beauty of nature, it makes the bourgeois home appear as an expansive as well as a cosmopolitan space, beyond the everyday world of labor and work. Its location within the temporality of "d'autrefois," in Carl Hopf's terms, another time when "a sensibility of profound joy is awakened by a natural and healthy life that drew abundance and opened out in richness, force, and beauty."[36] The carpet, when identified as emerging from the "the inner abilities of Orientals," then serves to assure the Occidentals about their own modernity and internal ability for progress.[37] The counterpoint creates a new site for the consumption of particular commodities including the Oriental and Persian carpet. According to the connoisseurs, the Persian carpet completes the European private space: "Home without a carpet is not a home. Peace, intimacy, and forgetfulness of the outer world are impossible without the absolute and complete absence of intruding sounds," and "carpets are essential to the man who thinks, to the woman who loves—and to the child who falls."[38]

The carpet also becomes a site of differentiation between the taste of Orientals and the taste of Westerners. Herbert Coxon writes,

> Oriental carpets, in their evenly distributed colouring, all in quiet and subdued harmony, are a relief to the eye that has been exposed to the brilliant glare of the sunny East, and this probably accounts for the successful blending of colour peculiar to the Asiatic. An attempt has been made to introduce into the industries brighter and harsher colour to suit Western taste and a duller climate. But this was calculated to impair the Oriental theory of harmony of colour, and destroy the designs; it is, therefore, satisfactory to learn that the present Shah, Nasr Eddin, has forbidden the importation of foreign wools and dyes, and ordered that all carpets manufactured in his dominions must be made in the old recognized Persian patterns, free from European designs.[39]

In this text, the question of design and its transformation is defined in terms of geographic differences, causing both the desire for change and a resistance to innovation. So the climate and geographic area are collapsed within the framework of enlightened modernity—the West synonymous with innovation, as opposed to the stern resistance to new designs shown by the Oriental monarch of the Qajar dynasty. While an ordered life is the center of modern forms of everyday life, carpets with geometrical designs and cosmic plates, referring to the circularity of life, are desired as the mobile place of Asiatic harmony that can be owned by middle and upper classes in the West through cosmopolitan consumerism. While women's comfort becomes an important site of advertisement, men remain the main consumers of the carpet.

The Spectacle of the Tribal

While the Oriental carpet was displayed and represented as a sign of wealth and a domesticated commodity, the weavers of the carpets and the labor process remain the most abject aspect of the connoisseur literature. Although a significant number of weavers are located in urban areas, the connoisseur books depict weavers as mostly rural and tribal women. The idea of rural women as naturally endowed with the ability to weave carpets converges with the market economy to create a homogenized and permanent basis for the production of certain commodities.

The trope of the subaltern is produced specifically through repetitious images of rural and tribal female weavers without any explanation in the text. Each book has one or two images that are exactly the same or are very similar to each other in depicting peasant women weaving at the carpet loom. Figures 9.2 and 9.3 show the kind of images of rural and tribal women that appear in many connoisseur books and that are now widely displayed on carpet-selling websites. Both images portray the weavers from an angle either from above or from the back. These two recurring images, frequently used in various carpet-selling sites, are part of a scopic economy that interpellates both consuming and producing subjects. As I have argued elsewhere, the image is supposed to be a form of evidence of a rather coherent narrative of the Persian carpet's production in what Anne McClintock calls "anachronistic spaces," where colonized people, working classes, and women do not inhabit history but exist in a permanently atavistic time, irrational and bereft of human agency.[40] Both images put the viewer in the position of seeing without being seen, and the display of the labor becomes a spectacle for modern

Fig. 9.2. "Carpet Weavers, Ghashghaie tribe, Fars Province." (Anavian.com, "Rug History")

Fig. 9.3. Rural and tribal women at the loom. (Rug Zone UK, "Persian Oriental Handknotted," http://www.rugzone.co.uk/rugstore/shop.php/traditional-rugs/persian-oriental-handknotted/c_16.html)

regimes of visuality and control. It echoes Foucault in making the point that the automatic functioning of power is to arrange things such that "the surveillance is permanent in its effects, even if it is discontinuous in its action."[41] In each image, there is a convergence of surveillance and control in the position of the camera (from above or from behind), in the depiction of the tribal and rural female carpet weaver, and in the ways in which through the scopic economy the power makes itself permanent.

The inclusion of these images sometimes goes along with such statements as, "And how intrinsically interesting is the carpet; how unique its long eventful story; what an ancestry it has! Back to the time of Adam and Eve, . . . she is still spinning in the East—goes the history of weaving, which is also the story of the carpet."[42] Both images depict the weavers in proximity with the natural, the tribal, and the uncivilized, making productivity a necessary condition. They also make the conditions of the labor normal, endurable, and tolerable. The image substitutes the body of the weavers, both male and female, through an ideological invasion. In broader terms, the Orient is portrayed as tribal and traditional, while the Occident is referred to as urban and modern. As a result, civilizations are described as having radically different narratives of origin which will never come to an end. Being lower on the hierarchy of civilizations, the tribal will always be positioned not only as the other of the urban but also as inferior in the evolutionary stages of civilization in modern narratives of progress and development. In both images, "the primitive," "the tribal," and "the female subject" as "the other" of civilization wipes out the labor and the process of production. In the Oriental spectacle of the Persian carpet, subaltern labor is invisible in the frame of value.

The Blood Bond of Transnational Masculinity

> The true Oriental carpet is vigorous, robust, and of fine-bred strength in texture, design, and coloring, and can claim in all its essential characteristics to be thoroughly masculine.[43]

Connoisseur books complement the masculinized and masculinist politics of mediation. Given that most of those who mediate the process of carpet circulation are men, the imagined audience of the connoisseur books is described in terms of masculinity. Women are depicted either as passive consumers, mostly in voyeuristic roles rather than being the buyers of the carpet, or as rural and tribal weavers, with not much information on the labor process. In addition, the carpet is mostly associated with private property, which is aesthetically appreciated and owned by men. In the most common visual representation of the carpet, a woman sitting on the carpet, the carpet is associated with private property and women. Both the carpet and European women are depicted as objects of the gaze rather than its subjects.

For example, Adam and Charles Black, Oriental carpet connoisseurs and collectors, claim that women have no knowledge of home decoration:

> I am doing a good turn to my own sex in writing in this strain, and I offer no apologies to the fair sex: there is the danger of every woman being infected by the prevalent "suffragette" microbe, and of becoming persuaded that she really knows something about housekeeping—save the mark! The French superiority in matters domestic may be owing to the fact that the French housemaid is a "man," with his own sex, which forms the connecting-link with the Oriental, who from the beginning of things knew how to construct a fabric, which his sense of fitness and justice later taught him to appreciate and understand as the prime minister to his comfort and ease.[44]

Another early carpet connoisseur and trader, Herbert Coxon, in his travelogue *Oriental Carpets: How They Are Made and Conveyed to Europe*, published in 1884, calls on a masculinity which is defined by the imperial culture of travel, adventure, and trade. At the closing of his book, which could be considered one of the earliest connoisseur books, he writes, "On this account, I think I have demonstrated that my journey has been a successful one, and if nothing more, it should prove that provincial firms in England may emancipate themselves of the metropolis, and obtain their wares first hand from the East."[45]

While the carpet becomes a site of ultimate cultural and religious difference between the East and the West, Coxon depicts Oriental masculinity as benefiting from the weaving skills of wives, concubines, and slaves. Here Oriental and Persian women become a natural labor force, eternally sustaining the production of carpets and sustaining men as the natural beneficiary of their work. He writes,

> The Mohamedan law allows a man four wives, but he can take as many concubines and slaves as the length of his purse will allow. The women are largely employed in carpet making, chiefly confining themselves in Persia to the sizes that would come under our definition of a rug. The larger sizes are made by men. Almost all well-known embroideries of Persia are the work of the women of the harem. In the East, as the reader is probably aware, it is the women who mostly toil, while their lords indulge in the sublime pleasure of doing nothing.[46]

In this early observation about cultural difference, gender is constructed as a category, which goes beyond ethnic, class, and urban/rural differences. In this context, all Muslim men indulge in the pleasure of taking advantage of the women of their harem. For example, for Fernand Windels, a French carpet connoisseur, this gender division mirrors the natural division of labor in Oriental societies. He writes, "Durant des siècles la production des tapis d'Orient fut exclusivement familiale. Les femmes s'occupaient du tissage tandis les hommes recueillaient les produits tinctoriaux d'origine naturelle" [For centuries the Oriental carpet was exclusively produced by families. Women engaged in weaving while men collected dyeing products of natural origin].[47] Such a depiction of the Orient is very much consistent with gendered notions of Orientalism. Gradually, this genre of observation is replaced with the naturalization of the cheap labor force of women and children in the so-called East and its justified exploitation in the new international division of labor of the empire. H. J. Whigman (the author *The Persian Problem* in 1903) elaborates on the cost of women's labor and the reasons the carpets were made in Persia and under European supervision rather than in Europe. He writes, "Fortunately for the British and American householders, the Persian woman is still a slave. If ever she is emancipated or raised out of the Mohammedan abyss to a higher level in the scale of existence Persian carpets will become a thing of the past."[48] The exploitation of Persian women in the carpet industry was not only blamed on their religious difference but also cathected as beneficial for the consumptive production of the British and U.S. imperialism.

Subsumption or Sublime

> Knowledge of the unknown world was mapped as a metaphysics of gender violence—not as the expanded recognition of cultural difference—and was violated by the new Enlightenment logic of private property and possessive individualism.[49]

The carpet's ability to express, among other things, the possibility of community, collaboration, and a form of territorialization which does not need to be attached to a defined national territory other than the imaginary landscape of plants, animals, sky, clouds, and colors becomes a threat to the humanist subject of connoisseur books. The humanist subject of connoisseur books is profoundly defined by the cultural values of an enlightened and civilized West, which is radically distinguished from the not-yet-civilized culture of the East. Such potential for territorialization of space conceals and defers the anxieties of cultural and artistic singularities that may interrupt and induce a new relation to desire, a relation which would create more perplexity than yearning in the interests of the imperial powers. Such potential for territorialization of what is being dislocated is exploited by, on the one hand, the discourse of nationalism in order to create national feelings for "there" and, on the other, the discourses of old and neo-Orientalism and self-Orientalization in order to create an exotic landscape which is domesticated and brought "here."

As elaborated in this chapter, both the subject figure produced in the discourse of connoisseurs and the subject/viewer who is subjected to these discursive practices to make sense of it are located within a scopic economy. This scopic economy links colonial exceptionalism with masculinist consumerism as it brings the national and transnational spaces together by creating pedagogic and affective relations to material objects that are targeted to display total mastery of the Other's culture. In this process, the figure of the Other, feminized and abjectified as an extension of nature, as opposed to culture, is used to mediate such transnational encounters to rationalize and legitimize the mastery of the knowledge-producing subjects over the process of subject formation. In other words, this process of subject formation cannot be separated from the practices of knowledge. Connoisseur books bring the power of science and money into conversation with the power of lifestyle values through the abstraction of the commodity. Such mediation brought various cultures into the same temporal and spatial framework through the vision and perspective of expert knowledge of a particular kind, in the case of connoisseurship with the power to abstract the commodity from the conditions of its existence and the economy of needs in the endless possibility of extracting material objects for circulation.

I am grateful to Radha Hegde for her careful reading and comments on this chapter. An earlier version of this chapter was presented in a panel at the American Studies Association conference in October 2007, and I wish to thank Caren Kaplan, Inderpal Grewal, and Jennifer Terry for a very stimulating dialogue in this panel.

1. On intertextuality, see Stuart Hall, *Representation: Cultural Representations and Signifying Practices* (London: Sage, 1997), 232.

2. Arjun Appadurai, "Introduction: Commodities and the Politics of Value," in Arjun Appadurai, ed., *The Social Life of Things: Commodities in Cultural Perspective* (Cambridge: Cambridge University Press, 1986), 6. I use the concept of commodity to refer to three ideas: commodity as an object of material culture, commodity as an object invested with value, and commodity as the object of circulation and exchange.

3. Sarah B. Sherrill, "America and the Oriental Carpet: Seventeenth and Eighteenth Centuries," in Jere L. Bacharach and Irene A. Bierman, eds., *The Warp and Weft of Islam: Oriental Carpets and Weaving from Pacific Collections* (Seattle: Henry Art Gallery, 1978).

4. Barbara Maria Stafford, "Presuming Images and Consuming Words: The Visualization of Knowledge from the Enlightenment to Post-Modernism," in John Brewer and R. Porter, eds., *Consumption and the World of Goods* (New York: Routledge, 1994), 462–477.

5. Ibid., 463–464.

6. Roland Barthes, *Critical Essays* (Evanston: Northwestern University Press, 2007), 6; for example, Onno Ydema notes that a survey of pictorial sources from the Netherlands within the years 1540–1700, relating to the study of Oriental carpets, has resulted in the cataloguing of about 960 representations. See Onno Ydema, *Carpets and Their Datings in Netherlandish Paintings, 1540–1700* (Zutphen, the Netherlands: Walburg Pers, 1991), 123.

7. Abdul R. JanMohamed, "The Economy of Manichean Allegory: The Function of Racial Difference in Colonialist Literature," in Henri Louis Gates, Jr., ed., *"Race," Writing, and Difference* (Chicago: University of Chicago Press, 1986), 86.

8. Edward Said, *Orientalism* (New York: Vintage Books, 1979).

9. Mark Crinson defines informal imperialism as a "form of imperialism by which control was established through ostensibly peaceful means of free trade and economic integration." Mark Crinson, *Empire Building: Orientalism and Victorian Architecture* (New York: Routledge, 1996), 2.

10. Carol Bier, *Woven from the Soul, Spun from the Heart: Textile Arts of Safavid and Qajar Iran, 16th–19th Centuries* (Washington, DC: Textile Museum, 1987), 254.

11. John Brewer and Roy Porter, introduction to John Brewer and Roy Porter, eds., *Consumption and the World of Goods* (New York: Routledge, 1994), 6.

12. Peter Pets, "The Spirit of Matter: On Fetish, Rarity, Fact, and Fancy," in Patricia Spyer, ed., *Border Fetishisms* (New York: Routledge, 1998), 99–100.

13. Ibid., 102.

14. Minoo Moallem, "Nation on the Move" (digital project designed by Erik Loyer), in Tara McPherson and S. Anderson, eds., *Vectors: Journal of Culture and Technology in a Dynamic Vernacular Difference* 3, no. 1 (Fall 2007).

15. For my work on the regimes of visibility and gendered citizenship in Iran, see Minoo Moallem, *Between Warrior Brother and Veiled Sister: Islamic Fundamentalism and the Politics of Patriarchy* (Berkeley: University of California Press, 2005).

16. Bruno Latour, *Science in Action* (Cambridge, MA: Harvard University Press, 1987), 220.

17. See Inderpal Grewal, *Transnational America: Feminisms, Diasporas, Neoliberalisms* (Durham, NC: Duke University Press, 2005), 200.

18. Herr R. G. Hubel Exhibition Catalogue, *Oriental Carpets* (Liverpool, UK: Paragon Books, 1972).

19. C. J. Delabère May, *How to Identify Persian Rugs: A Text-Book for Collectors and Students* (London: G. Bell and Sons, 1920), 107.

20. Rugs Direct, "Tips on Decorating with Persian Rugs," http://www.rugs-direct.com/popularthemes/persianrugs.htm (accessed May 9, 2010).

21. David Sylvester, "On Western Attitudes to Eastern Carpets," *Islamic Carpets from the Joseph V. Mcmullan Collection* (New York: Metropolitan Museum of Art Bulletin, 1972), 4.

22. M. K. Zephyr Amir, *Supreme Persian Carpets* (Singapore: self-published, 1972).

23. Cecil Arthur Edwards. *The Persian Carpet: A Survey of the Carpet-Weaving Industry of Persia* (London: Duckworth, 1960), i.

24. C. R. Clifford, *Rugs of the Orient* (New York: Clifford & Lawton, 1911), 71.

25. As noted by James Essinger, there was definitely a crucial link between the Jacquard loom and the analytical engine invented by Babbage. See James Essinger, *Jacquard's Web: How a Hand Loom Led to the Birth of the Information Age* (Oxford: Oxford University Press, 2004), 138.

26. E. Gans-Ruedin, *The Great Book of Oriental Carpets* (New York: Harper and Row, 1983), 7.

27. No source given. From the catalogue Herr R. G. Hubel Exhibition Catalogue, *Oriental Carpets.*

28. May, *How to Identify Persian Rugs,* 107.

29. In my view, Orientalia includes any material object attributed to what is referred to as Muhammadan, Musulman, Oriental, and Persian in nineteenth- and twentieth-century European and American writings. The concept is marked by the history of religious, racial, and cultural difference.

30. Cited in Sylvester, "On Western Attitudes to Eastern Carpets," 4, 6, 10.

31. A famous and precious Persian carpet that was made in the mid-sixteenth century during the Safavid dynasty and was sold to the Victoria and Albert Museum by a British broker with the advice of William Morris, the prominent English textile designer and artist.

32. "Souvenir Brochure to Commemorate the Visit of the Duke of York" (Kidderminster, UK: July 21, 1926).

33. Thomas Richards, *The Commodity Culture of Victorian England: Advertising and Spectacle, 1851–1914* (Stanford, CA: Stanford University Press, 1990), 16.

34. Fernand Windels, *Le tapis: Un art—une industrie* (Paris: Les éditions D'antin, 1935), 144. Author's translation.

35. René Huyghes, *Tapis: Présent de L'orient a L'occident,* Exposition associée au project de l'UNESCO "Routes de la Soie: Routes de la Dialogue" (Paris: Institut du monde Arabe, 1989), 7.

36. Carl Hopf, *Oriental Carpets and Rugs* (London: Thames and Hudson, 1913), 32.

37. Ibid., 34.

38. *The Carpet Book* (London: Waring and Gillow, 1910), 3.

39. Herbert Coxon, *Oriental Carpets: How They Are Made and Conveyed to Europe* (London: T. Fishr Unwin, 1884), 56–57.

40. Anne McClintock, *Imperial Leather: Race, Gender and Sexuality in the Colonial Contest* (New York: Routledge, 1995), 30. For more information, see Moallem, "Nation on the Move."

41. Michel Foucault, *Discipline and Punish,* trans. Alan Sheridan (New York: Vintage Books, 1979), 201.

42. *The Carpet Book*, 3.

43. Adam Black and Charles Black, *Oriental Carpets, Runners and Rugs, and Some Jacquard Reproductions* (London: Macmillan, 1910), 293.

44. Ibid., 232.

45. Coxon, *Oriental Carpets*, 74.

46. Ibid., 55.

47. Windels, *Le tapis*, 137.

48. H. J. Whigham, *The Persian Problem* (New York: Scribner, 1903), 300–301.

49. McClintock, *Imperial Leather*, 23.

Violence, Technology, and the Transgressive Gendered Body in India's Global Call Centers

Radha S. Hegde

As India defines its place in the global economy as the high-tech solution center for business operations, new forms of work and work environments have emerged in the communication and information-technology sectors. These new work environments have radically altered the social and cultural experiences of everyday life. The outsourcing phenomenon, which casts India simultaneously as a threat, a cost-saving option, and an irritant, has occupied a spectral presence in the Western imaginary. However, unraveling on the ground is a complex transnational narrative about the neoliberal framing of flexible work, enabled by the presence of new forms of mediated connectivity. The high-tech environments of India provide a site from which to examine the dynamics of globalization as it unfolds and to see how local realities of work are embedded within global frames. As global capital is instantiated in everyday practices, it plays on local instabilities and hierarchies.[1] In this process, a series of hot buttons are pressed, especially as women find their place in the neoliberal economy and face a grid of old and new power structures. This chapter explores how the growing influence of new media technologies and networks has created conditions of labor for women that disrupt everyday life and entangle the categories of the national and transnational, the private and public.

Call centers with rows of young people working the phone lines have become iconic of India's global presence. With time rearranged to service the Western world, call centers come alive in the middle of the night, when the computer screens light up and phones start ringing. What do these newly scripted jobs and work practices mean for the everyday life of Indian women? Hired for their English-speaking skills and/or technical competence, call center workers provide a variety of services for typically U.S., British, and Australian customers. The media in the United States and India glamorize these jobs and depict the employees as enjoying their fiber-optic journey into a new identity. A popular thread of reportage claims that call-center jobs have liberated Indian youth and turned them into avid consumers, thereby providing a necessary nudge to the traditionalism of Indian society, especially with regard to women.[2] However, the ways in which gender issues are set into motion by globalization are far more

Fig. 10.1. Colleagues and friends remember Pratibha after her brutal murder.
(Aruna Raman)

complex than these linear trajectories suggest. This chapter examines how new media technologies are reorganizing labor practices and everyday life for women in India. How does the binary of tradition and modernity get deployed and reworked in the context of technological change?

In December 2005, Pratibha Srikantamurthy, a young woman employed in a multinational corporate call center, was raped and murdered en route to her place of work, the Hewlett Packard (HP) Global Delivery application services. Around 1:30 a.m., a driver, one of many hired to transport employees to work, picked up Pratibha from her residence in Bangalore. The cab company, to whom HP had outsourced its transportation needs, later discovered that the driver who picked up Pratibha was not registered on their daily roster. Pratibha's husband, also a call-center worker, was not able to reach her on the phone at night and hence assumed she was busy. He began to panic when she did not return home at 11 a.m. the next morning. On calling HP, Pratibha's family was told that she did not report to work the previous day. After a day of waiting and police investigation, the driver who had raped and murdered Pratibha confessed to the crime. Her body was found in a ditch outside of Bangalore's technology corridor and had scratch marks, suggesting a struggle before her brutal rape and strangulation.[3] Her death shook up her colleagues, who held prayer meetings in her memory (see figure 10.1).

179   Spaces of Exception

The details of the case sent tremors around the country. The Indian media went into high gear, calling into question both the conditions of call-center work and the responsibility of multinational corporations for employee safety. It was a highly charged case that drew sharp responses from across the social spectrum, evoking discussions about sexuality, violence, modernity, and the erosion of tradition—all articulated within the binary of the national and the global. The topic of safety is one that arises quite frequently in conversations with call-center workers, and the "Pratibha case" is recalled as a moment of crisis in the recent life and history of Bangalore as India's premier technological city. I use the events and responses surrounding this violent crime to describe the narratives that are mobilized around the global call-center worker and the labor through which she is drafted into streams of global connectivity. In the construction of these elite global workspaces, local and national processes are circumvented, leading to intraurban schisms and new twists on the familiar patriarchal discourse around rape and the nomination of the victim. A reading of the discourse surrounding this rape and murder in Bangalore reveals how the figure of the "globalized" woman is constructed as sexually transgressive.

Transnational Exceptions and Gendered Transgressions

Violence against women is certainly not new to urban life. However, the fact that Pratibha's rape and murder drew the level of media attention it did was precisely because it instigated discussion about the conditions of public life in the context of global economic transformation. Both the local and national media went into a reporting frenzy, prying open details about new forms of work in the outsourcing industry. Reports claimed that her death offered insight into an unseen world of work within the glass and cement citadels of globalization.[4] In these offices, where access is highly restricted, young people solve problems at night for geographically remote customers. An aura of secrecy and global allure envelops both the work and worker within the call centers in urban India, which are cordoned off both symbolically and materially from the local environment.

The state also plays an active role in managing the intersection of national and transnational interests, which, in turn, intensifies the contradictions posed by these highly technologized workspaces. The information-technology industry advertises its jobs as exciting and offering opportunities to learn global competencies through interactions with international customers. The global call centers are compared to American college campuses, and the larger call centers pride themselves on being modern, egalitarian workplaces where gender discrimination is a nonissue.[5] According to a study of the vulnerabilities of labor in the new economic order in India, the emergence of this new type of work has effectively enabled the industry to maintain a "productively docile workforce within a changed framework of human resource management."[6]

Call centers within the information-technology corridor in Bangalore pride themselves on offering world-class facilities and state-of the-art technology. This visible separation from the local environment establishes the call centers as distinct islands of hypermodernity on the global fast track. Responding to demands of global capital, the state government of Karnataka has provided various forms of juridical relaxations to maintain Bangalore's magnetic draw as a technology hub. Aihwa Ong argues that neoliberalism, as a technology of governing, relies on calculative choices to produce conditions and possibilities for governing and for optimal economic productivity. Departing from the formulation of sovereign exception, in which the subject who is deemed excludable is denied protection, Ong argues that neoliberal exceptions are often decisions to include selected populations and spaces. Market-driven calculations, for example, are invoked in sites of transformation to create "spaces of exception" that in turn enjoy extraordinary political benefits and economic gain.[7] Spurred by the logic of the marketplace, the state strategically flexes its policies to make the local environment conducive to the flow of capital. Illustrative of this move is the creation of spaces in India designated as Special Economic Zones, which are advertised by the state as "hassle-free environments" promising various types of incentives for foreign investments. In order to encourage the growth of the information-technology sector, the state government of Karnataka notes in its "Millennium" policy statement that "the State is committed to simplify all the relevant enactments for the Business Process Outsourcing (BPO) sector. The barriers including employment of women at night, flexi-working hours and mandatory weekly off have all been removed by necessary amendments to the relevant Acts to create an optimal environment for the growth of the BPO sector in the state."[8] Through these exceptions and governmental suspension of policies, urban spaces of privilege are created as Bangalore is emplaced within technocratic globality.

What do these spaces of global optimization mean for reorganizing the politics of women's work life in the technology sectors of Bangalore? Call centers have reversed the work day in order to take advantage of the twelve-hour time difference between India and the West. This does not translate into conventional understandings of flexibility or other worker-negotiated models of work. Rather, there is a clear switching of the time span of work to nighttime hours in order to reap the benefit of international time differences between India and its customers in the Global North. The very presence of women in call centers was made possible due to the suspension of a state ban on nighttime work. In 2002, the state government of Karnataka, with its eye focused on economic growth, gave the information-technology industries an exemption from section 25 of the state's

Shops and Commercial Establishment Act, which prohibits the employment of women and young persons during the night—twelve consecutive hours between 8 p.m. and 6 a.m.[9] This exemption was contingent on corporate employers meeting certain conditions concerning the provision of safe transportation to women employees. The original ban, which restricted women's mobility and choice, was justified by the state's appeal to a gendered politics of protection. The new amendment caters to the emerging industry under the premise that the work paradigm in the information-technology establishments requires flexibility and cannot be stipulated according to traditional time slots or even weekly holidays. This exemption from legislative control with regard to the temporal context of women's work was specifically intended to nurture the growth of global outsourcing and to make Bangalore attractive to foreign investors. Both the existence of the archaic law and its subsequent removal, for the purpose of preferential treatment of the information-technology industry, consolidate the state's patriarchal stance with its neoliberal leanings.

While the amendment to the labor laws opens up opportunities for night work, it does not change existing systems of power or change perceptions about women in public spaces.[10] The popular conception that night work has ushered in a social revolution is at best facile.[11] In a calculative choice, the state has repurposed the rule to fit the demands of the twenty-four-hour global economy. Gender roles and sexuality are naturalized within a discourse of protection attuned to the larger economic rationale. In the context of the new digital economy, the lifting of the ban does not automatically translate into women's agency or freedom to choose their hours of work. Instead, as A. Aneesh suggests, "technologies of virtual mobility are increasingly made to penetrate into local times, and thereby reconfigure local contexts and the social times of people's lives."[12]

The public and private life of young women like Pratibha, employed in Bangalore's call centers, revolve around the transformed rhythms of night work.[13] With the emergence of these new technology-related jobs, the networks of global commerce reconfigure the types of mobility permissible at night within the cityscape. The crossing of conventional time and space boundaries confers on women in call centers an aura of independence and new form of sexualized visibility. At the same time, when women are exploring new employment options enabled by media technologies, there is a heightened surveillance of sexuality and its performance. Debates on sexuality have consistently been mobilized in the saga of modernization when anxieties about transformations are tacked onto discussions about purity, morality, and sexual behavior. As the postcolonial society rewrites itself within the cosmopolitan discourse of neoliberal globalization, we have to take pause at how gendered positions are inducted into the global imaginary—

more specifically, as Arvind Rajagopal states, at how new gendering processes are braided with existing ones.[14] The opening up of night work brings into full view the gendered dynamics of power and social contradictions embedded within global capitalism and the information society.[15]

Bangalorians talk about call-center workers as a breed apart—young free spenders with questionable sexual mores and a worldview influenced by their mediated exposure to the West. With their youth and earning power, they are drafted into the growing new middle class and emerge as economic subjects of globalization.[16] As women are actively recruited as workers and consumers by the new global economy, there is a noticeable shift in the ways in which public discourse on sexuality is constructed. Advertisements and billboards across the urban landscape produce new fields of desire for the new Indian woman who is young with disposable income, thereby producing the Indian global woman, in Janaki Nair's view, both "as a consuming subject and as object to be consumed."[17] This consumer savvy, prized in the marketplace, takes a different inflection in everyday life, leading to stigmatization of the labor that operates by a different set of rules. The new female worker is now marked as sexually transgressive. As one newspaper reports, "A female Indian call centre worker who works late nights and chats to strangers for a living is not the kind of girl you bring home to your mother."[18] The responses that followed the rape and murder of Pratibha demonstrate the cultural contestation that takes place over the terms of global change and, in particular, about women's role and mobility. Consider this statement from the Joint Commissioner of Police in Bangalore: "Why was this girl (Pratibha) so careless even when she learnt he was not the regular driver? She went and sat with the driver in the front seat. She did not maintain the normal protocol and distance. For a criminal she became an *easy target*. In the past, call centre employees have been mugged, but this is the first time such a heinous crime has taken place."[19] The city police in Bangalore also issued guidelines which recommended a dress code and suggested that women employees refrain from dressing provocatively and interacting "freely" with male colleagues in front of the drivers, as this might send wrong messages about women.

The case opened up the ways in which the politics of gender is reinscribed within overlapping discourses of modernity and tradition, under the watchful eye of the neoliberal economy. As Rajeswari Sunder Rajan writes, gender becomes an issue usually as a crisis, a problem, or a scandal and when women are conspicuously visible in spaces of modernity; they are treated as having chosen the "risk" of harassment voluntarily.[20] The call-center worker, hypervisible and marked as contaminated by global exposure, becomes the easy target made eligible for violence.

Thresholds of Techno Space

The movement into globality is hinged on a series of highly localized processes, and hence transnational sexual politics is played out within these scalar disjunctures. Customized webs of services that meet the needs of the global technology industry hold together Bangalore's status as a global technology hub. Alongside the visible growth of the elite spaces of the new economy, there is a development of an informal labor network, resulting in a visibly tiered urbanism.[21] The outsourcing industry, which has built its very existence and transnational identity around the collapse of space and time, remains deeply dependent on support services that are highly bound and constrained by local conditions. The technology-enabled neutralization of geography rests on the access and customization of a complex infrastructure connecting the flow of laboring bodies, electricity, roads, and transportation. Bangalore is a standing example of Saskia Sassen's argument that the tasks that manage and coordinate the flow of capital are place bound, in contrast to the hypermobility of the capital they service.[22] This case study reveals the inherent tensions that inhabit the ways in which the global is accommodated within local contexts and structures.

In the new high-tech world of Bangalore, there is a clear demarcation between those who are included within the citadels of capital and those who service it from the margins, at the threshold of globalization. This space of the outside is served by a complex transportation system which ferries employees back and forth from home to office—from the peripheries to the center, from the local to the transnational. Transportation to the work sites is a key operation in the information-technology spaces of Bangalore. Due to the late work shifts, corporations advertise transportation to the work sites as one of the perks of the job. The unreliability of public transportation makes this offer very attractive to the employees. A human-resources manager in Bangalore mentioned to me, "We have to be on time to start as soon as the workday in America begins, so we cannot take chances with the Bangalore buses. We would rather pick our employees up and ensure they are on time." Transportation hence becomes another piece in the mechanisms of worker control, circumvention of public services, and the private customization of infrastructure.[23]

Outside the large call centers of Bangalore, it is commonplace to see a line of vans and minibuses parked (see figure 10.2). There is a flurry of activity as the cabs pick up employees from their homes, starting from the late evening into the night, and then drop them back home, in the early hours of the morning. The drivers have hectic schedules shuttling employees according to the time demands of the countries they service. Call-center vans speeding through the city are a familiar sight, as they pick up the employees from various parts of the city

Fig. 10.2. The transportation scene outside call centers. (Radha Hegde)

and suburbs and head toward Electronic City, Bangalore's technology enclave. These vans have notorious accident rates, earning them the name "rogue" cabs.[24] The drivers, according to some reports I received, log over fifteen hours of driving a day. They are also sleep deprived, snatching winks of sleep in the car or even dozing off at the wheel. At the gates of the larger call centers, food stands sell chai and samosas. In these outside spaces, it is a familiar sight to see drivers playing cards and wiling away their time, since a significant part of their job and daily routine is simply waiting between shifts. In contrast to the new technology-driven, distanciated interactions happening inside the call centers, outside, one hears local inflections of Indian languages, mostly Kannada and Hindi, against the background hum of vehicular noise. The drivers are routinely monitored by their companies through mobile phones and other more immediate and direct forms of surveillance. The drivers stand at the entrance of globality—denizens of a vernacular world, unassimilable yet necessary for the production of a global modernity.

Confessing to the rape and murder of Pratibha, the driver Shivakumar stated that he had set his eyes on women working in the Hewlett Packard offices. He had been randomly calling women from the employee list maintained by the transportation office with the hope of luring one of them. Before calling Pratibha, he had telephoned two of her colleagues who were already on their way with their regular cab drivers.[25] In the middle of the night, an unsuspecting Pratibha got into Shivakumar's vehicle assuming that he was a legitimate replacement for her usual driver. Later investigations revealed that Pratibha had also attempted to reach her husband on her cell phone after she left home. Ironically, the driver also stole her credit cards and her mobile phone—the symbols of her commercial presence and cultural identity. Thereafter, Shivakumar simply moved his contractual services of shuttling employees to another global corporation in the vicinity.

It is revealing that Shivakumar had specifically targeted call-center employees of a multinational corporation. To the driver, the female call-center worker represents a globally exposed and available body—one who works at night servicing strangers in distant lands. The consumer identity ascribed to call-center employees accentuates the stereotype of the Westernized, sexually available woman. Call-center workers, particularly women, are routinely associated with being "call girls" or are considered sexually permissive and "Westernized." As A. R. Vasavi notes, girls are viewed as being particularly susceptible to a culture of Westernization.[26] This eroticization of the woman worker who offers, in this case, her ear to an unknown public nominates her as the right victim. The violence met by Pratibha has to be contextualized within the emergence of Bangalore as a global city and the particular economic and cultural routes through which women's labor is made visible. Doreen Massey notes the very characterization of cities as global makes the part stand in for the whole, with the city being defined by its elite.[27]

Following the murder, there was intense public discussion about safety and accountability, during which the various players and their agendas collided. The corporate world blamed the police and attributed the tragedy to the growing crime rate in the city. The police in turn chastised the young women for their lack of morals and cultural values and then focused on the individual pathologies of taxi drivers at large.[28] A Bangalore police chief recommended a set of rules for call-center employees, with the warning that he was not engaging in moral policing:

> All of us should understand that drivers come from a certain socio-economic background. Their standard of education is lesser. These people cannot digest a girl talking to a boy freely in a cosmopolitan society and wearing a particular type of dress. They form certain opinions about the persons based on their dress and behavior and crime follows.[29]

These comments from a senior police official capture the contradictions and divisions that accompany the global reorganization of work and labor practices. Hierarchies of gender and class are first redrawn and then mobilized in ways that pit groups against each other. The drivers provide essential material labor to prop up the dematerialized product of technological services that are offered within the temples of technology. The life of the drivers, who provide transportation on the outside, and the call-center employees, who labor within the technology centers, are vastly different and kept apart. Linguistic hegemony of the English-speaking technology call-center agents compounds the class divide between various strata of workers. In Electronic City, drivers are merely instruments of transportation who cannot claim admittance into the portals of technology or the community of transnational workers. The driver enables transportation from home to the workplace but also stands outside, literally, as the embodiment of risk and terror that lurks in the liminal space between the local and the global. Shivakumar the driver is the private face of shame that stands in contrast to the public image of globality. The drivers represent localized raw energy incompatible with the West—the constitutive outside of global cosmopolitanism.[30]

The violence is interpreted as an interruption from the local world, an aberration that disrupts the smooth operations of the high-tech world of the information industry. In a strange reversal, work spaces are depicted as safe spaces requiring no protection, and the real problem lies in the process of getting through local infrastructures. The spaces of globalization are represented as places of order, control, and predictability, in opposition to the chaos, disorder, and violence of the local. When asked what precautionary measures have been taken, Som Mittal, then chief of Hewlett Packard, responded that the question was akin to asking, "What precautionary measures can be taken against a suicide bomber?"[31] The transportation companies asserted that this was a stray incident and that the driver in question was just one bad example in an otherwise flawless system. This claim, also echoed by the technology industry, either downplayed or summarily dismissed the politics of sexuality set in motion by the transnational mediatization of work. Pratibha's murder, with its gory details, was sensational news that rocked Bangalore briefly, but it remains a glaring example of the violence underwriting these urban transformations brought about by the culture of technology and outsourcing.

New Salve for Old Wounds

In the aftermath of Pratibha's murder, public attention turned quickly to the quality of life and security in urban spaces. Bangalore, the city whose name has gained notoriety as a verb in the global lexicon—the pride of the Indian information-technology industry—was now a tarnished brand name. In media discourse, the city which signified code and computation had publicly revealed infrastructural loopholes. The city was abuzz with speculations about how the incident could have been prevented and even predicted. Far from approaching the gendered violence and classed oppression within the larger systemic structures, the response focused on fixing Bangalore through the reassertion of old ideologies of safeguarding women's morality, fused with projections of a digital nirvana.

The outrage and anger about Pratibha's rape and murder soon morphed into an obsessive focus on technology and informational devices. The speculations offered by the industry, the police, and the media focused mainly on how the city and its citizens should be viewed, read, marked, mapped, arranged, or recorded in order to prevent such incidents. The accounts asserted that this was a freak incident that happened due to a systems breakdown and that if only the technological infrastructure had been in place, the violence could have been prevented. In short, the city had to be rearticulated in technological terms in order make up for its machinic lack. In a studied move, the discussion veered away from material bodies and their locations within new time/space configurations. The industry used technology as an opportunistic salve to respond to the issue of violence against women.

The fact that Pratibha was driven to a remote, inaccessible area of Bangalore was used in public discussion to establish the fact that parts of the city remain outside the visual and virtual radar and, hence, fall outside the safety net or the regulatory gaze of technology. In general, the response and speculations adhered to common assumptions about the relationship between modernity and technology.[32] The first is a belief in the linear trajectory of progress guaranteed by technological growth; machines that can map, hear, and scan people will create utopic living conditions. Next follows the assumption that security and predictability can be achieved by drawing in more domains of everyday life into the realm of code, networks, and databases. Various types of gadgetry and informational devices were suggested as solutions to manage the uncertainties of urban life. As a symbol of the new economy, Bangalore was asserting its digital muscle with promises to deliver systems that would regulate mobility and track social interaction.

With increased dependence on surveillance technologies, cyberspace, according to David Lyon, is being mapped onto physical geographies.[33] Prompted by the need to provide an around-the-clock workforce for transnational corporations, the information-technology sector furnished easy justifications for scanning and cataloguing personal information and records. After the incident, private firms marketing security devices were quick to point out that "the eye in the sky"—referring to global positioning systems, or GPS, that were used mainly for distance tracking—could now be mined for its profiling and security potential.[34] One corporate official in Bangalore noted that the need of the moment was to accelerate the possibilities of moving scanned sensor data from one place to another using wireless network. Others speculated whether modest technologies, such as a text message from the company and the taxi service detailing the vehicle number, could have saved Pratibha's life.[35] Various suggestions followed for the institution of control rooms, help lines, digital cameras, digitized rosters for drivers, data bases compiling drivers' criminal records, and other informational devices to strategically monitor the space and movement of both technology and transportation workers. It was also suggested that speed control devices should be installed and radio frequencies should be shared with the police.[36]

Technologies of surveillance use a calculus of risk to identify certain individuals as potential threats to urban security, leading to forms of surveillance-as-social-sorting.[37] The industry and police also added cautiously that software cannot plug all stops in the security system or, in particular, capture criminal pathologies. A corporate representative lamented, "We can monitor the cars, but how can we stop the driver from committing the crime? By the time we manage to track an errant driver, it might be too late." Or as the owner of a car service added, "How can we guess what is in someone's mind? Police can only give a certificate about a person's past, but what about the present and future?"[38] Therefore, the ultimate solution, cited by police and industry alike, was to institute rules along gendered lines: no female employee will be dropped last or picked up first on the route, and she will always be accompanied by a male employee or a security guard. In addition, as cited in the media, both police and members from the industry encouraged women to carry camera phones and to try and have a male friend accompany them.

The machinic solutions to security serve as new regulatory mechanisms that operate within existing gender ideologies. Security is another infrastructural problem that has to be managed in order to streamline corporate operations and ensure that there is no foreseeable disruption of services. The focus on technological devices isolates gendered violence as a breakdown, which can be predicted through the production of an informational hum around the city.[39] A predominant assumption is that the more the city is wrapped up in software and information, the more the city and its inhabitants can be monitored and hence be more secure. Surveillance is never neutral, and social relations between those with power and those without are constituted by technologies of surveillance. In the call centers, the movements and performance of employees within the workplace have also been monitored digitally.[40] Now post-Pratibha, the strategy shifts to extending the reach of the surveillance assemblage outside the workplace, thereby recuperating modernist claims about techno-efficiency and discipline. Gendered lines of power are now digitally incorporated into the infrastructure. Pratibha's tragedy exemplifies how capital with the aid of technology restrains and tethers the laboring body to the global infrastructure of the city.

Damage Control and Laboring Bodies

The tragedy in Bangalore was followed by other, very similarly scripted acts of violence in other Indian call-center locations, in Delhi, Pune, and Mumbai. The events that unfolded around the rape and murder of Pratibha exposed a series of disjunctures in the fabric of everyday life which were set into motion by the modalities of transnational work. The insistence on technological explanations using corporatized language of best practices and efficiency narrowed the window of public discourse and altered the very conception of the citizen-subject. When the imperatives of consumption and the market forces are in place, the first casualty, notes Henri Giroux, is a language of social responsibility.[41] What happened in Bangalore was an active depoliticization of the events, rendering the violence as an aberrant event that happened because an employee was careless about her transportation arrangements. A brand consultant asks, "Why should the murder of someone working in another BPO firm affect and bother you?" Because "crises will come and go but brands will remain," and hence the consultant concludes that "every crisis represents an opportunity for a brand."[42] In this discourse of gadgets, brands, and damage control, any political discussion about material conditions of work, transnationally defined power structures, or the question of responsibility in global work environments were strategically avoided.

The question of accountability—how it was distributed, deferred, or sidestepped—assumed significant public attention in the aftermath of Pratibha's death. The demands and interpretations of feminist and trade-union activists stood in sharp contrast to explanations from the industry, whose main goal was to ensure continuity of services for the global corporations. The violent incident opened up the call-center industry for public scrutiny, and feminists and trade unionists wanted to pry open the case and all the overlapping issues. The industry, however, was mainly preoccupied with damage control to preserve the brand and value of their services.

In a protest staged symbolically near the statute of Mahatma Gandhi in Bangalore, banners called for safer working conditions and for justice and punishment for the rapist. Despite the rounds of text messages, the turnout at the rally was small, and by some reports many of the protesters were not employees of the call centers but rather interested union activists and feminists. K. S. Vimala, a spokesperson of the All India Democratic Women's Association, attributed the poor response to the apolitical, individualistic focus of the "me generation" in India.[43] The feminist organization forcefully condemned the corporations for negligence and emphasized that transportation services have to be managed by the corporation directly, since outsourcing this key operation puts employees at risk, with no structure of accountability in place. Adopting an antiglobalization

Fig. 10.3. Scene of the protest in Bangalore following Pratibha's death. (Aruna Raman)

stance, the feminist groups wanted a guarantee of security and accountability without restricting women's places and times of work.

Trade-union activists blamed the information-technology industry for blocking any type of collective bargaining or union organizing of their employees. Information-technology firms, they claimed, were pampered with special preferences by the state instead of being treated as profit-oriented companies. To them, the death of Pratibha served as a catalyst to address serious problems related to material conditions of work in the call-center industry. While the trade-union groups stressed the need to establish grievance-redressal machineries, management argued that unions were essentially an anachronism. The new information-technology environments, as claimed by the industry, were designed from the outset as highly democratic and employee-sensitive workspaces. Kiran Karnik, president of the National Association of Software and Service Companies, pointed out that unions made sense when worker exploitation was a reality at individual and collective levels: "None of these conditions apply in the case of the IT worker." In his critique of union activism after the Pratibha case, Karnik stated, "Some people fish in troubled waters. This incident should not be used as a peg to drive agendas."[44] After two and a half years, the state of Karnataka's Supreme Court did rule that the police could in fact prosecute the chief executive officer of Hewlett Packard for not providing for the safety of women employees, which led to the violent death of Pratibha. Though it was a token and weak gesture by the Indian state, it was intended to send a message to the global corporations. At the same time, the information-technology industry seized on a local proposition which suggested curbing women's work hours as a safety measure. Karnik opposed it vehemently, using the opportunity to brand the industry's position on women's rights: "We believe this will be a retrograde step and everyone including women have a right to work any time they want."[45] Ironically, all the players, from different vantage points, spoke to the issues of security, trying to beat each other in their role as protectors of women. The discourse around the Pratibha case stayed firmly within the two registers of technology and protection.

Blots and Brands

Pratibha Srikantamurthy's murder is marked as the first blot in the otherwise upbeat story of brand Bangalore and global outsourcing in India. When I spoke to people in Bangalore, they would inevitably connect the incident either to the crassness of drivers or the immorality of the women in call centers. What I have tried to show is how diverse actors and social logics are set into motion in the context of the new technology-enabled economy. Violence against women and the discourses around it remain part of a larger story. First and foremost, the myth of a seamlessly connected globalized world came apart as the various folds of the story unraveled. For an industry that prides itself on transcending time and collapsing geography, this incident underscored how transnational work environments are firmly tied, even violently so, to local geographies and temporally bound cultures. Ironically, Pratibha met her violent end in the very process of traversing space for a late-night shift in order to be present in another time zone and cultural context.

This case shows how the deterritorialization of work reorganizes social life in ways that are socially disruptive and often violent and yet necessary for the transnational circuits of capital. The layers of this narrative speak to Sassen's argument that global-economic features such as hypermobility and time-space compressions are not self-generative but have to be actively reproduced and serviced.[46] Women in India's global call centers come into public view in hyperexaggerated terms as either docile gendered bodies of a new service economy or transgressive bodies contaminated by transnational night labor. It was the intrigue of a call-center crime involving a multinational corporation and the new software generation of India that drove the massive coverage about the Pratibha case. Rape and murder are too chaotic, ugly, and political for the new technological spaces of exception, which are showcased as apolitical islands of progress, nourished by transnational capital flow and technological connectivity.

NOTES

I am immensely grateful to Allen Feldman for the inspiring conversations as I launched into this project. I deeply appreciate the suggestions from Rajeswari Sunder Rajan, Arvind Rajagopal, Arjun Appadurai, and Robert Wosnitzer. I thank Aruna Raman for her competent and diligent research assistance in Bangalore. A version of this chapter was presented at the Institute for Public Knowledge (New York University) in December 2009 and at the Department of Women's Studies at the University of California, Berkeley, February 2010.

1. Nigel J. Thrift, *Knowing Capitalism* (London: Sage, 2005).

2. Joanna Slater, "Call of the West: For India's Youth, New Money Fuels a Revolution," *Wall Street Journal* (January 27, 2004): A1; T. L. Friedman, *The World Is Flat: A Brief History of the Twenty-first Century* (New York: Farrar, Straus and Giroux, 2005).

3. See DH News Service, "Pick-Up Driver Rapes, Murders HP Techie," *Deccan Herald* (December 17, 2005): 1; "City Shocked at Heinous Crime," *Deccan Herald* (December 17, 2005): 3.

4. Kalpana Sharma, "Can Women Ever Be Safe?" *The Hindu* (December 12 2005), http://www.hinduonnet.com/thehindu/mag/2005/12/25/stories/2005122500240300.htm (accessed April 18, 2005).

5. Kiran Mirchandani, "Gender Eclipsed? Racial Hierarchies in Transnational Call Center Work," *Social Justice* 32 (2005): 105–119.

6. Babu Remesh, "'Cyber Coolies' in BPO," *Economic and Political Weekly* 39, no. 5 (2004): 492–449. Remesh's study drew sharp critique from the industry for his characterization of the work conditions within the call centers.

7. Aihwa Ong, *Neoliberalism as Exception: Mutations in Citizenship and Sovereignty* (Durham, NC: Duke University Press, 2006), 5–7.

8. Karnataka Udyog Mitra, "Karnataka State Government Millennium BPO Policy, 2002," http://www.kumbangalore.com/Htmlpages/policy/161/index.htm#b13 (accessed March 25, 2009).

9. For details, see P. Venugopal, "How Safe Are Girls on Graveyard Shift?" *MSN News India*, http://news.in.msn.com/columns/article.aspx?cp-documentid=1262964 (accessed March 21, 2008); DH News Service, "30,000 Bangalore Women Work in Night Shifts," *Deccan Herald* (March 20, 2008), http://www.deccanherald.com/content/Mar202008/scroll2008032058463.asp (accessed August 17, 2008).

10. See Reena Patel, *Working the Night Shift: Women in India's Call Center Industry* (Stanford, CA: Stanford University Press, 2010).

11. For example, see Joanna Slater, "Call of the West: For India's Youth, New Money Fuels a Revolution," *Wall Street Journal* (January 27, 2004): A1.

12. A. Aneesh, *Virtual Migration: The Programming of Globalization* (Durham, NC: Duke University Press, 2006), 92.

13. See Preeti Singh and Anu Pandey, "Women in Call Centres," *Economic and Political Weekly* 40, no. 7 (2005): 684–688.

14. Arvind Rajagopal, "Thinking about the New Indian Middle Class: Gender, Advertising and Politics in an Age of Globalization," in Rajeswari Sunder Rajan, ed., *Signposts: Gender Issues in Post-independence India* (New Delhi: Kali for Women, 1999), 57–100.

15. A. R. Vasvai notes that there is an entanglement of multiple logics as the young workers are drawn into the transnational economic order. A. R. Vasavi, "Serviced from India: The Making of India's Global Youth Workforce," in Carol Upadhya and A. R. Vasavi, eds., *In an Outpost of the Global Economy: Work and Workers in India's Information Technology Industry* (New Delhi: Routledge, 2008), 211–234.

16. For more on teleworkers as a community of consumers, see Vibodh Parthasarathi, "Beneath IT: Formations of Business, Labour and Identity in the IT Sector," issues paper (New Delhi: Centre for Culture, Media and Governance, Jamia Millia Ismalia, 2007), 1–15.

17. Janaki Nair, *The Promise of the Metropolis: Bangalore's Twentieth Century* (Oxford: Oxford University Press, 2005), 302.

18. Amrit Dhillon, "Dating Site Brings Indian Call Centre Workers Closer," *Telegraph* (August 9, 2008), http://www.telegraph.co.uk/news/worldnews/asia/india/2530292/Dating-site-brings-Indian-call-centre-workers-closer.html (accessed August 25, 2008).

19. Sugata Srinivasaraju, "The Wolf Strikes: Lax Security, Cost-Cutting Measures Lead to the Rape, Murder of a Call Centre Staffer," *OutlookIndia.com* (January 9, 2005), http://www.outlookindia.com/full.asp?fname=BPO%20(F)&fodname=20060109&sid=1 (accessed February 6, 2007).

20. Rajeswari Sunder Rajan, introduction to Sunder Rajan, *Signposts*, 1–16.

21. Manuel Castells, *The Informational City: Information, Technology, Economic Restructuring and the Urban-Regional Process* (Oxford, UK: Blackwell, 1989).

22. Saskia Sassen, "Introduction: Locating Cities on Global Circuits," in Saskia Sassen, ed., *Global Networks: Linked Cities* (New York: Routledge, 2002), 1–36.

23. See Stephen Graham, "Communication Grids: Cities and Infrastructure," in Sassen, *Global Networks*, 71–91.

24. Rama Lakshmi, "Ferrying the Night Owls Who Fix the World's Glitches," *Washington Post* (August 30, 2007): A12.

25. DH News Service, "Pick-Up Driver Rapes, Murders HP Techie."

26. Vasavi, "Serviced from India."

27. Doreen Massey, *World City* (Malden, MA: Polity, 2007), 88.

28. Writing about the murders of women in the industrial city of Juarez, Mexico, Melissa Wright makes a similar point that the focus was on restoring women's cultural values rather than finding the perpetrators of the crime. See Melissa W. Wright, "The Dialectics of Still Life: Murder, Women and Maquiladoras," *Public Culture* 11, no. 3 (1999): 453–474.

29. Times News Network, "Bangalore Police Lack Manpower, Equipment," *Times of India*, Bangalore (December 18, 2005): 7.

30. For the notion of the constitutive outside, see Timothy Mitchell, *Questions of Modernity* (Minneapolis: University of Minnesota Press, 2000), xiii.

31. DH News Service, "No Lapse on Our Part: HP CEO," *Deccan Herald* (December 19, 2005): 1.

32. See David Morley, *Media, Modernity and Technology: The Geography of the New* (London: Routledge, 2007); Timothy Mitchell, *Rule of Experts: Egypt, Techno-politics, Modernity* (Berkeley: University of California Press, 2002).

33. David Lyon, "Security, Seduction and Urban Sorting: Urban Surveillance," in *In the Shade of the Commons: Towards a Culture of Open Networks* (Delhi: Waag Society Amsterdam, 2006), 30–42, available online at http://www.sarai.net/publications/occasional/in-the-shade-of-the-commons (accessed September 28, 2008).

34. R. Raghavendra, "BPOs to Rely on an Eye in the Sky," *Times of India* (December 24, 2005): 2.

35. Times News Network, "SMS Could Have Saved Her," *Times of India*, Bangalore (December 19, 2005): 3.

36. "BPOs Go on High Safety Gear," *Deccan Herald* (December 20, 2005): 1.

37. Lyon, "Security, Seduction and Urban Sorting."

38. DH News Service, "She Was Misled," *Deccan Herald* (December 17, 2005): 3.

39. The idea of an informational hum is drawn from Ash Amin and Nigel Thrift, *Cities: Reimagining the Urban* (Cambridge, UK: Polity, 2002), 102.

40. Remesh, "'Cyber Coolies' in BPO."

41. Henri Giroux, *Public Spaces, Private Lives: Beyond the Culture of Cynicism* (Lanham, MD: Rowman and Littlefield, 2001), 82.

42. Ramanujam Shridhar, "Today's Crisis, Tomorrow's Opportunity," *Business Line* (July 6, 2006), http://www.thehindubusinessline.com/catalyst/2006/07/06/stories/2006070600180200.htm (accessed September 29, 2008).

43. K. Raghu, "Tech City Tepid to Pratibha's Fate," *DNA India* (December 17, 2005), http://www.dnaindia.com/india/report_tech-city-tepid-to-prathibha-s-fate_1002734 (accessed March 30, 2009).

44. Times News Network, "Call Centres Are like Udupi Hotels," *Times of India* (December 22, 2005): 2.

45. Times News Network, "Scrapping Night Shifts for Women Impractical: Karnik," *Times of India* (December 21, 2005): 2.

46. Saskia Sassen, "Spatialities and Temporalities of the Global: Elements for a Theorization," *Public Culture* 12, no. 1 (2000): 215–232.

11 Maid as Metaphor

Dagongmei and a New Pathway to Chinese Transnational Capital

Wanning Sun

The World, Jia Zhangke's poignantly titled and widely acclaimed film, is set on the rural outskirts of Beijing in a theme park studded with replicas of iconic global tourist destinations such as the Eiffel Tower, Big Ben, and the White House. There, visitors, many of whom are wide-eyed Chinese villagers visiting Beijing for the first time, vicariously experience the exotic West. To authenticate the experience, the theme park employs rural migrants to move around the theme park wearing exotic costumes. Visitors can also simulate transnational mobility by boarding a defunct airplane complete with a crew also played by rural migrants. During the day, these rural migrants perform transnational mobility, global modernity, and Western exotic; at night, they sleep in dark and dingy basements along train lines, speak with a thick Shanxi accent, and live out broken dreams. Also working in the theme park are Anna and her compatriots, migrant women from Russia, who are hired for their cheap labor and authenticity as Westerners. Xiao Tao, a migrant woman from Shanxi, befriends fellow worker Anna but remains ignorant of the unevenness of the global economy and Russia's relative disadvantaged position in it. When Anna first comes to work in the theme park, Xiao Tao remarks, "How I envy you! You are free to go abroad." Toward the end of the story, Xiao Tao is suitably shocked when, by chance, she discovers that Anna has become a prostitute since leaving the theme park.

On the surface, Xiao Tao and Anna could be read as yet another embodiment of the gendered nature of transnational processes. After all, examples of the gendered nature of Chinese transnationalism abound, ranging from the mainland Chinese popular representation of hypermasculine entrepreneurs to the lived reality and mobilities of the "astronaut families" of Hong Kong.[1] The circuit of transnational capital is inhabited not only by the movers and shakers but also by the invisible people in global cities and urban centers, which emerge as the nodal points of global trade and capital. The embodiment of the Occidental exotica articulated on and through the body of the Shanxi rural migrants and Russian labor migrants alike in a theme park outside Beijing poignantly point to the imbrication of the transnational within the translocal. Furthermore, the film underscores an often underexplored connection between transnational imagination and global mobility. The lives of the migrant workers demonstrate that mobility can be understood as both a material and a mental process, one predicated on the consumption of transnational images. Although the translocal is not defined by mobility, it is still shaped by a global imaginary and the representation of distant places. Transnational places and spaces feature prominently in the imagination of Chinese tourists and rural migrants alike, even though they lack the means to travel overseas.[2] For them, transnationalism is often a vicarious experience, but their spatial imagination is nevertheless stimulated by representations of travel.[3]

Aihwa Ong and Donald Nonini, in their work on the cultural politics of Chinese transnationalism, define modern Chinese transnationalism as an "emerging global form" that "provides alternative visions in late capitalism to Western modernity and generates new and distinctive social arrangements, cultural discourses, practices, and subjectivities."[4] Hence, to understand the nature of Chinese transnationalism, we must pay attention to how global capitalist forces and local communities interact to produce, on one hand, specific versions of modernities and, on the other, "oppositional narratives of modernity expressed by subalterns divided along class, ethnic, and gender lines, who are marginalised or even suppressed and elided by the dominant constructions of modernity."[5] This, according to Ong and Nonini, would entail shifting the locus of investigation from the village to the travel itself.

However, these "oppositional narratives of modernity" rarely exist in popular visual media. Despite Jia's international reputation, his films command a small audience and cannot compete with commercial blockbusters. How do popular media and visual culture construct mobility, and what role does travel play in the formation of a range of subject positions? Despite widespread recognition that the visual media play a significant part in the forging of new identities,[6] little sustained attention has been paid to the ways in which these "public allegories"[7] shape the subject formation of both transnational elites and subaltern individuals. To start addressing these questions, one must consider the specific signifying practices (format, genre, metaphor, trope) engaged to negotiate the mobility of socioeconomic elites and that of those marginal social identities.

This chapter seeks to contribute to this endeavor through a juxtaposition of media critique and engaged ethnography.[8] Focusing on the figure of the maid and the particular labor of Chinese *dagongmei* (female migrant worker), I demonstrate both the cultural construction and the stratified and variegated nature of mobility itself. I trace a number of often contradictory ways in which the migrant maid is configured in the narratives of nationalism and global capitalism, establishing the maid as an evolving metaphor in Chinese popular mediatized narratives of modernity. I then globally situate the discussion by juxtaposing the figure of the *Filipina maid* against that of the *provincial Chinese maid*. Finally, I describe the consumer economy that links domestic workers and employers alike in the circuits of popular culture.

The Emergence of the Dagongmei Identity

Currently, an estimated two hundred million people, China's floating population, have left home to seek work in China's prosperous cities. *Dagong* means "working for the boss" and is a term that bespeaks the commodification of labor, distinct from the term *gongren* (worker) in state enterprises from Mao's socialist period.[9] The addition of *mei* to *dagong, dagongmei* signifies the inferior status of migrant women, who are at once subject to the triple oppressions of the respective regimes of global markets, the Chinese state, and the rural patriarchal traditions.[10] Industrialization and development in south China, including the Shenzhen Economic Zone (SEZ), the Hong Kong Special Administration Region (SAR), Taiwan, and Macau, are distinctly gendered processes.[11] The export-oriented sector in the globalizing south China both sets the conditions for and shapes the formation of the social identity of *dagongmei*, young migrants from rural, and increasingly inland, areas of northern China who are recruited to the highly segmented market as cheap labor. The figure of the *dagongmei* stands in as an example of China's exploitation of its vast rural population—a reminder of how class and gender produce specific conditions of subjugation to accelerate capital accumulation in China's increasingly globalized capitalist market.

More controversial than the *dagongmei* but equally integral to the process of capital accumulation are the figures of the prostitute, mistress, and karaoke hostess. The proliferation of highly sexualized migrant workers from southern coastal China, such as *beimei* (northern girls) and *dalumei* (mainland Chinese girls), in the export-oriented industrialization regime testifies to the reproduction of patriarchal conditions in the new Chinese market economy, in which women's labor contributions are marginalized while their sexualized identities are made hypervisible and exploited.[12] By patronizing these places, transnational business professional elites think that they are doing their bit of charity work to bring income to the poor migrant women.[13]

Paid domestic work has emerged as a viable urban employment option for migrant women from rural areas. Many rural women choose this occupation, as their perceived "low *suzhi*" (personal quality)—low literacy, lack of employable skills, rural (hence "uncivilized") habits and outlook—would preclude them from pursuing other options.[14] These women are told by both the state and the market that they must engage in ceaseless "self-improvement" or they risk becoming irrelevant.[15] The domestic worker has been configured as an object of civilization and neoliberal governmentality.[16] Many married rural women with children also opt for domestic work, since factories in south China only hire single women. Despite lower pay and poor working conditions, rural women prefer work as domestics, since urban homes are perceived as safe work environments in comparison to spaces such as restaurants or massage parlors.[17]

Migrant domestic workers differ from other *dagongmei* identities in two paradoxical ways. First, the migrant domestic worker is largely invisible in the public domain, being confined to the private, domestic spaces of urban employers. Unlike workers in sweatshops or on the assembly lines of global factories, domestics and their labor conditions are not protected by Chinese labor law, nor do they attract the attention of international human rights activists. Second, despite this invisibility, the figure of the maid (*baomu*) has captured the public imagination in a way that is unrivaled by other *dagongmei* identities and is featured prominently in media narratives, including television dramas.[18] This "mediated publicness,"[19] via a proliferation of ambivalent and fraught popular representations, can be attributed to the fact that due to living alongside elite urban residents, domestics and their otherness become a perennial source of class-based fear and anxiety. Furthermore, although factory *dagonmei* in south China are the foot soldiers of transnational capital accumulation, it is domestic workers, particularly those who work for foreign and expatriate families and wealthy Chinese families, who are considered to have the most direct and embodied contact with transnational elites. The world of everyday interactions of Chinese migrant workers opens a rich space from which to understand the performance of multiply articulated difference in the transnational arena. The homes of the transnational families are *the* "site of cultural and emotional clashes and negotiations" and, as such, are what Haiyan Lee describes as a "quasi-public sphere where Chinese women engage in transitional object play to mourn the loss of socialism and effect their rebirth as citizens of the world."[20]

Maids in the Cosmopolitan Circuit

Running parallel to the internal rural-to-urban migration in the economic reform era was the outbound emigration out of China. In the mid-1980s, hundreds and thousands of urban Chinese became the first batches of *liuxuesheng* (students studying overseas) in the affluent countries of the West, particularly the United States, Canada, Australia, New Zealand, and, to a lesser extent, European countries. The story of Wang Qiming, the protagonist in *Beijing Natives in New York*, the most well-known television drama series on this topic, for instance, is a typical rags-to-riches story. He starts from the gutters of Manhattan and ends up becoming a rich entrepreneur/philanthropist on Long Island. Two decades later, many of these former, well-educated students from mainland China, as depicted in the series, stayed back in the host country, acquired citizenship, and, in turn, became professionals in white-collar jobs and entrepreneurs in their host country. To be sure, not everyone has succeeded to the extent marked by the iconic Wang Qiming, who has since then become a household name among both domestic and diasporic Chinese communities. Nevertheless, a new echelon of diasporic Chinese elites was indeed born, constituting the most recent, ambitious, and dynamic members of global Chinese capitalism. Settled in the host countries but freely moving in and out of China for business, pleasure, and family connections, they are enthusiastic propellants of China's growing integration to the global capital. The transnational mobility of cosmopolitans such as Wang Qiming is dependent on the easy availability of the cheap domestic labor of rural migrant women. Similarly, many mainland Chinese migrants who now live overseas have purchased a second home in China, enticed by the comparatively cheap real estate and easy availability of domestic service. This new transnational practice results from a range of considerations, from the desire to exploit their business connection in China to maintaining emotional and cultural connections with Chinese culture, in particular, for the sake of their children. In those spontaneous daily chit-chats in the gathering of domestic workers in the communal areas of the neighborhood, transnational activities in faraway places are featured prominently. For example, one of workers I interviewed volunteered the information that her charge was a toddler who could only speak English, as the parents had just moved from Chicago to Beijing for business reasons.

Cashing in on the *chuguo re* ("going abroad" fever), popular narratives—in the form of television dramas, novels, and autobiographical accounts—have flourished, chronicling the hardship and struggles of surviving in a foreign country. Although alluring images of the global cities such as New York and the successful stories of individuals have captivated the domestic audience's imagination and fueled their longing for the modern West, these "Chinese in the New World" stories are nevertheless told with a strong nationalistic undertone.[21] Although narratives of the Chinese in the New World have been exhausted in the media, there are new media genres which incorporate the figure of the maid in transnational configurations. *Bailaohui Yibaihao* (100 Broadway), a twenty-episode series produced in the early 1990s for domestic Chinese television, tells the story of a group of Chinese students living in a house in Los Angeles. The wife of a stereotypically diligent Chinese doctoral student finds a job with a wealthy, mean-spirited American woman, who has a powerful son who is also abusive to the maid. The Chinese maid decides to sue her employers, and everyone in the group house helps out in moral and financial terms. The series ends on a triumphant note, with the Chinese maid winning the case against her American employer and a face-to-face apology from her employers.

Both the motives and the consequences of the outbound migration of Chinese students and scholars to the global cities are framed in terms of China's desire to shed its isolationist image and integrate itself with globalization processes. The Chinese word for integrating into the globalizing world is *jiegui*, which literally means "switching railway lines so as to join the main system." In the realm of visual storytelling, this collective desire for the Western world manifests itself in a common trope of departure and arrival. Therefore, it should not come as a surprise that many of these visual narratives of Chinese-in-the-New-World begin with the image of an airplane in flight, with Chinese travelers crossing the border. Overriding the aspirational account of travel, it is the transnational experience of these cash-strapped and ill-adjusted students roughing it overseas and suffering from humiliation at the hands of the powerful Westerners that profoundly resonates with Chinese audiences.

The uneasy combination of strong transnational yearning and intense nationalistic feeling has promised extremely good television. Capitalizing on the supposedly true story of the maid in *Bailaohui Yibaihao*, Liaoning TV, a provincial television station, also produced an eight-episode drama in 1998. Titled *Dignity*, the series faithfully reproduces the storyline of *Bailaohui Yibaihao* but focuses on a court case brought by a Chinese student against her employers. When the verdict against her employers is read out, the Chinese maid makes a scathing speech to the Americans in the court:

> I am demanding an apology. It's not money I want. It is dignity. America takes pride in its human rights record, but my experience tells me that this is a society governed by money. But money isn't the most important thing. It would be wrong to assume that a nation can get away with murder simply because it is rich and powerful.[22]

The message from the scene is unambiguous: China wants to integrate itself into the global economy. And in order to modernize itself and become a stronger competitor, China needs the science, technology, and capital from the West, but it is only prepared to play on equal terms. The Chinese maid in the American court is clearly a politicized figure, signifying national dignity and respect. She is allegorical of the us-them boundary in racial and national terms, thereby inviting instant identification from national viewers, both urban and rural, rich and poor. In fact, Chinese viewers would not tolerate anything else other than defiance in the face of U.S. bully. This anti-U.S. undertone has been recurrent in the past few decades, despite or because of China's increasing integration with the global capital, as demonstrated by the sizable body of populist texts on this topic.

Stranger in the Home

If the Chinese maid overseas exemplifies the trope of the injured female body to signal national pride and humiliation, the rural maid in urban China is configured in a much more complex and ambiguous way. In contrast to stories of Chinese going to live overseas in the early 1990s, which provide a united and reasonably unproblematic point of identification for Chinese domestic viewers, the "villagers in the city" in the new millennium have to speak to a national audience stratified socioeconomically and divided by urban-rural disparity. Unlike the Chinese-in-the-New-World narratives which direct the viewers' gaze outward, to the world outside China, villagers-in-the-city narratives speak to the emerging urban middle class's fear and anxiety about China's internal Other—the intimate stranger intruding on the private spaces of urban residents.

For instance, *Professor Tian and His Twenty-Eight Maids*, the earliest and best known drama series about domestic workers in China, features a parade of rural maids who are unemployable because of perceived incompetence, uncleanliness, or moral deficiency—low *suzhi* in general. Although the depiction of migrant women is somewhat caricatured, Professor Tian's failure to gain the service of a good maid meets with widespread recognition and sympathy from urban viewers. The holy grail that every middle-class employer is in search of is a docile body who knows her place and never forgets her station. A more recent television drama series, *Baomu*—the title of the series means "maid"—again pits the figure of the rural maid against her urban employers. Maids are frequently reminded by their employers that people in their position should not "speak out of turn." An employer's adult daughter tells her mother's maid, "As a *baomu*, you should know when to ask questions and when not to ask questions." When the rural maid protests her innocence over a charge of lying, her employer tells her that "a defiant personality doesn't suit someone who works as a *baomu*."[23]

Comparing the difference with which the maid is configured in two clusters of popular televisual narratives reveals one fundamental tension, as well as complicity between the ideology of nationalism of the Chinese nation-state and the pragmatics of the neoliberal logic of global capital. The Chinese-in-the-New-World narrative, which was popular in the 1990s, charges the maid with the ideological and political burden of patriotism and showcases China's moral superiority in relation to technologically developed, economically strong, but morally deficient Westerners. In the villager-in-the-city narrative, in contrast, the figure of the maid is divested of the ideological content of patriotism. The maid—both rural and urban—is instead cast in the "*suzhi*" discourse, which justifies claims of her inferiority in relation to her urban compatriots in neoliberal market terms and explains social disparity in nonpolitical and nonideological terms.[24] This narra-

tive also offers a technical rather than political or social solution to their exploitation, which again, as Ong points out, is an attendant discursive strategy of neoliberalism. Within this reconfiguration, rural domestic workers are told that as
long as they work hard on self-improvement, including improving their literacy
(including learning English), manners and habits, and occupational skills, they
can end up like urban maid Qiaoyun. Or they risk going down the slippery slope
toward becoming "one more number among an abjected surplus" in the already
competitive labor market.[25]

The hegemonic discourse of "low *suzhi*" is usually deployed in the dominant
visual narratives with the domestic workers as the recipient of civilization and
development. Employers, local or transnational, are charged with the burden
of teaching civility to their employees. This discursive order, however, is often
turned upside down in everyday practice. A number of domestic workers I interviewed told me that they had experience working for foreigners, transnational
Chinese, and local residents. Some would even volunteer their knowledge of the
relative merits of employers based on their nationality, stating that Westerners
tend to be more generous than employers from Hong Kong, Taiwan, or Korea.
Japanese, they said, are fastidious about cleanliness, and local Chinese are the
strictest employers. The statements of domestic workers appropriate the discourse of *suzhi* and turn it around to assess the moral quality of employers. At
the same time, their moral assessments seem to do little more than reproduce and
reinforce the already established global pecking order of not only people but also
the place (nation, province, localities) from which individuals come.

Suzhi and Branding

Perhaps the most telling illustration of the power and reach of a neoliberal language of *suzhi* quality can be seen in the ways in which domestic workers establish
a pecking order among themselves through the deployment of *suzhi* discourse.
Domestic workers' direct exposure to transnational elites through close everyday interaction engenders a process of self-transformation, whereby one's sense
of the self is continuously reshaped. My conversations with domestic workers in
Shanghai and Beijing reinforced this point. Local Shanghai domestic worker Ge
Xiuying, in her early forties, is employed by an Australian couple—the husband
a Chinese Australian citizen who works for an American advertising company
and the wife an Australian who works for an American-owned market-research
company in Shanghai. Prior to her employment as a domestic, Ge Xiuying was a
worker in a state-owned enterprise. Her current status as a local Shanghai *baomu*
working for a foreign family meant that her wages were twice as much as her
rural migrant counterpart.[26] When asked to comment on the quality of domestic

workers from the countryside, her answer suggested that she thought she was a cut above the average *baomu* working for a local Chinese family:

> These *baomu* from the provinces and countryside have low *suzhi* and do not know the first thing about domestic work. Local Chinese families surviving on limited income have no options but employ these *baomu*, as they are cheap. People like us cost more and are usually sought after by foreign families, expatriate Chinese, or at least white-collar professionals.

The naturalization of such a pecking order is achieved through a consistent deployment of *suzhi* discourse. According to the logic inherent in the *suzhi* discourse, rural female migrants are underpaid and overworked not because of structural inequality but because they have lower *suzhi*. For the same reason that the *suzhi* discourse justifies the inequality between the employer and the employee, it also reinforces the implicit hierarchy of transnational spaces. Tracing how the domestic worker is configured in various national contexts helps unravel the ways in which the migrant body serves as a dislocated signifier of place. In other words, this particular form of mobility—leaving home to become a domestic in someone else's home—is often a result of, as well as a metaphor for, the unequal relationship between the sending zone and the receiving zone. Places are constituted not only by their location and physical features but also by the specific, often related, forms of bodies that inhabit them.[27] Experiences of domestic workers in a number of places in Asia, including Taiwan, Singapore, Malaysia, Hong Kong, and Southeast and South Asia, offer ample evidence of the racialized as well as gendered and classed nature of globalization.[28] In other words, if a maid stands for the place of her origin—be it Anhui, China, or the Philippines—then her relationship to her employers becomes a metaphor for the asymmetrical relationship between the two places/nations. The operation of this symbolic border guard in various national and historical junctures attests to the importance of theorizing inequality in symbolic as well as in material terms.

Domestic workers who travel overseas as contracted laborers are also caught in the paradoxical desire of the nation-state both to uphold nationalism and to facilitate the flow of transnational capital. Rural domestic workers from poorer, "developing countries" such as India, Sri Lanka, Indonesia, and the Philippines become live-in maids in the homes of their urban middle-class employers in the richer host societies, with their race, ethnicity, and, in some cases, religion becoming the defining marker of their taken-for-granted "inferiority." Although Filipina women are promoted by their own neoliberal government as industrious, flexible, and docile—hence, ideal choices in the global domestic service market[29]—they also embody an injured nationalism. When Flor Contemplacion, a Filipina domestic worker in Singapore, was sentenced to death for killing another Filipina domestic worker and a four-year-old Singaporean boy, she became a Janus-faced figure. In the media representations of the host country, she was a murderer who embodied risk, which once publicized becomes dramatically amplified.[30] Back in the home country, however, she was constructed in the media as a national hero/martyr. As Nefertia Xina Tadiar points out, the maid in these transnational narratives represents "two kinds of bodies": the individual body of the domestic worker and the collective body of the nation.[31] Above all, as widely noted, the transnational domestic worker in East and Southeast Asia embodies the unevenness of global modernity and transnational capitalism in the late twentieth and early twenty-first centuries.

Paid domestic work in post-Mao China is relatively recent and so far has been largely translocal, involving migration from rural China to urban China. Anhui Province, an inland and largely agricultural province in eastern China, is credited with having produced one of the most well-known brands of domestic workers in China, with its Wuwei maids—domestic workers from a particular county called Wuwei—having monopoly over the domestic-service market in Beijing in the 1980s.[32] Many employers in Shanghai and Beijing who employ Anhui domestic workers have little knowledge of Anhui as a province except that it is economically depressed. A Shanghai employer of Anhui maids admitted to me during an interview that he had never been to Anhui but was convinced that because of its reputation for producing domestic workers, Anhui is the "Philippines of China." The figure of Anhui maid embodies the gendered, unequal, and uneven relationship between Anhui and metropolitan centers of China.[33] The Shanghai urban resident's spatial imagination—Anhui is the Philippines of China—involves a mixing of metaphors, replicating global power relations within a national space. The arrival of the competent and supremely qualified Filipina maid in the home of transnational elites in China sends a clear message to China's domestic workers that even those who do not aspire to become transnational nannies have to contend with transnational competitors.

The 2004 July issue of *Migrant Women*, a magazine targeting migrant women workers, published a story entitled "Filipina Maids Are Crashing into the Chinese Market: Are You Ready for Them?"[34] According to the story, there are around 180,000 Filipina domestic workers in Hong Kong, and while the number is still small, some Filipina domestic workers are making inroads into Beijing and Guangzhou. Migrant women readers are told that these *feiyong* (Filipina maids) are well educated, speak good English, and are favored by transnational elites, and they naturally earn what seems to rural migrant domestic workers in China impossibly high wages. As if the moral of the story was not explicit enough, the story also comes with an editorial note for the Chinese migrant woman reader:

> How cool these foreign maids are! Of course in today's China, only those on the
> top of the social echelons can afford to hire a foreign maid, but this situation

is beginning to give rise to a sense of impending crisis among local domestic workers. As our society progresses, expectations for the *suzhi* level of domestic workers also grow. It is no longer adequate simply to be industrious and hard-working. . . . So a word of advice for those little maids: If you want to earn more money or have no job worries in the future, you'd better seize the day and "recharge your batteries."[35]

To "recharge one's batteries" (*chongdian*) is to engage in ceaseless self-development and capacity building. Here, we can see that the logic of the neoliberal production of the "right" worker impacts everyone, even the humble "little maid," even though she does not aspire to earn foreign money. The objectifying nature of the neoliberal language cannot be more obvious here: to become a desirable neoliberal subject, one must be constantly "plugged in," "switched on," and, as the quotation suggests, "recharged." The symbolic resourcefulness of the Filipina domestic worker is clearly demonstrated here. Already a much contested figure, as discussed earlier, once transported to China's neoliberal discourse, she is reconfigured yet again, her perceived high *suzhi* setting a formidable benchmark for success for her Chinese counterparts. The body of the maid is not only inscribed with the imbalance between the local and the global; it is also charged with the task of highlighting the difference between the self and the (un)desirable Other.

Between Translocal and Transnational

In the television series *Shewai Baomu* (Chinese Maids in Transnational Families),[36] Chinese domestic workers are told by their agency to work hard on self-improvement in order to meet the requirement of China's superior Other—the Americans. They must learn English, understand Western etiquette, adopt more civilized manners and habits, and give their best performance possible when serving their American employers working in Shanghai. The workers are warned that any problems they cause may reflect badly not only on the agency but also, more seriously, on the image of Shanghai as a favorable place for foreign investment. Rural domestic worker Xiangcao is keen, but her "uncivilized" (*bu wenmin*) habits seem to get in the way of pleasing her Mexican employer, a single woman working in Shanghai. What saves this maid is her humility and eagerness to improve. Toward the end of the series, we see that the rural maid has managed to shed most of her "undesirable" rural manners and behavior and has learned much along the way about how to behave like a polite, "civilized" city person. In the end she wins the approval and trust of both her city friends and her foreign employers, as well as the love of Donald, a young Canadian man teaching in Shanghai. In doing so, she proves herself to be the most successful practitioner of what geographers refer to as "scale jumping," moving from the rural to the urban and then to the global.

Shewai Baomu warrants careful reading since it reinforces the prevalent view that by providing domestic labor for urban, transnational Chinese and Westerners living in China, rural migrants will imbibe a little cosmopolitanism, which, in turn, will speed up their transformation into citizens who are useful for both the state's modernity project and the global market economy. A mythology is created that with the right attitude, rural domestic workers can indeed become participants in the mapping of Chinese transnationalism. In the same series, we follow the travails of a local city *baomu* caring for the children of an American couple, who eventually decide to take the maid, Qiaoyun, with them to the United States. In a dramatic final episode, we see Qiaoyun boarding a plane bound for America with her American employers. There she continues to work as a care provider and is helped by her employers to exhibit her designs of *qipao* clothing.

Domestic workers, of both rural and urban origin, are not only the subjects of popular cultural representation; they are also avid consumers of it. But consumption aside, this transnational imagination is also borne aloft by "secondhand" experience of transnationalism. The increasingly close connection between transnational imagination and actual transnational practice is played out for domestic workers on a daily basis. Conversations among domestic workers when they socialize often veer to the travels and relocations of their elite employers. During my interviews, the women would talk about how their own lives and labor would be accommodated into the transnational relocations of their employers. In the upscale gated community where I conducted my ethnographic work in 2006, names of global cities such as Chicago, Vancouver, or Sydney were no longer names which bore no direct connection with themselves. These places—or, to be more precise, the movement in and out of these places—have direct consequences on their everyday life. In these conversations, they would also sometimes speculate about what it would be like to work as a domestic worker overseas. One day, I was part of a spontaneous chat in which the conversation meandered to the topic of going abroad:

> *Maid A*: I heard that so-and-so *ayi* [meaning maid] has gone to the U.S. with her employers. She has been working for them for some time, and now suddenly, they are leaving. The employers are Chinese and want her to come with them to the U.S. I hear that she is making four times as much as we are making here. Mind you, her employers would still be saving heaps of money by taking her to the U.S. instead of hiring an American.
>
> *Maid B*: How can that be done? Surely not everyone can go abroad as they please?
>
> *Maid A*: The employers are their sponsors. I hear that they need sponsorship to get a visa.

Maid C: I am not sure if I want to work overseas even if I have the opportunity. I would be scared.

Maid A: What's there to be scared of? I would go, work hard, and make lots of money, and then I can get out of this job altogether! [*Laughs*].[37]

In my three-year ethnographic project on domestic workers in China, I did not come across one single domestic worker who made it to the West like their television counterparts—as Qiaoyun's move to the United States or Xiangcao's romance and marriage to a Westerner. However, it is not at all far-fetched to suggest that domestic workers' everyday practices and social-spatial imagination can be a result of the mobility of the social-economic elites they work for. For both translocal and transnational travelers, imagination and fantasizing about traveling is often the precursor to actual physical movement. For these reasons, the symbolic message which comes with the fantasies about the global warrant careful consideration. Where are what Arif Dirlik calls the "contact zones"[38] of Chinese transnationalism? Who are the key players in the grand theater of capitalism, and what are the secrets to success in building transnational linkage or breaking down transboundary barriers? The various television series engage with these questions by rendering the figure of the maid, both in local and transnational settings, as an evolving and powerful allegorical figure. Paid domestic work in post-Mao China is relatively recent, compared with its counterparts in other countries, and so far it has been largely translocal; the lure of transnational domestic labor trails are even more recent. China's growing status as the global economic powerhouse of the future is also fueling an intense surge of interest in the West, particularly in the United States, evidenced by the growing interest in teaching American children Mandarin Chinese, which has increased the demand for Chinese nannies.[39] Domestic workers' latent though stirring ambition to become a *dagongmei* overseas one day bespeaks of a paradoxical scenario confronting the subaltern class in the transnational capitalist order. While they have begun their apprenticeship in the global neoliberal order, domestic workers still remain transnational hopefuls destined to occupy the bottom of the chain of global mobility. The media portrayals of the lives and experiences of domestic workers construct the women as living in proximity to global modernity and the ambitions of an elite business class. Commenting on the television series, Haiyan Lee notes that it falls on these nannies "to act as the spy-apprentice-ambassadors who will link China up with the rail tracks of the world, starting at the intimate terminal of domestic life."[40]

Conclusion

This chapter has engaged with the multiple ways in which mobility as a mediated and cultural construct is embedded in and imbricated with mobility as a material process. The invisible yet intimate spaces that domestic workers inhabit situate them in the interstices between the translocal and the transnational. The domestic workers analyzed here vary widely in their ethnicity, location, and circumstance. Yet their embodied struggles as cheap labor constitute them as metaphors of the unequal, uneven terrain of transnational capitalism. The movements of transnational and internal migration are highly interconnected processes with overlapping consequences. And for both groups, social-spatial imagination is as important as the physical act of border crossing.

The figure of the maid stands as a metaphor for the unequal power relations between the place from which she comes and the places she goes to work. Whether it is a television series featuring translocal maids, Chinese maids overseas, magazine stories featuring foreign (e.g., Filipina) maids in China, or Chinese maids in transnational families, gender presents itself as a productive pathway to understanding both the political economy and the cultural politics of transnational capital. The challenge lies in unraveling the complex formations and everyday practices whereby gender, as embodied by the media's construction of the maid, intersects with class, geography, place, nation, and various modes of neoliberal governing to produce specific conditions of subjugation and possibilities of social mobility.

NOTES

1. In these "astronaut families," the male head of the household—Hong Kong businessmen—establish residency in Canada for their families but stay behind to continue business. For an account of the astronaut families, see C. Mitchell, R. Pe-Pua, R. Iredale, and S. Castles, *Astronaut Families and Parachute Children: The Cycle of Migration between Hong Kong and Australia* (Canberra, Australia: Bureau of Immigration, Multicultural and Population Research, 1996).

2. See Carolyn Cartier, "Symbolic City/Regions and Gendered Identity Formation in South China," in Tim Oakes and Louisa Schein, eds., *Translocal China: Linkages, Identities, and the Reimagining of Space* (London: Routledge, 2006), 138–154.

3. For a taxonomy of translocalism, see Wanning Sun, "The Leaving of Anhui: The Southward Journey toward the Knowledge Class," in Oakes and Schein, *Translocal China*, 238–261.

4. Aihwa Ong and Donald M. Nonini, "Introduction: Chinese Transnationalism as an Alternative Modernity," in Aihwa Ong and Donald M. Nonini, eds., *Ungrounded Empires: The Cultural Politics of Modern Chinese Transnationalism* (London: Routledge, 1997), 11.

5. Ibid., 16.

6. Mayfair Mei-Hui Yang, "Mass Media and Transnational Subjectivity in Shanghai: Notes on (Re)cosmopolitanism in a Chinese Metropolis," in Ong and Nonini, in *Ungrounded Empires*,

287–322; and Lisa Rofel, *Desiring China: Experiments in Neoliberalism, Sexuality, and Public Culture* (Durham, NC: Duke University Press, 2007).

7. Rofel, *Desiring China*, 26.

8. The ethnographic component of this chapter is based on two periods of three-month residence in a residential community in Beijing, in the summers of 2005 and 2006. Materials come from both informal conversations and interaction with around fifty domestic workers and interviews with employers. The fieldwork was funded by a Discovery Project grant from the Australian Research Council.

9. Pun Ngai, *Made in China: Women Factory Workers in a Global Workplace* (Durham, NC: Duke University Press, 2005).

10. Ibid.

11. Carolyn Cartier, *Globalizing South China* (Oxford, UK: Blackwell, 2001).

12. Ibid., 195.

13. Hsiu-Hua Shen, "The Purchase of Transnational Intimacy: Women's Bodies, Transnational Masculine Privileges in Chinese Economic Zones," *Asian Studies Review* 32 (March 2008): 57–75.

14. *Suzhi* is a Chinese term for "quality." It occupies a central place in neoliberal discourse of governmentality in reformed China. See Yan Hairong, "Neoliberal Governmentality and Neohumanism: Organizing *Suzhi*/Value Flow through Labor Recruitment Networks," *Cultural Anthropology* 18, no. 4 (2003): 493–523.

15. Hairong Yan, "Self-Development of Migrant Women and the Production of *Suzhi* (Quality) as Surplus Value," in Madeleine Yue Dong and Joshua Goldstein, eds., *Everyday Modernity in China* (Seattle: University of Washington Press, 2006), 227–259.

16. I follow Ong and others in using "neoliberal" to refer to the conception of government as a nonpolitical, nonideological agent of technical intervention, the logic of which "requires populations to be free, self-managing, self-enterprising individuals" in such matters as health, education, bureaucracy, and the professions, rather than citizens with a variety of claims on the state. See Aihwa Ong, *Neoliberalism as Exception: Mutations in Citizenship and Sovereignty* (Durham, NC: Duke University Press. 2006), 14.

17. See Tamara Jacka, *Rural Women in Urban China: Gender, Migration, and Social Change* (Armonk, NY: M. E. Sharpe, 2006); and Arianne Gaetano, "Filial Daughters, Modern Women: Migrant Domestic Workers in Post-Mao Beijing," in Arianne M., Gaetano and T. Jacka, eds., *On the Move: Women in Rural-to-Urban Migration in Contemporary China* (New York: Columbia University Press, 2004), 41–79.

18. For an account of domestic workers in China, see Wanning Sun, *Maid in China: Media, Morality and the Cultural Politics of Boundaries* (London: Routledge, 2009); and Yan, "Self-Development of Migrant Women."

19. John Thompson, *The Media and Modernity* (Cambridge, UK: Polity, 1995), 125.

20. Haiyan Lee, "Nannies for Foreigners: the Enchantment of Chinese Womanhood in the Age of Millennial Capitalism," *Public Culture* 18, no. 3 (2006): 508.

21. Wanning Sun, *Leaving China: Media, Migration, and Transnational Imagination* (Lanham, MD: Rowman and Littlefield, 2002).

22. These and other "New World" dramas are discussed in greater depth in Sun, *Leaving China*.

23. *Baomu* (Maid), a twenty-four-episode television drama series, was produced by Shanghai Blue Star Advertising Company and was initially screened on Chinese TV in 2007.

24. Ong, *Neoliberalism as Exception*.

25. Yan, "Self-Development of Migrant Women," 243.

26. When I interviewed her in 2005 in Shanghai, she was earning fifteen hundred yuan a month (a little over two hundred U.S. dollars at the exchange rate at the time). Although this does not sound like much, it was twice as much as what rural migrant domestic workers earned.

27. Louisa Schein, "Negotiating Scale: Miao Women at a Distance," in Oakes and Schein, *Translocal China*, 213–237.

28. There is a multitude of works on domestic workers in various national localities. There is no space to list them all here. For details, see the bibliography in Sun, *Maid in China*.

29. Ong, *Neoliberalism as Exception*, 200.

30. See James A. Tyner, *Made in the Philippines: Gendered Dimensions and the Making of Migrants* (London: Routledge-Curzon, 2003).

31. Neferti Xina M. Tadiar, *Fantasy Production: Sexual Economies and Other Filipino Consequences for the New World Order* (Hong Kong: Hong Kong University Press, 2004), 113.

32. Liu Yida, *Cangshen Fanjing: Beijing Yan* [Ordinary People, Extraordinary Times: The Eye of Beijing] (Beijing: Zhongguo Shehui Chubanshe, 1998).

33. See Wanning Sun, "Anhui *Baomu* in Shanghai: Gender, Class, and a Sense of Place," in Jing Wang, ed., *Locating China: Space, Place, and Popular Culture* (London: Routledge, 2005), 171–189.

34. Xie Haiyun, "Feiyong qiangtan zhongguo: Ni zhunbei haole ma?" [Filipina Domestic Workers Arrive in the Chinese Market: Are You Ready for Them?], *Lan Ling* [Blue Bell] 7 (2004): 21–23. Author's translation.

35. Ibid., 22.

36. *Shewai Baomu*, a twenty-two-episode series set in Shanghai, was first screened on Chinese television in 2002.

37. This conversation took place in July 2006 in Beijing.

38. Arif Dirlik, "Transnationalism, the Press, and the National Imaginary in Twentieth Century China," *China Review* 4, no. 1 (2004): 15.

39. "Meiguo huaren *baomu* nianxin qiwan meiyuan" [Chinese Maids Earn US$70,000 per Annum in the United States], *Xin: An Evening Post* [Xin An Wan Bao], January 23, 2007, B3.

40. Lee, "Nannies for Foreigners," 516.

12 Dial "C" for Culture

Telecommunications, Gender, and the Filipino Transnational Migrant Market

Jan Maghinay Padios

In recent decades, the transnational practices that tie migrants and immigrants to their families and friends "back home"—such as calling, visiting, and sending care packages and money—have become increasingly significant sources of profit for media and telecommunications corporations, airlines, shipping companies, and remittance centers.[1] Returns from the latter alone, for example, reached nearly fifteen billion dollars in 2007.[2] As more and more people from the Global South leave families to work abroad, what advertisers sometimes refer to as "cross-border" relationships have become more visible to corporate actors, who, in turn, search for ways to make their services and products visible to immigrant and migrant groups. They are aided in their efforts by a growing media network—including Internet social networking sites such as Facebook and Multiply and globally transmitted television channels such as India's Zee TV—that links migrants and immigrants to each other, their families, and the cultural products of their home country.[3]

This chapter situates the transformation of overseas Filipinos into a consumer group—what I call a *transnational migrant market*—within the context of Philippine neoliberalism and transnational media. I argue that advertisements and marketing campaigns to Filipinos overseas reinforce Philippine state-based discourse that frames labor migration as a source of Philippine national development and overseas Filipino workers (OFWs) as modern heroes (*mga bagong bayani*). These neoliberal characterizations privilege the notion that Filipino labor migration functions as a demonstration of familial love and a path to social mobility, rather than a neocolonial process of racial and gender exploitation. As such, they represent efforts by state and market actors to make Filipinos' individual and familial aspirations compatible with the large-scale neoliberal fantasies of Philippine national development and a global free market. In this chapter, I track the ways that both state and corporate actors integrate the notions of familial love and social mobility into neoliberal discourse and the way this discourse is reflected back to OFWs through various forms of global media. As Filipino labor migration has been and continues to be a gendered process through which a large number of women migrate abroad each year, I focus in particular on the way that

Filipino migrant and immigrant women are addressed within Philippine neoliberal discourse and in transnational media spaces.

This chapter also contends that Philippine state and corporate actors are similarly invested in the continued reproduction of Filipino labor migration and the transformation of Filipino workers and their families into transnational consumer subjects. On one hand, corporations reap profits from families separated by labor migration and their desire to stay connected over long distances. On the other hand, labor migration ensures the return of overseas workers' wages in the form of remittances, used by families in the Philippines to fund individuals' education, to invest in real estate, to build homes, and to purchase (often imported) goods. Although such activities support Philippine national development and the country's massive consumer economy, they also increasingly shift the burden of social reproduction and economic development away from the Philippine state and onto Filipino workers abroad. In this neoliberal context, the cultivation of consumer subjectivity is therefore a boon not only to the market but also to the Philippine state's market-based agendas.

The consumer realm has long been a site which hinges on people's imagination and aspirations: advertisements "hail" consumers with images that acknowledge and mirror their desires, and commodities are often doubly fetishized as signs of individual success. Yet corporate advertisers are not the only ones who deal in dreams. As Neferti Tadiar argues, since the late nineteenth century, the power of capitalism, modernity, and imperialism has worked, in part, through the transformation of human dreams into ideological fantasies of sovereignty, development, and free trade; in turn, these fantasies compel subjects toward specific actions, such as labor migration or consumption.[4] It is therefore no mere coincidence that the parallel efforts of the Philippine state and corporations to ensure the reproduction of Filipino labor in the global economy rely on the cultivation of consumer subjectivity. The latter is indeed part of what drives neoliberal projects. As Aihwa Ong writes,

> In short, the main elements of neoliberalism as a political philosophy are (a) a claim that the market is better than the state at distributing public resources and (b) a return to a "primitive form of individualism which is 'competitive,' 'possessive,' and construed often in terms of the doctrine of 'consumer sovereignty.'" It is important to note that neoliberal reasoning is based both on economic (efficiency) and ethical (self-responsibility) claims.[5]

Encouraging people to increasingly think of themselves as sovereign consumers thus constitutes an attempt to build consent for neoliberalism as a political philosophy, since consumer subjects ideally adhere to a core neoliberal practice: the definition and expression of economic success as the exercise of individual choice over a range of goods and/or services brought to the marketplace through the competitive, innovative, and profit-seeking processes of commodity production under capitalism.[6]

This chapter is concerned with two questions. First, how do Philippine as well as American telecommunications corporations market products and services to Filipinos overseas? The Philippine telecommunications industry is indeed a site that reveals the actualization of neoliberal agendas in the Philippines and the United States. In the mid-1990s, the Philippine government adopted a number of liberalizing reforms in air transport services, finance, retail, shipping, and telecommunications[7]—industries that would directly benefit from Filipino international labor migration by easing the movement of Filipino migrants, their earnings, and their care packages (*balikbayan* boxes) in and out of the country. The telecommunications industry in particular has grown remarkably: over two-thirds of the nation's ninety million people subscribe to mobile-phone services.[8] Without a doubt, consumers' increasing demand for reliable forms of communication and advances in the industry have "impacted the rhythms of life in local contexts":[9] mobile phones are ubiquitous in the Philippines, used for activities ranging from forwarding prayers to organizing protests.[10]

In particular, I look at telecommunications corporations' marketing during Filipino fiestas, weekend-long events held each summer in Los Angeles, San Francisco, and Secaucus, New Jersey, which draw tens of thousands of Filipinos every year. Topping the list of sponsors for these events are Philippine telecommunications, remittance, banking, and media companies, whose representatives showcase and sell their products in commercial booths at the fiesta venue. Filipino fiestas are not only saturated with the presence of Philippine media and telecommunications products; they are also structured by gendered notions regarding the role of women in global social reproduction and the reproduction of the Philippine diaspora and thus in transnational consumer culture. As such, Filipino fiestas mediate between Filipino immigrants, the Philippine nation, and Philippine and U.S-based corporations.

The second question is, what does the construction of a Filipino transnational migrant market suggest about the relationship between state and market actors pursuing neoliberal policies and philosophy and the role of consumer practices within them? Studies of globalization make clear that late-twentieth-century advances in telecommunications and transportation, coupled with neoliberal policies to deregulate capital and labor, have rendered people, goods, and capital more mobile and flexible.[11] Despite the suggestion that privatization and the dismantling of state services have rendered states less relevant in the neoliberal era, a growing body of research considers the ways states actively participate in global processes.[12] This chapter adds to that scholarship by analyzing Philippine neoliberal policies on labor migration and market liberalization along with Filipino fiestas and transnational advertisements. It shows how a neoliberal imaginary of the efficient, responsible, and transnational Filipino consumer-citizen is made possible through a global media machinery which operates within immigrants' and migrants' everyday lives.

Filipino Fiestas: Mediating Transnational Culture

A small but intense riot was erupting outside the VIP room at the Philippine Fiesta in America, inside the New Jersey Meadowlands arena. After waiting in line for hours to receive an autograph and picture with Bea Alonzo, star of Philippine television and film, many in the crowd were outraged to find that, unbeknown to them, those with special VIP bracelets were being granted first access to Ms. Alonzo. They announced their disapproval by shouting and finger-pointing directed at the Meadowlands' security guards and Philippine Fiesta staff in charge of crowd control. Inside the VIP room, however, the atmosphere was more calm and organized. The room itself was divided into two smaller spaces by a floor-to-ceiling partition. In the first space that fans entered, they were grouped together by a guard and told to wait along the partition, which blocked their view of the next space, where Ms. Alonzo was seated at a long folding table. Standing between the two spaces, where as a participant-observer I was in charge of holding back the line just before the point at which fans were finally free to approach and meet Ms. Alonzo, I heard sounds of frustration give way to loud whispers of admiration, such as "Ang ganda n'ya!" (She's beautiful!). Although asked by the Philippine Fiesta staff to move quickly through the room, many adoring fans insisted on bestowing Ms. Alonzo with kisses and hugs.

Filipino fiestas are special occasions for Filipinos in the United States to see the celebrities of Philippine mass media in person. The stars' appearance, performances, and autograph sessions are by far the biggest attraction of the fiestas for their attendees. For example, most of the people I spoke with at the U.S.-Philippines Expo told me that they had come to see Charice Pempengco, the Filipino teenage superstar who rose to national fame after her stunning renditions of American pop star Whitney Houston's hit songs were broadcast on YouTube. Although organized by different events-production companies, Los Angeles's "U.S.-Philippines Expo," San Francisco's "Fiesta Filipina," and Secaucus's "Philippine Fiesta in America" are structured in remarkably similar ways. Evening performances by the Philippines' top celebrities headline the event, while a beauty contest for Filipina teenage girls, local Filipino musicians, and traditional folk-dance groups fill the daytime lineup. While one purpose of the fiestas is to "showcase [Filipinos'] rich culture and heritage,"[13] another is to act as a marketing venue. As the Philippine Fiesta in America (PFIA) committee declared in its publication from 2007, "One of the Philippine Fiesta in America's key success factors is the ability to provide an avenue for businesses to sell to the lucrative Filipino-American market—a robust, multi-billion-dollar economic force with a high per capita income."[14] While ostensibly intended to attract corporate America, Filipino fiestas are increasingly attractive to Philippine and U.S.-based businesses, with profits tied directly to the transnational practices of Filipino migrants and immigrants. Money-transfer businesses such as Western Union and Money Gram and Philippine media conglomerates ABS-CBN and GMA are the most active and visible companies participating in the fiestas; along with telecommunications companies, they are also disproportionately represented among the fiestas' top sponsors. In return, the latter receive "top-billing" on the fiestas' collateral materials as well as prime locations for their commercial booths. These companies often mark their booths with giant banners or balloons touting their respective logos, organize games designed to engage consumers and educate them about the company's products, and have on hand a number of employees or volunteers giving away marketing gimmicks (e.g., pens, key chains, note pads). As with the 2008 Philippine Fiesta in America, Philippine media conglomerates even sponsor the celebrities who appear at the fiestas.

Like the "corporate pachangas" analyzed by Margaret Dorsey, Filipino fiestas bring together a public interested in participating in culture, with marketers interested in acquiring and keeping consumers.[15] Indeed, it is precisely Filipino immigrants' continued identification with people in the Philippines that make them worthy of attention from many of the fiestas' corporate sponsors. One marketing representative from a major Philippine telecommunications company present at the PFIA expressed this by saying, "We are really interested in those people who still have family in the Philippines. Migrants are really our market, not those Filipinos who have already built a life here [in the United States]." What makes this marketer's comment compelling is her definition of "migrant" as a transnational subject with ties to the Philippines, implying that those people who do not have intentions of returning to the Philippines on a permanent basis and/or who are U.S. citizens do not maintain such ties. Yet "newly arrived" Filipino migrants and immigrants with "permanent" lives in the United States also engage in the kinds of practices that companies have commodified.[16]

Fiesta organizers are explicit about the venue's serving as an opportunity for strengthening Filipinos' affective ties to the Philippines as "home." The opening statement of the Philippine Fiesta in America souvenir booklet explains this by claiming that "anchored on the Filipino values of community, solidarity, and friendship, the Fiesta provides a rare opportunity for families and friends to invigorate or renew ties while basking in the warmth of belongingness surrounded by their fellow countrymen."[17] Although supposedly "Filipino values" and the "warmth of belongingness" are certainly challenged by differences in class, regional origin, and citizenship status among Filipinos in the United States, fiesta organizers nonetheless cultivate a spirit of collectivity in order to strengthen Filipinos' sense of cultural and economic legitimacy as an ethnic minority group in the United States.[18] In addition to the sociality of the event itself, culture also plays a significant role in tying U.S.-based Filipinos to each other and to the Philippine nation. The latter is represented by performances of traditional and modern Filipino dances, the sale of "native" goods by local producers in the Philippines, and a range of Filipino dishes in the fiesta's food court. By "reinforc[ing] the connection between the young Filipino American generation and their parents' culture,"[19] these markers of Filipino ethnicity and history serve as pedagogical tools that encourage U.S.-born Filipinos to culturally and socially reproduce the Filipino diaspora.[20]

The draw of Filipino fiestas to Filipinos in the diaspora is not lost on Jim Finley, the president and CEO of NinjaTel, a small American telecommunications company whose presence has become palpable at these events in recent years. After years of experience in the telecommunications industry, Finley began a new NinjaTel service in which consumers can purchase prepaid credit for a Philippine mobile phone using a credit card and either the company's specialized website or its mobile phones themselves.[21] The service has a built-in feature through which a person in the Philippines can ask another person to pay for prepaid value for his or her Philippine phone. It is therefore especially suited for Filipinos in the United States who are accustomed to remitting money to family members in the Philippines; in fact, the process of transforming what might otherwise be a more conventional money transfer into payment for a product is referred to by corporate actors as "productizing remittances."

Filipino fiestas are important venues for Finley to brand his product and create "mindshare" with Filipino immigrants.[22] For example, fiesta attendees were often surprised to find that, instead of being granted direct access to the celebrities during autograph and photo sessions, they were first greeted by employees or volunteers of NinjaTel, who handed them a bag of marketing gimmicks and urged them to use the company's services. When fans were finally able to meet the stars and pose for a photo, they would find themselves standing in front of a backdrop or banner bearing the logo for NinjaTel's prepaid service. A NinjaTel employee would snap their picture and later upload it to the company's weblog, where fans and customers could view them anytime.

NinjaTel's efforts to insinuate its brands and products into consumers' lives go even deeper than photo ops and give-aways. Filipino fiestas are also spaces that demonstrate the ways that transnational culture casts women as reproducers of the nation and of the diaspora. The majority of the hundreds of people that pass through the celebrity-signing rooms are women, signaling what Lok Siu has called "gendered modes of participation" in diasporic gatherings.[23] Indeed, some women have constituted themselves as fan clubs of a specific celebrity: fans of Filipino American heartthrob Sam Milby, who performed at the Pinoy Musik Festival, had driven through two and a half states to see him, and Bea Alonzo's fan club showed up at the Philippine Fiesta in homemade fan-club T-shirts. Another, perhaps more important institution for the female-gendered reproduction of the Filipino nation and diaspora is the beauty contest for young Filipino women; there is one at every fiesta.[24] In the press conference held prior to the 2008 Miss U.S.-Philippines Expo pageant, for example, the contestants—most of whom were in their early twenties—were asked questions regarding their knowledge of "the economic situation" in the Philippines. When the first two girls were unable to respond adequately to the question, the next interlocutor settled on asking them where in the Philippines their parents were from. The contestants, in fact, competed in the knowledge of the names of the Philippine cities from which one or both of their parents had emigrated, although all of the contestants were born in the United States. The transnational significance of the contests was not lost on Jeannette, whose parents are from Davao. During the conference, she explained to the audience that this was "not only a pageant that represents where you live; it's also [a pageant that represents] where you come from."[25]

Such instances remind us that Filipino fiestas exist within a broader set of material and structural conditions that have feminized Filipino international labor migration by rendering Filipino women a large percentage of the Filipino global labor force. What happens when marketing to transnational migrants takes place within this gendered cultural and material context? After all, with the advent of both modern advertising in general and niche marketing in particular, advertisers look to the social roles and cultural practices of their target market to organize their strategies.[26] How do Filipino migrant and immigrant women workers get incorporated into these efforts?

Advertising: Reconnecting the Disconnected Family

The type of work or lifestyle Filipino women are able to secure overseas varies according to a number of factors: the region to which they migrate, their level of educational attainment and ability to obtain appropriate visa status, and their individual preference. In the United States, for example, where many Filipino women work as nurses, NinjaTel strives to reach nursing associations in order to gather potential customers. More recently, Jim Finley has considered ways to reach Filipino women in Japan who become sexual partners and/or girlfriends of Japanese men. Finley considers such an arrangement ideal for NinjaTel, since the men ostensibly provide financial support for the women, including keeping their mobile phones "topped up" with prepaid credit or minutes. Using language fit for the industry, Finley excitedly explained to me that "the culture is 'dialed-in'" for NinjaTel's service.

Such a comment bears even more weight when situated in the context of Philippine neoliberalism. Robyn Rodriguez has discussed transformations in notions of Filipino nationalism and citizenship that have arisen as a result of international Filipino labor migration. She argues that the Philippine state regards its citizens as profitable labor exports for the global economy because their remitted earnings—US$14.7 billion in 2007—substantially support the nation's economy.[27] A key way in which the state seeks consent for labor migration as government policy is the state-based discourse of modern heroism, whereby government agencies depict overseas labor migration as both an extension of Filipinos' goodwill and a means for national development.[28] The Philippines Overseas Employment Administration (POEA), in collaboration with the Bagong Bayani (Modern Hero) Foundation, even presents a number of *bagong bayani* awards to OFWs each year, "to pay tribute to OFWs for their valued role in nation-building."[29]

The official discourse of modern heroism is reinforced through various media. As Rodriguez mentions, the idea of OFWs as modern-day heroes has been popularized through Tagalog-language movies as well as online discussion forums and weblogs—even clothing design. It therefore comes as no surprise that the discourse is articulated by Philippine telecommunications companies that market their products and services to Filipinos overseas. Describing its Globe *Kababayan* (countrymen) list of products and services, Globe Telecom explains that it "cater[s] to our modern heroes—the OFW workers—from international remittance to prepaid cards and e-pins."[30] Globe further extended their recognition of overseas workers by sponsoring the fiftieth-anniversary celebration of the POEA.[31] Moreover, the extent to which market actors use the discourse of modern heroism *because* it is official government discourse is evinced by Rick Serrano, Globe's head of marketing to overseas Filipino communities. According to Serrano, Globe maintains a unique, informal relationship with the POEA which allows its marketing agents to conduct consumer education and market their products among Filipino workers who come to the agency to process papers, obtain information about employment, and so forth. The company thus promotes the heroic image of OFWs "because the government—the POEA, DOLE [Department of Labor and Employment], OWWA [Overseas Workers Welfare Administration]—would like to have that message, and since we're a partner. . . . We ride on their platform."[32]

In both state-based and popular representations of OFWs, a labor migrant's separation from his or her family in order to work abroad is what, in part, constitutes such labor as "heroic." For example, in most cases in which Filipinos take overseas contract work, migration is only by one, and in some cases two, members of a single household. This structure of labor migration has created what researchers refer to as "left-behind households" in the Philippines—that is, households in which a main provider works and lives away from the family.[33] The notion of a disconnected Filipino family in need of reconnection by telecommunication services is thus crucial to advertising by companies targeting the transnational migrant market. For example, to promote a special long-distance calling rate, the SMART Communications website posted an advertisement in which a young man working overseas sends a mock kiss to a young woman reciprocating from a domestic setting. The couple is separated by a thin line that bifurcates the page, while floating cartoon hearts display the call rate and the names of the Middle Eastern countries where the rate applies. While the advertisement alludes to a real premise of Filipino transnational labor migration—construction work in Middle Eastern countries does indeed represent a sizable portion of overseas contracts, and remittances are used to build homes—it also presents another reality made possible by telecommunications. The advertisement, that is, suggests a calling rate so good that it will bring the young lovers close enough that their lips could practically touch (see figure 12.1).

In a less saccharine but essentially similar approach, NinjaTel's primary direct appeal to consumers—its attempt at "hailing" them as consumer subjects—is to make consistent reference to "your loved one": using NinjaTel's prepaid service, one ad tells us, "is the easiest way to show your loved ones you are thinking of them."[34] This tactic is echoed in what is often the first question NinjaTel employees ask potential customers at Filipino fiestas: "Is there someone in the Philippines that you call often?"[35]

Affect: Reproducing Gendered Transnational Labor

By highlighting the separation of families entailed by Filipino labor migration, the aforementioned advertisements aim to capitalize on, and help resolve, the contradiction that family separation poses for capitalist production processes. For although Filipino workers provide labor on construction sites, in hospitals, and in homes outside the Philippines, their absence from their own homes disrupts the family as the site of social reproduction and, therefore, the production of new generations of workers. Moreover, being separated from one's family stirs feelings of longing and loss within workers themselves, which in turn causes them to question whether the ostensible economic benefits of labor migration are worth the pain of leaving their children, spouse, or parents for long periods of time. Such questions present a challenge to the ideology of labor migration,

Fig. 12.1. Advertising to the transnational migrant market. (SMART Communications website, www.smart.com.ph/)

which hinges on the notion that, despite the social costs, working abroad can be a source of national and familial development. Many of those who are involved in the process of labor migration thus seek resolutions to these contradictions for different reasons: the state, for the reproduction of its global workforce and their remittances; international companies, for profit; and workers, for the amelioration of the strain caused by fulfilling one set of social needs while inadequately meeting others.

Transnational migrant marketing combines these efforts using various media formats, therefore helping to reproduce the gendered and racialized division of Filipino transnational labor. Importantly, these marketing techniques operate on an affective register. In the SMART and NinjaTel advertisements, for example, *love* and *loyalty* are the common terms with which the respective companies communicate to their market. In a full-page advertisement in a Philippine fiesta booklet, one remittance company pictures an elderly Filipino woman clutching a cane. To the left of her photo are the Pilipino words "*ooperahan na siya. paano na ang ospital niya?*" (She's going to have an operation. What will her hospital stay be like?). Then, in English: "We ensure that your *sustento* [payment] reaches your loved ones in time for their medical needs."

Tracking the discourse of familial love within the media and the market, and the political economic conditions under which it is expressed, works against the notion of Filipinos as essentially "family oriented," a trope I sometimes heard expressed at NinjaTel. Yet if the disconnected Filipino family's transnational consumer practices are framed in terms of familial love and obligation, it is crucial to note that women in particular are often the subjects of this discourse. Indeed, as a result of the gendered structure of international labor migration, women make up a large portion of the Filipino diasporic body, implying their importance to companies targeting the Filipino transnational migrant market.[36] In this female-gendered context, migrant women are reported to remit more money than migrant men, and for purposes related to family reproduction—such as health, education, nutrition, and hygiene—rather than direct investment;[37] moreover, it is often the female figures in a household who take on the responsibility of compiling the clothing, home goods, school supplies, and luxury items desired by their family members back home and shipping them overseas. In the context of transnational media and marketing, migrant women thus face a number of forces compelling them to engage in transnational social reproduction through transnational consumption; they are far from being "natural" consumer subjects.[38] Some of these forces include marketers' use of *feminized* values such as familial love and obligation, as well as representations of women as reproducers of the diaspora, as seen in the Filipino fiestas.

Familial love and obligation thus constitute the terms in which to understand Filipino transnational consumption *and* transnational labor. Aihwa Ong describes the promotion of such values among "ethnicized production networks" of unskilled Asian women workers in electronics manufacturing, networks that "depend on disciplinary institutions of ethnic enclaves, factories, and families to instill feminine values of loyalty, obedience, and patience, and to mold docile labor."[39] Indeed, the global labor force—composed of a significant number of nurses, domestic workers, and entertainers—constitutes ethnicized production networks of Filipino women, as well women from the Caribbean and South Asia. This is not to say that love and obligation are social values and emotions that cannot appeal to men—only that the mobilization of feminized virtues through transnational migrant marketing and the state discourse of new heroism strengthens the discursive and material construction of women as both flexible labor for the global economy and flexible consumers for their global families. With the advent of transnational migrant marketing, loyalty, obedience, and patience do not simply tie individual workers to their families in the Philippines. They are also appropriated by marketers to build a loyal and docile consumer base and are upheld by the state to reproduce a stable and disciplined international workforce.

Conclusion

The neoliberal notion that the market is the most efficient and cost-effective generator of social welfare begs the question of *which* actors within the market are able to access goods and resources and under what kinds of conditions. After all, "the market" is not simply a collection of competing corporations or a system for exchanging goods and money. It also includes workers whose livelihoods are unevenly structured by gendered and racialized conditions of production and whose earnings must increasingly be used to purchase formerly public or partly public social services. The expansion of consumer sovereignty entailed by both mediatization and marketization thus also requires that consumers engage in increasing amounts of labor to meet their needs and desires. In this way, transnational consumption signals ways many people in various parts of the world are compelled to think and act less as citizens within a national arena and more as customers in a marketplace of social goods. This is not to say that globalized consumption renders acts of citizenship irrelevant in the neoliberal era—only that citizenship, or a relationship to a former national homeland in the case of diasporic subjects, may increasingly be tied to consumption in new and meaningful ways.

This chapter has analyzed and critiqued the ways that Filipino migrant women's engagements with their families, and the Philippine state, are shaped by transnational consumption, advertising, and media. It has demonstrated how Philippine corporate and state actors frame these engagements in ways that reinforce love and duty to family and nation as the dominant framework for understanding labor migration. State and corporate actors' appeals to feelings such as love and loyalty strengthen the ideology of the family as the core unit of social organization and the role of women within it. Thus, they represent an attempt to reinforce migrants' desires to endure the difficulty of labor migration. Rather than leave open to suggestion the possibility that familial love—or more specifically, the inability to immediately express familial love by being present with one's family—such advertisements contend that these emotions can be conveyed from distant places through the use of media and communications technology.

By pulling on the emotional strings that connect transnational migrants to their families abroad, advertisements for the transnational migrant market extend one of the projects at work in the Filipino fiestas: to reproduce affective ties that can be maintained and strengthened through consumer practices. Indeed, the tone of these advertisements echoes that of many images of OFWs and their families on television, in film, and on the Internet. These images often depict workers and their families shedding bittersweet tears while trying to maintain the conviction that one must suffer through loneliness and hard work for the good of one's family—a belief that sits at the core of the ideology of labor migration as a source of national development and of national heroes.

The transnational migrant market is thus a realm in which social values and emotions are mobilized in pursuit of exchange values and the reproduction of a global, female-gendered workforce. As a way for the state to support the continuation of its labor export policy, it appeals to migrants' dreams of providing for their families. At the same time, in the pursuit of profit margin, advertisers and other corporate actors use channels of global media to reflect back to their customers those same desires, building on the ideology of labor migration as a heroic act of patriotism. Both the state and the market thus benefit from the ways that transnational media forms help transform dreams from living things into abstract fantasies.[40]

Nestor García Canclini writes that "when we recognize that when we consume we also think, select, and reelaborate social meaning, it becomes necessary to analyze how this mode of appropriation of goods and signs conditions more active forms of participation than those that are grouped under the label of consumption."[41] The persistent circulation within transnational media and marketing of the affect and emotions associated with labor migration signals a struggle over the very meaning of obligation, loyalty, and the supposedly universal and timeless feeling of love within migrants' and immigrants' lives. Given the female-gendered division of Filipino transnational labor, the role assigned to women as reproducers of the diaspora, and dominant notions of motherhood as motivated by love and the desire to nurture, what is at stake in this struggle is women's labor—whether physical, social, or emotional. The extent to which women in particular are depicted as repositories of these feelings thus affects the extent to which the ideological notions that compel their presence within the global labor force are strengthened as well.

NOTES

I am grateful to Arlene Dávila, Emily Clark, Siddharth Iyer, and Radha Hegde for their comments on earlier drafts of this chapter. Special thanks to Arnold Alamon, of the University of Philippines, for a productive discussion of love, pain, Filipino labor migration, and the ideology of the family, on which much of the related material is based. Portions of this chapter were presented at the 2009 annual meeting of the American Studies Foundation. Funding for this research was provided by the Torch Fellowship foundation of New York University.

1. The names of all people who acted as informants for the research on which this chapter is based have been changed. However, celebrity names, the names of public events, and the names of those companies present at public events and in public spaces have been retained.

2. Orla O'Sullivan, "Once Rejected, Now Highly Valued," *Bank Systems and Technology* 45, no. 9 (September 2008): 11.

3. Throughout this chapter I use the terms "migrant" and "immigrant" to denote different social and physical locations of individuals relative to the country in which they live permanently and of which they are often citizens. Although migration clearly occurs *within* nation-states, here I use "transnational migrant" to refer to a person who travels away from the country he or she considers a permanent residence to another country, often to find gainful employment. More specifically, I characterize transnational migrants as individuals who return to their country of origin—or move on to another location—when not employed abroad. "Immigrant" refers to a person who travels away from the country he or she considers a permanent residence to another country (also often to find gainful employment) and, in contrast to a transnational migrant, considers the new country of residence a permanent place to live and work. While I recognize the slippery and contingent nature of these terms—which derive from the equally contingent and shifting ways that those people that I am calling migrants and immigrants achieve "permanency" in any place—I do think it is possible to make some distinctions between migrants and immigrants. Many of these distinctions rely on issues of citizenship (immigrants seek citizenship status in their new place of residence more often than migrants do), intent to stay (migrants often intend to return to their country of origin, whereas immigrants attempt to "set up a life" abroad), and family (most often, what constitutes the "life" immigrants want to establish in a new country is inextricably tied to a desire to raise or bring family there, whereas migrants seek to continue life with their family members in their country of origin, where those family members have remained). "Transnational migrant market," however, refers to *both* immigrants and migrants as a unified consumer demographic, since, as I discuss in the second section, both Filipino immigrants and migrants engage in the practices that make them attractive to advertisers.

4. Tadiar's Marxist formulation maintains that imagination is a form of *work*, making dreams akin to living labor and fantasies akin to abstract labor. Neferti Xina M. Tadiar, *Fantasy-Production: Sexual Economies and Other Philippine Consequences for the New World Order* (Manila: Ateneo de Manila University Press, 2004), 5–6.

5. Aihwa Ong, *Neoliberalism as Exception: Mutations in Citizenship and Sovereignty* (Durham, NC: Duke University Press, 2006), 11. Here, Ong also quotes Michael Peters, "Neoliberalism," in *Encyclopedia of Philosophy of Education* (London: Routledge, 1999).

6. I say "attempts to build consent" and "ideally" because I do not assume that neoliberal ideology—or any ideological project—is ever wholly complete.

7. Ma. Joy V. Abrenica and Gilberto M. Llanto, "Services," in Arsenio Balisacan and Hal Hill, eds., *The Philippine Economy: Development, Policies, and Challenges* (Manila: Ateneo de Manila University Press, 2003).

8. Darwin G. Amojelar, "Mobile-Phone Market to Fall amid Downturn," *Manila Times Online* (January 7, 2009), http://www.themanilatimes.net (accessed January 29, 2009).

9. Radha S. Hegde and Barbara DeCicco-Bloom, "Working Identities: South Asian Nurses and the Transnational Negotiations of Race and Gender," *Communication Quarterly* 50 (Spring 2002): 2.

10. See Raul Pertierra, *Txt-ing Selves: Cell Phones and Philippine Modernity* (Manila: De LaSalle University Press, 2002); Vicente L. Rafael, "The Cell Phone and the Crowd: Messianic Politics in the Contemporary Philippines," *Public Culture* 15, no. 3 (2003): 399–425; Chris Pritchard, "The World's Text-Messaging Capital," *Marketing Magazine* 6, no. 48 (December 2, 2002): 8; Wayne Arnold, "Manila's Talk of the Town," *New York Times* (July 5, 2000): C1.

11. David Harvey, *A Brief History of Neoliberalism* (Oxford, UK: Blackwell, 2005); Saskia Sassen, *The Global City: New York, London, Tokyo* (Princeton, NJ: Princeton University Press, 2001).

12. Robert Alvarez, *Mangos, Chiles, and Truckers: The Business of Transnationalism* (Minneapolis: University of Minnesota Press, 2005); Ong, *Neoliberalism as Exception*; Robyn Rodriguez, *Migrants for Export: How the Philippine State Brokers Labor to the World* (Minneapolis: University of Minnesota Press, forthcoming 2010).

13. "Philippine Fiesta in America, Summer 2007," souvenir booklet (New York: Special Edition Press, 2007), 1.

14. Ibid., 3.

15. As events which mix food, music, corporate marketing, and local politics, corporate pachangas are a way to "tie and create 'publics' and 'markets' as interconnected arenas." See Margaret Dorsey, *Pachangas: Borderlands Music, U.S. Politics, and Transnational Marketing* (Austin: University of Texas Press, 2006).

16. Furthermore, the marketing representative's comments suggest that, within the realm of the market, the term *migrant* may have more to do with transnational practices than politico-legal migration status, such that an immigrant who sends money and care packages (*balikbayan* boxes) home can be a migrant through his or her consumption practices. These attempts to define the transnational migrant market signal what Arlene Dávila has discussed as the "role played by marketing in the discursive construction of ethnicity and marginality." It is the former sense of the term *migrant* which compels me to use it in the term *transnational migrant market*, even though many of the people whom I include in my study are in the politico-legal sense of the term immigrants. Arlene Dávila, *Latinos, Inc.: The Making and Marketing of a People* (Los Angeles: University of California Press, 2001), 232.

17. "Philippine Fiesta in America, Summer 2007," 3.

18. For diasporic gatherings as a source of solidarity among ethnic minorities, see also Lok Siu, "Queen of the Chinese Colony: Gender, Nation, and Belonging in Diaspora," *Anthropological Quarterly* 78, no. 3 (Summer 2005): 519.

19. "Philippine Fiesta in America, Summer 2007," 3.

20. Siu, "Queen of the Chinese Colony," 520.

21. Unlike most mobile-phone users in the United States, where consumers purchase a phone plan which they pay for every month, the majority of the world's mobile-phone users prepay for discrete amounts of value which get stored onto their phone. Consumers use up this value whenever they make calls or send messages via their phone. In the Philippines, prepaid value is referred to as phone "load."

22. According to Jim Finley, Filipino fiestas are also good opportunities to demonstrate to the major Philippine telecommunications companies—with whom he collaborates—that NinjaTel knows and has access to the Filipino transnational migrant market in the United States. Indeed, NinjaTel's entry into the transnational migrant market signals the extent to which both Philippine and American corporations alike are targeting Filipinos abroad.

23. Siu, "Queen of the Chinese Colony," 523.

24. The fiesta beauty pageants function in a very similar way to those discussed by Lok Siu during the annual conventions for the Chinese diaspora in Central America and Panama. See

ibid. and also Lok Siu, *Memories of a Future Home: Diasporic Citizenship of Chinese in Panama* (Stanford, CA: Stanford University Press, 2005).

25. "Miss U.S.-Philippines Expo 2008 Press Conference," *YouTube*, http://www.youtube.com/watch?v=vsZjpdKACYE (accessed October 23, 2008).

26. On histories of advertising, marketing, and consumer history, see Lizbeth Cohen, *A Consumer's Republic: The Politics of Mass Consumption in Postwar America* (New York: Vintage, 2003); and David Steigerwald, "All Hail the Republic of Choice: Consumer History as Contemporary Thought," *Journal of American History* (September 2006).

27. Rodriguez, *Brokering Bodies*.

28. On "consent," see Antonio Gramsci, in Quintin and Hoare and Geoffrey Nowell Smith, eds., *Selections from the Prison Notebooks of Antonio Gramsci* (New York: International Publishers, 1971).

29. "Special Events: Migrant Workers Day and the Bagong Bayani Awards," *Philippine Overseas Employment Administration: Y2K Annual Report* (Mandaluyong City: Philippine Overseas Employment Administration, 2001), 17.

30. Globe Telecom, "International Services: Consumer," http://www1.globe.com.ph/contentrn.aspx?sid=1&artid=39 (accessed February 5, 2009).

31. Globe Telecom, "Globe Kababayan Events," http://www.globekababayan.com.ph/category.aspx?catid=3 (accessed February 5, 2009).

32. Interview with Rick Serrano, February 12, 2009.

33. Hector B. Morada, "Left-Behind Households of Overseas Filipino Workers," paper presented at the Asian Population Network Workshop on Migration and the "Asian Family" in a Globalising World (Singapore, April 16–18, 2001).

34. Louis Althusser, "Ideology and Ideological State Apparatuses," in *Lenin and Philosophy and Other Essays* (New York and London: Monthly Review Press, 1970). On the concept of hailing or interpellation in marketing, see Dávila, *Latinos, Inc.*

35. Moreover, that images of heterosexual relations, intergenerational families, and two-parent heterosexual households pervade print ads for the Filipino transnational migrant market suggests that families defined as normative by both capitalism and Catholicism are well deserving of reconnection.

36. The Asian Development Bank estimated that 65 percent of the overseas Filipino workforce in 2004 were women. In 2005, 70 percent of the nearly 285,000 newly hired overseas contract workers were women who took jobs as domestic helpers, entertainers, and factory workers. See Alex Pabico, "'Super Pinays' in Harm's Way," *Daily PCIJ* (August 17, 2006), http://www.pcij.org/blog/?p=1148 (accessed September 27, 2008). Moreover, the number of women hired as new overseas contract workers has surpassed that of men, and the number continues to increase. See Morada, "Left-Behind Households of Overseas Filipino Workers." For gender and Filipino transnational labor, see also Catherine Ceniza Choy, *Empire of Care: Nursing and Migration in Filipino American History* (Durham, NC: Duke University Press, 2003); Yen Le Espiritu, *Home Bound: Filipino American Lives across Cultures, Communities, and Countries* (Berkeley: University of California Press, 2003); Rhacel Parreñas, *Servants of Globalization: Women, Migration, and Domestic Work* (Stanford, CA: Stanford University Press, 2001).

37. Karol Ilagan, "ILO: Women at a Greater Disadvantage in Labor Migration," *Daily PCIJ* (September 27, 2008), http://www.pcij.org/blog/?p=2985 (accessed September 27, 2008).

38. A number of social scientists have remarked on the significant socioeconomic function of wages remitted from overseas by migrant women—and the nationalist discourses that characterize these workers as crucial for the economic development of their "homeland." See

Linda Basch, Nina Glick Schiller, and Christina Szanton Blanc, *Nations Unbound: Transnational Projects, Postcolonial Predicaments, and Deterritorialized Nation States* (Langhorn, PA: Gordon and Breach, 1994); Maria Mies, *Patriarchy and Accumulation on a World Scale: Women in the International Division of Labor* (London: Zed Books, 1986); Aihwa Ong and Donald Macon Nonini, *Ungrounded Empires: The Cultural Politics of Modern Chinese Transnationalism* (London: Routledge, 1997); Parreñas, *Servants of Globalization*; and Vicente L. Rafael, "'Your Grief Is Our Gossip': Overseas Filipinos and Other Spectral Presences," *Public Culture* 9, no. 2 (1997): 267–291.

39. Ong, *Neoliberalism as Exception*, 124.

40. Tadiar, *Fantasy-Production*.

41. Nestor Garcia Canclini, *Consumers and Citizens: Globalization and Multicultural Conflicts*, trans. George Yúdice (Minneapolis: University of Minnesota Press, 2001), 26. Originally published in Spanish in 1995.

IV   Technologies of Control

13   Digital Cosmopolitanisms

The Gendered Visual Culture of Human Rights Activism

Sujata Moorti

In the first decade of the twenty-first century, the Internet has become the pre-eminent medium from which international human rights campaigns have been publicized. Activists from around the world—whether it is Tibet, the Sudan, Iran, or Iraq—have increasingly turned to YouTube or independent websites such as the Hub to upload first-person accounts of human rights violations. These images have drawn international attention to "hot spots" of violation and local forms of activism that may have otherwise flown below the global media radar. Indeed, many human rights organizations now consider the Internet as the primary venue for exposing human rights abuses and mobilizing public opinion against them.

Scholars have parsed the do-it-yourself (DIY) culture that has come to pre-dominate the discourse and action of contemporary human rights campaigns, as well as the ways in which the reliance on visuality has transformed our understanding of human rights.[1] In this chapter, I focus on the representations of gender and sexuality in videos about the Oaxaca teachers' strike of 2006 and the Myanmar protests of 2007. Through a close reading of the visual grammar deployed in the videos posted on the Web, I highlight the cultural work of the images and signal how the representational grammar helps construct a transnational community of sentiment.

Updating Benedict Anderson's concept of imagined communities for the age of globality, Arjun Appadurai coins the term *community of sentiment* to designate a "group that begins to imagine and feel things together." He singles out electronic media as facilitating imaginings beyond the nation-state: "These are communities in themselves but always potentially communities for themselves capable of moving from shared imagination to collective action."[2] Working from this productive understanding of transnational community facilitated by the conjunctions of media and mobility, I examine the sentiment of cosmopolitanism that human rights videos effect.

The human rights digital uploads engender in viewers a shared sense of belonging and reinstate Western understandings of rights and justice. Notwithstanding the novelty of the technology and the poignancy of the evidence they provide, the images of human rights activism help reinscribe a digital colonialism.

Familiar themes of the North-South politics of representation are rewritten for the new digital era. Human rights as a discourse is once again authorized with themes central to the Western project of modernity, and the liberal subject of the Enlightenment is firmly recentered with accents and flavors from the Global South. Indeed, the promiscuous circulation of human rights videos serves as an alibi for the reinscription of Western modernity. These politics are keenly evident in the representations of gender; continuing asymmetries of power and existing geopolitical realities shape the ways in which human rights discourses continue to be articulated. The human rights videos facilitate new processes of governmentality, with incongruent effects in the Global North and South.[3] My analysis reveals that transnational circulations have a different valence in the South than they do in the North; often in the latter, the simple act of viewing the videos serves as an alibi for activism.

Over the past decade, the term *cosmopolitanism* has acquired the status of a catch-all term characterizing complex cross-cultural processes. Most commonly associated with a Kantian political philosophy of abstract universalism that transcends regional particularities, cosmopolitanism, however, cannot be conflated with a flaccid internationalism. There is also a growing consensus that like nationalism, cosmopolitanism is heterogeneous and is not opposed to nationalism.[4] Cosmopolitanism is located and embodied; it is not a postnational politics. The human rights videos are a fertile terrain from which to examine how two productive but unwieldy terms—*transnational* and *cosmopolitanism*—are referenced and translated. Notwithstanding the contradictory "local" effects that I document, I contend that digital media engender among viewers the capacity for flexible attachments to more than one community. They facilitate a cosmopolitanism that proclaims an abstract "universalism" and a form of activism, which dovetails with key principles of neoliberal capitalism. Above all, they make it possible for viewers to believe they belong to a transnational community of sentiment that allows them to think beyond the nation.[5]

I offer a brief outline of the teachers' strike in Oaxaca and the Myanmar protests and then offer a close reading of videos uploaded about human rights violations in these sites. The chapter concludes with an exploration of alternative possibilities that have the potential of breaking the existing mold of transnational media practices and the cosmopolitanisms they evoke.

The Transnationalization of Local Protests

In May 2006, teachers in the southern Mexican state of Oaxaca launched a (fairly routine) strike demanding higher salaries, better benefits, and improved facilities in their schools. A month later, the police tried to expel the teachers from buildings they had occupied in the state capital. However, the ensuing charges of police brutality helped mobilize other groups, such as peasant groups, and to enlarge the scope of the strike. From a demonstration narrowly focused on the educational enterprise, the protest was now transformed into a political movement against the state governor, Ulises Ortiz. Four months later, the local accents of this strike—which focused on inequalities characteristic of Mexican everyday life, such as those of urban-rural disparities and indigenous-European differences—were transformed by the death of an independent video maker, Brad Will, as he was filming clashes between demonstrators and state authorities.

As is characteristic of a lot of activist filmmakers, Will had arrived in Mexico in October 2006 to counter mainstream media coverage of the strike with reporting that would highlight the demands and experiences of the striking Mexicans.[6] As a representative of the self-proclaimed left-leaning Indymedia, "a collective of independent media organizations . . . offering grassroots, non-corporate coverage,"[7] Will hoped to bring more international attention to the growing civil crisis in Oaxaca. As he covered a skirmish between paramilitary forces and protesters, Will was shot a couple times, and he inadvertently ended up filming his own death. This stunning and morbid footage soon overshadowed all other aspects of the strike.[8] Indeed, Will's death catapulted the Oaxaca strike into the international limelight, with the U.S.-based Committee to Protect Journalists demanding an inquiry and the U.S. State Department warning against tourism in Oaxaca. Ironically, Will's death also provided Mexican president Vicente Fox the opportunity to deploy federal law enforcement authorities to forcibly remove protesters from the city center. On November 25, 2006, the strike ended officially with teachers promised a salary raise over six years as well as better facilities. None of the other demands was met. At the end of the six-month strike, eighteen people were killed and scores of protesters were arrested. The Oaxaca teachers' strike was covered by mainstream international media only momentarily; the numerous human rights violations that diverse watchdog groups and nongovernmental organizations (NGOs) have cited remain marginalized. In Western media coverage, the Oaxaca teachers' strike is now linked inextricably with Brad Will's death (see figure 13.1). This instance draws attention to a number of ethical and moral concerns about how local human rights activism is transformed by the transnational circulation of videos, as well as the troubling manner in which a universalized discourse of human rights has the potential to domesticate differences, often writing out the specificities of the local.

Across the globe almost a year later, bloggers and clandestinely recorded cellphone footage of protest marches offered the world glimpses into the closed society of Myanmar. Dubbed by the media as the Saffron Revolution, these protests were primarily aimed at contesting the rising prices of basic commodities. Begin-

Fig. 13.1. Shooting victim Brad Will. (http://elenemigocomun.net/wp-content/
uploads/2007/10/bradwill_261007.jpg)

ning in late 2006, commodity prices sharply increased, culminating in 2007 when
the military dictatorship abruptly removed fuel subsidies; in less than a week,
prices of petrol increased 100 percent and those of other good over 500 percent.[9]
As prices of basic commodities escalated, in a country which the United Nations
ranks as among the twenty poorest countries in the world, citizens started to
launch a series of protests. Initially, the protests were led by students and political activists, but a month later Buddhist monks joined in. Their vivid presence
remained on the streets for ten days before a military crackdown ended the strike;
the barefoot monks with their distinctively colored robes expanded the terms of
the protest, demanding greater freedom and the restoration of basic rights. The
monks' presence encapsulated in stark visual terms the contrast between the mili-

tary dictatorship and the citizenry of Myanmar. The military regime, however, raided monasteries and attacked monks within pagodas.

An Al Jazeera correspondent and some reporters for news agencies were the only "official" reporters at hand to cover the protests and the ensuing crackdown. Nevertheless, a number of "citizen-journalists" used their cell-phone cameras and rudimentary video equipment to clandestinely film the protests, especially instances of police brutality. In a thrilling reminder of the emancipatory potential of the Internet, these citizen-journalists either uploaded their videos from local Internet cafes (evading military censors by using proxy websites) or sent digital files to exiled activists across the border in India and Thailand to make the world aware of the human rights abuses occurring in Myanmar. On September 28, 2007, the military dictatorship arrested thousands of monks and civilians; more significantly, the government cut Internet access in the country and disabled international mobile-phone connections; they also started to target individuals with cell phones and cameras. The forty-day protest resulted in the death of over a hundred demonstrators,[10] as well as a Japanese photographer, Kenji Nagai, who was working for the French news agency Agence France Presse. There exists video documentation of a soldier shooting Nagai; however, the contents of Nagai's camera have not been disclosed. Existing video footage shows a soldier walking away with the camera Nagai was using when he was killed. Lacking the visceral elements of the Brad Will final footage, Nagai's death remains only a footnote in media coverage, which was dominated by the presence of monks. Similarly, the price hikes, which instigated the protests, were marginalized. Even as this instance highlights digital media's ability to draw global attention to human rights violations in a closed society, it signals also the ease with which an authoritarian regime could halt the flow of information. The Saffron Revolution underscores the intersection between politics and technology and has led several scholars to question the efficacy of the Internet to facilitate a transnational social movement.[11] Despite this pessimism, it is worth noting that the Internet images inspired protests around the world, with groups urging their governments to take action against the Myanmar military regime.[12]

Human Rights Discourses

Human rights is a capacious term through which politicoethical claims are made and sociopolitical transformations are initiated; the concept of human rights is inherently transnational in its address and scope. Technically, these rights are enshrined in the 1948 Universal Declaration of Human Rights (UDHR).[13] This document outlines the full range of human rights, including civil, political, economic, social, and cultural rights. Almost all the human rights videos that are uploaded on Internet sites primarily deal with violations listed under Articles 2 and 5.[14]

Scholars often characterize the concept of human rights as well as its juridical implementation as Western in nature and ideology. Human rights tend to focus on individual, civil and political, rights; the subject of these discourses tends to be the individual modeled on Western liberal humanist traditions. In contrast, third world communities appear to want to focus on the rights of collectivities and the right to economic development and self-determination.[15] Feminist philosopher Wendy Brown cautions that human rights ideology often serves as an alibi for specific economic-political purposes, often recasting collective justice projects into a discourse of suffering prevention.[16] Kenneth Cmiel and other scholars contend that contemporary human rights discourses and activism are the product of a particular kind of international realpolitik that came into being over the last third of the twentieth century (some contend that it is the discourse most appropriate to the latest stage of neoliberal capitalism).[17] The new politics of human rights entails a shift in focus from the sovereignty of nations to the rights of individuals, regardless of nationality.[18]

While noting the important interventions that such a counterhegemonic politics has been able to achieve, feminist scholars have pointed out the ways in which women's rights tend to be written out of this narrative of liberation and freedom; specifically they have highlighted how the human subject of these discourses is gendered male.[19] This is an insight that surfaces in several of the videos I analyze, in which it is male subjects whose rights have been violated by the state; the men are simultaneously positioned as agents of change seeking to reinstate their rights. Women appear primarily as those victimized by local cultural practices and needing to be rescued; rarely are they presented as being deprived of their rights by the state.

The central epistemology of human rights discourse is that of revelation and exposure; activists believe that the presentation of information of violations will shame nations into complying with the UDHR. Testimony and witnessing are thus central aspects of human rights discourses and activism; Thomas Keenan contends that such "mobilization of shame" is characteristic of the Enlightenment faith in the power of reason and knowledge. Human rights groups mobilize the language of visibility—bringing atrocities to light, the light of public scrutiny—and technologies of witnessing.[20] According to several scholars, the transnational circulation of images transforms human rights from national and regional events into tragedies that are "seen" and "felt" as part of the stream of everyday experience in the intimacy of homes thousands of miles away.[21] Inevitably, the quotidian experiences of violations "out there" help transform the practice of politics "here."

In the late twentieth century the media have been identified as critical to the diffusion of such information, and specific realist forms of representation and documentation have been privileged.[22] Meg McLagan identifies the proliferation of organizations and venues dedicated to the production, distribution, and circulation of rights-oriented media as constituting a "circulatory matrix," one that connects local grassroots activists with a global public sphere.[23] The digital videos belong to a similar type of multilayered, transnational circulatory matrix and utilize a specific representational grammar to construct a persuasive visual culture. As is the case with other human rights discourses, the videos I examine are structured around a central belief that seeing *is* believing. The community of sentiment they engender stems from a naturalization of viewing practices. There are specific modalities through which these videos participate in the construction of a regime of truth, a discourse that foregrounds the voices of the marginalized. Of equal significance is the culture of seeing that these videos engender. As numerous scholars have documented, the camera and photography have historically been conceptualized as providing incontrovertible proof that a given thing happened (it may be distorted, but it existed).[24] This presumption of veracity lends the human rights videos authority, interest, and seductiveness. The camera seems to furnish evidence that is otherwise unavailable and helps in the formation of a community of sentiment that naturalizes Enlightenment principles of objectivity.

The contemporary transnational circulatory matrix has rewritten the scopic regimes characteristic of the twentieth century. For instance, Allen Feldman contends in his eloquent work on the uses of visuality in Northern Ireland that state power is consolidated through optical surveillance; specifically, the state mobilized cameras to regulate its citizens.[25] The democratization of digital media technology has instead produced what human rights activist Sam Gregory calls a "participatory panopticon."[26] Today, everyday people have access to technologies of vision and possess the capacity to bring the state under regimes of regulation. This in turn has the potential to transform existing forms of governmentality.

An integral mode through which the concept of a participatory panopticon is mobilized is by abandoning journalistic principles of neutrality. Rather, human rights videos espouse overtly the point of view of those whose rights have been violated. How does this perspective shape our understanding of the violated subject(s) and human rights violations in general? Does this participatory panopticon facilitate a different gender politics?

Media scholars are only now beginning to address the ways in which the transnational circuits of human rights politics and digital media intersect to necessitate new communication models. While some scholars celebrate the freedom enabled by the Internet to make rights-based claims, others are more guarded and caution that technologies of freedom could easily become technologies of abuse.[27] James

Castonguay documents how different groups in the former Yugoslavia—Serbs, Bosnians, Croats—each mobilized the technology of the Internet to contest and establish rights claims, often upending taken-for-granted understandings of the civil war. He reminds us that progressive politics do not inhere in interactivity; instead he suggests that the Internet facilitates a general inter*passivity*.[28] Slavoj Žižek deploys interpassivity in his examination of video games to characterize a mode of relating in which emotions and activity are transferred to a surrogate self.[29] In a similar manner, viewers of human rights videos can claim to be active even as they "passively" experience a transnational sphere of violations; activism itself is transferred to the surrogate self wielding the camera.

Shooting with a Camera, Shooting with a Gun

The digitally uploaded videos of the Oaxaca teachers' strike and the Myanmar protests help to explicate how a regime of truth is constructed visually.[30] Unlike mainstream media coverage, these videos are not synchronous with events; instead there is always a time lag. Images of the actual protests enter the digital public sphere retrospectively. Watching these videos evokes the sensibility of a chronicle of a tragedy foretold. The viewing experience is thus suffused with a bathos, an affective emotion that is central to the constitution of a transnational community of sentiment.

While the Oaxaca teachers' strike continued for over six months, the majority of the DIY videos that are available on the Internet portray, without any commentary, scenes of protest marches.[31] These clips do not offer any context or explanation for the demonstrations. Visually, the protesting teachers are repeatedly cast in the image of the underdog fighting the military might of the state police. While the demonstrators are often shown with their hands raised in protest or carrying placards, images of the state forces are always from an oppositional viewpoint. The police always appear en masse as a group of men with shields, obstructing the teachers. For instance, a collage of photographs entitled "Oaxaca, Mexico Protests" is set to the tune of John Lennon's song "Power to the People." The camera is positioned amid the protesting teachers; thus, we see events from their angle of vision, and as viewers we are positioned to align with them. This portrayal of the demonstrators in combination with the evocative music helps draw viewers' identifications and sympathies through a familiar song whose politics and moral stance are readily identifiable.[32] These strategies of identification are heightened by the portrayal of the police and state forces. Repeatedly they are shown in isolation from the demonstrators or directly bearing down on them with force. Often these videos use the image of a loud helicopter to symbolize state authority—physically distanced and separate from the masses, the iconic image also captures the asymmetries of power. These ideas are captured in a November 2006 video, "Oaxacan Women March for Respect," documenting protests against the police rape of female demonstrators.[33] At one point, the camera suddenly swivels to focus on a police officer who has his rifle aimed directly at the camera lens. This startling moment is followed by a number of more banal images in which the police are located in a space and angle that appear inimical to the demonstrators and by extension the viewing audience. The video heightens viewers' sympathies with the demonstrators by showing the police from the point of view of the protesting women; much like the women in Oaxaca, we see the police as an intimidating block of expression-free, armed men. This is one of the few videos in which women appear as speaking subjects.

These videos, however, reached only a small audience, registering a maximum of about five thousand hits. The limited address of these videos can also be gleaned from the comments section, in which Mexican interlocutors predominate and the discussion is primarily conducted in Spanish. These commentaries are striking because pro- and antigovernment arguments are rehearsed in language characteristic of cyberspace. Thus, the claims of the striking workers tend to be occluded, and instead the discussion turns to whose assessment of the government is more accurate and correct. The posting of these videos on sites such as YouTube helps produce a regime of truth that seems to go against the intent of the video posters.

A year after the strike ended, Amnesty International conducted an investigation and distributed its findings and the government response to it in video format. Similarly, a local group, Alive in Mexico, uploaded its own anniversary video. Both videos recapitulate footage of street demonstrations and intersperse this footage with the testifying voices of individual witnesses. Representations of the police and state authorities are often reduced to images of a helicopter hovering over the narrow streets of Oaxaca. These videos give speaking roles to local Mexicans, who provide witness to specific police abuses and human rights violations. These witnesses restore the subjectivity of the violated; they help restore the individuality of those who experienced police brutality and thus translate the abstract concept of human rights violations into concrete form. Men's voices predominate in these videos, as they enumerate the specific ways in which the state has violated human rights. The voiceover accompanying both videos is that of an authoritative male, whose cadences closely resemble what is best characterized as anchor-speak (the soothing, assured tone of television anchors).

Women appear only as the victimized, as they testify to the losses they have suffered (such as the death of a husband or a son). Women do not appear claiming their demands as teachers; rather, they appear as objects of state brutality. Thus, these videos produce familiarly gendered narratives of women as victims.

As Carole Pateman and others have argued, these videos help reconstruct the difference between masculinity and femininity as the political difference between freedom and subjection. The videos also recapitulate a dominant theme of human rights discourse: that third world subjects need to be rescued from their own kind by Westerners (in this instance Amnesty International and more generally the UDHR). Thus, digital media amplify problematic aspects of human rights discourses and do not help us understand the specific ways in which Mexicans at the local level understand concepts of justice or civic and political rights. Instead, we learn to see the teachers' strike from the universalizing point of view offered by UDHR. These videos raise a number of other theoretical concerns about the role of the camera in local zones of activism and how the presence of the media transforms the practice of activism. Local forms of opposition as well as their modes of staging demands are overwritten by a universalizing drive; the local is rewritten in the idioms of the universal. Thus, rights violation and the resultant demands that may be unique to Oaxaca disappear from the sphere of visibility.

Also problematic is that the videos engender a voyeurism that results from construing suffering at a safe distance. As with the testifying Mexicans, the "video cameras take us into the intimate details of pain and misfortune," but without the social responsibility of real engagement.[34] The images of suffering appeal to our emotions and help establish evidentiary claims. The corporeal presence of the speaking subjects, however, does not facilitate the formation of a transnational social movement; rather, it permits a transnational community of sentiment. Affect thus trumps agency. The images promote a politics of pity; they center on the observation of the unfortunate and thus facilitate an aestheticization of suffering.

As noted earlier, the on-camera shooting death of U.S. citizen Brad Will has come to stand in for the Oaxaca teachers' strike and also functions as an allegory for Mexican police brutality. In contrast to the other videos related to the Oaxaca teachers' strike, "The Last Moments of Bradley Roland Will," a video hosted by Indymedia on YouTube, registered more hits than all the other videos about the teachers' strike. Viewed over seventy-five thousand times, this video offers raw footage from the tape in Brad Will's camera when he was killed. As with the other Oaxaca-related tapes, this sixteen-minute video too is aligned with the perspective of the demonstrators and repeatedly depicts paramilitary forces as threatening. The camera's point of view positions us as one with the protesters and hence as the recipient of police brutality. Most of the footage in this video offers a chaotic field of activities, with blurred images as Will runs along with demonstrators or hides behind parked trucks to protect himself from the paramilitary forces. The footage helps viewers understand the craft of human rights video making; we are transported with Will as he runs from site to site, seeking evocative visuals as well as actions of police brutality. In the final moments of the tape, we see images as Will cowers behind a vehicle along with other demonstrators as two armed gunmen bear down on them. Before the tape comes to an abrupt end, we witness the camera go askew as Will is shot and we hear him shout out for help before the camera fades out. Apart from the morbid curiosity this video undoubtedly evokes, it also resonates with Christian themes of martyrdom and individual suffering.[35] Abstract ideas of justice and equality are rendered apprehensible through this individual instance of violence, and we are made to understand the secular concept of what it means to be truly human.

More significantly, the camera serves as silent witness at the moment when the distinctions between subject and object collapse—Brad Will is no longer a journalist documenting atrocities but is himself a victim of these atrocities. The camera captures "the blurred intersection of what our impoverished theoretical vocabulary allows us to call only event and representation, occurrence and image."[36] The video offers viewers a sense of immediacy of witnessing suffering, or what Arthur and Joan Kleinman call the "appeal of experience."[37] The focus on individual experience has the potential to deny the social experience of suffering. More significantly, the videotaped death of this U.S. citizen gains more notoriety than the suffering of Mexicans. The imperial gaze of the video is worth remarking upon. Is the camera a predatory weapon? At least in this instance, the camera functions as more than a form of note taking; it serves as witness. In the absence of a new culture of seeing, the video serves to recenter the West and its ideologies. Thus, the asymmetries of the global political economy shape the ways in which human rights violations in the Global South are narrated and circulated. In a paradoxical move, neocolonial ideologies that recenter the West dovetail nicely with the digital democratic impulses central to Internet-based activism. Consequently, the local seems to become a site from which the West ventriloquizes its understanding of human rights. Brad Will comes to stand in for a hegemonic Western masculinity—courageous, driven by justice, he is a man of action who seeks to rescue beleaguered Oaxacans from other Mexicans, and he is willing to make the ultimate sacrifice for his principles. Although numerous other Mexicans died during the demonstrations, they remain nameless. Will's figure is the one that metaphorizes the event and represents the non-West as Other, needing to be rescued by the West.

Envisioning a Closed Society

Images are central to our understanding of the 2007 Myanmar protest; the event entered the (global) public sphere through clandestinely filmed footage—the local press and television stations ignored the protests. All Western media coverage of the events is based on images that were uploaded on the Internet or given to exiles across the border in Thailand or India. As mentioned earlier, demonstrations against the rise in prices of basic commodities fomented more expansive protests seeking the restoration of basic rights in Myanmar. Much like the Oaxacan teachers' strike, most of the footage of the protests was filmed by locals. However, in this instance, since the images were recorded clandestinely, most of them provide a bird's-eye view—we witness marches from rooftops, an angle of vision that offers a panoramic view of the masses of people demonstrating against the military junta. Visually these images are arresting also because of the vivid contrast drawn between the monks en masse, who are protectively ensconced within a human chain of citizens, and the gray mass of police. The blurred, shaky images adhere to the rules of photographic realism. The use of ambient sound and translations in subtitle cumulatively produce the seductive sense of verisimilitude characteristic of the realist aesthetic.[38]

The digitally uploaded images may have provided the information needed for mainstream media coverage, but the videos on YouTube and other sites appeared only after the government crackdown. To get an understanding of the difference between mainstream media coverage and the DIY videos it is instructive to examine Al Jazeera coverage of the demonstrations. Both during the protests and in the September 2008 coverage to mark the first anniversary, Al Jazeera's reports are framed by the authoritative voice of the off-camera reporter. The protest images, which are reinvoked during the anniversary coverage, are sharp and center on the protesting monks. The reports are punctuated by stunning images of the two pagodas with their distinct gold spires in the heart of Yangoon, often serving as a visual device to mark a transition in the narrative. Both sets of reports are bookended by images of monks at prayer—the serenity of this scene sets up a sharp contrast with the military brutality that the monks experience in the streets. These juxtapositions offer cues to the viewer on the identifications they are expected to form with the monks (since they are demanding freedom and the restoration of basic rights), as well as on the ways in which to interpret the police action on the streets. In addition, although many women participated in the demonstrations, the witnesses who appear in the reports are all men, and the camera focuses almost exclusively on the barefoot monks.[39]

In sharp contrast, the DIY videos offer grainy, blurred images of the protests with noisy ambient sound and often lack any kind of commentary. The video makers often indicate in accompanying text any significant action on screen, since the images are quite indistinct. For instance, "In Freedom's Cause" offers a composite portrayal of the events from the last week of September 2007, with a disclaimer that the editor has used all available "usable images" and cleaned up some clips for greater clarity.[40] This video is not accompanied by any commentary;

rather, it is set to music, which helps to underscore the emotions that the images are supposed to evoke: soaring Italian opera music, followed by music from the Philippines, and ending with a song called "You'll Be Safe Here," which is played as the military shoot the Japanese photographer. This key media moment remains indistinct, and the video maker has to alert viewers to the moment in the collage when we can expect to see the killing on screen. (There exist other minute-long videos documenting the precise moment when the photographer was killed, but these are equally indistinct.) "In Freedom's Cause" is one of the few videos of the Myanmar protests in which women appear on screen, either as nuns or as protesting students. Women tend to predominate in other digital videos uploaded on the Internet, which document different forms of state oppression. In most videos, such as the prosecution of the ethnic Karen in "Shoot on Sight," Burmese women are the ones who serve as voices testifying to the violence that their male kin have suffered under state persecution. Although the women have speaking voices, they always appear as victimized subjects.[41]

Other DIY videos offer, without any commentary, events on Yangoon streets. Many of them are taken from cracks in windows and thus show events from an eccentric angle. Often we see demonstrators using their cell phones to record incidents. These DIY videos offer quite a different view of Yangoon from that offered by Al Jazeera: although the golden pagoda shrines often appear on the screen, rarely are they the focus of the images. Instead, the videos focus on the movement of the demonstrators and capture some of the dynamism and vitality of the protests. The DIY videos also depict a Yangoon with huge billboards on street corners and cars, quotidian images rarely present in mainstream media depictions. Finally, even without any overarching commentary, viewers come to see how everyday citizens formed a human chain around demonstrating monks, in an attempt to shield them from state authorities. These videos are not centered on the barefoot monks; rather, they shift our perspective so we can see how the monks are part of a much larger demonstration. They help restore some agency to everyday Burmese. It is the collective rather than one individual who is foregrounded.

All the Myanmar videos were uploaded on popular websites after the military government imposed an Internet blockade. These videos do not enumerate specific violations of human rights, but the camera work captures evocatively the oppressive actions of the state forces. In the year after the protests, exile communities continued to provide information they had obtained clandestinely, and Myanmar monks disappeared from the media gaze. This instance offers a cautionary tale of the ease with which information on the Internet could be halted. The promise of the "participatory panopticon" was shattered by the military junta, which regained control of its disciplinary and regulatory functions through the use of force. Some scholars offer a mixed assessment of the Saffron Revolution. On the one hand, it was "an Internet driven protest which did not lead to tangible political change." On the other hand, the Internet may have restrained the military junta's violence and resulted in a more restrained response to the protests.[42] This instance nevertheless signals the failure of the "mobilization of shame" politics.[43]

Unlike in the Oaxaca case, the oppressive nature of the Myanmar military regime forced anonymity on the participants. Thus, the uploaded videos do not allow us to understand how individual lives were affected by the protests and the subsequent military action. Instead, our understanding of Myanmar is derived from the collective. With regard to gender, once again a hegemonic masculinity is promoted. While women are largely occluded from the field of vision, the only men we are expected to identify with are those who appear brave, daring, and willing to pit themselves against the might of the military (including the monks).

Replicating the ideologies of the public/private divide, human rights videos reproduce an analogous gendered discourse. Notwithstanding the broad circulatory matrix within which they operate, human rights videos, through their focus on actions within the public arena, reproduce men as the primary subjects of human rights discourses. Other forms of activism against human rights violations are marginalized. Thus, the videos on YouTube replicate familiar themes of political and civil rights violations, whereas economic and cultural rights tend to be marginalized. Similarly, collective action, which originates within the private domain, remains invisible. The gendered discourses that human rights videos inadvertently promote reinscribe modernity's deeply problematic geopolitical models of race, gender, and geography.

Within such an epistemological grid, human rights discourses remain largely about gaining a voice and are rarely identified as imparting collective agency. Both these protests reveal how the social and the economic are intertwined—yet the manner in which the videos depict these protests causes the economic underpinnings to disappear. Instead, the focus remains unrelentingly on the state's relation with citizens. Redress is also premised on a different relationship between the individual and the state. Thus, these digital human rights discourses recenter the state in emancipatory possibilities. The gendered nature of the state, or the role of the state in neoliberal capitalism, remains uninterrogated.

Of all the videos I observed, there was only one, "Oaxacan Women March for Respect," that outlined the particular ways in which human rights violations specifically affected women's rights and women's material bodies (differently than men's). This was also the lone video that allowed us to witness the innovative street theater that women had formulated to confront the police and ensure their safety. This particular form of activism moves beyond the binary discourse of woman-as-agent/woman-as-victim and allows us to conceptualize Oaxacan women as subjects whose identities come into being through their actions, both as teachers and as people challenging police brutality.

Transnational digital media such as the human rights videos I have examined, as well as Facebook campaigns, have the potential to constitute an alternative digital modernism—they transcend a range of boundaries central to the Western project of modernism, those between nations and cultures and between private and public, as well as providing subaltern subjects the opportunity to speak for themselves. They locate the viewer in multiple shifting positions—as voyeur, consumer, and activist. This array of possible identifications complicates any simplistic understanding of the horizon of actions as well as issues of ethical responsibility. But as I have illustrated, the visual evidence offered by the videos holds a deceptive immediacy and tends to facilitate outrage, horror, and indignation. The circulation of affect-intensive images and narratives has the potential to create a sense of connection but does not necessarily promote effective political action. In particular, as I have illustrated, these transnational videos tend to help reinforce existing binaries, especially our gendered conceptions of the rights-bearing subject and the arena of rights contestation. The videos I examined repeatedly rearticulated the gender binary constitutive of human rights discourses. Digital technologies have undoubtedly expanded the transnational public sphere, allowing people from remote locations to address a global audience. Nevertheless, as I have illustrated through the instances of Oaxaca and Myanmar, the transnational traffic of these images has backfired on the efforts of local activism.

Conclusion

Although I have outlined many of the failures and the squandered potential of digital modernisms, I conclude with the example of Witness and its subsidiary the Hub as offering a new way of considering the discussion of human rights activism. Witness is a nongovernmental organization from the 1990s which exploits the improved technologies of video production and distribution. Inspired by the video documenting the police beating of Los Angeles citizen Rodney King, rock musician Peter Gabriel helped establish Witness, with the utopic goal of providing ordinary people around the world the opportunity to use video cameras, thereby representing themselves, their violations, and their oppressions. After some initial hiccups, the program recognized the need to train video users and thus established Seeding Video Advocacy. Since then, a large part of Witness's activity has been collaborating with local activist groups and providing them with the tools to represent themselves.

In December 2007, Witness established the Hub, a human rights digital uploading site; its slogan urges viewers to "see it, film it, change it." Declaring itself the "world's first participatory media site for human rights," the Hub solicits people to upload digital media on the website. This information then becomes the foundation for the formation of a global community of shared sentiment, a transnational public sphere. This site was designed to mitigate against the decontextualized space of sites such as YouTube; it permits users to self-organize into affinity groups, comment on materials, and access online tools for action, and it offers guidance on how to turn video into compelling advocacy material.[44] In numerous interviews, Hub staff have highlighted the ideological biases that may inflect the videos they host; they have sought to provide greater context and to ensure that it is the local that is represented, rather than having the local routed through the West. The uploaded media bring into visibility "hot spots" of human rights violations, such as Chechnya, Myanmar, Afghanistan, and Israel. What makes the information on the Hub different from traditional media is the perspective from which these violations are documented. Rather than turn to official sources, inevitably Hub videos reveal the particular ways in which individuals are affected.

The Hub is also striking because of the didactic tone it adopts. Each video has a lengthy descriptive title, codes that document the violations that are depicted, and also a lot of background information about a particular country and event.[45] Thus, unlike the Oaxaca and Myanmar videos on YouTube, the Hub offers a lot of background information. In particular, with respect to the Brad Will video, Hub editors warn viewers that the outrage generated by the footage should not blind us to the sufferings and violations of Mexicans.

Despite this awareness of geopolitical asymmetries and the residues of colonial epistemologies, the Hub staff has not addressed feminist concerns. It is imperative that feminist and queer scholar-activists intervene in this burgeoning field of transnational media and help rewrite a digital modernism that creates the possibilities of new subject formations. Claims of universality have been central to Western discourses of modernity that erase historical differences and inequalities. Human rights discourses rely on a framework of a modernized North that should go in and rescue the South; similarly these discourses establish women's agency in dichotomous terms of those who act and those who are acted upon. The community of sentiment facilitated by existing digital media replicates these structures. The cosmopolitanism cultivated by the videos locates the viewer in a position akin to the nineteenth-century flâneur, a person who surfs the Internet in search of the dark, seamy side of the world. Visually, these imaging practices privilege a modernist regime of seeing, one that equates the camera and documentary form with realism. If the Internet and digitally uploaded videos are to rewrite these modernist scripts, they need to be able to visualize and foreground the local in the "vernacular." Contemporary conditions of globality require that we organize a new scopic regime and visual grammar—one that does not return to Enlightenment epistemologies. Third world postcolonial feminism has already laid the groundwork from which this new visual economy could be conceptualized. A digital grammar that makes visible a radical heterogeneity of rights, violations, and activisms could facilitate a cosmopolitanism that moves beyond the Kantian abstract universalism. This requires not just a new grammar but a new ethics of seeing.

NOTES

1. See Meg McLagan, "Making Human Rights Claims Public," *Visual Anthropology* 18, no. 1 (2006): 191–194; Thomas Keenan, "Publicity and Indifference (Sarajevo on Television)," *PMLA* 117, no. 1 (2002): 104–116; Henry Jenkins, "Human Rights Video in a Participatory Culture," *Mediashift Idea Lab* (April 6, 2008), http://www.pbs.org/idealab/2008/04/to-youtube-or-not-to-youtube-h.html (accessed April 26, 2010).

2. Arjun Appadurai, *Modernity at Large* (Minneapolis: University of Minnesota Press, 1996), 8.

3. Inderpal Grewal and Caren Kaplan, "Global Identities: Theorizing Transnational Studies of Sexuality," *GLQ* 7, no. 4 (2001): 663–679.

4. See Pheng Cheah and Bruce Robbins, eds., *Cosmopolitics: Thinking and Feeling beyond the Nation* (Minneapolis: University of Minnesota Press, 2008).

5. See Niamh Reilly, "Cosmopolitan Feminism and Human Rights," *Hypatia* 22, no. 4 (2007): 180–198.

6. Organizers of Witness, a key Internet site of human rights activism, specify that their videos do not aim for "neutrality"; rather, they are designed to give voice to marginalized people. See Gillian Caldwell, "Moving Pictures, Moving Mountains: A Primer on Using Video in Advocacy Campaigns," *Human Rights Video Project*, http://www.humanrightsproject.org/content.php?sec=essay&sub=moving (accessed April 26, 2010).

7. Independent Media Center website, http://www.indymedia.org/en (accessed April 26, 2010).

8. For the film, see "The Last Moments of Bradley Roland Will," *The Hub* (September 17, 2007), http://hub.witness.org/en/node/624 (accessed April 26, 2010).

9. Ironically, the World Bank and International Monetary Fund had long been urging the Myanmar government to align its economy with the rules of the free market, which meant eliminating government subsidies. None of the videos situate activism within the frames of neoliberal capitalism.

10. The Myanmar government acknowledges the deaths of thirteen to sixteen protesters; the UN Human Rights Council lists thirty-one, while prodemocracy groups list several hundred.

11. Mridul Chowdhury, "The Role of the Internet in Burma's Saffron Revolution," research pub. 2008-8 (Cambridge, MA: Berkman Center for Internet and Society at Harvard University, 2008).

12. The Global Day of Action for Burma was held on October 6, 2007, in over thirty countries.

13. United Nations, "The Universal Declaration of Human Rights," http://www.un.org/Overview/rights.html (accessed April 26, 2010).

14. Article 2 guarantees everyone freedoms without distinctions, and Article 5 prohibits the use of torture and inhuman treatment. See ibid., http://www.un.org/en/documents/udhr/index.shtml#a2 (accessed April 26, 2010).

15. See Margaret Jolly, "Woman Ikat Raet Long Human Raet O No? Women's Rights, Human Rights and Domestic Violence in Vanuatu," *Feminist Review* 52 (1996): 169–190.

16. Wendy Brown, "'The Most We Can Hope For . . .': Human Rights as the Politics of Fatalism," *South Atlantic Quarterly* 103, nos. 2–3 (2004): 451–463.

17. Kenneth Cmiel, "The Emergence of Human Rights Politics in the United States," *Journal of American History* 86, no. 3 (1991): 1231–1250. See also Meg McLagan, "Human Rights, Testimony and Transnational Publicity," *Scholar and Feminist Online* 2, no. 1 (2003), www.barnard.edu/sfonline.

18. Mark Bradley and Patrice Petro, eds., *Truth Claims: Representation and Human Rights* (New Brunswick, NJ: Rutgers University Press, 2002).

19. See Wendy Kozol and Wendy Hesford, eds., *Just Advocacy? Women's Human Rights, Transnational Feminisms, and the Politics of Representation* (New Brunswick, NJ: Rutgers University Press, 2005).

20. Thomas Keenan, "Mobilizing Shame," *South Atlantic Quarterly* 103, nos. 2–3 (2004): 435–449.

21. Arthur Kleinman, Veena Das, and Margaret Lock, eds., *Social Suffering* (Berkeley: University of California Press, 1997).

22. See Bradley and Petro, *Truth Claims*; Grewal and Kaplan, "Global Identities."

23. McLagan, "Making Human Rights Claims Public."

24. Susan Sontag, *On Photography* (New York: Farrar, Straus and Giroux, 1977).

25. Allen Feldman, "Violence and Vision: Prosthetics and Aesthetics of Terror," in Veena Das, Arthur Kleinman, and Mamphela Ramphele, eds., *Violence and Subjectivity* (Berkeley: University of California Press, 2000), 46–78.

26. Quoted in Jenkins, "Human Rights Video in a Participatory Culture."

27. See Jamie Metzl, "Information and Human Rights," *Human Rights Quarterly* 19, no. 4 (1997): 705–746.

28. James Castonguay, "Representing Bosnia: Human Rights Claims and Global Media Culture," in Bradley and Petro, *Truth Claims*, 157–185.

29. Slavoj Žižek, "The Cyberspace Real: Between Perversion and Trauma," World Association of Psychoanalysis, http://www.egs.edu/faculty/slavoj-zizek/articles/the-cyberspace-real/ (accessed April 26, 2010).

30. I draw on videos uploaded on YouTube, the Hub, and Indymedia.

31. For instance, see "Oaxaca Teachers' Strike," *YouTube* (June 7, 2006), http://www.youtube.com/watch?v=VcjyBNreUco&feature=related (accessed April 26, 2010).

32. "Oaxaca, Mexico Protests," *YouTube* (November 30, 2006), http://www.youtube.com/watch?v=IyZPIdH_t8g (accessed April 26, 2010).

33. "Oaxacan Women March for Respect, 02-15-2007," *The Hub* (August 3, 2007), http://hub.witness.org/en/node/548 (accessed April 26, 2010).

34. Arthur Kleinman and Joan Kleinman, "The Appeal of Experience; the Dismay of Images: Cultural Appropriations of Suffering in our Time," in Kleinman, Das, and Lock, *Social Suffering*, 1–23.

35. See McLagan, "Making Human Rights Claims Public."

36. Keenan, "Publicity and Indifference."

37. Kleinman and Kleinman, "The Appeal of Experience."

38. John Tagg, *The Burden of Representation: Essays on Photographies and Histories* (Minneapolis: University of Minnesota Press, 1993).

39. "One Year after the Burmese Uprising," *The Hub* (September 29, 2008), http://hub.witness.org/en/node/8872 (accessed April 26, 2010).

40. "In Freedom's Cause," *The Hub* (May 9, 2008), http://hub.witness.org/en/node/5377 (accessed April 26, 2010).

41. "Shoot on Sight," *You Tube* (April 17, 2007), http://www.youtube.com/watch?v=SPSsKcpxJMk (accessed April 26, 2010).

42. Chowdhury, "The Role of the Internet in Burma's Saffron Revolution," 2.

43. Keenan, "Publicity and Indifference."

44. Jenkins, "Human Rights Video in a Participatory Culture."

45. Mark Glaser, "Can Witness, Global Voices Make Human Rights Video Go Viral?" *Mediashift Idea Lab* (September 20, 2006), http://www.pbs.org/mediashift/2006/09/can-witness-global-voices-make-human-rights-video-go-viral263.html (accessed April 26, 2010).

Doing Cultural Citizenship in the Global Media Hub

Illiberal Pragmatics and Lesbian Consumption Practices in Singapore

Audrey Yue

The recent development of a global media hub in Singapore has enabled the emergence of a queer public culture despite the illegality of homosexuality. State-funded gay films, subsidized theater plays, Internet portals, and nightclubs are part of the new spaces and practices that have been direct beneficiaries of this policy initiative. In a city-state such as Singapore, cultural citizenship is contested through the way sexuality functions as a technology for the creative economy. While the government has mobilized sexuality as a policy tool to promote cultural liberalization, gays and lesbians have also seized on these practices to claim their right to produce and participate in public culture.

This chapter examines how lesbians "do" citizenship and carve out modes of expression through their consumption that allow them to fit in, use, and twist the governmental framing of media environments. The critical focus on governance will show how new sexual and gendered formations are produced in and through the developments of cultural and creative industrial policies. Singapore lesbians negotiate a nonnormative sexuality through the resistant and complicit practices of what I call the illiberal pragmatics of cultural and media policies. At the national level, their participation in public life shows the intensity of social networks and indicates strong civic engagement. At the transnational level, social capital is used to bridge global, diasporic, and inter-Asian cultural flows. Across these flows, lesbians' media consumption practices evince alternative rather than Western homonormative queer tastes, combining queer globalization, diasporic queer cosmopolitanism, and inter-Asian queer proximities. The global media hub produces a queer Singaporean identity without assimilating into the Western liberal discourse of homosexual rights. For lesbians, mediated networks have opened up new ways of making claims to and contesting cultural citizenship, as well as participating in trans/national life.

In the Global Media Hub

Singapore's strategic location between Asia and Europe has marked its symbolic and material presence as a hub for capital flows and postmodern consumption.

Fig. 14.1. Singapore's Chinatown riverside arts and nightlife hub, with the iconic Merlion and the Esplanade: Theatres on the Bay. (The photograph, entitled "Esplanade," was taken by Northernstar, from *Uniquely Singapore: Singapore in Pixels*, http://www.visitsingapore.com/pixels/)

Since its postcolonial independence in 1965, it has transformed from a transit for labor and food produce into a regional base for manufacturing, transportation, and multinational corporations.[1] In the 1980s, it began to establish itself as a global media hub, offering a knowledge-based economy and world-class digital infrastructure.[2] The arrival of international media production companies and venture capital led to a nationwide media restructuring that worked in conjunction with the service and consumer economy.[3] In 2002, the knowledge economy was consolidated into the creative industry, and media developments included the creation of a global media city, export of locally made content, and the growth of the media talent base through education.

Critical discussions of Singapore as a global media hub typically focus on the way technology is used for internal social control and external regional branding. While the embrace of digital media has expanded business opportunities, it has also allowed the authoritarian state to increase surveillance and suppress the civil society.[4] The cosmopolitan appeals to Eurocentric art and an English-language audience, while anachronistic, still remain hegemonic in the region.[5] These tensions problematize the hub's place-making capacity to "enhance individual potential, link communities locally and globally, and finally, improve the quality of life."[6] Celebrating the livability of the place through postmodern consumption, such strategies do not consider social stratification, inclusion, and cohesion.[7]

Aihwa Ong describes Singapore's hub strategy as replicating a "baroque economy," with its different clusters and multileveled scales of production.[8] As capital is used to leverage international collaborations to privilege knowledge workers and network participants, neoliberal governance has "reconfigur[ed the] relationships between governing and the governed, power and knowledge, and sovereignty and territoriality."[9] In this strategy, neoliberalism is mobilized as technologies of governance and self-governance, and it holds the potential to create new forms of inclusion and exclusion.

A few characteristics of the media hub emerge: the hub is engineered by neoliberal governance and uses market conditions as technologies of measurement for citizenship; it provides a milieu to critically consider the quality of life for the local population; it is a place of contradictory local/global cultural consumption; and it is also a hegemonic state that strictly controls social cohesion and suppresses the civil society. These characteristics are further complicated when sexuality is considered.

Cultural Citizenship and the Illiberal Pragmatics of Sexuality

As an authoritarian state that considers homosexuality a crime, creative industrial policies have paradoxically used sexuality as a tool to lure foreign talent and companies. The impetus for this strategy was drawn from Richard Florida's thesis that businesses will flock to cities that are tolerant, technology intensive, and talent rich.[10] Adopting Florida's thesis, the Singapore government has strategically used sexuality as a technology for cultural policy.[11] Elsewhere I have argued that sexuality is inscribed in the regulatory frameworks of the creative media city through new immigration policies that allow gay foreign talent to freely migrate for employment, new employment policies in the public service that do not discriminate against out homosexuals, and urban-planning and town-rejuvenation policies that encourage gay and lesbian businesses to cultivate a nighttime economy that enhances the vibrancy of the city.

These developments underpin what I have critically framed as the illiberal pragmatics of sexuality,[12] which suggests an illogical mode of governance that treats homosexuality through the pragmatics of illiberality. While homosexuality is continually policed at the level of everyday life, it is also pragmatically encouraged by the neoliberal demands of economic affluence and societal liberalization. In recent years, in spite of the increased police raids in gay saunas and the banning of public gay parties, creative queer cultures, from popular literature, the arts, broadcasting, and cinema, have flourished as sites of cultural production and consumption. More than simply a mode of commonsensical pragmatism, Singapore's illiberal pragmatics of sexuality, I argue, involves an active engagement with cultural politics and criticism.[13] For gays and lesbians in Singapore, this engagement

Fig. 14.2. Singapore's third gay and lesbian public party, "Nation: 03," held on August 8, 2003, at Sentosa island, where forty-five hundred people celebrated Singapore's thirty-eighth National Day. (The photograph was taken by Sylvia Tan for *Fridae*, from "Fridae Photo Vault," http://www.fridae.com/fotos/fotos20030808_2.php)

with pragmatism, coupled with the contradictory logic of the illiberal, has enabled them to actively use, fit in, and twist the governmental framing of culture.

The global media hub provides a rich arena to critically consider how the new cultures of consumption have impacted the quality of life of local gays and lesbians. What do the consumption practices of gays and lesbians reveal about their desire for acknowledgment, recognition, and inclusion? If the illegality of homosexuality has excluded them from the domain of social and political rights, what can their participation in the cultural sphere reveal about claims to citizenship in a neoliberal state? Here, I suggest cultural citizenship as an alternative framework to consider the ways in which gays and lesbians, as minority groups, make claims to culture, identity, and belonging. As sexual citizenship (the right of a citizen to a sexual subjecthood) does not exist in Singapore, gays and lesbians assert their identity not through sexual emancipation but by actively participating in cultural life.

Cultural understandings of citizenship are concerned not only with "'formal' processes, such as who is entitled to vote and the maintenance of an active civil society, but crucially with those whose cultural practices are disrespected, marginalized, stereotyped and rendered invisible."[14] These concerns highlight difference by emphasizing the "redistribution of resources" and a politics of "recognition and responsiveness."[15] In cultural policy studies, these conceptual developments are pragmatically applied to cultural institutions as key sites for facilitating the public sphere, engineering social conduct, and remaking new identities.[16] From art policies to urban rejuvenation strategies, the role of citizens as producers and consumers in shaping material culture is emphasized.[17] For Singapore lesbians, the global media hub has provided a mediated transnational conjuncture to consider the conditions of possibility for a certain type of public participation in national life. As Aihwa Ong attests, cultural citizenship is a dual process "of self-making and being made in relation to nation-states and transnational processes," shaped by "negotiating the often ambivalent and contested relations with the state and its hegemonic forms that establish the criteria of belonging within a national population and territory."[18]

Singapore lesbians perform cultural citizenship with resistant and complicit practices enacted through consumption. By focusing on the "doing" of cultural citizenship in an online survey with lesbians in Singapore about their practices of cultural participation and media consumption, I demonstrate cultural policy's pragmatic approach to cultural citizenship. A critical engagement with the "doing" of cultural citizenship among lesbians in Singapore reveals how everyday practices repeat and rework the illiberal pragmatic logic of neoliberal governance in Singapore.

"Doing" Cultural Citizenship

In a context in which the individual self is celebrated and the space of the political is kept invisible or compromised, how does one access the social fabric of lesbian life and understand the nature of lesbians' participation in the cultural life of the city? Ironically, it is the very tool of the marketplace—the survey—that provides access and a point of departure. Surveys measuring audience reception or the forms of cultural practices are used in market and social sciences research as instruments to truth. A technology designed for population surveillance, surveys are now widely used to tap into lifestyle trends and consumption patterns. They have become commonplace in the current climate, which values the individual and champions the public display of private selves. People not only readily and anonymously open up areas of their life; they are also socialized into survey instrumentation. Here, I read the survey and the responses received as a critical text that maps the complexities surrounding the quality of life, social capital, and cultural participation.

The survey was posted through e-mail and forum postings on the Red-queen e-mailing list, the Herstory forum, and the Sayoni forum, three of the largest and most popular e-lists for lesbians in Singapore.[19] The questions in the survey capture separate but related domains of life, such as family, job, leisure, and networks, in order to map how respondents perceive the satisfaction they derive from these aspects of their life. As the following analysis will show, the distinction of domains is increasingly blurred in the current culture of networked individualism that has produced new practices of social and cultural conditioning. Since cultural citizenship in the neoliberal context is assessed and evaluated by the performance of consuming, this logic frames the three market-driven frames of access that are incorporated in the survey: quality of life, cultural participation, and social capital. These framings provide a space to describe a contested and transnational lesbian public culture.

1. Quality of Life and Singapore Lesbians

The concept of "quality of life" (QOL) has gained popularity in recent years as a result of cultural-planning and urban-rejuvenation developments that emphasize the livability of a place.[20] In the survey, it served as a critical method of access and offered an instant portrait of lesbian lives as trends monitored in the urban structures of Singapore. The majority of the respondents are between the ages of eighteen and forty, with the dominant group in their mid- to late twenties. Chinese respondents predominate over Eurasians, Indians, and Malays, reflecting the Chinese hegemony in multicultural Singapore. Less than half of the respondents have tertiary education, and most are in full-time employment and earn less than five thousand Singapore dollars a month.[21] Although they work across professions in accounting, computer technology, engineering, hospitality, and sales, the creative arts industry dominates, with one in five respondents employed in design and media entertainment. While most live in public housing, more than a third live with their families, and only eight live with their partners.

These indices construct the profile of a working-class group of lesbians who are tertiary-educated, predominantly employed in the creative and service industries, and live with their families. This profile contradicts the earlier criticisms of the cultural hub as English-centric and promoting only a particular type of middle-class cosmopolitanism. As the site of the survey—the Internet—reveals, network access has enabled working-class lesbians to bridge the social stratifications that had earlier prevented their access to culture and information. The global media hub has also provided opportunities for working-class lesbians to work in the creative and service industries. Its promotion of a bohemian lifestyle and an attendant culture of flexibility suit the queer creative worker well, especially butch tomboys, who prefer the androgynous casualness of dress and disposition.[22] In concert with the way gays and lesbians in Asia negotiate their sexual coming out by not leaving the blood family, lesbians who live at home continue to conform to the communitarian demands of Confucian filial piety. Despite the potentially erosive impact of the hub's transnational flows, family values feature strongly. This is evident in the responses to questions about life satisfaction, overall well-being, and identity indicators.

Less than half of the respondents are satisfied with their standard of living (e.g., housing, car, furniture, material possessions, leisure time, income). Although almost all are comfortable with their sexual orientation, half bemoan a lack of sexual freedom. While only some have experienced discrimination, most do not feel that they have independence to do what they want to do or that they are included by others. And if given the opportunity, most will emigrate. These patterns suggest the deep discontent felt by the lesbian respondents about their position and lack of acceptance in the larger structures of urban politics.

QOL refers to more than just the economic definition of "the capacities or opportunities to have a life of well-being"; it also relates to the ethics of a person's behavior and how this is evaluated in terms of making choices.[23] As societal constraints prevent lesbians in Singapore from achieving the functionings of a good life, they carve out modes of survival through the importance they place on social capital and cultural participation. This is evident, first and foremost, through the hierarchy of indicators they feel are important to their identity.

All of the respondents list "friendship" as the most important indicator of their identity, above family and financial satisfactions, and about half belong to some form of community or social network. The need for a social life is ranked higher than career advancement or a personal relationship. Sexuality and gender are also more important than ethnicity, religion, and nationality. Interestingly, this hierarchy departs from a recent study of the mainstream population, who rank the family first.[24] By placing friendships above family, Singapore lesbians rely on the cultivation of social networks to make claims to inclusion, participation, and attachment. They poach the generic practices of social networking that are promoted in contemporary media culture to negotiate sexuality within the dominant logic of family values, by appropriating the structures of networked individualism to carve out a personal life and sexual identity that is compartmentalized between work, family, and friends. Clearly, for political and social reasons, they resort to such compartmentalization for reasons that are quite different from those envisioned by the market. This appropriation reveals how neoliberal governance has also paradoxically created new practices of sexual negotiation. The low regard the respondents have for nationality and ethnicity also shows how the flows of the global media hub have produced transnational rather than national affiliations.

What emerges from this analysis is a profile of an urban and hip generation of working-class lesbians who are filial, network savvy, and transnational in their affiliations. These qualities are further evident in their participation in cultural activities and in the way these activities enable the formation of social networks.

2. Cultural Participation

Given global trend for states to flex to market demands, the notion of cultural participation problematizes the connections of cultural citizenship to diversity, lifestyle, identity, and ethical governance. Cultural participation studies measure "the realization of cultural citizenship"[25] as contingent on capacity (the economic and social capability to participate), competency (the cultural capital to participate), and taste (possessing the shared cultural values to participate). For Singapore lesbians, it provides a critical pathway to examine how state-induced participation creates resistant identities that are complicit with and antagonistic to the new structures of neoliberal governance. In the survey, cultural participation is evaluated through the time devoted to lifestyle and leisure, the use of media and communication technologies, and participation in the nighttime economy and in arts and cultural activities.

The respondents' weekly leisure time is mostly spent with friends at a hawker center, restaurant, shopping mall, cafe, pub, bar, or club. These places have developed as a result of the creative economy's industrial policies that have supported the growth of the global media city. Hawker centers, usually located in the suburban heartlands, are food courts offering cheap local and regional food, while restaurants are usually more up-market, air-conditioned eateries serving European cuisine and located in shopping centers or bohemian clusters. Eating is a significant practice in the Singaporean lifestyle, touted by academics and tourism campaigns alike as the country's favorite pastime after shopping. Bars, pubs, and clubs are located in the inner-city creative enclaves of the Chinatown riverside and around the famous shopping precinct of Orchard Road. Bars and pubs are usually locally owned small businesses catering to different-language-speaking clienteles. They range from do-it-yourself retro chic to kitsch karaoke joints, and class distinction is measured through the quality and cost of the beer on tap. Dance clubs such as the Ministry of Sound franchise offer memberships and are more engineered large-scale sites of spectacle located in or near international hotels. As with other global dance clubs and parties, celebrity DJs usually stop over for a quick stint on their way to Bangkok, Hong Kong, or Tokyo.

Although hawker centers have been progressively "cleaned up" in the state's modernization of social hygiene, bars and clubs are more recent developments that have flourished in the new agenda of the creative city. Located in the creative media and tourism hub, they add to the vibrancy of a nighttime economy and create opportunities for new local entrepreneurships and joint global partnerships. For lesbians lacking private space in the family home and facing the high costs of rentals and homeownerships in land-scarce Singapore, these venues have shaped their lifestyle. Shopping, going to the movies, dining out at restaurants, and hanging out at cafes and bars make up the most common monthly leisure activities for these lesbians, and more than half engage in these activities with their gay and lesbian friends. Cultural participation clearly provides the requisite literacy to cultivate, embody, and perform lesbian sexuality. This is further evident in their media participation.

More than half the respondents watch gay and lesbian films at least once a month at home through online purchase or Internet download.[26] Most watch for a sense of identification, belonging, and support for the community. Here, the access to and spectatorship of queer cinema demonstrate the global media hub's contradictory logic of flow and control. While most of these films are banned from theatrical release, they are accessible on the Internet, a medium that is itself a policy outcome of the nationwide implementation of digital infrastructure. Lesbian film spectatorship has created a subcultural group that depends on media for its community; it has also shaped the conditions for an alternative queer transnationalism. In popular films and television series watched in the past six months—*The L Word*, *Saving Face* (Alice Wu, 2004), and *Spider Lilies* (Zero Chou, 2007)—global, diasporic, and regional queering practices are both incorporated and indigenized.

The L Word is a successful American television drama series hailed as the first in mainstream television for the lesbian community. Its popular appeal to Singapore lesbians shows the impact of global queering on local communities in non-Western societies. Like the cultural and media imperialism thesis, the globalization of queer cultures—global queering—has resulted in "the internationalization of gay, lesbian, and transgender identities and cultures."[27] While the series has been criticized for the sexual "Westernization of the Rest," its impact is evident in the local incorporation of its ideologies. Although banned from television broadcast in Singapore, it is still the most popularly watched DVD television series in the community. Despite the illegality of homosexuality and the fact that most lesbians live in high-rise apartment blocks with their parents, the anachronistic West Hollywood shared-household lifestyles of a bunch of professional lesbians, transgenders, and their friends are hailed as ideal lesbian identities. The series has themed local club nights. Two Queens Party, a lesbian event-management company, regularly screens the episodes in lesbian bars; for those who do not own the DVD and even those who have already watched it on their own, these fortnightly screenings present a collective opportunity to get together and cultivate a communal sense of belonging. The series's famous dating chart, kept by the protagonist, Alice, was also used as a motif for a January 2009 lesbian party, with the slogan "Are you L enough?" These spectatorship practices mediate a community and materialize a set of norms that replicate the nonmonogamous and pro-same-sex-marriage lifestyles proffered by the protagonists of the show. While the series's popularity shows how the clandestine Singapore viewership aspires to Western homonormative values, other film spectatorship practices reveal equally significant roles played by diasporic queer cultures.

Saving Face is an Asian American film about the "coming out" of a Chinese American doctor to her traditionalist mother. It was screened in a local multiplex and used as a fundraiser for various HIV/AIDS events. Contrary to the queer globalization of *The L Word*, *Saving Face* shows how diasporic identity is negotiated in Singapore. In Western queer Asian diasporas, gays and lesbians encounter the double marginalization of sexual and cultural difference from heteronormative mainstream and ethnic communities. The diaspora's ex-centric location, both culturally and sexually, enables diasporic queers to challenge the heteronormativities of the homeland and hostland, as well as local ethnicities. This tactical location of the ex-centric is also evident in Singapore, where postcolonial legacies and global flows have Westernized the population as much as the ideology of Asian values, initiated in the 1990s as a defense against the infiltration of Western values, has Asianized them. Like the queer diaspora, Singapore's queer culture is culturally and sexually ex-centric, a Western and Asian cosmopolitan hybrid. In such a context, the values promoted by the film's Westernized but well-educated and filial Chinese lesbian protagonist resound with the values of many lesbians in Singapore who have grown up in a rapidly developing country built by the contradictions of Westernization and indigenization. Like the protagonist, Singapore lesbians are not only Westernized; they also uphold the Asian values of filial piety. These similarities show queer Singapore, like the queer Asian diaspora, as a potential site that contests colonial heteronormativity and local patriarchy. It also reveals the global media hub as a space for the flows of diasporic queer cosmopolitanism.

Spider Lilies is a Taiwanese teenage lesbian melodrama about a webcam girl who falls in love with her tattooist, who used to be her old school flame.[28] The film belongs to the queer Asian genre of schoolgirl lesbian romance that revolves around teenage girls and their same-sex experiences in high school and that are usually set in the present context of the college or told as a flashback story by the protagonist.[29] The popularity of the film shows how Taiwanese high school lesbian cultures are also shared across the inter-Asian region through practices of cultural proximity such as the similarities of language (Mandarin), adolescent queer memories, and cityscapes of developmental progress, alienation, and media trends.

In these films and television series, lesbian spectatorship practices construct the global media hub as a space of alternative flows, including queer globalization, diasporic queer cosmopolitanism, and inter-Asian queer proximities. These forces expose the contradictory logic of illiberal pragmatism; while encouraging media globalization and maintaining media censorship, neoliberal governance has inadvertently provided the conditions for an alternative transnationalism and the self-fashioning of an unofficial lesbian subculture.

Internet use by lesbians in Singapore further shows how technology has cleared a space for new localisms.[30] The most popular Web portals visited are Fridae, Herstory, Sayoni, and Two Queens Party. These local sites are not only important to maintaining personal networks and group participation; they also show how the illiberal pragmatics of sexuality is operationalized in the global media hub. These portals have mushroomed as a result of new information-technology policies that encourage the uptake of new media in all facets of work and everyday life, despite the illegality of homosexuality, the prohibition of registered gay and lesbian groups, and the banning of public and collective group gatherings. Their popularity demonstrates the global media hub as a space for indigenized lesbian practices and queer media entrepreneurships. Online, these websites function as expressive spaces for minority groups; by advertising offline local lesbian venues and events, they materialize and anchor new social spaces and cultural practices. As sites of alternative transnationalism, these officially banned portals and material practices show indigenization as a form of translocality—how local social spaces have changed, as a result of the impact of transnational forces such as those of global and regional queering. They also highlight neoliberalism's optimizing technologies of subjectivity and subjection. As self-enterprising and net-savvy citizens, lesbians and lesbian businesses participate in capital accumulation afforded by the hub's new consumption cultures. In these neoliberal spaces of subjection, they self-engineer an unofficial culture that provides new conditions for sexual belonging and identity.[31]

Lesbian nightlife in Singapore, similar to the translocal websites just discussed, has proliferated as a result of creative industrial policies in the media hub that provide rent subsidies to enterprising businesses to complement the necessary nighttime economy of any self-described "creative" cities. The creative cluster by the riverside in Chinatown and Tanjong Pagar has emerged as an unofficial queer precinct as a result of these initiatives. This zoned area has gay saunas, lesbian bars, queer nightclubs, gay- and lesbian-owned restaurants, and queer-friendly boutique hotels. The most popular lesbian nightspots are Alternative and Taboo, two English-speaking bars in Chinatown, followed by Cows and Coolies, a Chinese karaoke pub in Chinatown. Similar to the mainstream bars and clubs discussed earlier, lesbian bars and clubs are also differentiated accord-

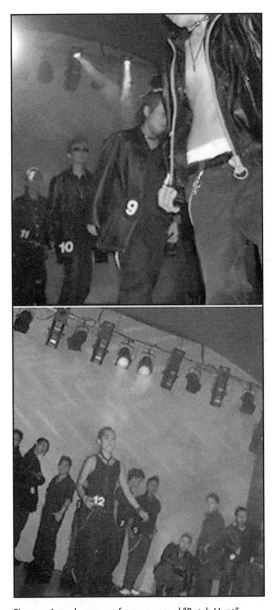

Fig. 14.3. A punk segment from an annual "Butch Hunt" competition final at Chinatown's Clarke Quay Gotham Penthouse dance club on June 9, 2005. (Photographs provided by the Butch Hunt competition organizers, Herstory)

ing to language and customer base. English-language-speaking bars are usually frequented by overseas-educated university students, oft-traveled professionals who work for multinational companies, and Western expatriates. Regional migrant workers, small-business entrepreneurs, and service-industry personnel usually prefer Chinese-language karaoke pubs.

Two-thirds of the respondents frequently attend mainstream arts and cultural activities, and slightly less than half participate in gay and lesbian activities.[32] Some of the factors cited as preventing participation in gay and lesbian activities include being unaware of their existence, affordability, lack of time due to paid work, no public transport, no one to go with, fear of discrimination, and fear of feeling unwelcomed. These factors highlight the subterranean nature of the unofficial lesbian culture, the high costs of entertainment, and the long hours of work in the global media city. Exacerbated by the mainstream prohibition of homosexuality, lesbians are usually required to be "in the know," to be literate about subcultural activities despite the proliferation of bars, Web portals, and cultural events. Where a jug of beer can easily cost up to thirty U.S. dollars and working hours can last until ten at night six days a week, the bright queer lights of the global media hub are also as exclusionary as they have been inclusive. Increasingly, more hip venues situated in bohemian enclaves such as the old colonial quarters of Dempsey and Rochester Park are also only accessible by cars or taxis.

Clearly, the hub's new media and creative arts development policies have inadvertently created the conditions for an unofficial lesbian culture. This culture has also been constituted by the flows of queer globalization, diasporic queer cosmopolitanism, inter-Asian queer proximities, and new localisms. Its practices provide a high degree of personal identification for the individual and a collective sense of belonging to and support for the community. It is crucial to note how these practices generate social capital conducive to the participatory democracy of this marginalized community.

3. Social Capital

The social capital approach, inspired by Pierre Bourdieu, has been applied in different contexts: "(a) as a source of social control; (b) as a source of family support; (c) as a source of benefits through extrafamilial networks."[33] A "by-product of cultural activities," social capital, according to Robert Putnam, refers to the skills in making cultural and social distinctions.[34] Key here is that participation breeds social capital, and social capital builds trust and reciprocity and cultivates social networks. The survey evaluates the duration of contact with others in various networks to consider how social networks enable social support and social integration. The following analysis uses the three types of social capital identified by Putnam: bonding, bridging, and linking.

For Singapore lesbians, family networks are crucial in bonding social capital. Bonding social capital refers to "social networks that reinforce exclusive identities and homogeneous groups."[35] Examples include bonds between family members and close friends that are good for getting by in life. Almost all the respondents say that their families are aware of their sexual orientation and that they are satisfied with their relationships to their families. The high priority placed on family (ranking second after friendship, as discussed earlier) indicates its importance to identity. Singapore lesbians "come out" not by leaving the biological family (as in the West) but by negotiating within the values promoted by the discourse of family values: social and economic reproduction and filial piety. This emphasis on the discourse of the family, rather than reinforcing the ideology of Asian values, shows how the social and economic value of the family has been reengineered to suit the self-regulating compliance of the neoliberal citizen.[36]

The social networks cultivated by lesbians demonstrate bridging social capital. Bridging social capital refers to "networks that are outward looking and encompass people across diverse social cleavages."[37] Examples include distant connections with acquaintances, groups, or social classes that are good for getting ahead in life. For minority lesbians, these networks are closely knit, formed with shared norms, values, and understandings that facilitate cohesion of sexual identity. Queer Internet consumption practices, discussed earlier, have enabled them to connect subculturally and transnationally across global, diasporic, and inter-Asian cultural flows. Participation in creative cultural activities has also expanded their local social networks. These practices not only generate enhanced information through increased networks of collaboration; they also extend network ties and the capacity for solidarity. All the respondents demonstrate that they have acquired high bridging social capital through media consumption and cultural participation: despite experiencing sexual discrimination and gender subordination, all unanimously claim a high level of support from and belonging to the community. For minority lesbians, bridging social capital adds to individual well-being and cultivates community development.

Lesbian cultural participation further links social capital. Linking social capital refers to relations of hierarchy with institutions of power. Consider, for example, the respondents' most frequented places in the past six months: Vivocity (shopping mall), Cathay Cineplax (shopping mall), Esplanade (a riverside theater and performing-arts venue), Chinatown (creative cluster), Holland Village (bohemian cluster), and Ministry of Sound (dance club). Consider, too, the most recent gay and lesbian cultural activity that the respondents have attended. Fourteen watched theater plays, one went to a queer poetry reading, one saw a photo exhibition, three participated in the events organized by "IndigNation" as part of gay and lesbian pride month, and six attended support groups and talks. These places and venues are official cultural infrastructures that have been developed as part of the global media hub's "livable city" agenda, and most of these are creative precincts with gay- and lesbian-themed bars and clubs. Lesbian practices in these places engage official cultural institutions, goods, and services that are enabled by the government's pragmatic approach to the cultural economy. Even plays, poetry readings, or lesbian photo exhibitions are also events officially subsidized to add value to the creative media city. These consumption practices reflect how, despite the exclusion of homosexuality from heteronormative laws and cultural institutions, nonnormative sexuality is pragmatically negotiated by cultural policy that has aided the development of queer businesses and arts in recent years.

The intensity of social networks generated from the high rate of cultural participation reflects strong civic engagement.[38] For Singapore lesbians, cultural literacy is used as a platform for political advocacy. Activities such as attending gay and lesbian activities, participating at pride events, talks, or social gatherings, signing petitions about homosexuality, and donating or helping to organize a gay and lesbian event enables lesbians in Singapore to express their role as citizens. These activities and practices confer the right to marginal citizens to tell their stories and provide the capacity for subcultural groups to engage official institutions to expose power hierarchies and sexual inequalities. These practices of civic engagement reveal what Nick Couldry has outlined as "the quality of people's 'mediated' public connection."[39] He defines "quality" as the networks of social opportunities that become available from the public knowledge and information gained from cultural consumption. For minority lesbians, linking social capital problematizes the points of connections and disconnections in the cultures of citizenship to reveal not only their exclusion and subordination but also the different ways that "being" and "doing" lesbian has allowed them to actively intervene in the politics of culture.[40] These politics expose the claims to cultural citizenship and reveal the global media hub as a site of competing flows, contradictory policies, and alternative identities. For Singapore lesbians, it has enabled their participation in trans/national life and the assertion of their sexuality.

Conclusion

This chapter has read the market survey as a critical text to deconstruct the performance of cultural citizenship by minority lesbians in Singapore's global media hub. The hub has emerged as a result of a neoliberal governance that has adopted the demands of a creative economy and the market conditions for citizenship. While cultivating transnational media and capital flows and engineering new competencies, it has also strictly enforced social cohesion and civil suppression. As a contradictory site of local/global consumption, it is a space for new inclusions and exclusions.

For the minority and unofficial urban lesbian subculture, the hub's media, cultural, and creative policy developments have constructed an illiberal logic of sexuality that has paradoxically enabled lesbians to pragmatically fashion a sense of their self and well-being. In such a city-state, working-class lesbians make claims to citizenship through their high rates of cultural participation. At the national level, they create strong social networks that are active in civic engagement. At the transnational level, they further cultivate social capital through diverse queer consumption. Despite the global media hub's normative flows, it has facilitated new mediated networks that allow lesbians to engage in participatory democracy and to create a local lesbian identity without assimilating into the liberal Western discourse of sexual rights and emancipation.

NOTES

1. Chia Siow Yue and Jamus Jerome Lim, "Singapore: A Regional Hub in ICT," in Seiichi Masuyama and Donna Vandenbrink, eds., *Towards a Knowledge-Based Economy: East Asia's Changing Industrial Geography* (Singapore: Institute of Southeast Asian Studies, 2003), 259–298; Clive Edwards, "Singapore: Reflections and Implications of Another Smart State," *Queensland Review* 10, no. 1 (May 2003): 53–69.

2. Mike Crang, "Singapore as an Informational Hub in a Space of Global Flows," *DISP* 154 (2003): 52–57.

3. Michael Curtin, *Playing to the World's Biggest Audience: The Globalization of Chinese Film and TV* (Berkley: University of California Press, 2007).

4. Garry Rodan, "Embracing Electronic Media but Suppressing Civil Society: Authoritarian Consolidation in Singapore," *Pacific Review* 16, no. 4 (2003): 503–524.

5. Kenichi Kawasaki, "Cultural Hegemony of Singapore among ASEAN Countries: Globalization and Cultural Policy," *International Journal of Japanese Sociology* 13 (2004): 22–35.

6. Crang, "Singapore as an Informational Hub in a Space of Global Flows," 54.

7. Brenda S. A. Yeoh and T. C. Chang, "Globalising Singapore: Debating Transnational Flows in the City," *Urban Studies* 38, no. 7 (2001): 1025–1044. On the hub's place-making strategy as a livable, creative city, see Caroline Y. L. Wong, Carla C. J. M. Millar, and Chong Ju Choi, "Singapore in Transition: From Technology to Culture Hub," *Journal of Knowledge Management* 10, no. 5 (2006): 79–91.

8. Aihwa Ong, *Neoliberalism as Exception: Mutations in Citizenship and Sovereignty* (Durham, NC: Duke University Press, 2006), 180.

9. Ibid., 3.

10. Richard Florida, *Cities and the Creative Class* (New York: Routledge, 2005). On criticisms of the way Singapore's policies follow this "institutional" trend, see Kai Wen Wong and Tim Bunnell, "'New Economy' Discourses and Spaces in Singapore: A Case Study of One-North," *Environment and Planning* 38 (2006): 69–83; Lily Kong, Chris Gibson, Louisa-May Khoo, and Anne-Louise Semple, "Knowledges of the Creative Economy: Towards a Relational

Geography of Diffusion and Adaptation in Asia," *Asia Pacific Viewpoint* 47, no. 2 (2006): 173–194.

11. Audrey Yue, "Hawking in the Creative City: Rice Rhapsody, Sexuality and the Cultural Politics of New Asia in Singapore," *Feminist Media Studies* 7, no. 4 (2007): 365–380.

12. Audrey Yue, "Creative Queer Singapore: The Illiberal Pragmatics of Cultural Production," *Gay and Lesbian Issues and Psychology Review* 3, no. 3 (2007): 149–160.

13. Ibid., 156.

14. Nick Stevenson, *Cultural Citizenship: Cosmopolitan Questions* (Maidenhead, UK: Open University Press, 2003), 23.

15. Renato Rosaldo, "Cultural Citizenship, Inequality, and Multiculturalism," in Rodolfo D. Torres, Louis F. Miron, and Jonathan Xavier Inda, eds., *Race, Identity and Citizenship: A Reader* (Malden, MA: Blackwell, 1999), 255.

16. Toby Miller stresses the need to account for culture, policy, and citizenship through the political economy of television and popular culture, in *Cultural Citizenship: Cosmopolitanism, Consumerism and Television in a Neoliberal Age* (Philadelphia: Temple University Press, 2007); see also Toby Miller and George Yudice, *Cultural Policy* (London: Sage, 2002).

17. David Chaney, "Cosmopolitan Art and Cultural Citizenship," *Theory, Culture and Society* 19, no. 2 (2002): 151–174; Franco Bianchini and Jude Bloomfield, "Urban Cultural Policies and the Development of Citizenship: Reflections on Contemporary European Experience," *Culture and Policy* 7, no. 1 (1996): 85–113.

18. Aihwa Ong, "Cultural Citizenship as Subject Making: Immigrants Negotiate Racial and Cultural Boundaries in the United States," in Torres, Miron, and Inda, *Race, Identity and Citizenship*, 262, 264.

19. Data were collected from April 14 to June 11, 2007. Fifty-six responded, and fifty-one were usable. The questions followed closely those used by Tony Bennett, Michael Emmison, and John Frow in *Accounting for Tastes: Australian Everyday Cultures* (Cambridge: Cambridge University Press, 1999).

20. See, for example, David Phillips, *Quality of Life: Concept, Policy and Practice* (New York: Routledge, 2006).

21. In Singapore, five thousand Singapore dollars a month is the socioeconomic marker for the middle class.

22. On the dominant culture of doing butch in Singapore, see Yue, "Creative Queer Singapore," 157–158.

23. Joel Kupperman, *Ethics and Qualities of Life* (New York: Oxford University Press, 2007), 4.

24. Ah Keng Kau, Jung Kwon, Tambyah Siok Kuan, and Soo Jiuan Tan, *Understanding Singaporeans: Values, Lifestyles, Aspirations and Consumption Behaviors* (Singapore: World Scientific, 2004), 219.

25. Catherine Murray, "Cultural Participation: A Fuzzy Cultural Policy Paradigm," in Caroline Andrew, Monica Gattinger, M. Sharon Jeannotte, and Will Straw, eds., *Accounting for Culture: Thinking through Cultural Citizenship* (Ottawa: University of Ottawa Press, 2005), 40.

26. Television consumption is omitted from the survey because of the strict censorship laws that prevent the broadcasting of gay- and lesbian-related content on free-to-air and subscription television.

27. Fran Martin, Peter Jackson, Mark McLelland, and Audrey Yue, introduction to Fran Martin et al., eds., *AsiaPacificQueer: Rethinking Genders and Sexualities* (Urbana: University of Illinois Press, 2007), 6.

28. A webcam girl is a young woman, usually of college age, who performs live sex acts or chats in front of a web camera to an individual or group online audience for free or for a fee.

29. Asian lesbian films in this genre include *Blue Gate Crossing* (Chin-yen Yee, 2002), *Butterfly* (Yan yan Mak, 2004), *Memento Mori* (Tae-Yong Kim and Kyu-Dong Min, 1999), and *Tempting Heart* (Sylvia Chang, 1999), from Taiwan, Hong Kong, and Korea.

30. Singapore lesbians are more e-oriented than is the mainstream population. Of my respondents, 94 percent reported Internet access, while only 59 percent have access in the mainstream population. For statistics on mainstream communities, see Kau et al., *Understanding Singaporeans*, 103–108.

31. On the new neoliberal technologies of optimization, see Ong, *Neoliberalism as Exception*, 6. On the indigenization of localization, see Arjun Appadurai, *Modernity at Large: Cultural Dimensions of Globalization* (Minneapolis: University of Minnesota Press, 1996).

32. This rate of 67 percent is higher than the reported 6 percent of the mainstream population who show an interest in arts and culture. For statistics on mainstream communities, see Kau et al., *Understanding Singaporeans*, 135–152.

33. Alejandro Portes, "Social Capital: Its Origin and Applications in Modern Sociology," *Annual Review of Sociology* 24 (1998): 9.

34. Robert Putnam, *Bowling Alone: The Collapse and Revival of American Community* (New York: Simon and Schuster, 2000). See also Bennett et al., *Accounting for Tastes*, 37.

35. Bennett et al., *Accounting for Tastes*, 22.

36. Ong discusses how neoliberalism has led to the demise of Asian values and the rise of an effervescent citizenship. Ong, *Neoliberalism as Exception*, 164. On the new value of the neoliberal "queer" family in Singapore, see Yue, "Hawking in the Creative City," 372–373.

37. Putnam, *Bowling Alone*, 22.

38. Henry Milner, *Civic Literacy: How Informed Citizens Make Democracy Work* (Hanover, NH: Tufts University Press, 2002), 18.

39. Nick Couldry, "Culture and Citizenship: The Missing Link," *European Journal of Cultural Studies* 9, no. 3 (2006): 330.

40. For more on "being" and "doing" lesbian in relation to Singapore's butch-femme cultures, see Yue, "Creative Queer Singapore," 157–158.

15 Gendering Cyberspace

Transnational Mappings and Uyghur Diasporic Politics

Saskia Witteborn

> I want to be the mother of the Uigurs, the medicine for their sufferings, the cloth to wipe their tears, and the shelter to protect them from the rain.
> —Rebiya Kadeer[1]

Positioning herself as a compassionate "Mother of the Nation," Rebiya Kadeer has emerged as a central figure in the transnational advocacy campaigns of the diasporic Uyghurs—a Turkic-speaking and predominantly Muslim minority community from the Xinjiang Uyghur Autonomous Region (XUAR) in China.[2] Her words and message, like the one quoted in the epigraph, from her biography, are displayed on various Internet websites and social networking sites such as YouTube and Facebook, projecting Kadeer as a spokesperson and human rights activist for the Uyghur people. Kadeer's maternal image serves as a representational counterpoint at a time when diasporic Uyghurs have become visible in the Western media through the frames of terrorism and radical Islam. While Kadeer's advocacy is perceived as subversive by the Chinese media, she claims status as an activist, author, and mother figure who sets the political agenda for the Uyghur diaspora and articulates a highly mediated politics of visibility for the community. Kadeer's life is a story of success and suffering—a transformation from laundress to millionaire to her current status as a media-savvy international advocate. Through the recuperation of traditional gender roles and a strategic use of her image and personal narrative on the Internet, Rebiya Kadeer is able to create diasporic linkages and to mobilize an identity politics scripted for a transnational audience.[3]

The human rights story of Uyghurs has not traveled globally and made the same impact as the cause of the Tibetans.[4] International audiences are aware of Tibet mainly due to the Dalai Lama's media presence, the exoticization of Buddhism, and celebrity involvement with the issue of Tibetan autonomy and human rights. Uyghurs, in contrast, are little known outside China, despite the fact that XUAR is a neighboring province of Tibet and that there are 8.4 million Uyghurs living in XUAR.[5] As a Muslim minority, Uyghurs are perceived as posing a threat and a danger. After the uprisings in XUAR in the 1990s and the attacks on September 11 in the United States, the Chinese government and the U.S. government under George W. Bush tried to link Uyghur separatism with fundamentalist branches of Islam and terrorism—allegations which have not been proven.[6]

The Uyghur diaspora, under the leadership of Rebiya Kadeer, strives to raise global awareness about the problems faced by this community in China and also to challenge existing perceptions of them as dangerous. In a 2009 interview, Kadeer states emphatically, "I have become the No. 1 enemy of the Chinese authorities because I am the voice of my people."[7] Kadeer's profile as a political dissident has a sensational trajectory—a former entrepreneur and millionaire from a remote region of China who lost all her wealth and now lives as a human rights activist in Washington, D.C. As spokesperson and "Mother of Uyghurs," keeping alive the diasporic political spirit has become Kadeer's life mission.

The Rebiya Kadeer narrative and the shape of Uyghur diasporic politics are deeply embedded within the realm and possibilities of new media technology. It is through the virtual circulation of exilic discourse and emotional appeals that Kadeer is able to get the attention of a global audience to focus on the Uyghurs and their claim of cultural autonomy. An audience base spread across nations and borders, especially when formed around a platform of common values such as human rights and social justice, plays a significant role in strengthening diasporic activism and forging transnational connections. The Uyghurs have responded to this exigency by using the persona of Rebiya Kadeer as a focal point for scripting her charisma to the needs of their global activism and publicity.[8]

Uyghur cultural politics is being defined outside the nation through a particular deployment of gender and cultural scripts that travel between tradition and modernity, the local and the transnational. Through an analysis of the embodied presence and persona of the leader of Uyghurs, Rebiya Kadeer, this chapter demonstrates how this leader appeals for global support by combining images of motherhood and a discourse of protection addressed to her diasporic "family," whose very presence she claims is being threatened.[9] The chapter demonstrates how new media technologies mobilize diasporic politics through the circulation of gendered and cultural representations.

Producing Minorities

Uyghurs are one of the fifty-six officially recognized nationalities in China and are largely concentrated in the most northwestern province in China.[10] There are reports that Uyghurs have been underrepresented in the political sphere, suffer high rates of unemployment, and have been marginalized through restrictions on their cultural and religious expression.[11] Other incidents in the wake of the War on Terror, such as the arrest of some Uyghurs in Pakistan and Afghanistan, the detainment of Uyghurs in Guantánamo Bay, and the reluctance of the international community to accept Uyghur prisoners who were cleared of charges, have associated the community with terrorism—a connection that Rebiya Kadeer repeatedly disavows. Uyghurs therefore have emerged in the global imaginary as victims facing the loss of their cultural heritage and homeland and at the same time as potential terrorists capable of striking at any time.[12] Kadeer herself is routinely portrayed in the Chinese media as a terrorist disrupting national unity. For example, the English edition of *People's Daily Online*, which has been launched by *People's Daily*, the official newspaper of the Communist Party of China, identifies Kadeer as a member of the "East Turkistan" terrorist forces and states that she poses a "great terrorist threat to China at present and in future."[13] By referring to Xinjiang as "East Turkistan," the Chinese press constructs the Uyghur diasporic leadership as supporting an ethnonationalist and secessionist project and, therefore, state terrorism.

Uyghurs are also rendered visible as hypereffeminized Others. In China, like in many other countries, the majority society defines and normalizes itself by disciplining its minority populations through visual forms of diminishment. Commenting on this hierarchical social structure, Dru Gladney writes, "Minorities are to the majority as female is to male, as Third World is to First World."[14] Gladney further argues that minority groups are perceived as wearing costumes, while majorities wear clothes; minorities are portrayed as finding happiness in "primitive" ways of living, while majorities are portrayed as longing for a return to nature while at the same time rationalizing their own status as modern subjects.[15] The public performances of ethnic diversity in the gala entitled *Colorful China*, staged in Hong Kong before the opening of the Beijing Olympics in 2008, offers a specific example. The event, which took place on Hong Kong Island after the torch relay, represented cultural diversity and harmony in China to a mainland China and Hong Kong audience. Television celebrities from Beijing and Hong Kong moderated the show, which featured speeches by politicians and members of the Olympic organizing committee, music bands, and a fashion show.

The fashion show was organized in chronological order and displayed the clothing of Chinese dynasties such as Tang and Ming. Juxtaposed were the costumes of ethnic groups, among them Uyghur, Tibetan, Mongolian, Korean, and Miao (also known as Hmong). This exhibition successfully produced the minoritized communities as exotic Others frozen in time and out of touch with modernity. The spectacle was accompanied by dance interludes with fanciful titles such as "Passion in the Border Villages," referring to the pastoral quality of village life on the border between China and the Southeast Asian nations. One of the performances, for example, featured a man with a dagger in his mouth and a woman engaged in a mating dance, leaving the viewer with an image of the Other as sexualized and animalistic. Underlying the colorful spectacle of Chinese multiculturalism was a clear demarcation of the hierarchical ordering and positioning of minority populations.

The seemingly harmonious coming together of various ethnic groups is hardly reflective of the complex layers of community politics and social realities that encircle the everyday lives of the Uyghurs. After communal uprisings in the 1990s, Uyghurs fled to countries such as Kazakhstan, Kyrgyzstan, Sweden, Germany, Australia, Canada, and the United States.[16] The largest diasporic Uyghur communities are in Central Asia, followed by Turkey, Australia, the United States, Germany, Norway, and Sweden.[17] During the course of my ethnographic fieldwork, I had the opportunity to interact with a cross-section of Uyghur migrants living in Germany and the United States and to hear their stories about their situation and politics. Many Uyghurs in Germany live in and around Munich, which is also the seat of the World Uyghur Congress (WUC). The WUC serves as an umbrella organization for several other diasporic Uyghur organizations from Central Asia to Australia, all of which focus on cultural and political issues for the recognition and human rights of Uyghurs. Many Uyghurs came to Germany as asylum seekers, often from the smaller towns and rural areas in XUAR. Several still live in asylum shelters, while others, who have been recognized as refugees by Germany, now hold a variety of occupations, including information technology, political advocacy, cleaning, and working in or owning restaurants. I met several people in the community who were members of the World Uyghur Congress and other diasporic organizations and actively involved in organizing activities. Bridging their private and public worlds under the banner of these organizations, diasporic Uyghurs participated in demonstrations against human rights abuses in China, taught Uyghur language and cultural traditions to their children, or organized community celebrations for festivals such as Nowruz (spring festival).

Uyghurs in the United States have a slightly different profile with regard to their premigration status, since many came to U.S. universities as students from urban centers in XUAR and with educational backgrounds. Uyghurs in and around Washington, D.C., tend to be actively involved in political advocacy and use their networks to promote their cause publicly in government circles. Most Uyghur exile organizations, in the United States and in Germany, also typically combine cultural and political goals such as promoting awareness of Uyghur culture, providing local platforms for Uyghurs to network, and reporting on human rights violations in XUAR. The charter of the Uyghur American Association (UAA) for example, raises awareness about the cultural and political situation in Xinjiang/East Turkistan and provides a virtual forum for Uyghurs to engage with each other locally and worldwide. Other programs such as the Uyghur Human Rights Project under the umbrella of the UAA focus exclusively on human rights, religious freedom, and democracy in Xinjiang/East Turkistan. Kadeer's singular contribution has been to found action-oriented programs which advocate for the rights of women and children and protest gender-specific human rights violations, especially concerning the forced migration and resettlement of Uyghur women into central and eastern China.[18]

The World Uyghur Congress, with Kadeer as elected president, is regarded by the diaspora as the main representative organization of the Uyghur people in East Turkistan and abroad.[19] It was in the offices of this organization that I first interviewed Kadeer in the summer of 2007. Dressed in the traditional four-corner hat, the *doppa*, and with braided hair, Kadeer, who had just turned sixty, was characteristically passionate, energetic, and outspoken. In the course of the interview, Kadeer told me that she wanted the world to know about the story of Uyghurs.[20] Having just published her biography, Kadeer talked at length about her childhood and the painful memories of forced relocations at the age of thirteen—a formative experience in shaping her political commitment. She talked about knocking on doors of nongovernmental organizations and U.S. politicians to make visible the state of affairs regarding the marginalized position of Uyghurs. During the interview, Kadeer was clearly emotionally overwhelmed by the situation of the Uyghurs. It was obvious that she was a woman with a mission and that the challenge she had assumed was to strategically orchestrate publicity and gain support for the Uyghur cause in a highly mediated global environment. In a 2009 media interview, she reiterated the ways to gain support:

> Only the rest of the world can save Xinjiang now.... Now, I have to rally support from democratic countries. We reach out to parliaments, senates, religious organizations, mosques, and human rights organizations. Uighurs rely on the world now. That's the only thing we have. What I do when I visit parliaments and senators and governments is ask that the Uighurs become part of their foreign-policy [agenda].[21]

Technology, Ethnicity, and Advocacy

Kadeer makes astute use of media and technology in order to firmly establish the visibility of the Uyghur cause in the transnational public sphere and to mobilize a transnational diasporic public for political action. Technological space both reproduces and archives the "homeland" and fuses the political goals of securing self-determination for Uyghurs with the diasporic story of forced dispersal. Kadeer's persona serves as the gendered, ethnic link in virtual space threading together the politics of diasporic imagination, homeland, and a transnational sense of community. Her advocacy demonstrates the extent to which new media defines the social context and provides political coherence to advocacy.

The advocacy efforts of the Uyghur diaspora have been assisted by different new media genres, such as websites hosted by exile Uyghur associations,[22] interactive discussions for podcasts and videos on YouTube, entries on Facebook,[23] online newspapers, and government reports. The Uyghur Human Rights Project website (www.uhrp.org), for example, in 2009 received 160,000–190,000 requests per month on average, up from around 80,000 in 2006.[24] A message board on the Uyghur American Association website enables Uyghurs to interact, socialize, and debate with one another. In my interview with Kadeer in 2007, she told me that the rationale for the creation of the message board was strategic and meant to increase the level and intensity of democratic dialogue about political and social issues pertaining to Uyghurs.

The visual display of the websites maintained by the Uyghur American Association and the World Uyghur Congress capture the spirit of a nation-in-exile through user-generated content. For example, the Uyghur American Association website,[25] colored white and blue, representing the colors of the East Turkistan flag, combines symbols of multiple allegiances and transnational connections. The horizontal head bar contains a symbol with the combined Uyghur and U.S. American flag, followed by pictures of glacial mountains, a mosque, and the U.S. Capitol. The juxtaposition of the blue flag with the crescent and white star inside, the mountains, and a mosque re-create the Uyghur nation, situated within transnational space. The snow-capped mountains convey an image of the lost homeland—a pristine and timeless place that stands uncontaminated and one with nature.

On the page entitled "About UAA," one can see the various accomplishments of Rebiya Kadeer, including an image of her biography and several pictures of her with various political leaders or while giving talks in impressive venues, including the U.S. Capitol. On the right-hand side, there is a hyperlink to access the "UAA Image Gallery," which showcases nature images from Xinjiang/East Turkistan, people, cultural artifacts, current diasporic events, and evidence of Kadeer's international activist work. Cultural artifacts in the image gallery, such as carpets and musical instruments, claim, archive, and essentialize an ancient culture in virtual space. Kadeer's image stands out prominently not only as the political leader but also as the cultural presence symbolizing the community. Hyperlinks provide further access to Uyghur history, culture, religion, news, and research reports and link the work of the Uyghur American Association to other Uyghur organizations.

The World Uyghur Congress website, designed in blue, conveys a similar image but speaks more to a global audience, offering a choice of five languages: Uyghur, English, German, Japanese, and Chinese.[26] The site offers an instantaneous overlap of tradition and technology as it expands its reach through connections with Radio Free Asia and Uyghur TV, as well as through videos of Uyghur lobbyist work. Hyperlinks to Uyghur history, geography, language, culture, and society not only serve as navigational signposts but embed a connective logic that reinforces a homogeneous Uyghur culture as a rationale for an identity politics. With a first click, users access information and political news pertaining to Uyghurs and East Turkistan; a second click brings users back to the diaspora and information about the World Uyghur Congress. Similarly, users can choose to learn more about human rights or get a heads-up on upcoming events such as political demonstrations. In short, hyperlinks serve as forms of appeal to cultural memory and diasporic imagination while at the same time inviting new and sympathetic world audiences.

Deterritorialization, as Arjun Appadurai notes, impacts the imaginative resources of lived local experiences in the transnational worlds of diasporic communities.[27] Media technologies offer new vistas to forge a culture in exile—a nation articulated within virtual space. The posts in the discussion forum run by the UAA tend to present the Uyghurs as a homogeneous group united by a political cause. The WUC and UAA websites have daily news updates and information about XUAR/East Turkistan, including the key points of contention such as human rights violations in XUAR, marginalization of the Uyghur language and culture, and the forced work migration of young Uyghur women. Through these discussions and representations, the diaspora reconstructs an endangered locality with the immediacy and affect enabled by media technology. The websites create the utopic props for an imaginary return to a reclaimed homeland that is already mapped in virtual space. Unlike a palimpsest that consists of layers of overwritten and erased texts, hyperlinked websites enable the existence of multiple texts and realities that are interconnected and provide ways to (re-)create diasporic life and purpose in visual space.

Political causes gain momentum in new mediated spaces through the hyper-circulation of symbols and the reproduction of overarching cultural logics. In the Uyghur case, Rebiya Kadeer's presence not only assumes iconic status but stands in for the contested place of tradition in the Uyghurs' larger story. A Google image search I conducted resulted in approximately ninety-one different photographs of Rebiya Kadeer;[28] seventy-nine of those images showed her with the traditional *doppa*. Pictures posted on the Internet and in Kadeer's biography do not often show her with the *doppa* before she went into exile. She had been represented, for the most part, as dressed in Western clothes, a white headscarf, or the *Tomak*, a fur hat. After she went into exile and became active on the political world stage, she has come to be represented mostly with the *doppa* and over time has started wearing her hair in braids. Images of Kadeer alongside politicians and heads of international organizations that are circulated on websites of Uyghur organizations, human rights organizations such as Amnesty International, Wikipedia, and social networking sites such as Flickr represent her in the traditional headwear and hairstyle. Therefore, one could argue that Rebiya Kadeer performs a version of ethnicity, after arriving in the West, by adorning her body with cultural symbols to draw attention to her Uyghur identity and the cause she stands for.

The intentional use of these cultural symbols seems to be for the purpose of reasserting a sense of cultural authenticity, tradition, and belonging to a larger social and political collectivity. In addition, the *doppa* and the braided hair stand in as gendered markers of Uyghur personhood. On the one hand, essentializing Uyghur culture visually through cultural artifacts can be regarded as a necessary move to project a unified media presence on the global stage. On the other hand, ethnicizing the body appeals to a global audience and the Orientalist image of the native woman fighting for the preservation of her culture and people. The *doppa* and the braids serve as cultural exclamation marks that stir Western sensibilities about the protection of threatened ethnic cultures. These are not apolitical accessories, but they are intended to capture the cultural politics of a group that struggles to claim its political rights of expression in the face of suppression and censorship. Kadeer's performance of ethnic alterity is a studied rhetorical move in this direction.

The positioning of the ethnic body alongside celebrities is another way in which the Uyghur cause is circulated and transnationalized through symbolic association. Kadeer is portrayed with symbols of spiritual and political importance such as the Dalai Lama, Kofi Annan, or former U.S. president George W. Bush. The fact that Bush was responsible for turning Guantánamo Bay into a terrorist detention camp where Uyghurs have been incarcerated for years becomes secondary to the visual triumph of having secured the political and financial support for Uyghur political advocacy from the United States. Strategic positioning of the Uyghur story and gaining the support of the United States seem more important to Kadeer's diplomacy than do political inconsistencies.

Images of Kadeer and the Dalai Lama serve as visual statements linking the Uyghur and Tibetan causes. The availability of those images on social networking sites such as Flickr[29] publicizes Kadeer's political goals and actions to a worldwide audience and projects her as a resistance leader of the caliber and stature of the Dalai Lama. Images of her with the Dalai Lama are strategic, given the Dalai Lama's well-established stance of dissent against the Chinese government's politics in Tibet. Circulated online are also images portraying Kadeer and the actor Richard Gere, one of the most important celebrity supporters and public-relations catalysts for the Dalai Lama and the Tibetan cause in the West.[30] These images of Kadeer, when circulated online, create symbolic links that translate

Fig. 15.1. Rebiya Kadeer and Richard Gere, August 5, 2008. (*Flickr*, licensed by Creative Commons, http://www.flickr.com/photos/62585343@N00/2735451958/)

and extend international sympathies for the Tibetan cause to include the Uyghur cause. In an orchestrated move, Kadeer rides in the wake of the Dalai Lama's popularity and support in the West for his attempts to influence China's human rights policies.

However, Kadeer is not merely riding the support wave of celebrities and politicians but is actively pursuing her own agenda with regard to political and cultural freedoms for Uyghurs. Her use of the visual space and dialogic possibilities of the Internet provides a logic and coherence for the Uyghurs to gather transnational political momentum. While media technology provides the framework for communicating locality and difference, at the same time, it influences the terms of transnational activism. Traditional gender ideologies become emblematic of Uyghur culture, and the deployment of these gender ideologies in the advocacy campaign is the subject of the next section.

Advocacy as Continuity and Change

Kadeer makes use of traditional gender roles, motherhood in particular, and mobilizes their symbolic capital as part of her strategy. The use of tradition enables her to create a unified cultural and political position, which in turn strengthens resistant action. Feminist scholars have long argued that such homogenization of social groups tends to naturalize gendered categories, which in turn obscures power relations and existing hierarchies.[31] For Kadeer, gendered symbols such as motherhood seem to be a statement about cultural resources and the preservation of authenticity but also serve as an expedient political move.

Kadeer's image as a mother figure is evoked by the community, the media, and herself; the affective overtones of motherhood become a way of gaining transnational visibility. There are emotionally charged videos on YouTube in which young torture victims reach out to Rebiya Kadeer as "Mother."[32] Other interviews abound on Uyghur TV, where she is addressed as "Mother Rebiya."[33] The gendered details of her personal life make great journalistic copy: an arranged marriage, divorce, a mother suffering the pangs of her own children's imprisonment. The details of Kadeer's forced separation from her children, imposed on her by the Chinese government, and her long imprisonment are publicized on the websites of Uyghur organizations, endowing a mythical stature to Rebiya Kadeer and to her political position. Kadeer's personal struggles become symbolic of the larger political issues faced by Uyghurs at large. Diasporic mobilization gains visibility by merging Kadeer's personal suffering with the emancipation movement for Uyghur self-determination. The statement "I want to be the mother of the Uigurs, the medicine for their sufferings, the cloth to wipe their tears, and the shelter to protect them from the rain," from her biography, is a political manifesto and a declaration of Kadeer's maternally inspired political leadership.[34]

In virtual space, the Uyghur and pro-Uyghur sites represent Kadeer first and foremost as an archetypal mother with limitless and selfless love. The nation of Uyghurs in exile is transformed into her personal family waiting for her protection, and the image serves as Kadeer's rallying symbol for political action. Her maternal presence appears in online discussion boards, human rights websites, diasporic organizational sites, and websites dedicated to sociopolitical and cultural analyses of Asian affairs.[35] To further her political goals, Kadeer utilizes the trope of suffering and the mediated circulation of her image as the self-sacrificing hero who transcends her personal traumas through mothering the nation.

The maternal image was also the subject of mockery and derision by the Chinese media during and after the riots in XUAR in the summer of 2009. For example, a front-page article in the *People's Daily Overseas Edition* stated, "On July 5, it is by this mother's hand that many mothers lost their children and many children lost their mothers. This mother is the chairman of the WUC, Rebiya."[36] Nur Bekri, former deputy chairman of Xinjiang, told the newspaper *Wen Hua Bao*, "She could not even raise her own children, how dare she claim to be the mother of an ethnicity which has a population of millions?"[37] Kadeer's standing and success as an activist leader is not only reduced to the stereotype of the bad mother but propagated as destructive for Chinese and Uyghurs alike.

The image of mothering used in Rebiya Kadeer's own advocacy shares similarities with other historical ethnonationalistic liberation movements and their use of normative gender scripts. Women have been instrumentalized, in various contexts, as active producers and transmitters of national cultures, as symbols of the nation, and as guardians of tradition.[38] Anne McClintock notes that "women are typically construed as the symbolic bearers of the nation, but are denied any direct relation to national agency."[39] Kadeer appropriates the logic of women as protectors of culture as a way of reaching out to women in the Uyghur community. She frequently notes that the Uyghurs have been reduced to a position in which they have lost their moral coordinates and that women in the community need to take on the responsibility of restoring values.[40] By inserting an essentialized idea of Uyghur womanhood into a normative script of cultural values and moral behavior, for example, she calls on women to assume the task of protecting the values and culture of the Uyghurs.

Given the precarious situation faced by the Uyghurs, connecting with the past and traditional values becomes part of the romance and nostalgia for a lost homeland. Uyghur music, which often uses the image of the mother to symbolize the spirit of the nation, has recently begun to represent, rather poignantly, the passing of a way of life and the fading dream of an independent motherland.[41] In this context, the work of remembering is relegated to women by assigning them the function of preserving tradition. Once again, the stereotypically gendered assignment of roles is seen as a legitimate and political move to draw diasporic women into action.

Rebiya Kadeer has used the trope of motherhood to promote her campaign at least since 1997, when she initiated the Thousand Mothers Movement. This movement attempted to create solidarity among Uyghur women and to provide various types of developmental programs for women and assistance for women to start their own small business enterprises. This movement, started when Kadeer was still in China, was soon dissolved by the Chinese government.[42] However, it continues to have a presence on Uyghur websites,[43] where picture galleries offer a cascading array of photographs of Kadeer as Mother of the Nation and draw attention to the now terminated Thousand Mother Movement as one of her key humanitarian accomplishments. In the disappearance of the homeland, the new transnational diasporic space is constructed with the familiar terms of family and gendered embodiments. In her global campaign, Kadeer reclaims domesticity as a location from which to articulate a politics of recognition.

Conclusion

In the process of changing the political conditions and status of the Uyghur people, Rebiya Kadeer resorts to history, memory, and forms of myth making to focus world attention on the situation of Uyghurs. Writing about activism for Tibet in the West, which has several parallels to the Uyghur situation, Meg McLagan notes that political activists today have to adapt to image-driven media practices in order to achieve international visibility and render their actions politically significant.[44] At the same time, she argues, we need to ask "from what experiential or cultural reserves do Tibetan political practices and historical consciousness in the diaspora emerge?"[45] This question rings true in the case of the Uyghurs as well as in their strategic use of virtual space. Rebiya Kadeer, once considered a symbol of modernization in China for her economic success,[46] is now re-creating her image in mythological terms in order to insert herself into alternative forms of mediated publicity and political action. Rebiya Kadeer inhabits a liminal space between tradition and modernity in her attempt to define what it means to be modern in the context of displacement and marginalization. In the persona and politics of Rebiya Kadeer, the flow of tradition and modernity takes on unexpected, sometimes contradictory and contested turns. It is as Mother of the Nation that Rebiya Kadeer has gained world attention for herself, and even nominations for the Nobel Peace Prize. As a cultural and political symbol, a change agent, Rebiya Kadeer moves local stories of suffering to the transnational media stage. Kadeer operates with the full awareness that human rights activism in the current geopolitical context has to be articulated in transnational terms and that her campaign has to reach culturally distinct publics and at the same time elicit sympathy, support, and outrage. Kadeer's strategies are reminiscent of other nationalist movements in which women's political relations to the nation were mediated through their familial relations.[47] Kadeer turns this gendering into a strategy to win her diasporic constituency and a larger global public.

Tapping into normative scripts of maternal care, sacrifice, and nurturance, the Uyghur leadership resurrects what they see as a universally appealing yet historically situated archetype. This beatific image of Rebiya Kadeer strikes a chord with global audiences, thereby making the distant familiar and turning the local struggles of an ethnic group in a remote part of China into a transnational cause. Within the community, Kadeer reaches out to Uyghur women to assert their agency as upholders of traditional values to build communal ways of preserving Uyghurness. Rebiya Kadeer was a powerful influence to the Uyghur women I talked to in Washington, D.C., who took their role as cultural reproducers very seriously, some even mentioning that it was critical for their survival as a community. For the Uyghur community, the recuperation of a normative discourse of femininity seems to conserve an imagined homogeneity and a continuous sense of history that validates the group's existence and struggle for human rights and self-determination.

Rebiya Kadeer's advocacy is a narrative of technology, homelands, and domesticity. In all these aspects, it is the gendered thread of meaning that stands out at different levels, both in her own embodied presence and in the construction of diasporic subjects. Through technology, Kadeer re-creates and circulates the sensory appeal of the homeland as a feminized space with maternal protection, hoping to forge bonds within a dispersed community and evoke the support of global publics. In this mediated realm, a private discourse of motherhood and family is used to publicize a politics of human rights. For this purpose, she both uses her maternal presence and prescribes adherence to tradition as a prerequisite for political participation. So while women are relegated to the private sphere, domesticity itself is made the center of Kadeer's politics of advocacy.

In the current geopolitical context, taking on China and the human rights issue is an extraordinary challenge. In an orchestrated move to become a globally recognized human rights activist, Kadeer strategically promotes the image of a lone woman against China in what she terms "an epic struggle."[48] A description of Kadeer on the website of the Swiss-Tibetan Association reads, "A short, fragile woman with soft facial features sits in front of me. . . . Somebody unfamiliar with her could assume her to be a simple grandmother from somewhere in Central Asia."[49] It is this Orientalist image of Rebiya Kadeer from "somewhere" that positions her as both endearing and nonthreatening to a global public. The image of a lone ethnic woman against the powerful Chinese state piques public imagination and stirs sympathy and support for her struggle.[50] In the new spaces of technologized publicity, Rebiya Kadeer's conventional visions of gender politics are reinserted into the service of a transnational human rights agenda.

"I am the voice of these people and I want peace."[51]

NOTES

The work described in this chapter was supported by a grant from the Research Grants Council of the Hong Kong Special Administrative Region, China (Project Number: CUHK 2120316), and a Direct Grant from the Chinese University of Hong Kong. I would also like to thank my research assistant for searching Chinese media reports about Uyghurs and translating them into English.

1. Rebiya Kadeer and Alexandra Cavelius, *Die Himmelsstürmerin* (Munich, Germany: Heyne, 2007), 18. Translation from the original German by the author.

2. Uyghurs also call this region East Turkistan.

3. In 1992, Kadeer became delegate to the National People's Congress of China. During a meeting, she openly criticized the policy of the Party toward Uyghurs in the wake of uprisings in XUAR in 1997. She eventually lost her seat in Congress. Kadeer was imprisoned in 1999 on her way to meet a U.S. congressional delegation and has been living in Washington, D.C., since her release in 2005. See also Uyghur American Association, "Biographical Sketch of Rebiya Kadeer" (October 12, 2006), http://www.uyghuramerican.org/articles/595/1/Biographical-sketch-of-Rebiya-Kadeer/Biographical-sketch-of-Rebiya-Kadeer.html (accessed March 7, 2008).

4. During my interviews with the Uyghur community in Germany, people pointed out that unlike the Tibet cause, which has received much attention in the West, the Uyghur situation is little known, as it is only since 2005 that they have had a leader in exile.

5. National Bureau of Statistics of China, "Geographic Distribution of Ethnic Minorities (2008)," *China Statistical Yearbook 2009*, CD-ROM (Beijing: Zhongguo Tongji Chubanshe, 2009), 1–11. Also see Dru Gladney, *Dislocating China: Reflections on Muslims, Minorities and Other Subaltern Subjects* (London: C. Hurst, 2004).

6. James A. Millward, *Eurasia Crossroads: A History of Xinjiang* (New York: Columbia University Press, 2007).

7. Annie Lowrey, "Seven Questions with Rebiya Kadeer," *Foreign Policy* (August 20, 2009), http://www.foreignpolicy.com/articles/2009/08/20/seven_questions_with_rebiya_kadeer?print=yes&hidecomments=yes&page=full (accessed February 25, 2010).

8. For more on the contextual nature of charisma, see Douglas Madsen and Peter G. Snow, *The Charismatic Bond: Political Behavior in Time of Crisis* (Cambridge, MA: Harvard University Press, 1991).

9. Rebiya Kadeer is vocal about the urgency to protect Uyghur cultural practices and about the forced resettlements of the Uyghurs, particularly women, to factories in central and eastern China. I gathered these views from a personal interview with her, on April 7, 2009, and also from her presentation at the Human Rights Watch Office in Washington, D.C., on May 20, 2009.

10. Xinjiang Uyghur Autonomous Region (XUAR) has many international borders, among them Mongolia, Kyrgyzstan, Kazakhstan, Pakistan, and Afghanistan, and it is located above the Tibet Autonomous Region. The area was conquered by the Qing in 1754, and the oasis cities were incorporated into the Chinese empire in 1821. In 1933 and 1944, two short-lived East Turkistan Republics were declared. See Millward, *Eurasia Crossroads*. Uprisings by the Uyghur population in Ghulja in February 1997, the explosions in Kashgar and Kuqa briefly before and during the Olympic Games in August 2008, and the deadly riots in summer 2009 are evidence of the ongoing tensions between Uyghurs and Han Chinese in the region.

11. A Human Rights Watch report from 2005 and the annual report of the U.S. Congressional-Executive Commission on China in 2007 (www.cecc.gov) verified structural job discrimination against Uyghurs and mentioned underrepresentation of Uyghurs in higher positions in the political and economic spheres and restrictions on religious practices as reasons for marginalization of Uyghurs in China. Human Rights Watch, "VI. Controlling Religion in the Education System," in *Devastating Blows: Religious Repression of Uighurs in Xinjiang,* available at http://hrw.org/reports/2005/china0405/8.htm#_Toc100128631 (accessed November 2007).

12. "Bermuda Takes Guantanamo Uighurs," *BBC News* (June 11, 2009), http://news.bbc.co.uk/2/hi/8095582.stm (accessed February 27, 2010).

13. "'East Turkistan,' Major Terrorist Threat to China," *People's Daily Online* (September 6, 2005), http://english.peopledaily.com.cn/200509/06/eng20050906_206700.html (accessed March 7, 2007).

14. Gladney, *Dislocating China*, 51.

15. Ibid.

16. Uyghur asylum seekers and recognized refugees in discussion with the author, Munich, Germany, in July 2007, 2008, and Washington, D.C., April–May 2009.

17. Member of the Uyghur American Association in discussion with the author, April 13, 2009.

18. U.S. Congressional-Executive Commission on China, *Annual Report* (Washington, DC: U.S Government Printing Office, 2007), 107.

19. The international board of the WUC is composed of Uyghurs from the United States, Germany, Canada, Sweden, Turkey, the Netherlands, Kyrgyzstan, Kazakhstan, and Norway. The organization, with an elected board and president, serves as the switchboard for all Uyghur organizations worldwide, organizes and coordinates rallies and demonstrations, and answers questions from the media.

20. The one-hour interview was conducted with Alim Seytoff translating my questions and Kadeer's responses.

21. Lowrey, "Seven Questions with Rebiya Kadeer."

22. Examples of websites are the Uyghur American Association (http://www.uyghuramerican.org/), the World Uyghur Congress (www.uyghurcongress.org), and the International Uyghur Human Rights and Democracy Foundation (http://www.iuhrdf.org/).

23. See, for example, he Facebook group "We All Support Uyghurs and Muslims," http://www.facebook.com/group.php?v=wall&gid=207576935253#!/group.php?gid=107309528219&ref=mf (accessed March 2, 2010).

24. A. Reger, Uyghur Human Rights Project coordinator in Washington, D.C., e-mail communication (April 14, 2009).

25. Uyghur American Association, http://www.uyghuramerican.org/ (accessed February 25, 2010).

26. World Uyghur Congress, http://www.uyghurcongress.org)/ (accessed February 25, 2010).

27. Arjun Appadurai, *Modernity at Large: Cultural Dimensions of Globalization* (Minneapolis: University of Minnesota Press, 1996), 52.

28. Search terms were "Rebiya Kadeer, Rabiye Kadir, or Rebiya Qadir" (accessed January 10, 2009).

29. "Dalai Lama con Rebiya Kadeer," *Flickr* (August 5, 2008), http://www.flickr.com/photos/62585343@N00/2735451958/ (accessed September 8, 2008).

30. Uyghur1 News, "Rebiya Kadeer and Richard Gere" (April 9, 2008), http://www.uyghur1.com/uyghur_images/Rebiya_Kadeer_RichardGere1.jpg (accessed June 22, 2009).

31. For example, see Nira Yuval-Davis, *Gender and Nation* (London: Sage, 1997).

32. "China 'Crushing Uighurs' (Rabiya Kadeer)," *YouTube*, http://www.youtube.com/watch?v=7sK8woLHKU0 (accessed December 17, 2008).

33. Aygul Yusup, "Meniwiy animiz Rabiya Xanim bilen söhbet" (A Conversation with our Spiritual Mother Rebiya Kadeer), *Uyghur TV* (September 6, 2006), http://www.uygur.tv/ (accessed February 16, 2009).

34. Kadeer and Cavelius, *Die Himmelsstürmerin*, 18.

35. Free Uyghur (message poster), "A Letter to Rebiye Kadeer, the Mother of All Uyghurs," Uyghur American Association website (July 30, 2008), http://www.uyghuramerican.org/forum/showthread.php?t=9848 (accessed May 2008). Also see Yitzhak Shichor, "Changing the Guard at the Uyghur World Congress," Association for Asian Research website (October 1, 2007), http://www.asianresearch.org/articles/2986.html (accessed June 20, 2008).

36. Ye Xiaowen, "It's Sorrowful to Say the Word 'Mother'" (English translation from Chinese by Allison Yang), *People's Daily Overseas Edition* (August 6, 2009), http://paper.people.com.cn/rmrbhwb/html/2009-08/06/content_313524.htm (accessed October 10, 2009).

37. "Rebiya: the Separatist Conspiracy of the Xinjiang 'Richest Woman,'" *Wen Hua Bao* (June 25, 2009): A1, quoting former deputy chairman of Xinjiang, Nur Bekri (translated from Chinese).

38. Radha S. Hegde, "A View from Elsewhere: Locating Difference and the Politics of Representation from a Transnational Feminist Perspective," *Communication Theory* 8, no. 3 (1998): 271–297. Also see Nira Yuval-Davis and Floya Anthias, eds., *Women-Nation-State* (London: Macmillan, 1989).

39. Anne McClintock, "No Longer a Future in Heaven: Gender, Race and Nationalism," in Anne McClintock, Aamir Mufti, and Ella Shohat, eds., *Dangerous Liaisons: Gender, National and Post-colonial Perspectives* (Minneapolis: University of Minnesota Press, 1997), 90.

40. Carneades (interviewer), "Women of Xinjiang: An Interview with Rebiya Kadeer," *Meshrep*, http://www.meshrep.com/Politicals/interview.htm (accessed March 10, 2008).

41. Rachel Harris, "Reggae on the Silk Road," *China Quarterly* 183, no. 1 (2005).

42. Kadeer and Cavelius, *Die Himmelsstürmerin*, 315.

43. Carneades, "Women of Xinijang."

44. Meg McLagan, "Spectacles of Difference: Cultural Activism and the Mass Mediation of Tibet," in Faye D. Ginsburg, Lila Abu-Lughod, and Brian Larkin, eds., *Media Worlds: Anthropology on New Terrain* (Berkeley: University of California Press, 2002), 90–111.

45. Ibid., 106.

46. "Rebiya Kadeer: Exiled Uighur Leader once a Chinese Success Story," *Times of India*, online edition (July 7, 2009), http://timesofindia.indiatimes.com/world/china/Rebiya-Kadeer-Exiled-Uighur-leader-once-a-Chinese-success-story-/articleshow/4747036.cms (accessed January 15, 2010).

47. McClintock, "No Longer a Future in Heaven." Also see Beth Baron, *Egypt as a Woman: Nationalism, Gender, and Politics* (Berkeley: University of California Press, 2005).

48. Rebiya Kadeer, *Dragon Fighter: One Woman's Epic Struggle for Peace with China* (Carlsbad, CA: Kales, 2009).

49. Chompel Balok, "Interview with Rabiya Kadeer," *Tibetfocus* (November 19, 2007), http://www.tibetfocus.com/gm/archives/00000450.html (accessed December 15, 2008).

50. In support of this claim, see Society for Threatened Peoples, "After the Disturbances in Xinjiang/East Turkistan China Maligns Uighur Human Rights Workers" (August 3, 2009), http://www.gfbv.de/pressemit.php?id=1944&highlight=Kadeer (accessed February 28, 2010).

51. Lowrey, "Seven Questions with Rebiya Kadeer."

16   Ladies and Gentlemen, Boyahs and Girls

Uploading Transnational Queer Subjectivities in the
United Arab Emirates

Noor Al-Qasimi

In recent years the United Arab Emirates (UAE) has witnessed multiple transgressive discourses pertaining to heteronormative structures of sexuality, with
cybertechnology serving as a primary platform for the enactments of subaltern
sexual subjectivities. In this chapter, I explore how state apparatuses and technologies of control both shape and govern the expression of queer subjectivities
in cyberspace.[1] As a result of intense economic restructuring, regional integration,
and technological growth, the UAE has garnered increasing global prominence
as a pioneering model for post-oil development over the past decade.[2] Despite
steps toward unification of the seven original "Trucial States" over the past forty
years,[3] the UAE presents a challenge to notions of a unified national hegemony,
which bears directly on the ways in which queer subjectivities are regulated by
technologies of control enforced not only by the federal government but also by
local police, families, and religious clerics.

It is important to note that there is a distinction between the governance of
queer subjectivities in the realm of cyberspace and in "real" space, the latter being
subject to a greater multiplicity of social power. In an illustration of this regulatory move, the Ministry of Social Affairs recently launched an "awareness initiative" targeting young women within educational institutions and youth detention
centers identified as *mustarjilaat*, or young women who "[give] up the characteristics of femininity, [try] to imitate boys in clothing and mannerisms, and [are]
attracted to females only."[4] The role of regulating queer subjectivities is also
adopted by nonbureaucratic entities; female students at the multicampus Higher
Colleges of Technology, for example, are required to sign a *ta'ahhud* (agreement)
that they will "behave" in their sexual conduct, and students at the all-female
Zayed University in Abu Dhabi, similarly, have long been surveilled for public
displays of affection.[5] Given the extensive regulation of both gender and sexuality
in real space, it is not surprising that UAE Internet users have the second-highest
rate of membership in social networking sites in the world.[6] The extension of
queer subjectivities into online discursive communities within the region of the
Arab Gulf states is also undoubtedly linked to the UAE's concerted investment
in the development of information technologies. Because of its greater interest in

joining the global community compared to its neighboring states, the UAE presents a particularly interesting context within which to examine the relationship between the national development of telecommunications and the emergence of new mediated forms of queer subjectivities.

Recent scholarship has critically engaged with the argument that online discourse is inextricably linked to off-line worlds.[7] Moreover, it has been argued that online communities are offered a certain transgressive agency that would otherwise be denied in "real" space. However, there has been a relative paucity of area-focused scholarship on specifically queer phenomena and telecommunications in the region of the Arab Gulf. I take the position that on- and off-line worlds are coconstituted rather than distinct and separate. The relatively lower visibility and heightened policing of queerness in off-line spaces impacts and is impacted by the heightened visibility and relatively less prevalent policing of queerness online. Using a textual and ethnographic analytical framework, I extend the argument of transnational sexual democratic space into the context of the UAE. First, I engage with the dissemination of queer subjectivities in the public sphere, demonstrating how this phenomenon is simultaneously accommodated and denied in current Emirati sociopolitical discourse. I then examine the expression of queerness in cyberspace and interrogate the extent to which a pan-Gulfian transnational queer imaginary is being produced in the context of new social networking technologies such as Facebook. As part of this discussion, culturally specific understandings of embodied practices will be juxtaposed with discourses of cultural protectionism and authenticity as voiced by religious clerics online. Drawing on firsthand interviews with representatives of Etisalat, a large national telecommunications company, and the governing body Telecommunications Regulative Authority (TRA), I argue that the state is currently attempting to restructure its image and media presence according to paradigmatic notions of Islamic autocracy by denying free speech and regulating the visibility of sexuality in cyberspace.

I use the notion of the transnational in the context of the "disrupted" surveillance of cyberspace, as opposed to the surveillance of national space on the ground, which is concerned solely with national citizens. This process, however, is also situated against a backdrop of the Emirates' transnationalistic turn insofar as national investments in cultural heterogeneity are posited against an increasing concern over the issue of Emirati national identity.[8] For example, Dubai, in its rigorous embrace of the Western metropolis as the dominant referential point and model of modernity,[9] has made a concerted effort to invest in the importation of "new" migrant communities. In addition, the anxiety over national identity operates with respect to a demographic imbalance: the position of the Emirati population is threatened not only by the UAE's efforts to implement Western models of multiculturalism but also by the fact that noncitizens constitute 79.9 percent of the population.[10] I argue that this emergent transnationalistic ethos has engendered a rupture in the sociopolitical field, with Emirati national identity rendered the vessel of collective national anxiety.

This chapter focuses on what I delineate as the "post-oil" generation: those who are directly subjected to a national collective imaginary regarding the state's troubled identity—its simultaneous strivings toward Western models of progress and its attempts to construct and preserve an authentic Arab Islamic identity. Not only is this generation distinctive in that they are the first to be born after the establishment of the Emirates as a country in 1971; they have borne witness to a landscape of excess, expatriate-national demographic imbalance, and values that appear in contradistinction to those upheld by indigenous groups, all of which are directly tied to the first oil boom in this region from 1973 to 1982. Although the national population as a whole carries the burden of embodying the essence of an Emirati identity under threat, with Emiratis outnumbered by expatriates by more than eight to one and with 51.1 percent of the Emirati population under age nineteen,[11] it is arguably the youth who are especially vested with the responsibility of defending against the erosion of "authentic" Emirati national cultural identity. Although this responsibility comes with both power and subjugation, the sociopolitical field is ambivalent as far as the articulation of power is concerned: those who are in receipt of the state's privileges are simultaneously subordinated—subject to discourses of cultural preservation that dictate the extent of acceptable transgression. Within this terrain, the post-oil generation is producing multiple discourses that challenge the very identity which they have been tasked to uphold.

The Dissemination of Queer Subjectivities

In recent years the proliferation of queer subjectivities in the UAE has been detected in greater magnitude, instigating a national moral panic. Contemporary manifestations of queer subjectivities, such as cross-dressing, have become increasingly visible in the public realm. Among men, sartorial queer culture is evident in the wearing of fitted *kandorahs*, long, white, male-body clothing that is stitched tightly at the waist, taking the form of a tight-fitting dress. Among national women—although they were once relegated to expressing queerness primarily in the semipublic realm (universities, "family spaces"), given the limitations inherent in the social necessity of wearing the *abayah* (Islamic national dress/body veil)—queer expression has been increasingly detected in the public sphere (e.g., butch self-stylizations in shopping malls).

In tandem with the increased visibility of queer culture in the form of dress, condemnatory proclamations made by conservatives are drawing contemporary queer culture into the discursive realm. In an unstructured interview I conducted at the women's campus of Zayed University in Abu Dhabi, a group of students described the popularity of the American series *The L Word*, which portrays the lives of a group of lesbian, bisexual, and transgender women. Contrary to conservative readings of queer politics as solely a product of the Western world, the students explained how screen representations of homosexuality are in fact being articulated regionally. As an example, the women cited the Kuwaiti television series *Adeel Al Rouh* (2005), which portrayed a lesbian character who, although socially marginalized, was nonetheless represented in her homosexuality.[12] It could be argued that although the portrayal was one of condemnation, the visibility provided by the Kuwaiti television series contributes by drawing queer politics into the discursive realm, with homosexuality no longer subalternized or, at least, not considered wholly taboo.

The launch of a "Social Values" campaign in 2008 in the UAE stands as another example of the ways in which queer politics is allowed to enter sociopolitical discourse—here, through its articulation by the conservative bloc itself. Released in collaboration with the Dubai Police and several governmental and private organizations, the campaign targets, arrests, and puts on trial youth who are seen to imitate the opposite gender, aiming to "protect society from any social deviancy."[13] The chief of Dubai Police, Brigadier Khalfan, has placed particular emphasis on the corrupting role of satellite channels, which broadcast "deviant behavior" throughout the region of the Gulf States, stating to the *Al-Bayan* newspaper that "young people believe what they see in the media and apply it to their lives without considering the content of the message they are getting."[14] It is perhaps an unintended consequence of the policing of sexuality that queer culture becomes more visible. What is particularly striking is that the brigadier describes how the national youth's expression of subjectivity lies at the intersection of globalization and cultural displacement, with the media functioning as the vehicle for contamination:

> The discovery of oil . . . has resulted in a change in society's habits. . . . Our surveys conducted on mostly youth show that some of the most profound foreign additions to our lifestyles have been in attire, strange hairstyles, use of foreign words in our everyday speech, not to mention imitating celebrities. The source of the most influence has been the satellite channel and the Internet, from which imitators have received material that is alien to Emirati society.[15]

With the national youth here upheld as the social group most vulnerable to the displacement of gender norms, such narratives of cultural protectionism seek to combat globalizing "alien" forces that contaminate constructions of cultural authenticity, such as spoken local dialect and national dress, among others. The media is seen to serve as a vehicle, producing and influencing the dissemination of queer subjectivities.

Gender Governance and the Resignification of Female Space

In the region of the Arab Gulf, the governance of gender and the regulation of private and public space have been historically interdependent. In the UAE, the regulation of space operates in tandem with a nuanced sociojudicial installment of hegemonic power.[16] Socially, public and private spaces are regulated through parental surveillance, and female dress and conduct through Islamic modesty codes. These forms of power are not as strictly and categorically defined in terms of society versus the law. Those executions of power that might fall under the purview of familial structures (e.g., youth dressing in drag) are in fact regulated by the police; conversely, sociofamilial structures often regulate that which might be thought of as the provenance of government (e.g., gender-based conduct in public spaces). A common trend is families arranging marriages for their lesbian daughters, either in the hope that they will "change" or to protect family honor.[17] Despite the power of the family to implement such marital laws, however, it is not uncommon for homosexual men and women to marry one another willingly, enabling them to conduct independent homosexual lives within the constraints of heteronormative subordination.

Recent models of governmentality have reinscribed what constitutes gendered space within the context of the public and the private.[18] Unlike Saudi Arabia, for example, the UAE is not subject to strict notions of gendered segregation within the public sphere, and interaction in both work and social spheres is common. Among upper- and middle-class female society, however, gendered segregation exists and, as noted earlier, is largely implemented within the context of societal norms as opposed to judicial power. Weddings and formal social events continue to be segregated, and "ladies' clubs" or "women's clubs" are widespread and popular. However, the recent surveillance, such as that on college campuses, has reinscribed the meaning of private, female space. Both the public expression of homosexuality and queer subjectivities through drag have proliferated within female spaces, since until recently these spaces have not been subject to parental surveillance or regulation by the state. It is widely believed that such spaces have enabled the dissemination of queer subjectivities among young Emirati women, and in response, various methods of social control have been employed. These include the introduction of female police and security guards into women's clubs, the implementation of dress-code regulations in women's colleges, and—as a result of observations of lesbianism in Al-Mamzar Park in Dubai and a skating rink in Abu Dhabi—the transformation of "women's day" into "family day." Due to such modes of governmentality, female spaces have been resignified, no longer considered private.

This resignification serves to shed light on the way in which female space is once again problematized as a categorical entity within a gendered hierarchical framework. In this regional context, traditional modes of gender segregation have allocated space by privileging the male through alignment with the public and subordinating the female through alignment with the private. Such structures of gender hierarchy have been established to the exclusion of homosexual narratives; however, their recent eruption has come to be accommodated solely within female, private spaces, rather than within male public space. That "women's day" is relabeled "family day" heralds the displacement of a gender norm, further complicating the subordination of female space, while male space remains unproblematized. Indeed, male homosexual narratives have been denied entry into this categorical framework altogether, excluded from the resignification of gendered space.

Technodialects and the Production of a
Pan-Gulfian Queer Imaginary

As noted earlier, the dissemination of queer subjectivities is largely seen as being related to the influence of the media. Whereas the statement issued by the chief of Dubai's police (as well as by other federal government bodies) implicates the media at large for its influence on queer communities, it is cybertechnologies alone that provide a platform for the actual dissemination of queer narratives. Unlike satellite television, whose influence is unidirectional, the Internet facilitates the creation of dialogic online communities. It has been established that Internet communication technology deemphasizes the gender-race-class triad, empowering the user and thus serving to democratize societies.[19] Furthermore, platforms within cybertechnology such as blogging arguably function as a tool of resistance against autocratic governments and state censorship.

Although I do not purport to celebrate cybertechnology as the sole site of resistant narratives, nor do I uphold online sociality as a domain uncontaminated by off-line reality, Internet usage by the post-oil generation has nonetheless served as a political vehicle for queer subjectivities. The phenomenon of the "boyah" identity in the Arab Gulf states exemplifies the extent to which cybertechnology has facilitated the dissemination of butch identities by female youth and produced resistant narratives with regard to patriarchal structures of heteronormativity and the sociolegal governance of gendered space. *Boyah* is a lexicalization of the English *boy*, followed by the Arabic feminine suffix *-ah*, and it is employed within local popular discourse to refer to the self-stylizations of butch identities.[20] Boyah identity is an outgrowth of an increasingly visible subculture within the Arab Gulf states. The articulation of boyahs in cyberspace, primarily through social networking websites such as Facebook, Flickr, and MySpace, has created a transnational pan-Gulfian community, with the Internet serving as a mediator for the production of a queer imaginary. Boyahs are popular on Facebook; entering the search term "boyah" yields scores of groups, including "The L Gurlz" and "BanoOotat & Boyat [Girlies and Boyahs]."[21]

The formation of Gulfian online queer communities is facilitated by "The Wall" on Facebook, where members from Saudi Arabia, Qatar, Kuwait, and the UAE discuss various themes such as fidelity, love, the proliferation of new boyah groups, lesbianism, and homosexuality at large. Members often use the forum to pose questions about relationships and boyah identities, such as the following from one user in a recent posting: "i wanna know 1 thing i'v meet alot of boyat in my life & none of thim wanted to have a real relationship y does all boyat r like that ??? is it in there blood or what !!!" Responses from other members are then posted, one example of which also demonstrates pan-Gulfian "technodialect," the lexicalization of Arabic and English, and numeric substitution common on such sites: "its not that its a boyah to do this bil3aks fe boyaz maRrah; [on the contrary, there are boyahs that are extremely] loyal n alL bs [but] its alL about love n jelousy !! thx 3algroup [for the group] n hope to c more posts :D." Social networking groups such as these provide a platform for the formation of queer communities that, although visible to some degree off-line, would be deemed transgressive. Transcending online alliances and national boundaries, boyah identities inhabit what Benedict Anderson terms "imagined communities,"[22] with boyahs signifying a shared system of cultural representation[23] within the region of the Arab Gulf. This system is intensified by the use of a common cyber dialect, with members using names such as "Boyah Q8 [Kuwait]" and "Jedda Altomboys."

That the dissemination of queer subjectivities has served to influence and alter notions of privacy underscores the necessity of cyberspace as a platform for transgressive expression. Users of such spaces challenge the state through their noncompliance with the judicial system and thereby at least partially transcend the public/private dichotomy found in "real" space. Moreover, the availability of anonymous identities and the vocabularies and tactics employed to suggest queerness, while still maintaining the status quo, further facilitate the articulation of queer politics online. Some examples of usernames that suggest female queerness through both content and the appendage of the Arabic feminine suffix *-ah* are "Sportyah" (Sporty One), "Boyah," "Rayalah" (Man), and "BanooTah" (Girly One); other names reflect a change from a real (female) name into a man's name (e.g., Hamdah becomes "Hamad," Mariam becomes "Muhammed").²⁴ Another popular means of conveying queerness online is the use of suggestive profile pictures, such as a caricature of a boyah from the state of Oman by the user "Kyoot [Cute] London Boyah" (see figure 16.1) and a picture of the popular lesbian character Shane from the television show *The L Word* by the Saudi Arabian user "Dode Boya" (see figure 16.2).

Fig. 16.1. Facebook user image: Kyoot London Boyah

Fig. 16.2. Facebook user image: Dode Boya

Queer Gulfian communities are expressed and formed not only online but in the real world. Among the Facebook groups recently established is one entitled "boyat w cutat in london (summer)" (boyahs and cute ones in London [summer]), which was uploaded to create a social network in London over the summer of 2008. Since the first oil boom in the Arab Gulf, London has for decades served as a place in which many Gulf Arabs spend their summer holidays. There is in fact a distinct Arab cosmopolitan presence in London, to the extent that "Arab Season" has recently been coined by the retail industry to refer to the summer months, when Gulf Arabs are in the city. The formation of the London boyah group on Facebook thus not only points to the manifestation of a pan-Gulfian transnational discursive community but further demonstrates the material realization of such communities in (real) spaces that are not subject to the principles of the governance of sexuality found in the Arab Gulf states. Indeed, usage of the Internet and of social networking profiles such as Facebook illustrates the manner in which the transnational space afforded by cybertechnologies challenges and displaces the governance of sexuality within the public sphere, producing expressions of queerness both on- and off-line. This process reflects what Nick Couldry describes as the "broader landscape" of how media is resurrected in everyday life, contributing to social life and politics both beyond and within the "centralizing pressures of the nation state."²⁵

The case of the London Facebook group demonstrates the intersection of media and everyday life insofar as the expression of queerness is concerned: the transcendence of the governance of sexuality offered by cybertechnologies is not only realized and made intelligible but moreover allows for the production of an imaginary that unsettles notions of sovereignty, territoriality, and local structures of domination. What is important here is not so much that cybertechnology displaces the governance of sexuality in mediating a transnational queer imaginary but, rather, the way in which the media and the everyday intersect to produce that imaginary.

"Exposure," Politics, and Protectionism

In a Facebook group entitled "WHY AL Boyat Like These????," which references Saudi Arabia as its host location, the overarching theme of discussion is "authenticity," with Islamic moralism rendered a central premise of attack by conservative members. The Facebook group displays several videos whose subject is the condemnation of the boyah identity and its dissemination within the region. One video's montage begins with a series of photographs that depict the boyah stylizations. The text states,

> The Messenger of God, peace be upon him, cursed female-impersonators who are males, and the male-impersonators who are women. There's a phenomenon growing among us of male impersonators, or what they call "boyat"—even children know about them. It is a disgusting phenomenon, but some call it a "trend." . . . Dear male impersonator, are you comfortable with yourself? Do you feel happy when you change the nature which God created? . . . Is it your intention to imitate the West? . . . I just want to make one thing clear before I continue. These pictures were displayed on Flickr, by boyat. Which means I am not the one who is *exposing them; they expose themselves.* . . . I curse the West, which has promoted this corruption and have sent us their filth. And some of you emulate them as if they are role models. Let's see what the West has given us. [Pictures from *The L Word* then appear, followed by pictures of anti-Islamic sentiment, including people urinating and stepping on the Quran and illustrations of Danish cartoon caricatures of the prophet Muhammed].[26]

This excerpt demonstrates the extent to which queerness is seen as part of a Western global ethos—an imposition and a threat to an Islamic cultural identity, as well as a byproduct of anti-Islamic sentiment. This stance is reminiscent of the scholarly assertion that queerness within non-Western regional contexts is seen as a product of Westernization and as an influence emanating from the West.[27] That which is construed as external and deviant is rendered a Western product, namely, through the alignment of condemnatory rhetoric with images from *The L Word*. The overarching stance of the statement is positioned with regard to

Fig. 16.3. Facebook video from the group "WHY AL Boyat Like These????"

a discursive structure of binary opposites: deviant sexual identities are placed alongside the Danish cartoons and images of the Quran being obliterated (see figure 6.3). Finally, the statement that the images were found on Flickr (uploaded by boyahs themselves) underlines the extent to which cyberculture is seen as a vehicle and platform of visibility and resistance. By highlighting the idea that the boyahs have "exposed themselves," the video attempts to circumscribe them within a complex of honor and shame. It is through the very act of uploading, however, that agency is achieved, transcending sociocultural norms and operating against culturally specific understandings of identity and embodiment.

In another video posted on the same Facebook group, the religious cleric Muhammed Al-Awadhi condemns the dissemination of the boyah identity, citing the notion of the body in Islam, most especially in relation to drag. Addressing boyahs and the culture of cross-dressing in general, he states, "Your body is not of your own possession, it belongs to God. . . . So when we say that tattoos are forbidden [in Islam] or, for example, piercing the body or shaving half your head and hence changing your appearance, . . . it is forbidden because your body is God's possession."[28] Therefore, Al-Awadhi concludes, any form of inscription or alteration in the name of articulating an embodied identity—be it gendered, sexual, or otherwise—is condemned.

It is particularly interesting to cross-examine this argument in relation to post-modern readings of the body as a discursive and epistemological entity. Relevant here are Foucauldian techniques of understanding how apparatuses of control mark the transition between traditional order and what Foucault terms "scientific biopower."[29] Insofar as the queer body in Islam is concerned, it could be argued that its alterity stands as a threat, in need of containment. As already established, its entry into the sociopolitical discursive realm in the UAE demonstrates that queerness both is constituted within the dominant discourses of governance and, in its excess, stands as a site of potential transgression against the very bound-aries that seek to contain it.[30] In the UAE, the exercise of "scientific biopower" on the queer body is exemplified in the state's concerted effort to eliminate the expression of queerness from within the public sphere. Political prerogatives in this instance would include regulating not only the queer body itself but also the space the queer body occupies. What, then, of the *online* queer body, which does not corporeally exist?

Relevant here is a discussion of cyborgian identities, hybrids of the discur-sive and the material that represent a postgendered identity beyond domina-tion.[31] In their ability to transgress boundaries and resist domination, cyborgian identities can effect progressive political action, thereby disrupting the terms of governmentality of queer space and Islamic notions of embodiment. The politi-cization of the cyborg is of significance to Web-based expression of boyahs and the Islamic condemnation of bodily reinscription. Since the resignification of the body is an anti-Islamic act, cyborgian constructions of queerness resist similar condemnation since the body is not wholly present.

In cyborg identities' interdeterminate status, "neither wholly technological nor completely organic," Anne Balsamo writes that they evade not only dominant cul-tural frameworks but also the notion of the natural body standing in opposition to the technological body.[32] In the case of the boyah, and in that of queer sub-jectivities generally, transgression is more comfortably accommodated through online cyborg identities than through material manifestations of queerness in the Emirati public sphere. With the boundary between body and machine altered, Islamic readings of bodily materiality are to a large extent displaced, as (cybor-gian) bodily reinscription, and hence resignification, is made available. With the complex of honor and shame rendered central to culturally specific notions of gendered and sexual subjectivities, the mechanical apparatus allows for both the "exposure" of queerness and anonymity of identity in a way that would not be possible without hybridization. In other words, the mechanical apparatus limits the potential for shame, since unlike acts of transgression that can be identified, cyborgian identities provide anonymity through aliases that appear in various forums and chat rooms. The act of uploading one's queer subjectivity therefore becomes transgressive of the dominant culture order, with the question of transgression specifically located in the interdeterminacy of the hybrid design.

What is perhaps most significant about the conservative rhetoric seen in media such as the Facebook videos is that alternative sexualities are heralded as byproducts of Western cultural imperialism. Although the penal code in the UAE does not state that homosexuality is prohibited, public opinion is demanding it. The penal code does, however, prohibit men from dressing as women; despite this prohibition, manifestations of queer cultures, such as the popular male drag band Ma'alayah, have existed in the Emirates for many years.[33] More contemporary manifestations of queer culture, however, are seen as alien—equated directly with the West and not necessarily seen as a product of globalization. This is manifest in a video posted on Facebook entitled "WHY AL Boyat Like These????," in which the Kuwaiti cleric Nabeel Al-Awadhi argues, "The coinage of 'boyah' in itself is problematic because it is not ours—it imitates the English word 'boy' and combines it with an Arabic feminine suffix. . . . This is an example of how this sexual phenomenon is a direct imitation of the West." What could be said of the boyah identity is that it is not merely an imitation of the West achieved through globalizing forces but a reappropriation of it—an integration of a Western linguistic term with an Arabic suffix that results in a coconstitution not only of sexual subjectivities but also of cultural logics. Their disjuncture from the local ought to be read within the context of the region's enthusiastic embrace of globalization and the Emirates' presentation of itself as a nation belonging to the global community.[34]

New Censures: Local Apprehensions and Global Realities

In recent years, international exposure of autocratic oppression has engendered a sense of urgency on the part of the Emirati government to revamp its self-image. With the establishment of the Telecommunications Regulative Authority (TRA) in 2004 and its aim to provide transparency with regard to censorship, the government has increasingly endorsed what is seen as a more progressive attitude toward freedom of speech. The government's position is in part a response and in part a byproduct of continuing human rights discourses in the world press about recurring democratic violations—the use of children as camel jockeys, poor living conditions for migrant workers, and the imprisonment of homosexuals—as well as control of the media by local governments.

As part of the government's preoccupation with its self-image, the National Media Council (NMC) was established to train journalists and diplomats. A representative of the NMC explained to me that there has been a desire to limit the negative publicity of Dubai because of its tourist industry, since any hint of attack for human rights violations could be seen as a threat to that industry and as something to be controlled.[35] Dubai thus stands as an example of the uncomfortable relationship between progressive democratic ideals and state control. In fact, Dubai has established a "Media Free Zone," where restrictions have been loosened on print and broadcast media produced for audiences outside the UAE. Inside the UAE, however, government officials continue to ban websites deemed "morally objectionable." For example, apart from those sites whose content is obviously anti-Islamic or sexual in nature, the reach of censoring bodies extends to blocking any website ending in Israel's domain, ".il." Furthermore, the government has banned technologies that allow voice-over-Internet communication, such as Skype, so it can continue to regulate and profit from the telecommunications industry.[36]

The installment of new censorship regulations has been forced to coexist, often uncomfortably, with the preservation of "authentic" national and cultural values. The TRA has played an important role in this dialectic, particularly with its establishment of an Internet regulatory department, known as Internet Access Management—"a 'regulatory framework' that ensures safe access onto the Internet in an effective and organized way." One of the TRA's primary mandates is that of transparency. As Muhammed Al-Ghanim, director of the TRA, notes,

> We are targeting the public sector for transparency. We created a common face for our blocked websites: when you click a link, a feedback form is sent to the operators regarding why certain websites should be blocked. . . . Transparency is one of our values and the values of our committee, most especially to the government and to the public.[37]

Before the development of the TRA, the communications industry operated in a somewhat unstructured manner with regard to censorship in the UAE. Through my interviews, I found that many websites were blocked for "no valid reason," since the primary mechanisms on which the system of censorship was based was a list of catchwords and catchphrases that filtered through the Internet.[38] For example, a website on breast cancer was blocked since it was prohibited under the catchword *breast*. A representative from the NMC explained how this period of censorship was not particularly well defined in what was prohibited; however, sex and anti-Islamic sentiments constituted the "basic premises" of the censorship. Intermittent shutdowns and reversions of websites back into the public sphere also demonstrate the level at which censorship guidelines remained uncategorized before recent developments. For example, Flickr—a social networking website—faced intermittent shutdown over a period of three years due to the fact that photographs uploaded by users are often unauthorized for public viewing.[39]

In my interviews, I was struck by the comprehensiveness and sophistication of the TRA's structure for regulating the Internet industry, in contrast to previous unsystematized approaches. Its modus operandi is expressed not only in its guidelines and procedures—that is, in the detail in which it was working—but in its presentation of itself as a product of cosmopolitanism: bilingual, technologically sophisticated, and retaining an essence of tradition through gendered social conduct and national dress. The TRA, which falls under the auspices of the government, stands as a product of the Emiratization program installed in the country to encourage civic participation in the sphere of employment. It could be said that the TRA's hiring of national youth is a way in which it can ensure that its employees are attuned to values and traditions or to what would be considered prohibited or culturally transgressive. However, the TRA's employment of nationals—as well as its advocacy of transparency—is an attempt to present discourses of "modernity" and "authenticity" as not necessarily mutually contradictory. The fact that a newly established governing body is able to reinscribe this progression within the local (with regard to national employment) not only serves to affirm the Emirates' discursive embrace of national identity but also facilitates its accommodation within the global arena. Its progressive agenda is not presented as an alternative to "authentic" discourses but rather as one that is coexistent.

The UAE's dilemma about how to maintain its global image has been in many ways thrust upon the post-oil generation. Facilitated by social networking sites, this generation has produced a pan-Gulfian queer imaginary within the context of transnational sociopolitical discourse. The dialectic between visibility and control is critical to the understanding of how queerness is simultaneously contingent on dominant formations.[40] The policing of sexuality off-line and its attendant dissemination and visibility of queers online has engendered the production of more rigorous censorship laws in the UAE. So while cybertechnology in this context has the potential to transform sexual power structures, it simultaneously reaffirms and violently reproduces others.

Noncensorship and "the Freedom of Subjects under the Law"

My analysis of the interviews presented here reveals that the UAE's simultaneous inscription of democratic ideals regarding freedom in the media and preservation of tradition is inseparable from its preoccupation with its global image and paranoia about regulating bodies. It is through the installment of the governmental technologies detailed herein—Internet Access Management and, as will be described, Content Follow-Up—that the Emirates' dilemma between the global and the local agenda is "discursively codified."[41] Al-Ghanim explained how before the genesis of Internet Access Management, the provider Etisalat, and its competitor Du, implemented censorship categories that were never published. He further explained, "We are now going to publish these guidelines and categories, [which constitute] what is against the moral, cultural, and religious values of the country." He added, "It is an aspect of protecting young people . . . in terms of 'censorship,' if you want to call it that—we prefer to call it Internet Access Management." The most crucial element in Al-Ghanim's statement is his ideological rhetoric, particularly his modification of the term "censorship" into "Internet Access Management." In fact, a similar alteration of terminology was made by the director of the NMC when he noted that "the NMC is currently in the process of producing something called 'Content Supervision' or 'Content Follow-Up,' as we prefer to call it."[42] This adjustment of language points to a vigilance regarding the issue of censorship and the nuances inherent in the preferred terminologies of "management" and "supervision."

Describing the mechanisms of Internet regulation alongside the denial of censorship itself, the NMC director stated, "It does not mean that we would have censorship. . . . We will have guidelines, and we expect the 'user providers' to be able to monitor themselves." Although here he explains that there is neither censorship nor supervisory committees but rather "guidelines," my research has found that this is in fact not the case. The TRA representative explained to me that Web-based expressions of homosexuality were to be categorized under "pornography" and that new guidelines will explain in fuller detail the heterogeneous nature of queer subjectivities and their censorship. Moreover, Flickr's battle against intermittent shutdown and its labeling as a "dispute case" with regard to its partial censorship has engendered the implementation of new laws against *tashheer* (fame), designed to protect identities against social abjection.

Although governing bodies are bent on restructuring the media in the name of "progress," the installment of Internet Access Management appears to have engendered the production of a more rigorous and specialized categorical nature to censorship laws in the UAE. The ideological and rhetorical stance articulated in my interviews points to a significant transition from traditionally unorganized modes of censorship to ones that are extremely lucid and transparent. Furthermore, there has been a significant change in the nature of censorship material itself; censored content is no longer determined by a crude categorization along binaries of permissible/forbidden but, rather, is acknowledged in its heterogeneity and evaluated with engaged and nuanced approaches, such as partial blocking, dispute cases, and feedback forms. This particular change sheds light on the nature of the new image of authority: the censor is no longer an untouchable force, endowed with infallibility; rather, he is attentive, sympathetic, responsive to feedback, and a potential promoter of agency. However, despite the seemingly progressive nature of this approach insofar as the implementation of strict censorship is denied, the new laws under the auspices of Internet Access Management and Content Supervision are in fact more demanding of the subject, who may have greater access to once-forbidden material but now finds him- or herself more powerfully regulated within it.

Arguably, this repositioning of noncensorship reflects a shift toward a neoliberalist ideological stance. In contradistinction to discussions of neoliberalism that highlight its negative relation to state power, Aihwa Ong conceptualizes neoliberalism as a mechanism by which government recasts its activities as "nonpolitical and nonideological problems that need technical solutions."[43] In the UAE, although social networking tools such as MySpace and Facebook are available, certain group memberships relating to queer subjectivities and homosexualities will be blocked, classified under the rubric of pornography. Users are aware of what is available in cyberspace but are denied full access into that realm. As the NMC director stated, "We want the law to be accepted and absorbed, and we want to respond to the needs of society," and he added, "We are not going to have a supervisory committee; we will leave it to the people to monitor themselves." This position recalls Rose and Miller's observation that political power in the context of liberalism becomes not so much a matter of imposing constraints on citizens as of creating citizens capable of living with regulated freedom.[44] Unlike in neighboring states such as Saudi Arabia and Iran, where hegemony dictates subordination and consent, in the UAE, the subject is regulated within a nuanced hegemonic field, one that demands tolerance of bearing witness to freedom as well as self-regulation in accordance with the law. It is through the freedom of subjects under the law that the state is discursively codified in governmental technologies: "management" and "supervision" affect governmental ambitions of continuing to regulate the subject under the guise of progress. These modes of governmentality seek to replace outright autocracy with a neoliberalist rhetoric, with the effect that regulation masquerades in the name of transparency.

NOTES

1. The term *queer subjectivities* is here used to capture the liminality inherent in the expression of sexual practices, as opposed to more fixed, categorical terms, such as *butch identities*. In my analyses there were no clear references to self-identified homosexualities; the utility of *queer* is to recognize multiple social positions that extend beyond reductive categorizations.

2. Christopher Davidson, "After Shaikh Zayed: The Politics of Succession in Abu Dhabi and the UAE," *Middle East Policy* 13, no. 1 (Spring 2006): 42.

3. For a detailed historical study of the UAE and its position with respect to modernization and globalization, see Christopher Davidson, *The United Arab Emirates: A Study in Survival* (Boulder, CO: Lynne Rienner, 2005).

4. Faten Hamoudi, "Excuse Me I'm a Girl: A Preventative Initiative Targeting 'Mannish Women' (*Mustarjilaat*)" (February 12, 2009), http://www.emaratalyoum.com/articles/2009/2/pages/02122009_6144b605bbd0493a8f48d88e49e2cf63.aspx (accessed February 21, 2009).

5. Salma Al-Darmaki (Zayed University student), personal e-mail communication to author, February 21, 2009.

6. Vineetha Menon, "UAE Second in World List for On-line Social Networking," *ArabianBusiness.com* (September 30, 2008), http://www.arabianbusiness.com/532785-uae-second-in-world-list-for-online-social-networking (accessed February 12, 2009).

7. See, for example, Radhika Gajjala, "Studying Feminist E-spaces: Introducing Transnational/Post-colonial Concerns," in Sally R. Munt, ed., *Technoscapes: Inside the New Media* (London: Continuum, 2001), 113–126; Adi Kuntsman, *Figurations of Violence and Belonging: Queerness, Migranthood and Nationalism in Cyberspace and Beyond* (Oxford, UK: Peter Lang, 2009); Lisa Nakamura, *Cybertypes: Race, Ethnicity, and Identity on the Internet* (New York: Routledge, 2002); Kali Tal and Gene Lyman, "Room Full of Mirrors: Virtual Tourism and First World Technogaze," Kali Tal personal website (2000), http://www.kalital.com/Text/Articles/artbyte.html (accessed March 3, 2009).

8. In recent years, the federal government has made efforts to disseminate discourses of Islamic nationalism through conference forums and scholastic competitions, declaring 2008 to be the Year of National Identity.

9. For a critical reading of Dubai's political stance in relation to its program of modernization, see Mike Davis, "Fear and Money in Dubai," *New Left Review* 41 (September–October 2006): 47–68.

10. United Arab Emirates Ministry of Economy, "UAE in Numbers 2007," http://www.economy.ae/English/EconomicAndStatisticReports/StatisticReports/Pages/UAEinNumbers.aspx (accessed March 7, 2009).

11. Ibid.

12. Students at Zayed University (members of the International Studies Council and participants of the Women as Leaders Conference), interview with author, June 2008, Abu Dhabi, UAE.

13. Mustapha Al-Zar'ouny, "Dubai Launches 'Let's Maintain Our Values,'" *Al-Bayan* (Abu Dhabi; May 26, 2008): 18.

14. Ibid.

15. Ibid.

16. For example, on the judicial level, in accordance with *sharia* (Islamic jurisprudence), which dictates that women are subject to structural frameworks of *walee al amr* (male guardianship) in multiple realms, a signature of approval from a male representative is required for national women to obtain a driver's license in the UAE.

17. Ruba Al-Hassan (Project Management Office member at Abu Dhabi Government Restructuring Committee), personal e-mail communication to author, February 17, 2009.

18. See Michel Foucault, "Governmentality," in Graham Burchell, Colin Gordon, and Peter Miller, eds., *The Foucault Effect: Studies in Governmentality* (Cambridge, MA: MIT Press, 1991), 87–104.

19. Gail Dines and Jean Humez, eds., *Gender, Race, and Class in Media*, 2nd ed. (Thousand Oaks, CA: Sage, 2003), 673.

20. Noor Al-Qasimi, "The Codes of Modesty: Reconfiguring the Muslim Female Subject," Ph.D. diss., University of Warwick, 2007.

21. I use *boyahs* to refer to the plural form of *boyah*; however, throughout this chapter various forms appear in both plural ("boyat," "boyaz") and singular ("boya") usage.

22. Benedict Anderson, *Imagined Communities: Reflections on the Origin and Spread of Nationalism* (London: Verso, 2002).

23. Anne McClintock, *Imperial Leather: Race, Gender and Sexuality in the Colonial Contest* (London: Routledge, 1995), 353.

24. Wijdan Al-Mutairi (Zayed University student), personal e-mail communication to author, February 21, 2009.

25. Nick Couldry, "Transvaluing Media Studies, or, Beyond the Myth of the Mediated Centre," in James Curran and David Morley, eds., *Media and Cultural Theory* (London: Routledge, 2006), 178.

26. Posting on "WHY AL Boyat Like These????" group, *Facebook*, http://www.facebook.com/group.php?gid=18687390228, translation of text by Noura Al-Noman (emphasis added).

27. This debate has been broadly discussed in relation to various non-Western contexts within queer diasporic scholarship. See, for example, Arnaldo Cruz-Malavé and Martin F. Manalansan IV, eds., *Queer Globalizations: Citizenship and the Afterlife of Colonialism* (New York: New York University Press, 2002); Cindy Patton and Benigno Sánchez-Eppler, eds., *Queer Diasporas* (Durham, NC: Duke University Press, 2000).

28. Posting on "WHY AL Boyat Like These????" group.

29. Michel Foucault, *The Will to Knowledge: The History of Sexuality, Volume 1* (London: Penguin, 1976), 143.

30. Anne Balsamo, *Technologies of the Gendered Body: Reading Cyborg Women* (Durham, NC: Duke University Press, 1999), 28.

31. Donna J. Haraway, "A Cyborg Manifesto: Science, Technology, and Socialist-Feminism in the Late Twentieth Century," in *Simians, Cyborgs and Women: The Reinvention of Nature* (New York: Routledge, 1991), 149–181.

32. Balsamo, *Technologies of the Gendered Body*, 11.

33. Over the past decade, however, government bodies have implemented measures to limit the presence of drag musical groups.

34. Tom Boellstorff, "I Knew It Was Me: Mass Media, 'Globalization,' and Lesbian and Gay Indonesians," in Chris Berry, Fran Martin, and Audrey Yue, eds., *Mobile Cultures: New Media in Queer Asia* (Durham, NC: Duke University Press, 2003), 173.

35. National Media Council representative in discussion with the author, May 29, 2008, Abu Dhabi, UAE.

36. Representatives of the Telecommunications Regulatory Authority, presentation to author, June 2, 2008, Abu Dhabi, UAE.

37. Muhammed Al-Ghanim (Director, Telecommunications Regulatory Authority), interview with author, June 2, 2008, Abu Dhabi, UAE.

38. Representatives of the TRA, presentation to author.

39. Ali Ahmed (Director, Etisalat), interview with author, May 29, 2008, Abu Dhabi, UAE.

40. Jasbir Puar, "Q&A with Jasbir Puar," *Darkmatter* (May 5, 2008), http://www.darkmatter101.org/site/2008/05/02/qa-with-jasbir-puar/ (accessed July 10, 2009).

41. Nikolas Rose and Peter Miller, "Political Power beyond the State: Problematics of Government," *British Journal of Sociology* 43, no. 2 (1992): 176.

42. Ibrahim Al Abed (Director, NMC), interview with author, May 29, 2008, Abu Dhabi, UAE.

43. Aihwa Ong, *Neoliberalism as Exception: Mutations in Citizenship and Sovereignty* (Durham, NC: Duke University Press, 2006): 3.

44. Rose and Miller, "Political Power beyond the State," 172.

About the Contributors

Noor Al-Qasimi received her Ph.D. in film and television from the University of Warwick in 2007. Her research interests include sexuality, cybertechnology, the region of the Middle East, critical theory, postcolonial feminism, transnational feminism, queer theory, biopolitics, governmentality, and affect theory. She is currently a research fellow at the Center for Gender Studies at SOAS, University of London. She recently held a research fellowship at the Center for the Study of Gender and Sexuality at New York University, where she also taught in the Department of Media, Culture, and Communication.

Spring-Serenity Duvall is Assistant Professor of Communications at the University of South Carolina, Aiken. Her research interests include celebrity culture, girlhood studies, and commodity activism. Her published work includes "Dying for Our Sins: Christian Salvation Rhetoric in Celebrity Colonialism," in *Celebrity Colonialism: Fame, Representation, and Power in (Post)Colonial Cultures* (2009). She has also presented her work at the International Communication Association, the Political Studies Association (UK), the National Communication Association, and the Association of Educators in Journalism and Mass Communication. Forthcoming publications include "Perfect Little Feminists? Young Girls in the U.S. Interpret Gender, Violence, and Friendship in Cartoons," in the *Journal of Children and Media*. She has served on the AEJMC Commission on the Status of Women.

Nabil Echchaibi is Assistant Professor in the School of Journalism and Mass Communication at the University of Colorado–Boulder. His recent research focuses on the intersections between Islam, Arab popular culture, and the media. His current research in the political economy and reception of Islamic satellite media is an attempt to document and analyze the new public articulation of identity and religion among young Arabs. His book on the role of diasporic media among young Muslims in France and Germany is forthcoming. He is also interested in new media and their impact on journalism. His coedited book *International Blogging: Identity, Politics and Networked Publics* was published in 2009.

Karmen Erjavec is Associate Professor at the Faculty of Social Sciences, University of Ljubljana, Slovenia, where she teaches mass communication, journalism, and media education. Her research interests extend to the areas of media and

303

minorities, nationalism, racism, media education, and the quality of journalism. Her numerous publications include "Eastern European Media Representation of the Discrimination against the Roma," in *Discourse and Society* (2001); "Beyond Advertising and Journalism," in *Discourse and Society* (2004); and "Hybrid Public Relation News Discourse," in the *European Journal of Communication* (2005).

Radha S. Hegde is Associate Professor in the Department of Media, Culture, and Communication at New York University. She has published in the areas of postcolonial and transnational feminism, globalization, and diaspora. Her earlier work examined violence and reproductive politics in south India. Her publications have appeared in journals such as *Communication Theory*, *Critical Studies in Media Communication*, *Feminist Media Studies*, and *Violence against Women*. Her current projects include a monograph on media and migration and an ethnographic project in India examining the role of language and training in the construction of digital futures. She has been the chair of the Feminist and Women's Studies division of the National Communication Association. She serves on the editorial board of several major journals in the field of media and cultural studies. She is also the cofounder of Manavi, an organization that addresses issues of gender and violence in the South Asian immigrant community.

Minoo Moallem is Professor and Chair of Gender and Women's Studies at the University of California, Berkeley. She is the author of *Between Warrior Brother and Veiled Sister: Islamic Fundamentalism and the Cultural Politics of Patriarchy in Iran* (2005). She is also the coeditor (with Caren Kaplan and Norma Alarcon) of *Between Woman and Nation: Nationalisms, Transnational Feminisms, and the State* (1999) and the guest editor of a special issue of *Comparative Studies of South Asia, Africa and the Middle East* on Iranian immigrants, exiles, and refugees. She has recently ventured in digital media, and her online project "Nation-on-the Move" (design by Eric Loyer) was recently published in *Vectors: Journal of Culture and Technology in a Dynamic Vernacular* (special issue on difference, fall 2007). She is currently working on a book manuscript on the commodification of the nation through consumptive production and circulation of such commodities as the Persian carpet, a research project on gender, media, and religion, and a project on Iran-Iraq war movies and masculinity.

Sujata Moorti is Professor of Women's and Gender Studies at Middlebury College. Her research explores the intersections of feminist and cultural studies theories. She has published extensively on U.S. television programming and South Asian diasporic media. She is the author of *Color of Rape: Gender and Race in Television's Public Spheres* and coeditor of two anthologies, *Global Bollywood: The*

Transnational Travels of Hindi Song-and-Dance (2008) and *Local Violence, Global Media: Feminist Analyses of Gendered Representations* (2009). She is currently working with international media activists to develop a protocol for human rights media representation.

Susan Ossman is Professor of Anthropology and Director of the Global Studies program at the University of California, Riverside. Her research has developed comparative approaches in the study of globalization. Her current work explores new forms of transnational social life and political engagement from the perspective of serial migrants. Her other publications include *Picturing Casablanca: Portraits of Power in a Modern City* (1994), *Miroirs Maghrbins, Itinéaires de soi et Paysages de Rencontre* (1998), *Three Faces of Beauty: Casablanca, Paris, Cairo* (2002), and *The Places We Share: Migration, Subjectivity, and Global Mobility* (2007).

Jan Maghinay Padios is a doctoral candidate in the American Studies Program in the Department of Social and Cultural Analysis at New York University. Her dissertation tracks the emergence and implications of consumer cultures in the Philippines and among Filipinos in the United States, in relation to the neoliberal policies of the Philippine state. Her primary fields of research include global political economy, consumption, U.S. imperialism, and media and technology. She is also a cofounder of an international partnership program between New York University's Asian/Pacific/American Studies program and the Department of English at the Ateneo de Manila University and is a guest editor for the Manila-based journal *Transpacific American Studies*. Her work is supported by the Torch Fellowship program at New York University.

Radhika Parameswaran is Associate Professor in the School of Journalism at Indiana University, Bloomington. She holds adjunct appointments in the cultural studies and India studies programs. Her research spans transnational feminist cultural studies, postcolonial studies, qualitative methods, and South Asia. Her recent publications have appeared in the *Journal of Communication Inquiry*, *Critical Studies in Media Communication*, the *Journal of Communication*, *Communication Theory*, and *Journalism and Communication Monographs*. Her forthcoming publications include an article in *Communication, Culture and Critique* and a book chapter in the *Handbook of Critical Indigenous Methodologies*.

Felicity Schaeffer-Grabiel is Assistant Professor in the Feminist Studies Department at the University of California, Santa Cruz. Currently she is working on a book manuscript, "Cyber-brides across the Americas: Transnational Imaginaries, Marriage, and Migration." Her research interests include borderlands and trans-nationalisms, sexuality and migration, affect and capitalism, race, technology and subjectivity, and Chicana/Latina cultural studies. Some of her publications include "Flexible Technologies of Subjectivity and Mobility across the Americas," in "Rewiring the 'Nation': The Place of Technology in American Studies," special issue of *American Quarterly* (2006), and "Planet-Love.com: Cyberbrides in the Americas and the Transnational Routes of U.S. Masculinity," *Signs: Journal of Women in Culture and Society* (2006).

Wanning Sun is Professor of Chinese Media and Cultural Studies at China Research Centre, University of Technology Sydney (UTS). Wanning was a visiting professor at the Asian and Asian American Studies Program at the State University of New York from 2005 to 2006. Wanning's research extends to a number of areas including Chinese media and cultural studies, gender, migration, social change in contemporary China, and diasporic Chinese media. Wanning is the author of two monographs, *Leaving China: Media, Migration, and Transnational Imagination* (2002) and *Maid in China: Media, Morality and the Cultural Politics of Boundaries* (2009), and the editor of *Media and the Chinese Diaspora: Community, Communications and Commerce* (2006). She is a member of the editorial board for *Media International Australia* and a member of the executive advisory board of the *Asian Journal of Communication*.

Julie Thomas is Associate Professor of Global Communications at the American University of Paris, where she teaches courses in material culture, the museum as medium, and communicating fashion. She has written widely on museum exhibitions, the museum and citizenship, interactivity and attention, and ethical fashion. Her chapter "The Manipulation of Heritage and Identity in Museums of Migration" is forthcoming in the *Cultures and Globalization Series*, edited by Helmut Anheier and Yudhishthir Raj Isar.

Angharad N. Valdivia, Research Professor of Communications, Latina/o Studies, and Gender & Women's Studies, is the head of the Department of Media and Cinema Studies, University of Illinois, Urbana-Champaign. She is currently the editor of *Communication Theory*. Her research and teaching focus on issues of gender, race, and ethnicity in transnational popular culture, combining political, economic, and cultural aspects. Her work on Latina/o studies, girls studies, and transnational feminist studies has generated two single-authored books, *A Latina in the Land of Hollywood* and *Latina/o Media Studies*, as well as several edited collections including *Latina/o Communication Studies Today*, *A Companion to Media Studies*, and *Feminism, Multiculturalism, and the Media*. She has published in a range of journals including *Girlhood Studies*, the *Journal of Com-*

munication, the *Journal of Communication Inquiry, Sociological Quarterly, Camera Obscura*, the *Journal of Children and the Media*, and others.

Zala Volčič is a postdoctoral fellow at the Centre for Critical and Cultural Studies at the University of Queensland, Australia. She is interested in the cultural consequences of nationalism, capitalism, and globalization, with a particular emphasis on international communication, media, gender, and cultural identities. Her numerous publications include "The Machine That Creates Slovenes: The Role of Slovene Public Broadcasting in Re-affirming the Slovene National Identity," in *National Identities Journal* (2005); "The Notion of 'The West' in the Serbian National Imaginary," in *European Journal of Cultural Studies* (2005); "Blaming the Media: Serbian Narratives of National(ist) Identity," in *Continuum: Journal of Media and Cultural Studies* (2006); and "Yugo-nostalgia: Cultural Memory and Media in the Former Yugoslavia," in *Critical Studies of Mass Communication* (2007).

Saskia Witteborn is Assistant Professor in the School of Journalism and Communication at the Chinese University of Hong Kong, where she also coordinates the M.A. program in Global Communication. Her work focuses on migration, the construction of translocal spaces, and diasporic identity politics. She has published in the areas of culture and communication, language and social interaction, and diaspora studies in journals such as the *Journal of Communication, Research on Language and Social Interaction*, and the *Journal of International and Intercultural Communication*. She is chair of the Communication as Social Construction Division at the National Communication Association and associate editor of the *Journal of International and Intercultural Communication*.

Audrey Yue is Senior Lecturer in Cultural Studies at the University of Melbourne, Australia. She is the author of *Ann Hui's Song of the Exile* (forthcoming 2010) and coeditor of *AsiaPacifiQueer: Rethinking Genders and Sexualities* (2008) and *Mobile Cultures: New Media in Queer Asia* (2003). Her recent essays on diasporic queer cultures have appeared in *GLQ, Sexualities, Feminist Media Studies*, and *Gay and Lesbian Issues and Psychology Review*. She is currently Chief Investigator in two Australian Research Council–funded projects on Asian Australian cinema and transnational large screens.

Index

Abu Ghraib, 3
Abu Lughod, Leila, 16n30, 101n4, 283n44
Activism, 140–142; and Christianity, 107; local human rights, 233, 240; and neoliberal, 140, 153; and trafficking, 113. *See also* Celebrity
Advertisements: and transnational markets, 215. *See also* Transnational
Advertising: and fields of desire, 183; global, 78; in India, 71–75; and sex trafficking, 110–112, 117–119
Africa, 145, 146, 149, 151; African Americans, 58, 110; and women, 75. *See also* Slavery
Ahmed, Leila, 101n4
Ahmed, Sara, 16n26, 17n41, 122n26
Al Jazeera, 242, 243
Alarcon, Norma, 16n26
Alexander, Jacqui M., 5, 16n25, 16n26
American Girl, 58–59
Anderson, Benedict, 231, 301n22
Aneesh, A3, 193n12
Appadurai, Arjun, 6, 14n6, 16n31, 16n36, 33n1, 137n4, 139n30, 175n2, 231, 247n2, 267n31, 274, 282n27
Archive, 124
Arkan, Zeljko, 40–42
Audience/s: *60 Minutes*, 79; Arab Muslim, 91, 97; and celebrities, 140, 141; Chinese, 197, 200, 201; and DIY, 238; ethnic, 64; Filipino women, 218; French, 129,132; global, 26, 64, 65, 127, 245, 268, 269, 273–275, 279; Hong Kong, 270; imagined, 172; interpretations, 76; male, 154n9; Mexican American, 63; and

museum, 126, 128; outside UAE, 296; Serbian, 41,45; Singapore, 251; as spectators, 132, 134; and surveys, 254; Tamil, 81; and Tibet cause, 268

Balikbayan, 214, 226n16
Balsamo, Anne, 294, 301n30, 301n32
Bangalore, 179; as brand, 192
Banlieu, 131
Basu, Amrita, 14n2
Beale, Alison, 138n23
Bennett, Tony, 124, 137n1
Berlant, Lauren, 122n26
Biopower, 294n29
Body: of Afghan woman, 2; of Balkan diva, 35, 48; of carpet weavers, 171; and dress, 99–100; as covered, 21; as discursive entity, 294; as docile, 181, 192; 202; economic imaginations, 70; ethnic gendered body, 275; foreign male, 116,119; gendered, 128; as globally exposed, 186; as infrastructure, 189; Latina body, 53–54, 64–65; as light/dark-skinned, 68; maternal, 143; and media policing, 154n9; Muslim woman, 3; normative beauty, 75; opacity, 127; and Orientalist frames, 46; raced bodies and beauty, 75–77; racialized, 116; of the sex worker, 115; women's bodies, 244; worthy of being saved, 106. *See also* de Certeau; Islam/ Islamic
Books: as travelogues, catalogues, 161; *See also* Carpet; Connoisseur
Bourdieu, Pierre, 99, 102n23, 133, 139n31, 262

Mufti, Aamir, 15n26
Muhajiba, 30. *See also* Clothing
Multicultural/multiculturalism, 3, 54, 82, 136, 145, 154n9, 286
Museum, 124–126; and spectators, 132. *See also* Citizenship
Muslim: anti-Muslim, 89; identity post -9/11, 90; modern man 94–97. *See also* Mediatization
Mustarjilaat, 284
Myanmar, 233–235, 242–243; Buddhist monks, 234; Saffron Revolution, 233, 235; and technology, 235; 239

Nair, Janaki, 194n17
Nakamura, Lisa, 300n7
Narratives: adoption, 144; civilizational, 171–172; of conjecture, 165; and desire, 7; Latinidad, 57, 60; media, 29, 90, 99; mobilizing of, 180; and Muslims, 89–90; oppositional, 197; protectionism, 287; purity, 55; queer, 289; transnational, 205; visibility, 30; visual, 201–203; of women as victims, 239
Nation: body of, 119; normative scripts, 10; as savior, 105; as visual grammar, 10
Nationalism: and cosmopolitan discourses, 182; as exception, 181; and flexible work, 178; and Milosevic, 41; as mode of consumption, 44–45; Serbian nationalism 35– 38; U.S., 3
Neoliberal: capitalism, 236; and citizenship, 223; commodity culture, 80; and cultural citizenship, 255; and Filipino Nationalism, 219; as governance, 252; and immigration policies, 104; individual heroism, 114; markets and depoliticization in Balkans, 44–46; and Philippine state, 212–215; and postsocialist capitalism,

43–49; as project, 213–214; values, 119; version of modernity, 126; and Western feminism, 116. *See also* Activism
Nikolaidis, Andrej, 50n3, 50n6, 50n15
Nonini, Donald M., 197, 209n4, 209n6, 228n38

Oaxaca, 232–233; Brad Will's death 233, 240; teacher's strike, 233
Occident, 168, 196; and exotica, 196
Ong, Aihwa, 12, 16n41, 17n45, 123n39, 181, 193n7, 197, 203, 209n4, 209n5, 209n6, 210n16, 210n24, 213, 222, 225n5, 226n12, 228n38, 228n39, 266n18, 267n31, 302n43
Orientalism, 52n41; and Africa, 145; discourses of, 174; and domestic Orientalia, 166; and gender, 173; music, 96; and Muslim men, 89; Oprah, 80; and spectacle, 167, 172
Ossman, Susan, 33n4, 33n5, 33n7, 34n24
Other: and Balkan bodies, 46; fear of, 199; minority communities, 270–271

Panopticon: as participatory 237, 243
Parameswaran, Radhika, 150, 155n38
Parrenas, Rhacel, 123n46, 227n36, 228n38
Patrimoine, 136
Persian carpet: and consumerism, 168; as cosmopolitan product 162; as exotic commodity, 16; as motif, 167
Pink TV, 38
Political advocacy, 272–278
Post-oil generation, 289
Postfeminism, 61, 151, 153
Puar, Jasbir, 3, 14n3, 15n14, 301n40
Public: creation of, 226n15; cultural policy, 254; and Emirati, 294; Habermasian 23n6, 237; mediated publicness, 199; and opinion, 231; as

Technology: as archive, 272; and diasporic communities, 274; and everyday life, 260

Thompson, John, 210n19

Tibet, 275, 276, 279, 280. *See also* McLagan, Meg

Three worlds model, 23, 33n7, 25–28

Tradition: gender roles, 277; and Latina femininity, 65; and Rebiya Kadeer, 274–276; and televangelism, 98. *See also* Modernity

Translocal: and the transnational, 196–197, 206–209; and websites, 260

Transnational/transnationalism: advocacy campaigns, 268, 276; aesthetic and ethos, 36–37; alternative, 260; audience, 36; and China, 197, 208; circulation of images, 236, 237, 240, 245; community, 231; community of sentiment 232; and consumer culture, 214–215; and consumption, 197; cultural practices, 55; diasporic space, 278; digital media, 245; as gendered, 196; heuristic, 8; and identities, 124, 127, 131, 134; image management, 23; and Indian modernity, 80; as invisible, 137; and malleable identities 50; media environment, 36, 41; and media spaces, 213; mediated conjuncture, 254; and metaphors of slavery, 105; optic, 8; and Other, 162, 164;participation 250; and politics of care,147, 153; public culture, 255; public sphere, 245, 272; and publicity, 38–39; and sexual politics, 184; social movement, 235; as space 291; sphere of violation, 238; staging of Latinadad, 64; and subaltern class, 208; subject,

4; taming of, 136; *Ummah,* 99. *See also* Humanitarianism; Lesbian; Muslim; Public; Queer; Translocal

Turbo-folk, 37–38

Turner, Graeme, 40, 51n24, 93, 100

Ugly Betty, 55–57; *Betty La Fea,* 55; *Yo Soy Bea,* 55

Umah, 96, 99

United Arab Emirates: and Social Values campaign, 287. *See also* Facebook; Islam; Queer; Social Networking

Upadhya, Carol, 186n26

Uyghur: as minorities, 269–272; and Tibetan cause 275–276

Valdivia, Angharad, 10, 65n4, 66n16, 67n37

Vasavi, A.R., 186, 194n15; 194n26

Veil: and French ban, 3; and Jack Straw, 3. *See also* Clothing

Visibility: politics of, 1–2; forms of, 8

Visual: of cues, 111; economy 69; and knowledge, 163, 167

West/Western: as avatar, 79; and Balkan society, 44, 46; and beauty, 48, 80; as claims, 90; commodities, 125; as ethos, 292; and etiquette, 206; as exotic, 196; as feminine empowerment, 141; feminism, 116; happiness, 118; imaginary, 178; imperialism, 78, 95, 295; incompatibility with 187; Indo-Western, 7; Islam split, 2; liberal scripts, 11; materialism, 95; metropolis, 285; as morally deficient, 202; pastoral power, 2; and taste, 169, 250; and understandings of rights, 231, 265; as Westernization, 258, 259, 292; as Westernized, 4, 81, 186; values, 109,